The Expository Pulpit Series

REVELATION

Unveiling Christ and His Prophetic Program

DR. GLEN SPENCER JR.

Dr. Glen Spencer Jr.
15 Pine Ridge Road — Tunkhannock, Pa. 18657
PastorGlenSpencer@gmail.com

Revelation: Unveiling Christ and His Prophetic Program
Copyright © 2005 by Glen Spencer Jr.

All Rights Reserved. No part of this book may be reproduced, stored in a retrieval system or transmitted in any form by any means, electronic, mechanical, photocopy, recording, or otherwise, without the prior permission of the author, except as provided by USA copyright law.

All Scripture Quotations From The King James Bible

This Printing 2022

Contents

Introduction 9
Blessed Is He That Readeth 17
The King Is Coming 25
A Vision Of The Glorified Christ 47
The Church Age 67
Ephesus: The Lacking Church 73
Smyrna: The Loyal Church 83
Pergamos: The Lax Church 93
Thyatira: The Loose Church 105
Sardis: The Lifeless Church 121
Philadelphia: The Loving Church 131
Laodicea: The Lukewarm Church 143
The Rapture 161
Heaven's Throne Room 195
Worthy Is The Lamb 207
The Wrath Of The Lamb 221
The Sealing Of The 144,000 239
The Still Before The Storm 249
The First Four Trumpet Judgments 255
The Day All Hell Breaks Loose 263
Hell's Hideous Horseman 273
Time No Longer 283
The Temple Measured 293
The Two Witnesses 299

The Third Woe	309
War In Heaven	315
The Rise Of The Antichrist	329
The Coming World False Prophet	337
Victory On The Mountain	345
Angelic Messengers	353
When The Wicked Reap The Wrath of God	359
Preparing For The Vial Judgments	369
The Seven Vial Judgments	377
The Judgment Of Religious Babylon	389
God's Judgment Of Political Babylon	399
Heaven's Alleluia Chorus	411
The Marriage Of The Lamb	419
The Conquering King Returns	425
The Battle Of Armageddon	433
The Millennial Reign	441
The Great White Throne Judgment	451
All Things New	457
The New Jerusalem	467
The Protected Book	479
The Old Account Is Settled	485
God's Final Invitation	491
Even So Come, Lord Jesus	497

Recommendations From Our Readers

Pastor Spencer is not only a gifted preacher, but a gifted writer as well. As a fundamentalist and pastor, I am careful about the books I endorse, but Dr. Spencer is at the top of my list of writers. So, it is with great honor that I recommend his Expository Pulpit Series to you.

Michael D. McClary, Th.D.,
Pastor, Community-Bainbridge Baptist Church,
Founder/Executive Director, Good Samaritan Ministries

I have enjoyed reading your books in the past and look forward to getting newer ones. The thing I enjoyed about your books were that when I read them, I said, "I have to teach this to my people. I want others to know this". I appreciate your study, work and insight.

Dr. Jeff Fugate
Pastor, Clays Mill Road Baptist Church
President of Commonwealth Baptist College

To those who love to study the Bible, I want to take the time to highly recommend Pastor Spencer's expository series. For years, it has been one of my favorite resources when I study the Bible. When I study a passage, this material is consistently consulted. I find the material rich in practical applications, word studies, and clear explanation of passages in the Bible. The outlines are excellent. Any investment that you would make in this study material will be worth it. You will be glad that you did.

Dr. Rod Mattoon
Author of Treasures from Scripture Series
Pastor of Lincoln Land Baptist Church
Springfield, Illinois

It is with great delight that I recommend to you, "The Expository Pulpit Commentary Series." Dr. Glen Spencer Jr.

combines years of exhaustive research and practical ministry experience to bring to the church, the pastor, the teacher, and the student of the Scriptures a sound, in-depth and yet very practical set of study tools. This ongoing verse by commentary series will be a great addition to your library. This is not just more rehashed information but wise insight from a seasoned Bible Scholar. I know Dr. Glen Spencer Jr. the man and have found him to be a great Christian, a compassionate pastor and a true champion of the authorized King James Bible, believing it to be God's Preserved Word For English speaking people.

This trustworthy commentary series is, Dispensational in theology, pre-Tribulation and pre-millennial in its eschatology, literal in its hermeneutical approach and expository in its format. I am thrilled that this good work is now available to you and I as we seek to benefit from its invaluable help to deepen our knowledge of God's perfect, preserved word.

Dr. Jon M. Jenkins,
Pastor, Grace Baptist Church
President of Grace Baptist College

You have written an excellent study on the Book of Revelation. This will be a great help to preachers and teachers everywhere. This work is informative, inspiring, and encouraging. Your alliterative outlines are excellent! Your study of this book will be a great help to many, many Christians.

Dr. Lee Roberson
Founder of Tennessee Temple University

The Expository Pulpit Series by Glen Spencer Jr. is outstanding in its exposition, practical in its application and powerful in its presentation. Pastor Spencer is a man of character who upholds the integrity of God's Word in a world that has lost its way. These commentaries are written from a successful pastor with a servant's heart and not someone who has no burden for souls or no experience dealing with people. Pastor Spencer is a man of integrity, and he has had a consistent testimony that is above reproach. He is a man of deep conviction and who refuses to compromise in his personal life or ministry.

There has been a great lack of doctrinal preaching in many pulpits across America. This series by Pastor Spencer addresses that need, and I encourage every pastor, missionary, evangelist, and student of the scriptures to get them. Pastor Spencer is an excellent communicator of the Word of God in his writing and public speaking. I have had him several times in the churches I have pastored, and he always does an excellent job and my people love him. In my opinion he is the best bible expositor in America, and you would be doing yourself a favor by getting these books. If you want to grow as a Christian and learn how to communicate truth better, then I suggest you get this entire series.

Kurt John LaCapruccia
Pastor, Keystone Independent Baptist Church
East Greenville, PA

Dr. Glen Spencer's commentaries are practical and valuable, they are a great resource for personal Bible study and for teaching God's Word to others.

Dr. Don Woodard, Pastor
Beacon Baptist Church, Salem, VA

I have been a pastor in the Independent Baptist movement for over thirty years and have used various Bible commentaries that have much good printed therein, but quite often are lacking with regards to true Bible doctrine. The Expository Pulpit Series, written by my dear friend, Dr. Glen Spencer, is a breath of fresh air. It is quite obvious that Dr. Spencer has spent long hours studying and researching in order to provide an honest and accurate commentary that is worthy of notice. It will prove to be of great value to the seasoned minister of the Gospel of Jesus Christ as well as to the man who has recently been called to preach. The series not only will enhance the sermon preparation of pastors and evangelists but will also prove to be of great value to the average Christian whose heart seeks to know the Lord better through the study of God's Word. I fully endorse and highly recommend The Expository Pulpit Series.

Pastor Phillip Paul Thomas
Bible Baptist Church, Meadville, PA

I recommend all individuals to explore the readings of Dr. Glen Spencer Jr. His books are very inspirational, informative, powerful, and purposeful. I often reference his work within my own professional realm of ministry.

Pastor Chris Traylor

INTRODUCTION

The Book of Revelation is a rich and rewarding book. In this book the Lord Jesus Christ is revealed in all His glory and His plan for the ages laid out for all to see. J. Vernon McGee wrote:

> *This book is like a great union station where the great trunk lines of prophecy come in from other portions of Scripture. Revelation does not originate but consummates. It is imperative to a right understanding of the book to be able to trace each great subject of prophecy from the first reference to the terminal.*

It records the end of things as we know them but the restoration of all things to God's creating perfection. Revelation has twenty-two chapters, four hundred and four verses and twelve thousand words. The major theme of the book of Revelation is the Lord Jesus Christ. It is the grand and glorious unveiling of Christ. In Revelation we see Jesus as the Divine Overseer walking in the midst of His Churches, the Keeper of the Keys of death and hell, the Author of the Word of God, the Protector of His people, the Righteous and Wrathful Judge, the great and glorified Lamb of God, the Rightful Possessor of His Creation, the Mighty Conqueror over Satan and his demons, the Light of Heaven, and the King of Kings and Lord of Lords.

THE PENMAN

While God is the Author of the Scriptures, the Holy Spirit used the Apostle John as the human penman of this book. Four times in this book, the author is clearly identified as John (Revelation 1:1, 4, 9; 22:8).

> **For the prophecy came not in old time by the will of man: but holy men of God spake as they were moved by the Holy Ghost. (2 Peter 1:21)**

The Revelation Of Jesus Christ

The Apostle John identified himself as his (Christ's) **servant**: (Revelation 1:1) This is the same John, the beloved disciple, who wrote the Gospel and the books of First, Second, and Third John in the New Testament. He is the human penman God used to record the Revelation.

THE PLACE

The visions recorded in the book of Revelation were seen by John the beloved disciple while banished to the Isle of Patmos for preaching Christ and the way of salvation (Revelation 1:2). The Isle of Patmos was a small rocky island in the Aegean Sea, about forty miles off the coast of modern Turkey. Revelation was written about 96 AD.

THE PURPOSE

The first verse of Revelation reveals to us that the purpose of the book is **to shew unto his servants things which must shortly come to pass; (Revelation 1:1)** The word **Revelation** means *"to unveil, uncover, reveal, to manifest."* It carries the idea of pulling the cover off something to reveal that which has previously been unseen. The last book of the Bible is called the **Revelation** because it is an unveiling of the events associated with the Second Coming of our Lord Jesus Christ to establish His Millennial Kingdom here on the earth. Revelation is the unveiling of things previously hidden and unknown. The very title of this book shows the purpose of God in giving the Revelation to His people.

In the book of Revelation, the veil is pulled back and Jesus Christ is shown in His Divine fullness. The veil of His humanity is pulled back and we see Him as the Eternal God. (1:17-18); the Lion of the Tribe of Judah. (5:5); the Lamb endued with power and glory. (5:12-13); the Sovereign King of all the world. (11:15); the Commander in Chief of Heaven's forces. (19:11); the King of kings and Lord of lords. (19:16); the bright and Morning Star (22:16). He is no longer the lowly Babe in Bethlehem's manger, but **He cometh with clouds** in all His glory. No more are the Herod's who sought the young child's life, but now...

Introduction

The kingdoms of this world are become the kingdoms of our Lord, and of his Christ; and he shall reign for ever and ever. (Revelation 11:15)

The ungodly once declared Him a blasphemer worthy of death, but here kings and priests fall down and worship...

Him that liveth for ever and ever. (Revelation 5:14)

The one of whom it was said:

His visage was so marred more than any man, and his form more than the sons of men. (Isaiah 52:14)

... now stands out in all His beauty, majesty, and glory!

His head and his hairs were white like wool, as white as snow; and his eyes were as a flame of fire. (Revelation 1:14)

Oh, how men have misunderstood the Lord Jesus down through the ages. No longer is He the carpenter's Son, the Man from Nazareth, but rather the Divine Creator of the universe crying:

Behold, I make all things new. (Revelation 21:5)

Gone is the wicked bloodthirsty mob shouting, **crucify Him.** Their voices have been silenced by His wrath. Instead, kneeling before Him are:

... ten thousand times ten thousand and thousands of thousands. (Revelation 5:11)

... of His saints and angels, all crying out and proclaiming with a mighty voice that will ring throughout Heaven saying ...

Worthy is the Lamb that was slain to receive: power, and riches, and wisdom, and strength, and honour, and glory, and blessing ... Blessing, and honour, and glory, and power, be unto him that sitteth upon the throne, and unto the Lamb for ever and ever. (Revelation 5:12-13)

No longer does He ride into Jerusalem on a borrowed ass, but we see Him in all His splendor, riding out of Heaven on a fiery white steed, as a mighty conqueror going to war (Revelation 19). In Revelation, He who once hung upon the cross sits upon His throne—alive for ever more. We are reminded that He was once dead, but now He is alive for evermore and holds the keys of death and hell. He has gloriously triumphed over the last enemy, death. This is what is meant by "*The Revelation of Jesus Christ, which God gave.*" It is God's picture of His Son, unveiled in the galleries of time that we may see Him as He truly is. We see God's people triumphant, taken into Heaven at the shout of the archangel. Then, in sharp contrast, we have a revelation of sin in its worst form, of the depth of depravity, of the devil and his angels in their last futile attempt to overthrow God.

THE PROPHECY

One must employ proper hermeneutics in the study of the Bible. Hermeneutics is the *"method and techniques used to interpret written texts."* In theology is speaks of the laws that govern the interpretation of Scripture. Unfortunately, not everyone follows the biblical laws of interpretation. Thus, there are several differing schools of interpretation when it comes to the book of Revelation and its eschatology. These are:

The Preterist

Preterists teach that all of the events of the Book of Revelation have already taken place. Thus, this view holds that Tribulation Period Revelation was all fulfilled in the early years of Christian persecution. The word *"preterist"* comes from the Latin and means *"past."* Those who hold to this view believe that John wrote this book prior to 70 A.D., when General Titus destroyed the temple and burned the city of Jerusalem. Thus, according to this interpretation, the persecutions described in the book of Revelation were those which occurred at the time of the Roman Empire. This view is rejected in this study!

The Historical

This view holds that the Book of Revelation gives a view of the history of the church from the time of John to the end of the

Introduction

age. The book is therefore in the process of being fulfilled throughout the Church age. This view is rejected in this study!

The Idealist

This is the view that the Book of Revelation is only a series of symbols which represent the struggle between good and evil. The book is therefore spiritualized, and the details are neither important nor do they need to be fulfilled. This view is rejected in this study!

The Futurist

Finally, there are those, however, who believe in a literal interpretation and hold that the larger part of the book is prophetic and yet to take place. This view holds that the events from chapter 4 onward are yet to be fulfilled, for nothing in history adequately fulfills the passages. No judgments have ever equaled those recorded in chapters 6 through 18. The Lord Jesus Christ has not returned as described in chapter 19. There have never been any resurrections to match those recorded in chapter 20. This view is the only one that matches up when we compare **spiritual things with spiritual** and **Study ... rightly dividing the word of truth.** This view allows a literal interpretation of Scripture and the fulfillment of all the prophecies and promises concerning the throne of David. Therefore, it is the view taken in this study. J. Vernon McGee said:

> *This book is like a great union station where the great trunklines of prophecy come in from other portions of Scripture. Revelation does not originate, but consummates. It is imperative to a right understanding of the book to be able to trace each great subject of prophecy from the first reference to the terminal.*

The Book Of Revelation is an exciting book to study. Some consider it hard to understand and simply avoid it. Hence their claim is that the Revelation can't be understood, so why so why waste our time. We strongly disagree! While there are some symbols and mysteries that we may not understand in this life, the day is coming when God's people will fully grasp the great truths of this book. God promises a blessing to those who read and hear the Revelation (1:3).

> **All scripture is given by inspiration of God, and is profitable for doctrine, for reproof, for correction, for instruction in righteousness: That the man of God may be perfect, throughly furnished unto all good works. (2 Timothy 3:16–17)**

Like all Scripture, Revelation is a profitable book. Read it, study it, love it, and look for its fulfillment!

General Outline Of Revelation

I. The Past: Things Which Thou Hast Seen. (1:1-20)
    a. His Plan 1:1
    b. His Prophet 1:1b-2
    c. His Promise 1:3
    d. His Purchase 1:5-6
    e. His Priority 1: 7
    f. His Partners 1:9
    g. His Preeminence 1:10-16
    h. His Power 1:17-18
    i. His Program 1:19
    j. His Pastors 1:20

II. The Present: Things Which Are. (2:1-3:22)
    a. The Lacking Church— Ephesus 2:1-7
    b. The Loyal Church— Smyrna 2:8-11
    c. The Lax Church—Pergamos 2:12-17
    d. The Loose Church—Thyatira 2:18-29
    e. The Lifeless Church—Sardis 3:1-6
    f. The Loving Church—Philadelphia 3:7-13
    g. The Lukewarm Church—Laodicea 3:14-22

III. The Prospect: Things Which Shall Be Hereafter. (4:1-22:5)
    a. The Throne Room—Rejoicing 4-5
    b. The Tribulation Period—Retribution 6-18
    c. The Triumphant Saviour—Return 19
    d. The Thousand Years—Reign 20
    e. The Timeless Ages—Reward 21-22

BLESSED IS HE THAT READETH
Revelation 1:1-3

The book of Revelation is one the most intriguing book of the Word of God. Due to its thorough description of the future, man can know for sure what lies ahead. The Revelation concludes the canon of Scripture. There will be new added to Scripture. It is now a completed book. Genesis and Revelation are like bookends. Genesis is the beginning; Revelation is the end. There is quite a contrast between Genesis and Revelation. Genesis, the first book of the Bible, unfolds for us the wonderful work of creation which brought the heavens and the earth into existence. In Genesis, we learn of man's creation, his fall into sin, and of the beginning of God's redemptive plan through the promised Seed of the woman. Revelation tells us about the completion of God's plan of creation and redemption, revealing to us the many wonderful events leading to Satan's defeat and Christ's victorious triumph. During this time, the promises of the Kingdom will be fully realized in the thousand-year earthly reign, in which Jesus the Christ will rule supreme over all the earth. After the Millennial Kingdom, our Lord will destroy this sin tainted earth and create a new one that will last for all eternity. This will be the eternal state. As we see in chapter one, it is Jesus Christ who is working His plan to bring about the consummation of the ages. In Revelation we see a contrast between ...

- The *Warfare* on earth and the *Worship* in heaven!
- The *Victims* on earth and the *Victors* in heaven!
- The *Judged* on earth and the *Judge* in heaven!
- The *anti-christ* and the *Almighty Christ*!

The Second Coming of Christ is a fact of Scripture. At His ascension, the Apostles stood gazing into Heaven as the Lord Jesus ascended. The assuring message of His return was given to

The Revelation Of Jesus Christ

the Apostles as they watched Him return to the Father after the resurrection.

> ... while they beheld, he was taken up; and a cloud received him out of their sight. And while they looked stedfastly toward heaven as he went up, behold, two men stood by them in white apparel; Which also said, Ye men of Galilee, why stand ye gazing up into heaven? this same Jesus, which is taken up from you into heaven, shall so come in like manner as ye have seen him go into heaven. (Acts 1:9-11)

Notice here that Jesus will return **in like manner** as He ascended. His was a literal and visible ascension, therefore His return will be literal and visible. When He returns to this earth, it will be a visible and glorious return (Revelation 19). The text dogmatically states that the **Lord himself shall descend from heaven.** This will literally be fulfilled when the Lord Jesus returns to earth in Revelation 19.

> **And I saw heaven opened, and behold a white horse; and he that sat upon him was called Faithful and True, and in righteousness he doth judge and make war. His eyes were as a flame of fire, and on his head were many crowns; and he had a name written, that no man knew, but he himself. And he was clothed with a vesture dipped in blood: and his name is called The Word of God. And the armies which were in heaven followed him upon white horses, clothed in fine linen, white and clean. And out of his mouth goeth a sharp sword, that with it he should smite the nations: and he shall rule them with a rod of iron: and he treadeth the winepress of the fierceness and wrath of Almighty God. And he hath on his vesture and on his thigh a name written, KING OF KINGS, AND LORD OF LORDS. (Revelation 19:11-16)**

Keep in mind that the Second Coming of Christ will occur in two stages. There will be a Rapture and a Revelation. The Bible is clear that there is a distinction between the imminent return of

Christ in the air for His people and His coming in wrath back to the earth (1 Corinthians 15:50-58; 1 Thessalonians 1:9-10; 2:19; 5:23; 4:13-18; 2 Thessalonians 2:1; Titus 2:13; 1 John 3:2-3). Just as surely as Jesus literally ascended into Heaven, He will literally return to this earth at the end of the Tribulation Period.

HIS PLAN

God knows what is going on and He is not without a plan. Someday He will enact His all-wise plan for the ages. This world is not merely winding down, rather it is on a downward spiral and it is not going to get any better. Nothing short of the Second Coming of Jesus Christ will salvage the world. The Word of God declares that He has a very specific plan for this world. In these first few verses we see that God's plan ...

Involves A Person

The Revelation of Jesus Christ... (Revelation 1:1a) The very title of this book shows the purpose of God in giving the book of Revelation to His church. The word **Revelation** comes from the Latin *"re"* meaning *"back,"* and *"velum"* meaning *"veil or covering."* It means to, *"pull back the veil or to uncover."* The Greek word is *"apokaloopsis"* and means *"to unveil, to lay bare, to expose."* With the usage of this word Revelation, it clearly establishes the fact that this book is a revealing of Jesus Christ. In Revelation the veil is pulled back and we see that which has been hidden up till now. You will notice that it is the **Revelation of Jesus Christ.** The Person revealed is the Lord Jesus Christ. In the Revelation we see His Person, Plan, Purpose, Promise, Priorities, and Power. In this wonderful revelation we are allowed to see things that were hidden up until John received this book on the isle of Patmos. For instance, the message to Daniel was:

> **...O Daniel, shut up the words, and seal the book. (Daniel 12:4)**

Praise God, He has pulled the veil back and declared His plan for the future. He has unfolded that with was hidden. No longer is God's future hidden behind the veil of darkness. Rather the veil is pulled back and God's shines throughout the book. The eternal plane of God is laid open before our very eyes. We further see that God's plan ...

Involves A People

... to shew unto his servants... **(Revelation 1:1b)** Now this is pretty clear. Divine mysteries are revealed only to God's people. Notice that the Revelation is for God's **servants**. It is not primarily written to the unsaved man.

> **But the natural man receiveth not the things of the Spirit of God: for they are foolishness unto him: neither can he know them, because they are spiritually discerned. (1 Corinthians 2:14)**

The unsaved cannot fully understand this book because it is revealed to **His servants** to show them His plan. Neither is the Revelation written to those who sit idly by with little or no concern for the things of God. It is given to His servants, those who are engaged in the work of God.

Involves A Program

... things which must shortly come to pass... **(Revelation 1:1c)** The word **must** speaks of the necessity of the prophecies of this book being fulfilled. God is not going to skip over the events of this book. He will execute His plan and judge the world and bring all these things to pass. These things **must** be.

The phrase **shortly come to pass** does not mean that the events will occur soon, but that when they begin, they will take place swiftly and rapidly. In other words, these events will take place in a short period of time. Foolish man does not understand the Word of God. The scoffers mock God saying:

> **...Where is the promise of his coming? for since the fathers fell asleep, all things continue as they were from the beginning of the creation. (1 Peter 3:4)**

God is not bound to our timetable. He is not looking at our calendar, He is looking at His own. He has the future planned out and will execute it according to His Sovereign will.

> **But, beloved, be not ignorant of this one thing, that one day is with the Lord as a thousand years,**

> **and a thousand years as one day. The Lord is not slack concerning his promise, as some men count slackness; but is longsuffering to us-ward, not willing that any should perish, but that all should come to repentance. (2 Peter 3:8-9)**

We can be assured that the events of the Revelation will take place just as they are written. The only reason they have not taken place so far is because of the grace of God. He wants all who will, to be saved.

Involves A Penman

...and he sent and signified it by his angel unto his servant John: Who bare record of the word of God, and of the testimony of Jesus Christ, and of all things that he saw. (Revelation 1:1d-2) The word **signified** means *"to expose, to make known."* This is a book that was written for the purpose of making it known to people. The Author whom God chose to pen the book of Revelation was John the Apostle, His beloved disciple. The name **John** means *"the Lord is gracious."* John learned a lot about the grace of God as he walked with Christ during His earthly ministry. However, he no doubt learned a lot more as he was banished to the isle of Patmos because of his faith and testimony. Often it is when we are alone in this world that we are closest to God. We have in this book the very truths that John saw on the isle of Patmos.

HIS PROMISE

While there are many who claim that the book of Revelation is beyond human understanding, we clearly see that such a statement cannot be substantiated. In fact, God promises a great blessing to those who read it. God has written His Word to reveal truth to His people. Thus, it must be an understandable book. Furthermore, God has given His people the Holy Spirit to guide them in truth,

The Offer

Blessed is he that readeth, and they that hear the words of this prophecy... (Revelation 1:3a) Revelation is the only book in the Bible that both opens and closes with a blessing. The blessing here in verse 3 is to those who receive, with meekness, the engrafted word. Contrary to popular opinion, Revelation is an understandable book. Yes, the book of Revelation was written to be understood. There are many who say, *"I can't understand it."* Yet, God has promised a special blessing to those who read, who hear, and who keep its inspired truths. Dr. M.R. DeHaan said ...

> *There is probably not a book in the entire Bible which is less read and understood than the book of the Revelation. To the average person the last book of the Bible is a deep mystery, consisting of strange, fantastic predictions which cannot be understood, and as a result the average Bible-reader knows little or nothing about either its contents or its meaning. No greater delusion, however, could occur than to call the book of the Revelation a dark book and one difficult to understand.*

Now, if God promises a blessing to all those who read, hear and keep its words, then surely this book must be understandable. It is a sad thing that many of God's people know little or nothing of the Revelation, or the rest of the Bible as far as that goes. The big problem with many professing Christians is that they are neglecting the Word of God. They fail to read and study it. They are like Ephraim of old. The Bible is a **strange thing** to them.

> **I have written to him the great things of my law, but they were counted as a strange thing. (Hosea 8:12)**

Jesus said:

> **...Ye do err, not knowing the scriptures... (Matthew 22:29)**

The world is in spiritual ruin. Men have made a wreck of their lives. Most have no hope. Such is the life of those who reject God's truth. A Christian who neglects the Word of God will err in his walk with God. Every believer sooner or later must face trials, tribulations, and troubles. However, he faces his foes with the Word of God. It is God's Word that admonishes us to press on and reveals the promises of God for those who persevere. We will be sustained regardless of our problems.

> **Unless thy law had been my delights, I should then have perished in mine affliction. (Psalm 119:92)**

Anyone who will read and study the Bible, and store it in their heart, will tend to be victorious in the battle of life.

> **Thy word have I hid in mine heart, that I might not sin against thee. (Psalm 119:11)**

The Word of God also builds and sustains our faith.

> **So then faith cometh by hearing, and hearing by the word of God. (Romans 10:17)**

God's Word instructs us in the hour of need, comforts us in the time of trouble, and gives us hope for the future. The way to keep our mind on Christ is to stay in the Word of God.

> **This is my comfort in my affliction: for thy word hath quickened me. (Psalm 119:50)**

Nothing comforts the Christian's heart like God's Word. The Bible will bring peace and inner rest to the troubled heart.

The Obligation

... and keep those things which are written therein...: (Revelation 1:3b) We have an obligation to **keep** the **things which are written** in this book. The word **keep** comes from *"tereo"* and means *"to keep an eye on, watch, and hence to guard, keep, obey."* The idea is that we are to learn this book and guard its truths diligently and obey it whole heartedly. This is a military word that speaks of guarding and watching over one's post. In Bible times, guards were posted on the walls of the city to watch against intruders. These guards watched over the city's diligence and dedication. Nothing or no one was allowed in. This is how we ought to guard the truths of God's Word.

The Occasion

... for the time is at hand. (Revelation 1:3c) This is a solemn statement! The phrase, **at hand** denotes nearness from the viewpoint of prophetic revelation. The imminent rapture of God's people from this earth is the next great event on God's timetable. The Rapture could come at this moment or next week. This is the next event on God's prophetic calendar. Not a single prophecy needs to be fulfilled before Jesus comes back. It could happen at any moment. The coming of Christ is **at hand**. Are you ready?

THE KING IS COMING
Revelation 1:4-11

The Second Coming of Christ is a major theme in God's Word. This event will take place in two stages. There will be the Rapture when Jesus comes in the air for His people and the *Revelation*, when He comes back to earth in His glory. In this section, we read about His return in glory.

HIS PARISHIONERS

John to the seven churches which are in Asia: Grace be unto you, and peace, from him which is, and which was, and which is to come; and from the seven Spirits which are before his throne; (Revelation 1:4) In this section, we have the first mention of the seven Churches of Asia Minor. The recipients of Revelation were the **seven churches which are in Asia.** Asia refers to the Roman province of Asia Minor, which is part of modern-day Turkey. These specific Churches are mentioned by name in verse 11 and they are dealt with in greater detail in chapters two and three. We will deal with each of these congregations in more detail when we get to those chapters.

The Stunning Sevens

The number seven is a prominent number in the Word of God. Revelation is a book of sevens. There are many other places in Scripture where the number seven is used. For instance, there are seven feasts of Jehovah (Leviticus 23). There are seven kingdom parables (Matthew 3). The Lord God labored six days and rested on the seventh day. Besides the seven churches of Asia, the book of Revelation refers to many other sevens. There are Seven candlesticks, Seven stars, Seven angels, Seven seals, Seven trumpets, Seven personages, Seven vials. In biblical numerology, the number seven speaks of completeness and perfection. The book of Revelation tells us about the end times and the completion of God's plan concerning things to come.

The Selected Settlements

John to the seven churches which are in Asia... (Revelation 1:4a) John directly addresses this book to the **seven churches which are in Asia.** Keep in mind that the **Asia** spoken of here is not the Far East continent of Asia that we are familiar with today. Rather, it refers to the Roman Province of Asia Minor, which is modern day Turkey. These were seven local Churches that existed in Asia Minor at that time. Of course, there were more than seven Churches there. There were at least three other churches in that region that we know of.

- The Church at Colosse (Colossians 1:2)
- The Church at Hierapolis (Colossians 4:13)
- The Church at Troas (Acts 20:6-7)

Jesus chose these seven specific Churches because they are representative of the types of Churches found throughout Church History. These types of Churches are still seen today. We will study these Churches in more detail in chapters two and three.

The Settling Salutation

... Grace be unto you, and peace... (Revelation 1:4b) In keeping with the custom of his day, John wished the recipients of this letter **grace** and **peace.** Someone has well said, *"These two words capture the richness of the Christian faith."* This reminds and assures us of the grace and peace we enjoy because of our relationship with God through the Lord Christ. The word **grace** reminds us of all we receive from the loving and merciful hand of God. Grace is one of the most needed things in the Christian life. Grace is the _Unmerited_ favor, _Unexplainable_ love, and _Undeserved_ gift of God. Grace saves us and keeps us in a right relationship with our Saviour. Charles H. Spurgeon said:

> *Grace outdoes sin, for it lifts us higher than the place from which we fell.*

By God's grace that the believer stands righteous before God. We sing that wonderful old Hymn; *Amazing Grace* and His grace is still Amazing! Therefore, the Apostle Paul encouraged Timothy ...

> **Thou therefore, my son, be strong in the grace that is in Christ Jesus. (2 Timothy 2:1)**

Lost man is spiritually bankrupt. He has nothing with which we can influence God or satisfy His righteous requirements. It is only by God's grace that a sinner can be brought into God's family, and it is only God's grace that secures and sustain a believer.

Peace speaks of the tranquility of the heart that results from trusting the Lord. Notice that grace comes before peace. No one can experience the peace of God until grace has done it's saving work in their heart. Zodhiates, in his Complete *Word Study Dictionary*, describes peace as ...

> *... tranquility, arising from reconciliation with God and a sense of a divine favor (Rom. 5:1; 15:13; Phil. 4:7 [cf. Is. 53:5]).*

This is a peace comes at a great price. It was purchased by the blood of Christ and made available to us at the moment of our salvation.

> **Therefore being justified by faith, we have peace with God through our Lord Jesus Christ: (Romans 5:1)**

Even in troublous times believers enjoy a God-given peace that the world knows nothing of. This is a promise of the Almighty.

> **... the LORD will bless His people with peace. (Psalm 29:11b)**

Over and over, the Word of God reminds us that peace is available to God's people. Even now we can have the peace of God. Jesus said:

> **These things I have spoken unto you, that in me ye might have peace. In the world ye shall**

> have tribulation: but be of good cheer; I have overcome the world. (John 16:33)
>
> Peace I leave with you, my peace I give unto you: not as the world giveth, give I unto you. Let not your heart be troubled, neither let it be afraid. (John 14:27)

Peace settles our heart and strengthens our soul. Peace helps us to endure conflicts and trials. We can enjoy peace because our Saviour has **overcome the world.**

> Thou wilt keep him in perfect peace, whose mind is stayed on thee: because he trusteth in thee. Trust ye in the LORD for ever: for in the LORD JEHOVAH is everlasting strength. (Isaiah 26:3-4)

Peace is the calm that comes from a right relationship with the Lord Jesus Christ. Too many believers are living in turmoil when they could be enjoying the peace of God. As believers in Christ, we can enjoy the ...

> ... the peace of God, which passeth all understanding. (Philippians 4:7)

God's people can have peace no matter what is happening around them. We must remember that peace is not dependent on the conditions around us, but on the condition of the heart. God's people are to view the circumstances of life through His eyes. Only then can we see as He sees. To the world this book deals with judgment, catastrophe, and war, but to the believer it is a message of hope, grace, and peace.

The Sovereign Saviour

... from him which is, and which was, and which is to come... (Revelation 1:4c) This describes the eternality of God. He is endlessly existent and limitless. He is the One who was past, is present and will come. This is God the Father. He is seen as the self-existent and eternal God. Jesus Christ is He that was, He that Is, and He that is everlasting. Harold B. Sightler wrote:

> *... He that was, and He is the everlasting one. He is the ancient of days; there was never a time when*

the Lord Jesus was not. He has always been, preexistent, and co-existent with God the Father as God the Son, the Lord Jesus, and described also as He which is to come.

There was never a time when the Lord Jesus was not. He has always coexisted with the Father. He declared of Himself ...

... I AM THAT I AM... (Exodus 3:14)

God did not come from anywhere. He has always been. God is, God has always been, and God always will be. God has no origin of existence. He is the self-existing, He is the Almighty God of glory. He is the Eternal God. He is timeless. Isaiah referred to Him as ...

...The everlasting Father... (Isaiah 9:6)

God is not subject to man's calendar. He transcends time and dominates eternity. He is not limited to time. He will never die. The Bible tells us that God ...

... inhabiteth eternity. (Isaiah 57:15b)

God dominates eternity. We are confined to our clocks and calendars. When we think of time we think of years, months, days, hours, and minutes. As humans we are limited in our finite understanding. But God is transcendent. He will never come to an end. God dwelt in eternity for the ages before creation and will dwell throughout the ages that are yet to come. John describes God the Father as the One who exists eternally in the past, present, and future. This reminds us that the eternal God is the source of all the blessings of salvation, grace, and peace. These blessings come as a result of knowing the Lord Jesus Christ personally.

The Seven Spirits

... and from the seven Spirits which are before his throne; (Revelation 1:4d) This speak of the Holy Spirit. Now we know there is only one Holy Spirt. But the number seven speaks of completeness and fullness. The phrase **seven Spirits** is a reference to the Holy Spirit in His sevenfold completeness. Isaiah lists the **seven Spirits**.

> **And the spirit of the LORD shall rest upon him, the spirit of wisdom and understanding, the spirit of counsel and might, the spirit of knowledge and of the fear of the LORD; (Isaiah 11:2)**

The entire Trinity, the Father, the Son, and the Holy Spirit have been mentioned in this passage. This tells us that the book of Revelation along with entire Word of God has the full force and authority of the Godhead behind it. God's Word the final authority in all matters of faith and practice.

HIS PURCHASE

In verses five and six we come to the great atoning work of Christ. Christ purchased our salvation with His own blood. The Word of God dogmatically teaches that without the blood there is no salvation (Hebrews 9:22). However, we see here that there are several great truths connected to the atonement of the Lord Jesus.

His Reliability

And from Jesus Christ, who is the faithful witness... (Revelation 1:5a) Jesus Christ is **the faithful witness**. This goes to the fact that what Jesus says is true. The word **faithful** means that Jesus is *"trustworthy and reliable, sure and true."* The Word of our Saviour is reliable and trustworthy. We can always trust what Jesus says. His Word is good! Isaiah prophesied of Christ as a faithful witness.

> **Behold, I have given him for a witness to the people, a leader and commander to the people. (Isaiah 55:4)**

Christ said of Himself:

> **To this end was I born, and for this cause came I into the world, that I should bear witness unto the truth. Every one that is of the truth heareth my voice. (John 18:37)**

When Jesus was here, He was faithful to do the will of God. Jesus witnessed the truth when the wicked people of His day refused to believe it. He witnessed the truth while they mocked and blasphemed God. He witnessed while they persecuted Him. He witnessed while they laughed at Him in scorn. He witnessed the truth to Herod. Again, He witnessed to Pilate, the Roman governor who delivered Him to the people to be crucified. Even on the cross He gave witness to God in the words He spoke and the way in which He died. We need to follow His example.

His Resurrection

... and the first begotten of the dead... (Revelation 1:5b) Jesus is also identified as **the first begotten of the dead.** Of course, there have been other people raised from the dead. The prophet Elisha raised the son of the Shulamite woman. Jesus raised the widow's son, Jarius' daughter, and Lazarus. These were all resurrected but eventually died again. These people were mortal beings., but Jesus is the eternal Son of God. He is the first to rise from the dead never to die again.

> **But now is Christ risen from the dead, and become the firstfruits of them that slept. (1 Corinthians 15:20)**
>
> **And he is the head of the body, the church: who is the beginning, the firstborn from the dead; that in all things he might have the preeminence. (Colossians 1:18)**

God raised Jesus from the dead to live forever. Jesus is immortal. He ...

> **... ever liveth to make intercession for them. (Hebrews 7:25)**

The phrase **first begotten** describes a position of authority and prominence. Jesus Christ was the first to be resurrected with a glorified body that will never die again.

His Rule

... the prince of the kings of the earth... (Revelation 1:5c) Jesus is described as the **prince**. He is ruler over the **kings of the earth**. He is King of kings and Lord of lords. God has declared ...

> **Also I will make him my firstborn, higher than the kings of the earth. (Psalm 89:27)**

This is an announcement of what is coming. When it is all said and done, Christ will sit triumphantly upon His throne and the kings of the earth shall be no more.

> **These shall make war with the Lamb, and the Lamb shall overcome them: for he is Lord of lords, and King of kings: and they that are with him are called, and chosen, and faithful. (Revelation 17:14)**
>
> **And he hath on his vesture and on his thigh a name written, KING OF KINGS, AND LORD OF LORDS. (Revelation 19:16)**

The Lord Jesus will reign as King when He establishes His Millennial Kingdom at the end of the Tribulation Period.

His Reasoning

... Unto him that loved us... (Revelation 1:5d) We see here is that He **loved us.** This was the reason behind His redemptive work. The wonderful love of Christ is a powerful subject. Jesus' love motivated Him to lay down His life for sinners. The Bible says:

> **Greater love hath no man than this, that a man lay down his life for his friends. (John 15:13)**

But that was not the love Christ had for us. No! A thousand times no! His death upon the cross was not the case of a man dying for His friends, but that of a Man dying to save His enemies. Paul wrote:

> **For scarcely for a righteous man will one die: yet peradventure for a good man some would even dare to die. But God commendeth his love toward us, in that, while we were yet sinners, Christ died for us. (Romans 5:7-8)**

As His enemies, we were lost, wicked, and full of unbelief—we had no right to Divine grace. Still, He loved us and gave Himself for us. That's the love of Christ.

His Redemption

... and washed us from our sins in his own blood, (Revelation 1:5e) Christ's love resulted in action. He **washed us from our sins in his own blood.** The doctrine of the blood seems to be out of fashion nowadays. It is being removed from new translations, some hymnbooks, and modern preaching. But God makes much of the blood. We are told that ...

> **... the blood of Jesus Christ his Son cleanseth us from all sin. (1 John 1:7)**

Concerning sin, the Bible declares:

> **... without shedding of blood is no remission. (Hebrews 9:22)**

We are redeemed by the precious blood of Christ.

> **Forasmuch as ye know that ye were not redeemed with corruptible things, as silver and gold, from your vain conversation received by tradition from your fathers; But with the precious blood of Christ, as of a lamb without blemish and without spot: (1 Peter 1:18-19)**

Blood is the redemptive price that Jesus paid for our salvation. There is only one ransom, God accepts nothing else. It is the blood of the Lord Jesus Christ that procures man's salvation. Blood is the Divine requirement to pay for sin. Therefore, Jesus shed His own blood on the cross of Calvary and met that Divine requirement, so that He might wash us from **our sins in his own blood**. Isaac Watts wrote ...

> *Not all the blood of bulls and goats on Jewish altars slain,*
>
> *Could give the guilty conscience peace or wash away the stain.*
>
> *But Christ, the heavenly Lamb, takes all our sins away;*
>
> *A sacrifice of nobler name and richer blood than they.*

The blood sacrifice is a major Bible doctrine. It is taught throughout the Word of God. A crimson river of blood flows through the Bible. It began back in the garden when Almighty God offered the first sacrifice for sin. This grand and glorious

The Revelation Of Jesus Christ

theme of the blood comes to a climax in the book of Revelation where God's people gather around Heaven' throne and sing the praises of the Lamb that was slain and

> **... redeemed us to God by thy blood... (Revelation 5:9)**

No wonder that Peter refers to the blood as precious. The Pure, Precious, Permanent, and Perfect blood of the Lamb is the only cleansing for the sinner. All mankind has sinned and come short of the glory of God.

> **Come now, and let us reason together, saith the LORD: though your sins be as scarlet, they shall be as white as snow; though they be red like crimson, they shall be as wool. (Isaiah 1:18)**

What a marvelous truth! He has **washed us from our sins in his own blood.** The wonderful and glorious work of redemption is complete.

> **In whom we have redemption through his blood, the forgiveness of sins, according to the riches of his grace; (Ephesians 1:7)**

All who come to Christ by faith in His atoning work will be washed and thoroughly cleansed of all sin. The blood atonement will be the subject of much singing in Heaven!

His Reward

And hath made us kings and priests unto God and his Father... (Revelation 1:6a) Not only does Christ Redeem sinners, He Rewards them also. The reward here is two-fold.

He Gave Us Power

First, when the Lord purchased us, He made us **kings**. A king is one who has the authority and power to rule. We are no longer slaves to sin, we are rulers. This is the Lord's promise to the overcomer.

> **And he that overcometh, and keepeth my works unto the end, to him will I give power over the nations: (Revelation 2:26)**

> **To him that overcometh will I grant to sit with me in my throne, even as I also overcame, and am**

> **set down with my Father in his throne. (Revelation 3:21)**

Christians who overcome the flesh and the world and live victoriously in this life exalted to rule in the world to come. These overcomers will be given the great privilege to rule under God's authority. This is not a blanket promise for every Christ, but only to the Christians who conquer the flesh and overcome in this world and live whole heartedly for God.

> **For whatsoever is born of God overcometh the world: and this is the victory that overcometh the world, even our faith. (1 John 5:4)**

Any Christian can be an overcomer and rule with Christ. Again, this is a promise to overcomers. In Heaven, not every Christian is going to share and share alike. Those who remain slaves to sin will not rule with Him.

He Gave Us A Priesthood

Secondly, when the Lord purchased us, He made us **priests.** As priests we have the privilege of direct access to God. All believers are **priests** and together make up a **royal priesthood.** Peter said:

> **But ye are a chosen generation, a royal priesthood, an holy nation, a peculiar people; that ye should show forth the praises of him who hath called you out of darkness into his marvellous light. (1 Peter 2:9)**

We belong to **a royal priesthood**. According to this truth every believer is a priest in God's eyes. A priest's work is to mediate between man and God. He is to minister on behalf of others. What a tremendous work to be a part of. Believers are to be busy about the business of bringing others to Christ. This is the work of reconciliation.

His Reign

... to him be glory and dominion for ever and ever. Amen. (Revelation 1:6b) The Lord Jesus Christ is worthy of our praise. The word **glory** comes from the Greek *"doxa"* and means *"to honor, to magnify, to invest with dignity."* Christ is worthy to receive the honor and praise of His people because of all that He has done for them. The word **dominion** speaks of *"power and strength."* He is the all-powerful One. His glory and power will be **for ever and ever.** Throughout eternity God's people will praise Him for His salvation and for His mighty works.

HIS PRIORITY

The primary theme of Revelation is the Return of Christ to judge evil and to establish His earthly Kingdom. We hear the scoffers say, where is the promise of His coming? However, don't let His delay fool you. He is right on schedule. He will return according to His all-wise plan. The Second Coming is a priority on God's calendar and will be accomplished in His timing.

The Warning

Behold, he cometh with clouds... (Revelation 1:7a) The world is warned. Jesus is coming again. His death not only assured salvation for all who believe and trust Him, but also assures of His return to this sin darkened earth to set things in order. The **clouds** speak of His power and glory.

> **I saw in the night visions, and, behold, one like the Son of man came with the clouds of heaven, and came to the Ancient of days, and they brought him near before him. (Daniel 7:13)**
>
> **And then shall appear the sign of the Son of man in heaven: and then shall all the tribes of the earth mourn, and they shall see the Son of man coming in the clouds of heaven with power and great glory. (Matthew 24:30)**
>
> **And then shall they see the Son of man coming in the clouds with great power and glory. (Mark 13:26)**

These clouds do have an important meaning. We find in the Bible that clouds are often symbolic of God's presence, power, and majesty.

> **And the LORD descended in the cloud, and stood with him there, and proclaimed the name of the LORD. (Exodus 34:5)**

> **Bless the LORD, O my soul. O LORD my God, thou art very great; thou art clothed with honour and majesty. Who coverest thyself with light as with a garment: who stretchest out the heavens like a curtain: Who layeth the beams of his chambers in the waters: who maketh the clouds his chariot: who walketh upon the wings of the wind: (Psalm 104:1–3)**

When Christ comes back to earth, He will come in great power, majesty, and grandeur. There will be no question as to Who He is or what He is here for. Oh yes! He is coming again, not as a babe born in a manger, but as King of kings and Lord of lords, descending from Heaven in wonderful glory (Revelation 19:11-16).

The Watching

John further declares that **every eye shall see him. (Revelation 1:7b)** We must keep in mind that the second coming of Christ will be in two stages. The first stage will be the *Rapture*, when all the righteous, both dead and living, will be caught up to meet Him in the air. The word rapture means "*a catching or snatching away.*" This is the event which is referred to in 1 Thessalonians 4:13-18. At this time Christ will come as a thief in the night, snatching away those who have been washed in the blood and delivered from the wrath to come. However, in out text John said, **every eye shall see him.** He is speaking of the second stage of Our Lord's Second Coming—the *Revelation*. This event will take place at the end of the Tribulation Period when the Lord Jesus comes back with His saints.

> **And Enoch also, the seventh from Adam, prophesied of these, saying, Behold, the Lord cometh with ten thousands of his saints. (Jude 1:14)**

This event will occur at the end of the Tribulation Period just prior to the establishing of the Millennial Kingdom. John described Christ's glorious return.

> **And I saw heaven opened, and behold a white horse; and he that sat upon him was called Faithful and True, and in righteousness he doth**

> **judge and make war. His eyes were as a flame of fire, and on his head were many crowns; and he had a name written, that no man knew, but he himself. And he was clothed with a vesture dipped in blood: and his name is called The Word of God. And the armies which were in heaven followed him upon white horses, clothed in fine linen, white and clean. (Revelation 19:11-14)**

This passage refers to the second stage of the Lord's return when He comes in judgment and after the judgment, the restoration of righteousness upon the earth. The Lord will also establish the Millennial kingdom will be established at this time. Of course, we will study this in more detail when we get to chapter 19. The first stage is in the air for His saints; the second stage is to the earth with His saints. We are told that during this second stage **...every eye shall see him.** It will not be as in the Rapture when He comes secretly for His people, and they are caught up into the air. This event, when **...every eye shall see him,** is when He comes back to the earth and reveals Himself to the whole world in His glory and might. Until the last few years this wasn't possible. But now, with satellite and cable and satellite television, and real time news, **every eye shall see him.**

The Wayward

... they also which pierced him... (Revelation 1:7c) This speaks of the unbelieving Jews who rejected the Messiah and orchestrated Christ's crucifixion. They have been set aside for two thousand years. They are the ones who conspired and instigated the Lord's death. They are the ones who **pierced him.** The first time Jesus came, the Jews rejected and crucified Him.

> **He came unto his own, and his own received him not. (John 1:11)**

The rejection of her Messiah is the most tragic event in the history of Israel. Because of her unbelief, she is in a state of spiritual blindness today.

> **What then? Israel hath not obtained that which he seeketh for; but the election hath obtained it, and the rest were blinded (Romans 11:7)**

As a result of their unbelief, God set Israel aside and began to call the Gentile people unto Himself. However, at the end of the Tribulation, many Jews will recognize the Lord Jesus as their Messiah when He returns. The God of the second chance will save His people. This will be the fulfillment of Zechariah's prophecy.

> **And I will pour upon the house of David, and upon the inhabitants of Jerusalem, the spirit of grace and of supplications: and they shall look upon me whom they have pierced, and they shall mourn for him, as one mourneth for his only son, and shall be in bitterness for him, as one that is in bitterness for his firstborn. (Zechariah 12:10)**
>
> **But one of the soldiers with a spear pierced his side, and forthwith came there out blood and water. (John 19:34)**

Finally, at this time Israel will realize who Jesus is and recognize Him as their Messiah. Jesus will restore the nation of Israel to Himself and establish His Millennial Kingdom upon the earth and rule as King of kings and Lord of lords.

The Wailing

... all kindreds of the earth shall wail because of him. Even so, Amen. (Revelation 1:7d) The word **wail** comes from *"koptō"* and carries the idea of *"beating the breast in grief, to lament, mourn."* All the people of the earth will beat their breasts in grief at the Second Coming of Christ. The judgment of God will be so great that the people living at that time will mourn as they have never mourned before. It will be a time of great wrath and punishment for those who have rejected Christ. Again, this verse refers to the end of the tribulation. This event will usher in the darkest hour the world will ever experience.

> **And then shall appear the sign of the Son of man in heaven: and then shall all the tribes of the earth mourn, and they shall see the Son of man coming in the clouds of heaven with power and great glory. (Matthew 24:30)**

Notice that Christ will return with **power and great glory**. The significance of this glorious event cannot be understated. We are told, **then shall all the tribes of the earth mourn** There is coming an awful time of judgment and reckoning. This will be a fierce time.

> **For then shall be great tribulation, such as was not since the beginning of the world to this time, no, nor ever shall be. And except those days should be shortened, there should no flesh be saved: but for the elect's sake those days shall be shortened. (Matthew 24:21-22)**

The Tribulation Period is also known as the **wrath of the Lamb**. This will be a time so horrific and terrible that men will pray for the rocks of the mountains to fall on them as they beg for death.

> **And the kings of the earth, and the great men, and the rich men, and the chief captains, and the mighty men, and every bondman, and every free man, hid themselves in the dens and in the rocks of the mountains; And said to the mountains and rocks, Fall on us, and hide us from the face of him that sitteth on the throne, and from the wrath of the Lamb: For the great day of his wrath is come; and who shall be able to stand? (Revelation 6:15-17)**

Over and over the Word of God speaks of His coming judgment upon the unbelieving world. This will be an awful time for those on earth. So severe will be the judgment of God in that day that Jesus said:

> **And except those days should be shortened, there should no flesh be saved: but for the elect's sake those days shall be shortened. (Matthew 24:22)**

This describes a time near the end of the Tribulation Period when the antichrist's armies invade Jerusalem. So severe will be the desolation and bloodshed that unless God steps in and shortens the time the very elect (the Jews) will not survive.

There is coming a day when this old world will face the most severe judgment it has ever seen. That judgment will be meted out by the Lord Jesus Christ

HIS PROPHET

As we learned a bit earlier, this book was given to the Apostle John, and He was instructed to write it down and give it to seven specific local Churches in Asia Minor. John was a man of faith and faithfulness. In these next few verses, we get a glimpse into the suffering and sacrifice of this faithful servant of God. Those who are faithful to God often suffer the hostility of the wicked.

The Tribulation He Derived

Tribulation can be a way of life for the believer. We are not promised easy days in a peaceful world. In the days in which John lived, it was not uncommon to suffer severely and even be put to death for the testimony of Christ. We see several truths about John's tribulation.

Involved Partnership

I John, who also am your brother... (Revelation 1:9a) John identifies himself as **your brother**. This reminds us that John was a human being just like you and me. The word **brother** describes one who comes from the same womb. John was a sinner saved by grace. He was born again. John was a brother in the Lord, a brother in the faith. All believers are brothers and sisters in Christ. We all come from the same spiritual womb as it were. Thus, all believers are blood kin brothers and sisters in Christ. Sometimes believers have the tendency to look at these Bible characters as superhuman. However, John reminds us that He is just like us.

Involved Partaking

... and companion... (Revelation 1:9b) Thank God for true companions in the ministry. The word **companion** means *"a partaker or a participant."* John shared in the same persecutions the other believers were dealing with. The Bible never puts preachers on a pedestal. We are mere men and as someone has well said, *"the best of men are only men at best."* John was partaking of the same troubles that all believers must deal with.

Involved Persecution

... in tribulation. (Revelation 1:9c) The word **tribulation** means *"persecution, anguish and affliction."* John was suffering because of his faithfulness to the Lord Jesus Christ. The Bible reminds us:

> **Yea, and all that will live godly in Christ Jesus shall suffer persecution. (2 Timothy 3:12)**

The word **persecution** means *"to afflict, harass or annoy."* The believer who lives for Christ will see persecution. Jesus warned His people that they would not be accepted by this world.

> **If the world hate you, ye know that it hated me before it hated you. If ye were of the world, the world would love his own: but because ye are not of the world, but I have chosen you out of the world, therefore the world hateth you. (John 15:18-19)**

Christ predicted the suffering that was ahead for this Church and all believers. There is no need to be surprised when it comes. The Apostle Peter wrote:

> **Beloved, think it not strange concerning the fiery trial which is to try you, as though some strange thing happened unto you. (1 Peter 4:12)**

Our Saviour has gone through the depths of persecution and death, but He has come out victorious, and so will His children. There is great comfort for the oppressed and persecuted to know that their Saviour has gone before them.

> **I am with you alway, even unto the end of the world. Amen. (Matthew 28:20)**

The Apostle John had been banished to the isle of Patmos because of his testimony of Jesus Christ. He was sent there to be silenced, yet Christ used him to give us one of the greatest books ever written—the Revelation. The unveiling of Christ's plan for the consummation of the ages was revealed on that forsaken island. No one successfully fights against God.

> **But rejoice, inasmuch as ye are partakers of Christ's sufferings; that when his glory shall be revealed ye may be glad also with exceeding joy. (I Peter 4:13)**

Persecution often moves God's message forward. His message will never be silenced. We can not to allow our afflictions to rob us of the privilege of serving Christ. Oliver B. Greene wrote:

> *The only reason some of us are not exiled or thrown into prison is simply because· we do not preach as fervently and as sternly as did Paul, John, Peter and others. This modem "santa claus" religion that is sweeping the country today is not the religion Jesus taught and John practiced.*

Not only did they fail to silence John, but he still speaks today through the book of Revelation.

Involved Patience

... and patience of Jesus Christ... (Revelation 1:9d) John was resolute in his work. The word **patience** means *"endurance, constancy, continuance."* It speaks of bearing up under a load. We see here that John's persecution didn't stop him. John endured the persecution and kept serving Christ. John lived during the time of the awful persecution of Domitian, the Roman Emperor, whose thirst for blood was unquenchable. The Christians of Asia Minor suffered greatly under his rule. John being the pastor of the Church at Ephesus, was especially a target.

Involved Patmos

... was in the isle that is called Patmos... (Revelation 1:9e) Patmos was not a desirable place. It was a terrible place. John was banished to Patmos in order to isolate him from the rest of the world. This was an attempt to silence him. Patmos was an awful place. It was the Alcatraz of the Roman world. It is a small rocky island about ten miles long and six miles wide, located seventy miles southwest of Ephesus in the Aegean Sea. John Walvoord points out:

> *According to Victorinus, John, though aged, was forced to labor in the mines located at Patmos. Early sources also indicated that about A.D. 96, at Domitian's death, John was allowed to return to Ephesus when the Emperor Nerva was in power.*

Joseph A Seiss said of Patmos:

> *"Less than a year ago I passed that island. It is a mere mass of barren rocks; dark in color and cheerless in form. It lies out in the open sea, near the coast of western Asia Minor. It has neither trees nor rivers, nor any land for cultivation, except some little nooks between ledges of rocks. There is still a dingy grotto remaining in which the aged apostle is said to have had his vision. That was John's prison!"*

So many of God's servants have suffered in awful ways in this world but let us keep in mind that this world is not our final home. John Walvoord said:

> *Moses wrote the Pentateuch in the wilderness. David wrote many psalms while being pursued by Saul. Isaiah lived in difficult days and died a martyr's death. Ezekiel wrote in exile. Jeremiah's life was one of trial and persecution. Peter wrote his two letters shortly before martyrdom. Thus, in the will of God the final written revelation was given to John while suffering for Christ and the gospel.*

By this time the Apostle John was an old man and suffered greatly for the cause of Christ. However, we shall see that his tribulation did not stop him. As the old gospel songs goes, *"This world is not my home, I'm just a-passing through."* That was John's attitude. He had his heart set on Christ.

The Testimony He Declared

... for the word of God, and for the testimony of Jesus Christ. (Revelation 1:9f) John was faithful in the ministry that

God had given him. He was a courageous and committed preacher of God's Word. But such preaching goes against the course of this world and that causes friction. John's faithful preaching of the Lord Jesus had gotten the attention of those who hated the Lord and His people. However, God had a divine purpose in John's trouble and persecution.

The Tenacity He Displayed

I was in the Spirit on the Lord's day... (Revelation 1:10a) John was not faint-hearted and timid. He just kept on doing what he had always done. It was the **Lord's day** so he went to Church as it were. Here is a child of God, imprisoned on a desolate island and what does he do? He worships the Lord just as he always had. Worship is a matter of the heart and men cannot take that from us. John's persecution did not hinder him from spending time with the Lord. Jesus said:

> **Blessed are ye, when men shall revile you, and persecute you, and shall say all manner of evil against you falsely, for my sake. Rejoice, and be exceeding glad: for great is your reward in heaven: for so persecuted they the prophets which were before you. (Matthew 5:11-12)**

That is what John was doing! He was rejoicing in his trouble. They can banish us to exile, lock us in prison, put us in chains and shackles, but the heart that knows and loves God can still connect with Him.

The Trumpet He Discovered

As John worshipped in the Spirit, he suddenly heard a great voice behind him. We read about these loud voices and sounds many times in this book. They stress the importance and solemnity of what God is about to say. There are two things we notice about this voice.

The Seriousness Of The Sound

.... and heard behind me a great voice, as of a trumpet, (Revelation 1:10b) This was the powerful voice of the Lord Jesus Christ. In Bible days, trumpets were used to summon people together so that a matter of public importance could be announced. Matters of great importance were about to be announced. The voice as a trumpet signifies that something of great importance is about to be said.

The Speaking Of The Saviour

Saying, I am Alpha and Omega, the first and the last... (Revelation 1:11a) These are titles of eternality. With this great voice, the Lord Jesus Christ identifies Himself as the Eternal God. We will look at this title in more detail a few verses down.

The Tidings He Delivered

... and, What thou seest, write in a book, and send it unto the seven churches which are in Asia; unto Ephesus, and unto Smyrna, and unto Pergamos, and unto Thyatira, and unto Sardis, and unto Philadelphia, and unto Laodicea. (Revelation 1:11b) The responsibility of the Apostle is clearly given. The command to **write in a book, and send it unto the seven churches.** Twelve times in the Book of Revelation John is commanded to write (1:19; 2:1, 8, 12, 18; 3:1, 7, 14; 14:13; 19:9; 21:5). The Lord Jesus names and identifies the seven Churches that were to receive the letters. Thus, those seven congregations were the immediate recipients of the book of Revelation.

A VISION OF THE GLORIFIED CHRIST
Revelation 1:8, 11-20

As the Apostle John began to write and record the book of Revelation, the first vision he received was that of the Lord Jesus standing among the seven golden candlesticks. This vision describes Christ's *Appearance*, *Apparel* and *Authority*.

THE PREEMINENCE OF THE GLORIFIED CHRIST

When John turned, he saw Christ in His glory and went on to pen down a seven-fold description of the glorified Christ. God turned John's banishment into blessing and allowed him to see the glorified Christ. In the following verses we see an eight-fold description of Christ.

His Supremacy

The supremacy of Christ is seen in the titles that He uses of Himself in verses eight and eleven. These are designations that clearly speak of His sovereignty.

His Deity Proclaimed

I am ... (Revelation 1:8a) The Lord Jesus referred to Himself as the **I am**. This is a definite proclamation of deity. This is a title first used of Almighty God.

> **And God said unto Moses, I AM THAT I AM: and he said, Thus shalt thou say unto the children of Israel, I AM hath sent me unto you. (Exodus 3:14)**

In presenting Himself as the great I Am, the Jesus proclaims His deity, self-existence, and sovereignty. He is the eternal God as much God the Father is. There has never been a time when Jesus Christ did not exist.

His Duration Pronounced

... Alpha and Omega, the beginning and the ending, saith the Lord... (Revelation 1:8b) This is Christ speaking here. He identifies Himself as the Alpha and Omega, the first and the last. There is a similar description of Christ given a few verses later.

Saying, I am Alpha and Omega, the first and the last: (Revelation 1:11a)

Alpha is the first letter of the Greek alphabet and **Omega** is the last letter of the Greek alphabet. Jesus declares Himself to be the Self-existent, Eternal, Omnipotent, Omnipresent, and Omniscient God. Praise God, He is not the Alpha and the Beta— He is the Alpha and Omega, the beginning, and the end. He is the:

Author and finisher... (Hebrews 1:2)

Jesus is not a created being as some of the cults suppose. Someone has well said, *"He is the first and the last, and everything in between."* Lehman Strauss said:

> *He is the one who created, controls, and will consummate all things (Ephesians 1:10; Colossians 1:16-17).*

The words Alpha and Omega are used in 1:8, 11: 21:6; 22:13 and always with the expression, **the first and the last** or **the beginning and the ending**. This phrase signifies completeness. Jesus is everything! Jesus is He that is, He that was, He that shall certainly come again someday.

His Determined Program

... which is, and which was, and which is to come... (Revelation 1:8c) Here we again have a clear proclamation of Christ **which is to come.** There is no one, or no power that can thwart Christ's planned return to this earth in judgment.

His Divine Power

... the Almighty. (Revelation 1:8d) He is the all-powerful God. The word **Almighty** comes from the Greek *"pantokrator"* and speaks of the all-powerful Sovereign God. In Isaiah we read:

> **Thus saith the LORD the King of Israel, and his redeemer the LORD of hosts; I am the first, and I am the last; and beside me there is no God. (Isaiah 44:6)**

Floyd Hitchcock in his book, *Lectures on the Revelation,* said of the title Almighty ...

> *These words express the eternal character of the Christ, and there is no higher expression of deity anywhere in Holy Writ than the words which Christ used here, concerning Himself, i.e., "The Almighty."*

J. Allen said ...

> *That which belongs inherently to deity is revealed in Christ. In Him is displayed the omnipotence of deity.*

Lehman Strauss says ...

> *This name of God, which appears not less than forty-eight times in the Old Testament, is here applied to our Lord Jesus Christ. It is the Hebrew word Shaddai, meaning "the sufficient One."*

The first use of this title is in Genesis 17:1, where the God assured Abraham of His blessing and provision in giving him a son. Isaac could only be given by divine intervention. Abraham tried it on his own and made a mess of things. God assured Abraham that only Himself, the Almighty One, could provide such a seemingly impossible blessing.

His Standing

When John turned toward the voice that spoke to him, he saw the Lord Jesus standing amid seven golden candlesticks.

His Action

And I turned to see the voice that spake with me. And being turned, I saw seven golden candlesticks; (Revelation 1:12) The **seven golden candlesticks** are no mystery. God did not leave us to dig and wonder what the candlesticks mean. God interprets the candlesticks for us.

> **the seven candlesticks which thou sawest are the seven churches. (Revelation 1:20)**

So then, these candlesticks represent the seven Churches to which this book was first given. Notice here that Christ is in the midst of the seven candlesticks takes us back to the tabernacle where the candlestick was in the Holy Place. It was the only light, for there were no windows. It was the Priest's duty to replenish the oil (a type of the Holy Spirit) and keep the wicks trimmed so the lights would keep burning bright. Here is Christ, our Great High Priest, walking in the midst of His churches trimming their wicks and replenishing their oil. What a fitting symbol of the Church. Candlesticks serve as a source of light and individual believers who make up local Churches are to shine. Jesus said:

As long as I am in the world, I am the light of the world. (John 9:5)

God's people who have been delivered from darkness and translated into the realm of Light.

Giving thanks unto the Father, which hath made us meet to be partakers of the inheritance of the saints in light: Who hath delivered us from the power of darkness, and hath translated us into the kingdom of his dear Son: (Colossians 1:12-13)

As Christ's people we are commanded to ...

... walk as children of light: (Ephesians 5:8)

We are no longer children of darkness. The local Church is made up of **children of light** who reflect the light of Christ. The believer is to live in such a way that the world sees Jesus Christ in him. Jesus said:

Let your light so shine before men, that they may see your good works, and glorify your Father which is in heaven. (Matthew 5:16)

Light is something the world desperately needs more of today. God's people are to shine as lights in a dark world. The redeemed are on constant display before the lost. Hence. we are to shine as lights before men that they may see our **good works.**

His Association

And in the midst of the seven candlesticks one like unto the Son of man... (Revelation 1:13a) The designation **Son of man** is a name that Jesus used often for Himself in the gospels. (Matthew 9:6; 10:23; 12:8, 40; 13:37; 16:13; 17:9; 18:11). The prophet Daniel used this title of the Messiah (Danial 7:13;

A Vision Of The Glorified Christ

Matthew 26:64). Stephen also when he saw Jesus at the right hand of God (Acts 7:56). The title **Son of man** has to do with the incarnation. It is a title that refers to Christ's humanity. The glorified deity speaking here is the same Jesus that ...

> ... **made himself of no reputation, and took upon him the form of a servant, and was made in the likeness of men: (Philippians 2:7)**
>
> **And the Word was made flesh, and dwelt among us, (John 1:14)**

The first time Jesus came He associated Himself with us by His incarnation. He was one hundred percent God and one hundred percent man at the same time. This title reminds us that the One who once came to this world as a man is about to return as King of kings and Lord of lords.

His Apparel

> ... **clothed with a garment down to the foot, and girt about the paps with a golden girdle. (Revelation 1:13b)**

In this vision Jesus was clothed with a **garment down to the foot** and He was wearing **a golden girdle.** These are garments that represent His office as High priest. As High priest He is now interceding for the saints, before the throne of God the Father.

> **Seeing then that we have a great high priest, that is passed into the heavens, Jesus the Son of God, let us hold fast our profession. (Hebrews 4:14)**

The **girdle** shows His preparation for service. The One who is now on the throne of grace is about to take His place on the throne of judgment. Once in humility He girded Himself and served His disciples. Now He is girded about the breasts, which speak of affection, with a golden girdle, which also speaks of Deity. John had seen Him at Calvary, naked and suffering, but now He is seen in His glory, clothed with His official garments.

His Superiority

His head and his hairs were white like wool, as white as snow... (Revelation 1:14a) These symbols reflect His seniority and superiority. Paul said:

> **And he is before all things and by Him all things consist. (Colossians 1:17)**

The **head** speaks of wisdom and **white** speaks of purity. Here we have a symbol of the incomprehensible wisdom and absolute flawless purity of the Judge Who is preparing to return in judgment. Here we see Christ as the **Ancient of Days** from the book of Daniel.

> **I beheld till the thrones were cast down, and the Ancient of days did sit, whose garment was white as snow, and the hair of his head like the pure wool: his throne was like the fiery flame, and his wheels as burning fire. (Daniel 7:9)**

The symbolic language here is rich. In the Word of God, white or gray hair speaks to wisdom, respect, and reverence.

> **... the beauty of old men is the gray head. (Proverbs 20:29)**

> **The hoary head is a crown of glory, if it be found in the way of righteousness. (Proverbs 16:31)**

Society today worships youth. Everyone wants to stay young. Since it is impossible to stay young, most try to look young. However, age and gray hair in the Word of God is an adornment, not a disgrace. The white hair denotes the reverence and respect that is due Christ because of His eternal wisdom and holiness.

His Search

His eyes were as a flame of fire; (Revelation 1:14b) Jesus Christ is the all-knowing God. Nothing can be hidden from Him. Fire is the thing that consumes and devours. Matthew Henry said the eyes of fire speak of His *"piercing and penetrating into the very hearts and reins of men."* His eyes, as a flame of fire, speak of the fact that God is a

> **... consuming fire. (Hebrews 12:29)**

His eyes as a **flame of fire** speaks of His righteous judgment. When Christ judges, nothing will be hidden from Him. The eyes of fire speak of His penetrating ability to search the hearts and minds of man.

> All things are naked and opened unto the eyes of Him with whom they have to do. (Hebrews 4:13)
>
> For the LORD seeth not as man seeth; for man looketh on the outward appearance, but the LORD looketh on the heart. (1 Samuel 16:7b)

His eyes will search in judgment. They pierce; they penetrate; they commend or condemn. There is no person or thing that will escape the examination of His eyes of fire. Everything will be laid open and exposed before His eyes.

His Sovereignty

And his feet like unto fine brass, as if they burned in a furnace... (Revelation 1:15a) The Lord Jesus is the omnipotent God Who will defeat His enemies. His feet speak of absolute authority and victory over His enemies. This is seen several times in Scripture.

> Thou madest him to have dominion over the works of thy hands; thou hast put all things under his feet: (Psalm 8:6)
>
> For he must reign, till he hath put all enemies under his feet. (1 Corinthians 15:25)
>
> And hath put all things under his feet, and gave him to be the head over all things to the church, (Ephesians 1:22)
>
> Thou hast put all things in subjection under his feet. For in that he put all in subjection under him, he left nothing that is not put under him. But now we see not yet all things put under him. (Hebrews 2:8)

His feet are like brass. **Brass** speaks of judgment. The brazen altar in the Tabernacle was the place where the sin offering was sacrificed. (Exodus 38:2), and the laver, also of brass, spoke of self-judgment, for here the priests washed their hands and feet as they went in and out of the Holy Place. The Brazen serpent was a type of the cross where Christ received the judgment of God for our sin (Numbers 21:9 & John 3:14). His feet looked as if they were **burned in a furnace.** A furnace is used for smelting. It is a place where impurities are separated from metal. Jesus is preparing to turn the heat up and pour out His wrath upon the earth.

His Sound

His voice as the sound of many waters. (Revelation 1:15b) Water symbolizes the Word Of God.

> **He that rejecteth me, and receiveth not my words, hath one that judgeth him: the word that I have spoken, the same shall judge him in the last day. (John 12:48)**

Many waters speaks of His power and majesty.

> **The LORD on high is mightier than the noise of many waters, yea, than the mighty waves of the sea. (Psalm 93:4)**

The voice, once so loving and gentle, is now as the sound of many waters. Wicked men reject Him and His word now, but when our Lord Jesus Christ comes back in judgment, His Word will be heard above all.

> **That at the name of Jesus every knee should bow, of things in heaven, and things in earth, and things under the earth; And that every tongue should confess that Jesus Christ is Lord, to the glory of God the Father. (Philippians 2:10-11)**

The many waters describe what the voice of Christ sounds like when He speaks in judgment. It will be the most powerful and terrifying thing that sinful man has ever heard.

His Sword

... out of his mouth went a sharp two edged sword ... (Revelation 1:16) The Word of God is referred to as a sword. Paul described the word of God as

> **... the sword of the Spirit... (Ephesians 6:17)**

A sword is used to protect and defend the righteous and punish and destroy the wicked. The Word of God is powerful and cuts to the heart.

> For the word of God is quick, and powerful, and sharper than any twoedged sword, piercing even to the dividing asunder of soul and spirit, and of the joints and marrow, and is a discerner of the thoughts and intents of the heart. (Hebrews 4:12)

The Word of Christ, at His coming in judgment, will go forth with power and force.

His Splendor

And his countenance was as the sun shineth in his strength. (Revelation 1:16b) When Jesus was here on earth, wicked men beat and spit in His face, but no more! Never again will sinful man lay a hand on the Lord Jesus Christ! In eternity all the Glory of God will be seen in Him. This reminds us of His transfiguration.

> And was transfigured before them: and his face did shine as the sun, and his raiment was white as the light. (Matthew 17:2)

Also see Exodus 34:30 where the face of Moses shined from being in the presence of God. The Scottish Preacher, Horatius Bonar wrote ...

> *Such is the excellence of the Lord Jesus Christ. All divine and all human perfections are in Him. 'In Him dwelleth all the fullness of the Godhead bodily.,' In Him are the unsearchable riches. He is 'the king in His beauty;' He is 'fairer than the children of men.' Thus, excellent is the Church's Head, and He is Head over all things to the Church. He is, moreover, 'Prince of the kings of the earth;' and all allegiance from earth as well as heaven, from nations as well as Churches, from kings as well as saints, is due to Him. All crowns are His, all scepters, all thrones. Heaven is now full of His glory, and ere long earth shall be the same.*

Just think about the fact that this same Jesus is the One Who came to earth, took man's place, and died under the judgment of

Almighty God for the sin of lost mankind. The day is coming when we will dwell with Him. We will see Him in His glory just as John did.

THE POWER OF THE GLORIFIED CHRIST

John's encounter with the glorified Christ had a powerful effect on him. The same is still true today. Anyone who has a significant encounter with Christ is changed.

The Terror Experienced

And when I saw him, I fell at his feet as dead... (Revelation 1:17a) Is there any wonder that John falls on his face when he sees the glorified Saviour? The effect of the glorious vision of the Lord Jesus Christ was overwhelming. This is the same John that walked with Jesus for three and a half years. But now he sees Him in all His glory and splendor and is unable to stand in His presence. He falls as a dead man. The same thing happened with Isaiah, Ezekiel, Paul and others in the Word of God.

> **As the appearance of the bow that is in the cloud in the day of rain, so was the appearance of the brightness round about. This was the appearance of the likeness of the glory of the LORD. And when I saw it, I fell upon my face, and I heard a voice of one that spake. (Ezekiel 1:28)**

> **So he came near where I stood: and when he came, I was afraid, and fell upon my face: but he said unto me, Understand, O son of man: for at the time of the end shall be the vision. (Daniel 8:17)**

> **And he fell to the earth, and heard a voice saying unto him, Saul, Saul, why persecutest thou me? (Acts 9:4)**

Likewise, upon seeing the Lord, John was immediately floored and fell in fear at the sight and voice of the glorified Saviour.

The Touch Endowed

And he laid his right hand upon me... (Revelation 1:17b) This is the life changing touch of God. John is overwhelmed and on his face in fear before the God of glory. However, as John lay on his face before Jesus, the God of the universe stooped down and laid His hand on him. Have you ever heard of a more tender moment? What a warming and precious moment we see here between God and one of His children. Here is Deity demonstrating compassion beyond comprehension on a mere man. What tenderness! God's right hand speaks of Strength and Satisfaction.

> **Strong is Thy hand, and high is Thy right hand. (Psalm 89:13)**
>
> **Thou openest thine hand, and satisfiest the desire of every living thing. (Psalm 145:16)**

The hand which was pierced for us also comforts us. To have the hand of God on a person is a powerful and satisfying thing.

The Tranquility Extended

... saying unto me, Fear not; I am the first and the last: (Revelation 1:17c) John is told to **Fear not.** These are words of comfort and calm. God's people do not have to live in fear.

> **For God hath not given us the spirit of fear; but of power, and of love, and of a sound mind. (2 Timothy 1:7)**

I am the first and the last refers to the eternality of Jesus. Jesus gives John assurance by assuring him of Who He is. This is a title used by God in the Old Testament.

> **Thus saith the LORD the King of Israel, and his redeemer the LORD of hosts; I am the first, and I am the last; and beside me there is no God. (Isaiah 44:6)**
>
> **Hearken unto me, O Jacob and Israel, my called; I am he; I am the first, I also am the last. (Isaiah 48:12)**
>
> **Who hath wrought and done it, calling the generations from the beginning? I the LORD, the first, and with the last; I am he. (Isaiah 41:4)**

Christ uses the same title three times in Revelation (Revelation 1:17, 2:8, 22:13). Jesus is the self-existing, ever-living, eternal God. Thus, this title is irrefutable proof of the deity of Christ and His absolute supremacy. As God's people we do not have to fear when we are right with Him.

> **Fear thou not; for I am with thee: be not dismayed; for I am thy God: I will strengthen thee; yea, I will help thee; yea, I will uphold thee with the right hand of my righteousness. (Isaiah 41:10)**
>
> **No weapon that is formed against thee shall prosper; And every tongue that shall rise against thee in judgment thou shalt condemn. This is the heritage of the servants of the LORD, And their righteousness is of me, saith the LORD. (Isaiah 54:17)**

These are the promises of the eternal God. God's promises are good as long as He lives. On the Mount of Transfiguration, when the disciple had witnessed the glorified Christ, it was the touch of Jesus' hand that satisfied the hearts and gave courage to His fearful disciples.

> **And when the disciples heard it, they fell on their face, and were sore afraid. And Jesus came and touched them, and said, Arise, and be not afraid. (Matthew 17:6-7)**

Likewise, the touch of the Lord Jesus stripped John of his fear allowing him to rise and record the marvelous book of Revelation. The touch of God is what we need. The eternal God gives us the encouragement and strength we need.

The Triumph Established

I am he that liveth, and was dead; and, behold, I am alive for evermore, Amen; and have the keys of hell and of death. (Revelation 1:18) What a statement of absolute victory! Jesus Christ is the only person who could honestly make such a statement. He is indeed the eternal God. There are four significant statements made in this verse.

The Resurrected Saviour

I am he that liveth... (Revelation 1:18a) This is the third **I am** statement of Jesus in the book of Revelation. The One who has appeared and is speaking to John is none other than the resurrected Son of God. He is the ever-living God. Oliver B. Greene points out:

> *He is the Living One from eternity through eternity. The incarnation did not originate the life of Jesus ... He was in the beginning with the Father. But the incarnation was the manifestation of the Christ who had existed from all eternity.*

Though infidels and liberals have done everything in their power to prove that He is dead, Jesus is the ever-living God. He is alive and well! Founders and leaders of various religions have lived and died—they remain dead. However, Jesus Christ, the founder of the New Testament Church died, and He is alive today seated at the right hand of God the Father in glory (Hebrews 12:2). Oliver B. Greene said:

> *The greatest bombshell ever to explode in the face of an unbelieving world was the bodily resurrection of Jesus Christ.*

God's Word proclaims the resurrection and man must believe it or remain lost. The testimony at Christ's tomb is simply:

He is not here: for he is risen ... (Matthew 28:6)

Praise God! Jesus is no longer in the grave! Rather, He is in Heaven seated at the right hand of God the Father. Furthermore, the Bible says He:

... is able also to save them to the uttermost that come unto God by him, seeing he ever liveth to make intercession for them. (Hebrews 7:25)

The devil hates the doctrine of Christ's resurrection because it is where He was defeated. What a death blow the resurrection dealt to Satan.

The Redemptive Sacrifice

... and was dead... (Revelation 1:18b) This reminds us of that fact that Jesus died for the sins of mankind. Jesus was dead. He came to this world for that purpose. He came to die for the sins of man. Jesus' death was necessary to pay the sin debt. Jesus took upon Himself a human body and as the God-Man, did what the law could not do.

> **For the law of the Spirit of life in Christ Jesus hath made me free from the law of sin and death. For what the law could not do, in that it was weak through the flesh, God sending his own Son in the likeness of sinful flesh, and for sin, condemned sin in the flesh: (Romans 8:2-3)**

We are told that when the Lord Jesus died on the cross, He tasted death for every man.

> **But we see Jesus, who was made a little lower than the angels for the suffering of death, crowned with glory and honour; that he by the grace of God should taste death for every man. (Hebrews 2:9)**

In His death and resurrection, Jesus conquered death, Hell, and the grave. On the basis of His atoning work whosoever will, may come to Him for salvation.

The Related Security

... and, behold, I am alive for evermore, Amen... (Revelation 1:18c) Jesus was crucified and buried in a tomb. But now He is alive and saying, **I am alive for evermore**. Here is the difference between Jesus and every other religious leader that ever or will ever exist, Jesus was dead, but He is now alive. Oliver B. Greene said:

> *He is alive forevermore, He will die no more, He has emerged from the darkness and the domain of death, He has conquered death, He has risen from the dead, and He announces to the saints in the Church that He will die no more.*

This is the truth that separates Christianity from every other religion. Christianity is the only religion that can claim a resurrected Founder. The word **evermore** stresses the fact that Jesus will never die again.

> But this man, after he had offered one sacrifice for sins for ever, sat down on the right hand of God; (Hebrews 10:12)

Jesus' death on the cross was sufficient to pay for man's sin and placate the righteous requirements of God Almighty for sinners. This is where the idea of security comes in. Jesus died to save me, and He ever lives to keep me saved. As long as God is alive, the true believer is secure.

The Royal Sovereignty

> **... and have the keys of hell and of death. (Revelation 1:18d)** Keys speak of authority. The one has the key to a building or room determines who will or will not be allowed in.

As the one who conquered death, He now has the keys of death and Hell. There is no reason for any believer to fear death. When Jesus walked out of the tomb, He conquered death. Keep in mind that death is Satan's handiwork. Hence, Jesus became man and died for the sins of man so that He could destroy him (Satan) that had the power of death.

> Forasmuch then as the children are partakers of flesh and blood, he also himself likewise took part of the same; that through death he might destroy him that had the power of death, that is, the devil; (Hebrews 2:14)

Keys lock and unlock doors. Here, the keys speak of access and authority. Whoever has the keys is in control. As the sovereign God, Jesus has full authority over death. Paul said:

> O death, where is thy sting? O grave, where is thy victory? (1 Corinthians 15:55)

Through His death and resurrection, the grave is defeated, and the chains of death are broken. At death, all bodies decay into dust. God has determined

> ... for dust thou art, and unto dust shalt thou return. (Genesis 3:19)

This is what sin did for man. But. Christ now holds keys of hell and of death. Thus, the grave cannot hold God's people. Because Jesus lives forever, believers will live forever.

Furthermore, His people are guaranteed new bodies like His glorious resurrection body.

> **For our conversation is in heaven; from whence also we look for the Saviour, the Lord Jesus Christ: Who shall change our vile body, that it may be fashioned like unto his glorious body, according to the working whereby he is able even to subdue all things unto himself. (Philippians 3:20-21)**
>
> **Beloved, now are we the sons of God, and it doth not yet appear what we shall be: but we know that, when he shall appear, we shall be like him; for we shall see him as he is. (1 John 3:2)**

When Jesus returns for His people, every grave of every saint will burst open and give up the body of the child of God. The corrupt body of sin and depravity will be changed, and every believer will receive a glorified body.

> **In a moment, in the twinkling of an eye, at the last trump: for the trumpet shall sound, and the dead shall be raised incorruptible, and we shall be changed. (1 Corinthians 15:52)**

What a promise! John said, **we shall be like him; for we shall see him as he is. (1 John 3:2)** At the time of the rapture, the blessed hope that God has given to every believer will be brought to pass.

> **For whom he did foreknow, he also did predestinate to be conformed to the image of his Son, that he might be the firstborn among many brethren. (Romans 8:29)**

This is God's plan for every one of His children. The Christiaan will be brought into the full likeness of the Lord Jesus Christ. Once we are ushered into our Saviour's presence, our glorification will become a reality and we will be fully conformed to the image of Christ. The child of God has a glorious future.

THE PROGRAM OF THE GLORIFIED CHRIST

Write the things which thou hast seen, and the things which are, and the things which shall be hereafter. (Revelation 1:19)

A Vision Of The Glorified Christ

This verse presents to us the threefold division of the book of Revelation. The Lord Jesus now instructs John to write down His design or His plan for things to come. It is important to understand that verse nineteen gives us the natural divisions of the book of Revelation. This is God's own outline of Revelation. The apostle John was to write three things:

- *First*, **things which thou hast seen**.
- *Second*, **things which are**.
- *Third*, **things which shall be hereafter**.

Verse 19 is the key that will unlock many doors in the Book of Revelation. Thus, it should be noted that this is the key verse to interpreting the book of Revelation. The Lord laid Revelation out in chronological order. Anyone who does not discern the correct interpretation of this verse will probably miss the message of the book. This verse breaks it down into three major divisions of the book.

The Past

The things which thou hast seen... (Revelation 1:19a) John was given instructions to write the things he had already seen. (Chapter 1). You will notice the past tense as this chapter ends. This refers to everything John has seen thus far. This would include Christ standing in the midst of the seven candlesticks and holding the seven stars in His right hand. This would also include the description of the glorified Saviour. These things took place on the isle of Patmos when Christ visited John. They are in the past. That is, all these things, along with everything else mentioned in chapter 1, were in the past as far as John's vision was concerned.

Present

...The things which are... (Revelation 1:19b) This speaks of the Church age and describes a period of time from the beginning of the Church to the Rapture. This is the age in which we live today. The messages are written to seven Churches of Asia Minor to represent the succession of seven different periods of Church history, from the beginning of the Church to the Rapture. The entire view of Church history is laid out here in a most wonderful and accurate way. Thus, we can look upon these Church periods as a prophetic chart of the entire history of the Church.

The Prophecy

...The things which shall be hereafter. (Revelation 1:19c) These are the things that will take place on earth after Christians are raptured out of the world. This will include the outpouring of God's wrath during the seven-year Tribulation Period, the regathering of the nation of Israel into her homeland, the battle of Armageddon, the Millennial Kingdom, and the eternal state (Chapters 4-22).

THE PASTORS OF THE GLORIFIED CHRIST

As we come to verse 20, we have a clear demonstration of how Scripture interprets Scripture. This verse breaks down into four thoughts.

The Mystery Proclaimed

The mystery of the seven stars which thou sawest in my right hand, and the seven golden candlesticks... (Revelation 1:20a) Jesus explains the mystery of the seven golden candlesticks and seven stars. The word **mystery** speaks of that which was previously unknown. In the New Testament it refers to the doctrine which is specific for the Church Age. It is called **the mystery** because its truths were never revealed in Old Testament Scriptures.

The Messengers Provided

The seven stars are the angels of the seven churches... (Revelation 1:20b) The Book of Revelation often interprets itself. The **seven stars** were first mentioned in verse 16 and are explained here as the **angels of the seven churches.** There is a great deal of controversy over the identification of the angels of the seven Churches. We need to keep in mind that the word for angel can speak of heavenly beings or human beings. The word **angel** comes from *"aggeloi"* and means *"messenger."* The holy angels are messengers of God in that they are ministering spirits sent forth by Him to accomplish His purposes (Psalm 104:4;

Hebrews 1:7). However, human beings can be messengers also. Many Bible scholars believe these stars are the Pastors of the local churches. John Walvoord says...

> *These messengers were probably the pastors of these churches or prophets through whom the message was to be delivered to the congregation.*

The stars are the pastors who are provided by God to the local Churches. This word comes from a Greek word, translated *"angels, messengers, pastors."* These pastors are in the right hand, the hand of power, the hand of authority, the right hand of Jesus Christ.

The Meeting Place

... and the seven candlesticks which thou sawest are the seven churches. (Revelation 1:20) The **seven golden candlesticks** also seen in verses 12 and 13 are identified as **the seven churches**. The purpose of a candlestick is to provide a place where a candle could be placed, thereby providing light for a particular area. These **candlesticks** represent the local Church. God has placed faithful local Churches throughout the world to provide gospel light to the lost world.

The Message Propagated

The **candlesticks** (Churches) and the **stars** (Pastors) give off light. Testimony is the main thought here. The lamp stand in the Tabernacle was to give light and never go out (Exodus 35:14; 27:20). Its source of light was the oil, which is a symbol of the Holy Spirit. The local Churches are God's light bearers in this world. The source of their shining is the Holy Spirit in the life of individual believers.

> **But ye shall receive power, after that the Holy Ghost is come upon you: and ye shall be witnesses unto me both in Jerusalem, and in all Judaea, and in Samaria, and unto the uttermost part of the earth. (Acts 1:8)**

In the Word of God soul winners are compared to shining stars.

And they that be wise shall shine as the brightness of the firmament; and they that turn many to righteousness as the stars for ever and ever. (Daniel 12:3)

The Lord Jesus described the believer's light bearing when He said:

Ye are the light of the world. (Matthew 5:14)

Back in verse twelve we learned that when John heard the voice and turned, he saw in the midst of the Churches, the Lord Jesus Christ. He had once hung on the cross, in the midst of two thieves, He had promised to be in the midst of His disciples when they gathered together for prayer, He appeared in their midst after His resurrection to encourage them. Here, Christ is seen in the **midst** of the seven churches. This is where Jesus longs to be. He died for the Church and is the head of the body. Today Jesus Christ is outside of many churches instead of being in the midst of them, as He ought to be. Many churches have their programs, possessions, properties, etc., but the one thing they need is Christ dwelling in their midst.

THE CHURCH AGE
Revelation 2:1-3:22

Chapters two and three of Revelation are comprised of letters written by our Lord to seven local Churches of Asia Minor. These Churches represent Church history from the beginning, on through until the Rapture of the Church. Therefore, in these seven letters, the glorified Christ gave to the Apostle John a prophetic outline of Church history. In his commentary on *Revelation*, Lehman Strauss quotes R. H. Clayton:

> *It can be no mere coincidence that these Epistles do set out the salient characteristics of the Church through the centuries, and no one can deny that they are presented in historic sequence.*

We can see from the names and characteristics of these seven churches that they align perfectly with the corresponding dates in Church history. Not only are they in perfect order, but the very characteristics and conditions are clearly seen in the history of the Church. There were more than seven churches is the Roman province of Asia Minor. There was Colosse and Hierapolis, for example, but they were not mentioned by John. Our Lord chose seven specific local Churches that would portray the Church age. As we study these letters, we see a sad decline in the spiritual condition of the Church, until we finally end in up in Laodicean times, with the Church in apostasy.

. While these periods of Church history have come and gone, we still see the characteristics of all these Churches today. Every Church out there fits in one of these seven church types. In fact, we have a threefold application:

- *Primary Application*—These letters were written to seven local churches in Asia Minor. As we mentioned before, there were more than seven Churches in this area. However, the Lord Jesus chose these seven specific

- *Prophetic Application*—These seven letters consist of a snapshot of the Church age. Again, the characteristics of these Churches perfectly represent the stages of Church history from its beginning till the rapture.
- *Personal Application*—The truth found in these seven letters can be applied to the individual believer. We are admonished, **He that hath an ear, let him hear what the Spirit saith unto the churches.** That is, we are to learn from these Churches an make a personal application to our lives. These letters were written to address various situations that prevailed at that time as well as in our day.

In his commentary on Revelation, John F. Walvoord said ...

These messages, therefore, contain divine revelation and exhortation pertaining to the present age; and, having special pertinence in the present situation in the church, they constitute one of the most incisive and penetrating exhortations in the entire New Testament in relation to church doctrine and Christian living.

In these letters we see the End from the beginning. Sit has been well said that prophecy is history in preview. That is certainly true and nowhere is it clearer than in these seven letters written to the seven Churches of Asia Minor. We can see in advance just what to expect as history unfolds.

THE CHURCH OF EPHESUS

The beginning of the Church to A.D. 100. **Ephesus** represents the Apostolic Church. Ephesus means *"desirable."* It speaks of the early church with all the zeal of its first love for the Christ. A great work was being done there. Dr. Harold B. Sightlier wrote:

The church at Ephesus, which is the first that John deals within chapter number 2 verse 1, is symbolic of the apostolic day-the day when the twelve apostles were yet alive, and the early believers were yet alive, and the days before they were scattered throughout all the area because of persecution that we read about in Acts chapter number 8. With chapter 8 of the Acts of the apostles, the church was persecuted, and they were scattered throughout all of Asia, throughout all of the Middle East. Now this church at Ephesus is symbolic of that early day, before the dispersion and before the rising tide of persecution.

The Ephesus Church started out with a great love for Christ and a burning desire to see souls saved, but toward the end of the first century she left her first love, and the fire went out and she no longer exists.

THE CHURCH OF SMYRNA

A.D. 100—312. The city of Smyrna was located about thirty-five miles from Ephesus. It was a city of about a hundred thousand people in John's Day. It was called the crown city because it was surrounded by hills resembling a crown. **Smyrna** represented the period of great persecution. Smyrna means myrrh. Myrrh is a fragrant spice which has to be crushed to bring forth its full fragrance. The Christians of this era were crushed and persecuted, but the more they suffered the more fragrant was their testimony. During this time thousands of Christians were brought into the theaters of Rome to be fed to lions while spectators cheered. Many were crucified, others were covered with animal skins and tortured to death by wild dogs. They were covered in tar and set on fire and used as human torches. They were boiled in oil and burned at the stake. These faithful warriors of Christ died vicious deaths to glory of their Saviour. It has been estimated that during this period over five million Christians were martyred for the testimony of Jesus Christ.

THE CHURCH OF PERGAMOS

A.D. 312—606. **Pergamos** was in the Roman providence of Asia west of what is now Turkey. The city was noted for its vast library, containing some two hundred thousand volumes. It is called **Satan's seat** by John (Revelation 2:13). Satan had a stronghold there. This city was one of the most prominent cities of Asia and was about fifty miles north of Smyrna. Pergamos represented that period of Church history when worldliness crept in, and the Church received the favor of the State. Pergamos means marriage and elevation. The church had just passed through the martyr period and now entered into a time ruled by Constantine. When he became emperor of Rome, he sent out an imperial decree, lifting the ban on Christianity. He showered favors on the Christian Church. Pagan temples were taken over by Christians and the government sponsored them. The Church of Pergamos received its true meaning by becoming married to the world and elevated in its sight.

THE CHURCH OF THYATIRA

A.D.606 to the end. **Thyatira** portrays the Church in the Dark Ages, as it was then filled with corruption. The word Thyatira comes from two words meaning sacrifice and continual. It was during this time that the Church of Rome took off. It's no doubt that the Roman sacrifice of the mass is foretold here. How remarkable is this prophecy, for every time a Roman priest celebrates the mass, he teaches that the Lord Jesus Christ is sacrificed again, not only for the sins of the living, but also for the dead. The doctrine of transubstantiation teaches that priests have the power to turn bread into the actual body of Christ and wine into the actual blood of Christ. The belief is that every time mass is celebrated the actual body and blood of Christ is offered again. This false theory belittles Christ's one sacrifice for sins fore ever (Hebrews 10:10-14).

THE CHURCH OF SARDIS

1520 to the end. **Sardis** was symbolic of the Church during the period of the great reformation period. The name Sardis means *"escaping Ones"* or *"remnant."* This church had the name that it was alive, but it was in fact dead. The characteristics Sardis parallels the denominational practices of the Protestant Reformation. Thus, this church gives us a prophetic picture of the reformation Church that escaped from the bonds of Rome. At this point spiritual darkness covered the land. It was only the so-called hierarchy that the Scriptures. However, with the invention of the printing press the word of God was put into the hands of the lay people. With this a new study of the Bible began, heresies were exposed, and the reformation started.

However, the reformation fell short of accomplishing all that it should have. While it protested the ecclesiastical hierarchy of Thyatira it went to the other extreme. Being free from the hierarchy they were split by the abuse of their own liberty and freedom and became divided into several sects and groups establishing their own hierarchical system. This is all a matter of Church history.

THE CHURCH OF PHILADELPHIA

1750 to the 1900. **Philadelphia** denotes the great Missionary period of Church history. Millions came to Christ to throughout this period of history. The word **Philadelphia** means brotherly love. This was one of the most blessed times of the church age. The light of the Reformation had just about burned out and Christendom had become cold, formalistic, and dead. The Lord at that time brought about a great revival. This revival centered largely in the United States, England, Scotland and Wales and was the beginning of one of the greatest Missionary movements of all times. People were being saved by the thousands and looking for the Saviour to appear at any moment. Being aware of Christ's possible return at any moment, they occupied themselves with holy living, the defense of the faith and the preaching of the gospel of Christ.

THE CHURCH AT LAODICEA

1900 to the end. This Church clearly represents the apostate Church of the last days. It speaks of the present stage of Church history. The name Laodicea comes from two Greek words, *"laos"*, meaning *"the people"* and *"dikao"* meaning *"to rule."* It means the peoples' rule or the peoples' rights. What a picture of the present day. Surely the church is lukewarm today. It is neither on fire for

God, nor is it completely cold. It is indifferent: we can see this church in the world today. We have many fancy church buildings, large denominations, and much money, but the church is poor. Many Churches have stored up great accounts in the banks of this world, but nothing in the bank of Heaven. Clayton Derstine said it well:

> "Magnificent buildings, imposing services, high salaried preachers, paid pews, expensive choirs, all furnished by Balak's gold, but the poor and sinful are not wanted. They know it and stay away. How sad! This church counts itself rich, but in the eyes of God is poor. This is the church that Christ will vomit out of His mouth."

When the characteristics of these seven churches are considered in view of Church history, we can easily see that these letters perfectly correspond to and represent the stages of church history. Therefore, we are compelled to look upon these seven messages to the early churches as a prophetic preview of the entire Church age.

These two chapters constitute one of the most enlightening and most unique portions of scripture in the book of Revelation. Why? Because they reveal to us the end from the beginning. They make known to us, in advance, just what to expect as history unfolds before our eyes. What is written here has always helped Christians to understand what would be next in the divine plan for the Church age.

Such truth, such foreknowledge, my friends, is priceless to the child of God, because it serves as a beacon of light to guide our steps, and it serves to comfort us as we labor on in a world of sin and sorrow, with tares among the wheat, and with difficulty on every hand. It helps us to understand that our present circumstances are not to be the eternal state of things, but that soon the long dark night will end, and a new day will dawn for the child of God.

EPHESUS: THE LACKING CHURCH
Revelation 2:1-7

The message to the Church of Ephesus—Beginning of the Church to A.D. 100. Ephesus represents the Apostolic Church. The word **Ephesus** means *"desirable."* It was the early church with all the zeal of its first love, burning for Christ. This Church started out with a great love for Christ and truth, but toward the end of the first century she left her first love and as a result, began to cool off. Our labor for Christ is to always to be based on our love for Him. We must be careful that we do not fall into the same trap that captured the Ephesus Christians. We must prioritize our life—it is love and then labor. We serve Him because we love Him—not simply because we have to. There are several important lessons learned from this Church.

THE PLACE OF THE EPHESIAN CHURCH

Ephesus was one of, if not the most important, cities in Asia Minor. It was a large city on the west coast of Asia Minor. Paul founded the Church of Ephesus and it had been a successful Church, but by the time of John, she had left her first love.

A Prominent Place

The city of Ephesus had the largest theatre in the world. It could hold up to fifty thousand spectators. It was a center of government and trade, and there was a great seaport there which resulted in a great deal of industry and wealth. It was also well known as a center of learning and art.

A Profitable Place

Ephesus was a great commercial center and there was a lot happening there. With the hustle and bustle of activity and the floods of people who did their shopping and business, it was a profitable place.

A Pagan Place

Ephesus was the center of the worship of Diana, the goddess of fertility. There were thousands who came to Ephesus to participate in the immoral practices of Diana.

THE PRAISE OF THE EPHESIAN CHURCH

Unto the angel of the church of Ephesus write; These things saith he that holdeth the seven stars in his right hand, who walketh in the midst of the seven golden candlesticks; (Revelation 2:1) We notice that the Lord Jesus Christ **walketh in the midst of the seven golden candlesticks.** This speaks of His presence in the early Church. However, when we get to the Church of Laodicea Christ is locked outside the Church and knocking on the door in an attempt to gain entrance.

Christ appears here as the Judge before whom every believer will stand. You will notice that the seven stars are in His **right hand.** The right hand speaks of power and authority. Christ searches their hearts, and he first commends them. He praises the Church of Ephesus for several things.

It was a Desirable Church

Unto the angel of the church of Ephesus ... (Revelation 2:1a) The word **Ephesus** means *"desired."* Ephesus was a desirable Church. The early Churches were the beginning of an eternal plan and purpose. The Church of Ephesus was started by the Apostle Paul. It began with great fire and was marked by its missionary and evangelistic zeal, as well as its uncompromising stand for the truth. The Church of Ephesus was Fundamental, Fiery, Faithful, and Fruitful—it was a desirable Church.

It was a Dedicated Church

Jesus said, **I know thy works, and thy labour... (Revelation 2:2a)** What a sobering thought! Jesus Christ knows! There is not one thing in our lives that He doesn't know about.

> **The eyes of the LORD are in every place, beholding the evil and the good. (Proverbs 15:3)**

He knows the sincere, loving desire of every child of God. He knows our hurts and heart aches. He knows our works. Likewise, Jesus knows all the bitterness, malice, and wickedness of the hypocrites. Sinful man will get away with absolutely nothing at the judgement. It is a definite fact that God knows about and

> **...shall bring every work into judgment, with every secret thing, whether it be good, or whether it be evil. (Ecclesiastes 12:14)**

God knew that the Ephesians were faithful in their work and commends them for their labor and hard work. They were workers—not shirkers. They got the job done. They weren't loafers, they were laborers. They weren't Greedy, they were Givers. They weren't Slothful, they were Servants. Solomon said:

> **Whatsoever thy hand findeth to do, do it with thy might; for there is no work, nor device, nor knowledge, nor wisdom, in the grave, whither thou goest. (Ecclesiastes 9:10)**

The word **labour** carries the idea of toiling or laboring to the point of weariness and exhaustion. It emphasizes the depth and measure of their labor for the Lord. There is coming a day when all opportunity to obey and serve God will be over. If the Lord tarries His coming, we will all go to the grave. They opportunity to serve will be over.

It as a Discerning Church

Jesus also commended them because they could not **...bear them which are evil. (Revelation 2:2b)** This is a lost truth in this day of ecumenical Christendom. Professing Christianity has little or no discernment. We expect the natural man, that is the unregenerate man, to be void of discernment.

> **But the natural man receiveth not the things of the Spirit of God: for they are foolishness unto him: neither can he know them, because they are spiritually discerned. (1 Corinthians 2:14)**

However, the child of God is to be the opposite. Being indwelt by the Spirit of God, he can discern right from wrong.

> **But he that is spiritual judgeth all things, (1 Corinthians 2:15)**

Yes! We are to judge all things. The Christian life calls for discernment. John warned us:

> **Love not the world, neither the things that are in the world. If any man love the world, the love of the Father is not in him. (1 John 2:15)**

Christians are supposed to hate the wickedness of the world. God's people are not to be part of this evil system.

> **... Let every one that nameth the name of Christ depart from iniquity. (2 Timothy 2:19)**

> **The highway of the upright is to depart from evil: (Proverbs 16:17)**

Separation is key to the success of the saint. It is a sad thing that most professing Christians today have no problem with associating and running with those who are evil.

It was a Determined Church

And hast borne, and hast patience, and for my name's sake hast laboured, and hast not fainted. (Revelation 2:3) Jesus commends their patience and determination to continue steadfastly in service. The word **borne** means *"to bear up under a load or to bear what is burdensome."* The word **patience** speaks of endurance. It is the ability to remain steadfast under pressure. These Christians were opposed, threatened, and persecuted—yet they stayed in the battle. They were courageous in conflict. They remained faithful in their work. They had learned from the best. Their first pastor was the Apostle Paul who had founded the Church thirty some years earlier. These believers had not become weary in well doing.

It was a Defending Church

But this thou hast, that thou hatest the deeds of the Nicolaitans, which I also hate. (Revelation 2:6) Jesus praised the Church of Ephesus because they detected and detested false doctrine and error. He commended them because they hated the deeds of the Nicolaitans, and in the same statement He announced His own Divine hatred of the same crowd. The word

Nicolaitan comes from two words, *"nikao"* meaning *"to conquer,"* and *"laos"* which means *"the laity."* The two words together means to *"conquer the laity."* The Nicolaitans were those who were attempting to become lords over God's heritage by dividing the Church into two groups of believers—the big shots and the laity. There were certain men who set themselves up to rule over the people. This perfectly describes the trend we see so much of today where elder boards sit around and make decisions for the Pastor and the people of the Church. If the Holy Spirit leads the Pastor on something, the Holy Spirit and the Pastor have to go to the elders to get it approved. Elder boards could rightly be called the board of **Nicolaitans.** The Ephesian believers hated these people and so does God.

It should be noted here that it is called **the deeds of the Nicolaitans.** However, when we come to verse 15 of this of this same chapter, it is the **doctrine of the Nicolaitans**. The Ephesians were fighting the deeds, but something went wrong, and the Deeds became Doctrine. Therefore, we stand uncompromisingly for truth. We don't ease up, back up, let up! If we allow evil to infiltrate our ranks, it will become full blown before we know it. The Apostle Paul warned that ...

A little leaven leaveneth the whole lump. (Galatians 5:9)

This a vivid illustration of how false teachers and their doctrine quickly spread and permeate a Church. This why the leaders and the people of the Ephesian Church hated the **Nicolaitans** and took such a strong stand against them.

THE PROBLEM WITH THE EPHESIAN CHURCH

Nevertheless I have somewhat against thee, because thou hast left thy first love. (Revelation 2:4) Jesus overlooks nothing. He sees not only what we have, but also what we do not have. He never becomes so carried away with our assets that He overlooks our liabilities. Along with the words of praise Jesus also had some words of rebuke. You say, *"What stinging words, what dreadful rebuke to fall from the tender lips of the Saviour."*

Yes, but look at the love and friendship behind the rebuke. Solomon said:

> **Faithful are the wounds of a friend; but the kisses of an enemy are deceitful. (Proverbs 27:6)**

Jesus is faithful even when He has to rebuke His own children. Jesus is the...

> **... friend that sticketh closer than a brother. (Proverbs 18:24)**

There is no doubt that the Church at Ephesus was solid and grounded in the truth. It was a church based and built on sound doctrine. They knew what they believed and practiced it with conviction. They were separated, both ecclesiastically and personally. Their purity of doctrine and continuance in service were unquestioned, but they had deserted their first love. They had gotten so caught up in duty that they had lost their devotion. Their <u>Labor was Commendable,</u> but their <u>Love was Contemptible</u>. Like Martha, they had become so busy that they had no time for Jesus. Their relationship with Christ was based on Performance rather than Passion. They were far more occupied with the work of Christ than with the person of Christ. They were straight, but they were empty. The love here is described as the **first love**. It is the honeymoon love of the newlywed. Jeremiah calls it the love of the espousal.

> **Thus saith the LORD; I remember thee, the kindness of thy youth, the love of thine espousals, when thou wentest after me in the wilderness, in a land that was not sown. (Jeremiah 2:2)**

Israel is pictured here as the loving bride who clings to her beloved bridegroom. Honeymoon love! The most intimate and cherished loved between the bride and groom. It is a time of absolute devotion, one to another. Notice the phrase used here, **... the love of thine espousals, when thou wentest after me in the wilderness.** It speaks of the wilderness wanderings, when God's people were separated from Egypt and totally dependent on God. This is the love that Jesus wants. Isn't it astonishing that the God of Heaven so values our love that He misses it when we fail to love Him as we should? Their accomplishments were the results of cold, dead, and dry orthodoxy. Duty without devotion does not satisfy our Lord. Our service must be carried out because of love for Christ. The Church of Ephesus was getting the job done. But, regardless of their accomplishments, they had failed in their most important task. Jesus said:

> **Thou shalt love the Lord thy God with all thy heart, and with all thy soul, and with all thy mind. (Matthew 22:37)**

No matter what else we may accomplish, when we fail in our love for Christ—we fail most miserably. There is no more dangerous Christian than one who is operating in the power of the flesh. A Church that does not labor out of love for the Lord will eventually become cold, pharisaical, and destructive. We see too much of this in our day.

THE PRESCRIPTION FOR THE EPHESIAN CHURCH

Jesus had put His finger on a problem that if left uncorrected would result in the death of the Ephesian Church. The Lord never corrects without offering a solution. Here Jesus tells the Ephesians how to get things right again.

Remember

Remember therefore from whence thou art fallen... (Revelation 2:5a) The Christians at Ephesus had **FALLEN**. They had not committed adultery. They had not committed murder. They had not committed robbery. Yet, they had fallen! What a note of seriousness! It is a terrible fall for a Christian to become so occupied and busy that his love for Christ fails. Few ever survive such a fall. The believer's love of Christ helps to regulate his relationship with the Saviour.

> **If ye love me, keep my commandments. (John 14:15)**
>
> **For this is the love of God, that we keep his commandments: and his commandments are not grievous. (1 John 5:3)**

The Christian who loves Christ will obey and stay close to Him. The believers at Ephesus were commanded to reflect upon the precious relationship that they once had. We need to slow down and remember what Christ has done for us. Remember those wonderful honeymoon days when we were first saved. Do you remember what it was like when you were first saved? You couldn't get enough of Jesus. You were in your Bible, you prayed, went to Church, fellowshipped with God's people. Why is it that you can skip Church now without it bothering you? You go through life without witnessing. When you were first saved you told everybody—now you are silent. Could it be that you have left your first love? The fire that once burned in your heart has been quenched. The honeymoon is over.

Repent

... **repent...** (Revelation 2:5b) The Ephesians started well but they had gotten off course. They had left their first love and were laboring in the flesh. Now they are called upon to turn back to their first work. Thayer defines repentance as:

> *The change of mind of those who have begun to abhor their errors and misdeeds, and have determined to enter upon a better course of life, so that it embraces both a recognition of sin and sorrow for it and hearty amendment, the tokens and effects of which are good deeds.*

These Christians needed to get back to serving God out of their love for Him rather than merely performing a duty. There are too many people sitting in our Churches today who are serving at the command of the preacher rather than out of a compassion for Christ. Dear friend, return to your first love. Return to a ministry that is motivated by love.

Return

... **and do the first works...** (Revelation 2:5c) It is not enough to simply say I repent. No! Repentance is a change of mind that leads to a change of direction. If there is no change, there has been no true repentance. Paul said...

> **... that they should repent and turn to God, and do works meet for repentance. (Acts 26:20)**

Repentance involves changing the mind, turning to God, and bearing fruit. John instructs the Ephesians not only to repent, but also **do the first works**. The work of genuine repentance is seen in action. John the Baptist told the religionists of his day to **bring forth fruit meet for repentance.** Matthew Henry says:

> *They must repent. They must be inwardly grieved and ashamed for their sinful declension; they must blame themselves, and shame themselves, for it, and humbly confess it in the sight of God, and judge and condemn themselves for it. They must return and do their first works. They must as it were begin again, go back step by step, till they come to the place where they took the first false step; they must endeavour to revive and recover their first zeal, tenderness, and seriousness, and must pray as earnestly, and watch as diligently, as they did when they first set out in the ways of God.*

Repentance is a change of mind that leads to a change of direction. The Ephesus Christians had voluntarily **left** their first love. Jesus had not left—they had left, and they must return. They needed to turn back to the Lord Jesus. There are a lot of folks today who simply need to turn back to Christ and serve Him the way they once did.

> **If my people, which are called by my name, shall humble themselves, and pray, and seek my face, and turn from their wicked ways; then will I hear from heaven, and will forgive their sin, and will heal their land. (2 Chronicles 7:14)**

The Lord Jesus makes it clear that the Ephesian Church would have to *Remember*, *Repent* and *Return*; or they would be ...

Removed

Jesus warns, **... or else I will come unto thee quickly, and will remove thy candlestick out of his place, except thou repent. (Revelation 2:5d)** The **candlestick** speaks of their light and testimony. If the Ephesians would not repent and return to

Him, He had no choice but to remove them. His warning is strong and serious. You see my friend, if your love for Jesus is not right, you have no light for Him.

THE PERISHING OF THE EPHESIAN CHURCH

Tragically, Christ's challenge to the Church of Ephesus went unheeded and He withdrew and passed judgement. . When God withdraws His blessing from a Church, it is over. God does not honor disobedience. History tells us that the people of the Ephesian Church did not repent and therefore, the Church of Ephesus does not exist today. The once great city of Ephesus itself is now reduced to mere ruin and desolation. The marketplace is in ruins: no more trade, no more wealth, no more art, no more learning! Scarcely a trace of the great theater of the Ephesians still remains to remind us of the ancient glories which the Ephesians once possessed. Her light has been snuffed out. Why? Because she would not repent and return to her Saviour. Our Lord warned that in the last days,

> ... because iniquity shall abound, the love of many shall wax cold. (Matthew 24:12)

Many Churches today offer no light for a dark world to see. The look like the world, live like the world and love the world. Have you left your first love? All over America there are defeated, dead, and dried up Churches that were once great light houses for the Lord. Many no longer exist at all—the doors are closed. Their light and testimony have been snuffed out.

SMYRNA: THE LOYAL CHURCH
Revelation 2:8-11

The message to the Church of Smyrna—A.D. 100-313. Smyrna represents a period of intense persecution. As pointed out earlier, the name **Smyrna** means myrrh. Myrrh is a fragrant spice which must be crushed to bring forth its full fragrance. Myrrh was used as a fragrance by the living and as an embalming agent for the dead. Believers this time were crushed by persecution. Yet the crushing released the sweet fragrance of their testimony. During this time thousands of Christians were brought into the theaters of Rome to be fed to lions as spectators cheered. Many were crucified, others were covered with animal skins and ripped apart by wild dogs. Many were covered in tar and set on fire as human torches. They were boiled in oil and burned at the stake. It was during this time that Justin Martyr was beheaded, and Polycarp was burned at the stake. When Polycarp was 86 years old, he was pressured by the Roman proconsul to renounce Christ to be set free. He answered:

> "Eighty and six years have I served Him, and He never did me any injury. How then can I blaspheme my King and my Savior?"

John Walvoord wrote:

> *The Faithfulness of Polycarp to the end seems to have characterized this church in Smyrna in its entire testimony and resulted in this church's continuous faithful witness for God after many others of the early churches had long lost their life ... The purifying fires of affliction caused the lamp of testimony to burn all the more brilliantly. The length of their trial, described here as being ten days, whether interpreted literally or not, is short in comparison with the eternal blessings which would be theirs when their days of trial were over. They could be comforted by the fact that the*

sufferings of this present time do not continue forever, and the blessings that are ours in Christ through His salvation and precious promises will go on through eternity.

It is estimated that during this period over five million Christians were martyred. J. H. Jowett has well said ...

Ministry that costs nothing, accomplishes nothing.

It costs to be a Christian. There have been thousands upon thousands who have died down through the years as a result of standing for the gospel of Christ. Every child of God must be ready to pay the price.

THE PERSON EXPLAINING

In difficult times, it is easy to lose our focus. Jesus comforts the persecuted Church by reminding them of Who He is.

His Perpetuity

These things saith the first and the last... (Revelation 2:8a) This title first appears in the book of Isaiah where God is described as the eternal One.

> **Thus saith the LORD the King of Israel, and his redeemer the LORD of hosts; I am the first, and I am the last; and beside me there is no God. (Isaiah 44:6)**
>
> **Hearken unto me, O Jacob and Israel, my called; I am he; I am the first, I also am the last. (Isaiah 48:12)**

Daniel describes God as the ...

> **Ancient of days... (Daniel 7:9; 13)**

Our Lord identifies Himself to Smyrna as One who is eternal. He is **the First,** He is before all in time, and above all in power. He is **the Last,** He is the consummation of all things. He speaks to the Church as the Eternal God—the Everlasting One.

His Power

... which was dead, and is alive. (Revelation 2:8b) He is the Victorious One who overcame persecution and death. He is the

Living One who was dead but is dead no longer. The resurrected Christ stands as the one Whom no power can overcome. He endured and had overcome the worst that persecution could do to Him. Death and the grave could not destroy Him, nor will it destroy His people. He is the all-powerful God. The point Jesus makes here is that He has gone through the depths of persecution and death and came out victorious and so will His people.

THE PRESSURE ENDURED

The Smyrna Christians were dealing with a great a good amount of pressure. They were a *Suffering* people, but they were also a *Steadfast* people.

Their Saviour

I know ... (Revelation 2:9a) The Lord Jesus says, **I know**. This Divine knowledge! Christ is the all-knowing, omniscient God. Surely, this is wonderful news for a suffering and hurting Church. Jesus is the all-knowing God, and we can be certain that nothing ever escapes Him.

> **For the ways of man are before the eyes of the LORD, and he pondereth all his goings. (Proverbs 5:21)**
>
> **The eyes of the LORD are in every place, beholding the evil and the good. (Proverbs 15:3)**

Jesus knew their weariness and the suffering that results from persecution. He knew pain and suffering like no one else.

> **Wherefore in all things it behoved him to be made like unto his brethren, that he might be a merciful and faithful high priest in things pertaining to God, to make reconciliation for the sins of the people. For in that he himself hath suffered being tempted, he is able to succour them that are tempted. (Hebrews 2:17-18)**

Jesus was **made like unto his brethren.** He took on human flesh and lived among sinful man. He felt persecution, pain, hunger, thirst, etc. Therefore, to the suffering Christian He can say out of His own experience, **I know thy works, tribulation and poverty.**

Their Service

... thy works... (Revelation 2:9b) Jesus commends these believers for their **works**. The difficulty they faced did not deter their service. Too often people fizzle out and quit when the pressure is on. Solomon said ...

> **If thou faint in the day of adversity, thy strength is small. (Proverbs 24:10)**

We have a lot of small strength Christian running around today. They have the strength for everything except serving God. One of the greatest proofs of genuine salvation is service. There are too many quitters in our Churches today. They don't have what it takes to stay by the stuff. God's people are exhorted to

> **... endure hardness, as a good soldier of Jesus Christ. (2 Timothy 2:3)**

The child of God will have to endure hardships for the cause of Christ. The Christians at Smyrna endured the hard circumstances and served Christ in the midst of affliction.

Their Suffering

... and tribulation... (Revelation 2:9c) The word **tribulation** comes from *"thlipsis"* and means *"trouble, pressure, affliction, trouble and anguish."* The awful persecution that the Christians of Smyrna went through would stop the average twenty first century Christian in his tracks. Vance Havner said:

> *We are wearing a lot of medals these days, but not many scars.*

With the Smyrna Christians it was the opposite. They suffered for the cause of Christ.

Their Sparsity

Jesus also assured them that He was aware of their **poverty. (Revelation 2:9d)** The word **poverty** comes from *"ptocheia"* and carries the idea of *"destitution of beggary."* The Smyrna church endured great poverty. This is another comforting statement to the struggling Christians of Smyrna. Jesus, the exalted Christ, understands the real value of a man's life, regardless of His earthly circumstances. They may not have had many coins, but they had crowns. Jesus reminds them, **but thou art rich.** Jesus had said:

> ... a man's life consisteth not in the abundance of the things which he possesseth. (Luke 12:15)

As a general rule, the richer a man is in this world's goods, the more this world looks up to him. However, Jesus says to these poverty-stricken believers, **but thou art rich.** When it comes to eternal things, anyone can be rich in Christ. The trials that they were experiencing resulted in great spiritual wealth. Christians who suffer through poverty in this life can take comfort in the fact that if they serve and remain faithful to God, they possess great spiritual riches in Christ. The Christians of the Church at Smyrna apparently were not men and women of wealth. They were poor, despised and rejected by those about them. They had suffered persecution and were reproached of others. Yet Jesus, who looks not upon the outward appearance, but upon the heart, knew what they suffered, and He sought to encourage them in the faith.

Their Struggle

... and I know the blasphemy of them which say they are Jews, and are not, but are the synagogue of Satan. (Revelation 2:9e) These believers had a constant struggle with the forces of Hell. The word **blasphemy** means *"evil speaking, railing and slander."* The Jews of Smyrna hated Christianity with a passion. Jesus describes the persecutors as those who **say they are Jews, and are not.** The people were Jews by birth, but not by faith. A Jew who understood the Scriptures would've received Christ. Back in the Gospel of John when the Jews boasted

> ... We be Abraham's seed... (John 8:33a)
> ... Abraham is our father... (John 8:39)

Jesus answered:

> Your father Abraham rejoiced to see my day: and he saw it, and was glad. (John 8:56)

Abraham was a man of faith. He believed God. By faith Abraham saw the day of Jesus and rejoiced. If these were true spiritual descendants of Abraham, they too, would rejoice rather than persecute the Smyrna Church.

THE PERSECUTION ENCOUNTERED

Fear none of those things which thou shalt suffer: behold, the devil shall cast some of you into prison, that ye may be tried; and ye shall have tribulation ten days... (Revelation 2:10a) Christ predicted the suffering that was ahead for believers. However, we are not to fear because we are partakers of Christ.

> **But rejoice, inasmuch as ye are partakers of Christ's sufferings; that when his glory shall be revealed ye may be glad also with exceeding joy. (I Peter 4:13)**

Fear is a crippling thing. This kind of fear does not come from the Lord. He has been given the child of God power over fear.

> **For God hath not given us the spirit of fear; but of power, and of love, and of a sound mind. (2 Timothy 1:7)**

Fear does not have to cripple the believer. Persecution is the norm for any Christian who is dedicated to living righteously. The child of God is to rejoice for the privilege of being counted worthy to suffer for Christ's sake.

> **Beloved, think it not strange concerning the fiery trial which is to try you, as though some strange thing happened unto you. (1 Peter 4:12)**

Peter describes this suffering as a **fiery trial.** The picture here is that of the intense heat of the refiner's furnace. These fiery trials serve to prove and purify God's people.

THE PRIZE EXPECTED

Our Lord then tells them, **be thou faithful unto death and I will give thee a crown of life. (Revelation 2:10b)** So, what are we to do when persecution comes? We are to remain **faithful**

unto death. This was a reality for these believers. They understood the consequences of sold out living for Christ. Christ assures them, **I will give thee a crown of life.** This promise has nothing to do with salvation which is a free gift from God to all who trust on the Lord Jesus Christ. At the Judgment Seat of Christ, where the believer will be judged for his works, Christ will give crowns to those who have earned rewards. The believer's works will be tested as by fire. Some works will be burned, causing the believer to suffer loss, while other works will endure, for which the believer will receive a reward. (1 Corinthians 3:10-15) The Believer's judgment is very real!

> **For we must all appear before the judgment seat of Christ; that every one may receive the things done in his body, according to that he hath done, whether it be good or bad. (2 Corinthians 5:10)**

When Paul said, **we must all appear**, he meant just that! It is certain that every Christian will stand before Judgement seat and give an account to the Lord for what he or she has done since their conversion. Contrary to modern theological jumble and popular opinion, the believer will stand before God and face judgment. God invested His best — His only begotten Son to pay man's sin debt. God is going to hold His people accountable for what they did for Him. It will be a wonderful day for those who have overcome the flesh and faithfully served the Lord Jesus. In the New Testament five crowns are mentioned as rewards to the believer for faithful service. These crowns will be given at the judgment seat of Christ.

Striving — The Incorruptible Crown

And every man that striveth for the mastery is temperate in all things. Now they do it to obtain a corruptible crown; but we an incorruptible. (1 Corinthians 9:25) This crown is the Victor's Crown. It is given to those who strive, overcome the flesh, and live victoriously for Christ. It is given to all who:

> **... keep under the body and bring it into subjection. (1 Corinthians 9:27)**

It is given to those who run the race well. It is for those who do not yield to fleshly lusts and allow worldly amusements and pleasures to interrupt or hinder their responsibility to do God's work. The greatest battles of life are fought in the heart. Christ has already won the battle and now He stands by to help us. We must set our eyes on Him and Him alone if we are to win the Victor's crown. Paul said:

> ... **let us lay aside every weight, and the sin which doth so easily beset us, and let us run with patience the race that is set before us. (Hebrews 12:1)**

A **weight** is anything that hinders a runner and makes it more difficult to finish well. Weights hinder the runner and prevents him from winning. Christians have weights that must be laid aside also.

Souls — The Crown Of Rejoicing

For what is our hope, or joy, or crown of rejoicing? Are not even ye in the presence of our Lord Jesus Christ at his coming? (1 Thessalonians 2:19) This is the soul-winners crown. Paul said, **my brethren dearly beloved and longed for, my joy and crown.** This crown will be given to those who have won souls for the Lord Jesus Christ. It will be a great reward just to see those whom we have won in Heaven with us.

> **And they that be wise shall shine as the brightness of the firmament; and they that turn many to righteousness as the stars for ever and ever. (Daniel 12:3)**
>
> **The fruit of the righteous is a tree of life; and he that winneth souls is wise. (Proverbs 11:30)**

Without a doubt, winning others to Christ is one of the most rewarding works of Christianity. May we do and say only that which can be used to see souls come to the Lord Jesus Christ.

Seekers — The Crown Of righteousness

Henceforth there is laid up for me a crown of righteousness, which the Lord, the righteous judge, shall give me at that day: and not to me only, but unto all them

Smyrna: The Loyal Church

also that love his appearing. (2 Timothy 4:8) This crown is for those who love and long for His appearing. Many people today do not believe in the personal return of Christ, in spite of the fact that Jesus said:

I will come again, and receive you unto myself; that where I am, there ye may be also. (John 14:3)

The doctrine of Christ's return is a forgotten and neglected truth in many Christian circles today. With no expectation of Christ's return many are living in sin and debauchery. There is no greater incentive to living a sanctified life than the imminent return of Christ. Dr. R. A. Torrey said:

"The imminent return of our Lord is the greatest Bible argument for a pure, unselfish, devoted, unworldly, active life of service."

There is absolutely no excuse for any professing Christian not to love the glorious return of Christ. His return is our blessed hope.

Shepherds — The Crown Of Glory

Feed the flock of God which is among you, taking the oversight thereof, not by constraint, but willingly; not for filthy lucre, but of a ready mind; Neither as being lords over God's heritage, but being ensamples to the flock. (1 Peter 5:2-3) This is the Pastor's crown. This crown is given to all who faithfully preach and teach the Word of God, faithfully leading God's flock into the green pastures and by the still waters of life. Faithful shepherds, who are often dishonored and ridiculed on earth, will receive a crown of glory, in Heaven, from chief Shepherd whom they followed.

Sacrifice — The Crown Of Life

Fear none of those things which thou shalt suffer: behold, the devil shall cast some of you into prison, that ye may be tried; and ye shall have tribulation ten days: be thou faithful unto death, and I will give thee a crown of life. (Revelation 2:10) This is sometimes called the martyr's crown. It is for those who suffer unto death. It is mentioned twice in the Scriptures. It will be given to those who suffer persecution for

Christ's sake. The reward for the overcomer is great. The crown of life is given to those who have lived the overcoming life. It pays to live whole-heartedly for the Lord Jesus. If you are half-heartedly and compromisingly stumbling along on spiritual crutches, with no real testimony for the Lord Jesus, you are not living an overcoming life for Him. God has something infinitely better for us, and He wants us to have the overcomer's reward.

THE PROMISE ENJOYED

He that hath an ear, let him hear what the Spirit saith unto the churches; He that overcometh shall not be hurt of the second death. (Revelation 2:11) The message of Jesus to this church ends with **He that hath an ear, let him hear** Is it possible to have ears and not hear? Some people have big ears, but they do not listen well. The Spirit is always saying to these churches:

> **He that hath an ear, let him hear what the Spirit saith unto the churches.**

What is the reward to the overcomer of the church at Smyrna? Even in times of peril and persecution Christians can enjoy the wonderful promise of Heaven. Jesus said:

> **...He that overcometh shall not be hurt of the second death.**

The overcoming one shall not be hurt by the second death. Oh! How glorious it will be when we get to the place where we will never die! There will be no undertakers, no flowers, no good-byes, no tears, no sorrow.

PERGAMOS: THE LAX CHURCH
Revelation 2:12-17

The message to the Church of Pergamos represents the time period from 312-590 A.D. The word Pergamos means *"marriage, wedded to."* The Church of Pergamos was married to the state. As a result, paganism as well as the worship of the Roman emperors common. This period in Church history was a time when a state church was developed. With such a close tie between the world and the Church God's people fell into a state debauchery and corruption. Pergamos was a place of extreme wickedness and paganism. These were challenging for God's people. There was great temptation and opposition from Satan. Unfortunately, this along with the depraved practices pf Pergamos had an adverse effect on the Church that God had located in that city. As we study, we find some in Pergamos who held fast to the name of Christ and remained true to the Word, while others embraced the false doctrines of Balaam and the Nicolaitans.

THEIR CITY

There are several characteristics (some good, some bad) about the city of Pergamos that makes it stand out as a unique city.

It Was A Prominent City

Pergamos was a prominent city in Asia Minor and the largest city in that area. It was located in the western part of Asia Minor some twenty miles from the Mediterranean Sea. Over the years many kings had made Pergamos their home. It was certainly an impressive and prominent city.

It Was A Progressive City

Pergamos was a great city of learning and progress. Located in Pergamos was the greatest library of the ancient world containing over 200,000 volumes. A library of such size was unfathomable in a day when there were no printing presses. Every volume had to be handwritten. It was in Pergamos that the method of producing very thin layers of animal skins was perfected. These thin layers made excellent writing material. These skins were called *"pergement"* and later became known as *"parchment."*

It Was A Pagan City

Pergamos was the great pagan religious center of Asia Minor. It was a stench in the nostrils of the True and Holy God. The people there worshipped many pagan gods. Zeus was believed by many to have been born there. Hence, the temple of Zeus was located there with its great altar standing one hundred and fifteen feet above the ground level. Animal sacrifices were offered around the clock by continuously rotating teams of priests. Our Holy God never looks at paganism lightly. It is certain that Pergamos was an evil place full of infidelity and idolatry. Hence it was known as Satan's throne. Our Lord called it the place ...

... where Satan dwelleth. (Revelation 2:13)

Asclepius was also worshipped in the city of Pergamos. Asclepius was the god of healing. It is interesting that the emblem used for Asclepius was a serpent. Snake venom was believed to be medicinal, and their skin-shedding was considered a symbol of rebirth. There was also a temple for Asclepius there. The city of Pergamos became a healing center connected to the worship of this healing snake god.

It Was A Perverted City

Pergamos was a depraved city of sin and worldliness. Jesus called it the place **where Satan's seat is. (13)** Unfortunately, the practices of the city found their way into the Church and contaminated God's people. Therefore, Pergamos represents that period of Church history when worldliness crept in and the Church received the favor of the State. Pergamos means *"marriage and elevation."* When Constantine became emperor of Rome in 312 A.D., he sent out an imperial decree, lifting the ban on Christianity. He bestowed many favors on the Christian Church, many pagan temples were taken over by Christians and the government gave money for their operations. Oliver B. Greene said that ...

> *Pergamos is the message to the church under imperial favor... the church settled in the world.*

Thus, Pergamos received its true meaning, because the Church became married to the world and, as a result, was elevated in the eyes of the world also. The Church became useless so far as the work of Christ was concerned. The Bible clearly warns against this kind of alliance.

> **And have no fellowship with the unfruitful works of darkness, but rather reprove them. (Ephesians 5:11)**

Throughout Scripture we have warning after warning about getting tangled up with the things of the world. Sadly, too many Christians are entangled in this temporal life and the things of this world. Their love for this present world has rendered them useless as a soldier of Jesus Christ.

> **No man that warreth entangleth himself with the affairs of this life; that he may please him who hath chosen him to be a soldier. (2 Timothy 2:4)**

We are warned that ...

> **... the whole world lieth in wickedness. (1 John 5:19)**

John instructs the believer to:

> **Love not the world, neither the things that are in the world. If any man love the world, the love of the Father is not in him. For all that is in the world, the lust of the flesh, and the lust of the eyes, and the pride of life, is not of the Father, but is of the world. (1 John 2:15-16)**

The word **world** comes from the Greek *"kosmos"* and has the basic meaning of *"arrangement or decoration."* It speaks of this world's order or system. This world system is contrary to the things of God. Hence, separation from the world is essential to the victorious Christian life. Any alliance with the world will kill the testimony of any Church or Christian just as it did in Pergamos. We will take note of several things concerning the Church of Pergamos.

THEIR CHRIST

And to the angel of the church in Pergamos write; These things saith he which hath the sharp sword with two edges. (Revelation 2:12) The Lord referred to Himself as the one, **which hath the sharp sword with two edges.** The sharp two-edged sword speaks of the Word of God.

> **For the word of God is quick, and powerful, and sharper than any twoedged sword, piercing even to the dividing asunder of soul and spirit, and of the joints and marrow, and is a discerner of the thoughts and intents of the heart. (Hebrews 4:12)**

The Word of God has the power to penetrate the very depths of the soul and expose the hidden secrets of the heart of man. There were manmade doctrines in Pergamos. These were mere inventions of paganism and man's reasoning. But like a **sharp sword with two edges**, the Word of God cuts through human reasoning and logic, exposes false doctrine for what it is.

The two-edged sword also speaks of sure and swift judgment. A twoedged sword cuts both ways. It is a powerful weapon. Jesus warned that sinful man would be judged by His word.

> **He that rejecteth me, and receiveth not my words, hath one that judgeth him: the word that I have spoken, the same shall judge him in the last day. (John 12:48)**

If Christians today would get hold of this reality, they would have a lot more respect for the Word of God. The very wording of this greeting testifies not only as to the authority of the speaker, but it points out that conditions existed in the Church at Pergamos which had to be rebuked and corrected. Jesus stands with the two-edged sword prepared to take the action necessary to correct His wayward people and bring them back to Him.

Pergamos: The Lax Church

For God shall bring every work into judgment, with every secret thing, whether it be good, or whether it be evil. (Ecclesiastes 12:14)

We live in a day when there is little preaching on the judgment of God. People do not want to hear that the God love is also a God of judgment. But that does not change the fact that God still judges His children, as well as the ungodly. There is coming a day when God's wrath will fall.

THEIR CIRCUMSTANCES

I know thy works, and where thou dwellest, even where Satan's seat is... (Revelation 2:13a) There has always been a great effort on the part of Satan to destroy the work and influence of the Church. Satan has always used persecution as one of his main methods. However, at Smyrna it didn't work for him. Real and dedicated Christianity has always flourished and spread under persecution. Someone has well said that *"the blood of martyrs is the seed of the Church."* It was true then and has been during every period of Church history. Persecution usually strengthens the determination and causes men to affirm their allegiance to Christ as nothing else seems to do. Having failed with persecution, Satan changed his method of attack from persecution to infiltration. Notice the phrase, **where thou dwellest, even where Satan's seat is.** Satan felt right at home in Pergamos. He couldn't stamp them out, so he would join the Church and destroy them from within.

During this time Constantine came to the throne of the Roman Empire. Constantine was a pagan who claimed to have seen a vision of a fiery cross burning in the heavens, and to have heard a voice saying, *"By this sign conquer."* Thus, he professed to be a Christian. However, there is no evidence that he was truly saved. His profession in Christ was nothing more than a clever political move.

By this time, the Christians had increased in numbers and rather than to oppose them, Constantine thought it would be far better to make peace with them. Constantine took the name of Pontifex Maximus, meaning High Priest. He was the High Priest of paganism. He continued to hold on to the ideas of the heathen and led the Church into a state of compromise with the world. This robbed the Church of its favor with God. God never blesses worldliness.

THEIR CONVICTIONS

... thou holdest fast my name, and hast not denied my faith... (Revelation 2:13b) We see that there were some Christians with conviction in Pergamos. Although they were right in the midst of battling Satan, they stayed by the stuff. Praise God for Christians who stand true in the heat of battle. I fear that the martyrs who died for their faith would be ashamed to stand beside the average preacher today. The concern of the average Christian today is not Conviction but, Convenience.

Let's keep in mind that conviction is the principle that life is built on. The idea of conviction is to be convinced of something. For instance, when one is convicted of sin, he has become convinced of what God says about that sin. That means that he now has a conviction about that sin. So, for the believer, convictions are personal beliefs based upon biblical principles which govern our lives. These beliefs determine our character, our course and our conduct.

THEIR COURAGE

... even in those days wherein Antipas was my faithful martyr, who was slain among you, where Satan dwelleth. (Revelation 2:13c) Their Christianity was more than lip service. They were willing to die for Jesus. Their stand was true and steadfast, even when those around them were being put to death for doing the same thing. This is indeed a hard time to stand but stand we must. Troublesome times will separate the fakes from the real Christians.

THEIR COMPROMISE

Jesus commended them for their works and faith, but He also found it necessary to rebuke them because of their compromise. Like so many of our own day, they had fallen into compromise.

Pergamos: The Lax Church

The road of compromise is a crowded highway today. It is crowded with men who at one time stood as separated Baptists but have gone down the road of compromise and popularity. They have sold the pulpit and embraced the ungodly philosophy of pleasure and popularity. We need more preachers who stand with Micaiah who said:

As the LORD liveth, even what my God saith, that will I speak. (2 Chronicles 18:13)

Bob Jones Sr. said, *"Take your stand, take your losses, and build from there."* Taking a stand does not make us very popular with this world, but far better it is to be popular with God, than with His enemies. Our Lord deals with two areas of compromise.

The Doctrine Of Balaam

But I have a few things against thee, because thou hast there them that hold the doctrine of Balaam, who taught Balac to cast a stumblingblock before the children of Israel, to eat things sacrificed unto idols, and to commit fornication. (Revelation 2:14) The **doctrine of Balaam** had also infiltrated the Church of Pergamos. Compromise is a dangerous and deadly thing, and it must be dealt with. Jesus hits the nail on head. In order for us to understand the doctrine of Balaam, referred to by our Saviour in this passage, it will be necessary for us to refer to the Old Testament account of Balaam.

In the book of Numbers, chapters 22-25 and 31, we find that the Children of Israel, on their way from Egypt to the Land of Canaan, had pitched in the plains of Moab. Balak, king of Moab, was afraid of the Israelites, so he called for Balaam the Prophet, and asked him to curse the king of Israel. The purpose was to defeat the children of Israel, thus he asked Balaam, a so-called prophet, to curse God's people that they might have the victory over them.

Almost every Sunday School child knows the story of how Balaam went on his way, riding on a donkey and how he was met by an angel on the way, The angel warned him against the purpose of his journey. Nevertheless, he was allowed to go on his way, but he was told to speak only those things which the Lord would direct him to say.

Every time Balak tried to get Balaam to curse the Children of Israel, he ended up blessing them instead of cursing them. Not being allowed to curse Israel, Balak the king of Moab was very angry, and Balaam himself was greatly disappointed for, being a hireling prophet, he had hoped to receive a great reward for cursing the Children of Israel.

Therefore, having been hindered in his purpose of cursing the Children of Israel, Balaam conceived another plan for securing the reward which he desired. Balaam reasoned with the King of Moab that if he wanted to overcome the Children of Israel, he could do so by breaking down their standards of separation. This he did by calling the people of Israel unto the sacrifice of their gods, and by leading the Children of Israel to commit whoredom with the daughters of Moab. Let's keep in mind that Moab was a staunch enemy of God and His people. Because of this unholy alliance with the children of Moab, God sent a plague among them, and twenty-four thousand of them died of the plague before the judgment of God was stayed. God deals seriously with unholy alliances.

Balaam was willing to see Israel robbed of her glory, and thwarted in her purpose, all for the love of money and a fleshly reward. Balaam, the hireling prophet, was willing to do anything for the sake of profit and in the Church of Pergamos there were those who held to the doctrine of Balaam. Therefore, Jesus made is clear that He was against them.

> **For the love of money is the root of all evil: which while some coveted after, they have erred from the faith, and pierced themselves through with many sorrows. (1 Timothy 6:10)**

Sadly, there is no shortage of Balaamites in our day. The Apostle Jude warned those who would follow in Balaam's footsteps.

> **Woe unto them! for they have gone in the way of Cain, and ran greedily after the error of Balaam for**

reward, and perished in the gainsaying of Core. (Jude 1:11)

Such men are not true shepherds. If they were, they would preach the Word of God and help the people live for Christ. They are simply hirelings. Jesus describes the hireling:

But he that is an hireling, and not the shepherd, whose own the sheep are not, seeth the wolf coming, and leaveth the sheep, and fleeth: and the wolf catcheth them, and scattereth the sheep. The hireling fleeth, because he is an hireling, and careth not for the sheep. (John 10:12-13)

There are those in many churches, even today, who are willing to do anything for the sake of reward. These are not true shepherds. Their true love is money, fame, applause, etc. These hirelings stay until things get a little rough and then go on their own way. Peter describes them as those:

Which have forsaken the right way, and are gone astray, following the way of Balaam the son of Bosor, who loved the wages of unrighteousness. (2 Peter 2:15)

Such is the doctrine Of Balaam. Pulpits are full of Balaamites! These are greedy men who are out for all they can get. They are not interested in helping God's people. They simply want their paychecks and will not do anything that might offend the sinners in their congregation.

The Deadliness Of The Nicolaitans

So hast thou also them that hold the doctrine of the Nicolaitans, which thing I hate. (Revelation 2:15) Another point of compromise was their allowing the Nicolaitan doctrine to infiltrate the Church. The Church of Ephesus took a strong stand against the Nicolaitans, but Pergamos allowed them in. Those who would corrupt the Church never rest. They continue their attack and work to get in. We must ever be on the lookout for those who would pervert Bible doctrine and destroy the people of God. Such are described as wolves and still operate today.

> **For I know this, that after my departing shall grievous wolves enter in among you, not sparing the flock. Also of your own selves shall men arise, speaking perverse things, to draw away disciples after them. (Acts 20:29-30)**

The word Nicolaitan comes from the two Greek words; *"nikao"* which means to *"conquer,"* and *"laos"* which means the *"laity."* The word, therefore, means to rule over the people. This was accomplished by setting up certain men to rule over the ordinary people in the Church. They divided the church into two divisions: the rulers and the laity. It was those in charge who ruled over and dominated the laity. This is much like our present-day situation with Church boards setting themselves up to rule the local Church. Christ hated this and so did the Church.

The Nicolaitan movement marks the beginning of a form of the priesthood in the Church. This is the doctrine of so-called church leaders oppressing the people and lording over God's heritage. We have seen this happen for years in Roman Catholicism and unfortunately it has crept into other movements. It is interesting to note that the Church of Ephesus hated the deeds of the Nicolaitans, but the Church of Pergamos was practicing the doctrine of the Nicolaitans. False doctrine takes root fast. This is why we must be careful not to trifle with it but purge it right away.

THEIR CHOICE

> **Repent; or else I will come unto thee quickly, and will fight against them with the sword of my mouth. (Revelation 2:16)**

Their choice was simple, repent or perish. If Christ's admonition was not obeyed, His judgment would follow. The word **fight** comes from *"polemeō"* and means *"to make war."* Imagine being at war with the omnipotent God.

> **Woe unto him that striveth with his Maker! (Isaiah 45:9a)**

Christ warned them that the Word of His mouth would be like a sword against their error. He had warned them about

Pergamos: The Lax Church

embracing the practices of Balaam. It's interesting that Balaam himself was slain by the sword.

> **And they slew the kings of Midian, beside the rest of them that were slain; namely, Evi, and Rekem, and Zur, and Hur, and Reba, five kings of Midian: Balaam also the son of Beor they slew with the sword. (Numbers 31:8)**

Those who refuse God's correction will receive His judgment. The sword they would have to face would be a far greater one than the one that took Balaam down.

THEIR CHALLENGE

He that hath an ear, let him hear what the Spirit saith unto the churches; (Revelation 2:17a) Here we find Christ's promises to the overcomer. Their challenge was the same as ours today. We are to **hear** the Word of God; obey it and receive the blessing. Here we have a most precious promise and one with great significance.

The Promise Of Provision

To him that overcometh will I give to eat of the hidden manna... (Revelation 2:17b) The children of Israel were fed and sustained with **manna** in the wilderness. Jesus Himself is the bread from heaven.

> **And Jesus said unto them, I am the bread of life: he that cometh to me shall never hunger, and he that believeth on me shall never thirst. (John 6:35)**

The Lord fed the children of Israel from Heaven. The overcoming life is for those who feed upon Christ, the eternal Bread of Life (John 6:31-35). Just as bread is the staple of physical life, so is hidden manna the sustainer of spiritual life. Christ will feed the overcomer with a Heavenly sustenance. The manna in the wilderness was temporal. It satisfied physical hungers for a while, but Christ, the Bread of Life, will satisfy spiritual hunger forever.

> **Blessed are they which do hunger and thirst after righteousness: for they shall be filled. (Matthew 5:6)**

Those who would repent and return to Him will find spiritual nourishment-real food for their souls.

The Promise Of Purity

... white stone, and in the stone a new name written, which no man knoweth saving he that receiveth it... (Revelation 2:17c) This promise was taken from the Hebrew custom of giving to one acquitted in trial, a white stone. The white stone became the symbol of innocence and of deliverance. The white stone here speaks of deliverance for all who will repent and return to Christ.

THYATIRA: THE LOOSE CHURCH
Revelation 2:18-29

Thyatira portrays the Church of the Dark Ages—590 to 1517. The word **Thyatira** comes from two words meaning *"sacrifice"* and *"continual."* It was during this time that the Church of Rome took off. It's no doubt that the Roman mass is foretold here. Every time a Roman priest celebrates the mass, he teaches that the Lord Jesus Christ is sacrificed again, not only for the sins of the living, but also for the dead. The doctrine of transubstantiation teaches that the priest's bread becomes body of Christ and wine the actual blood of Christ. Therefore, every time mass is kept, the actual body of Christ is offered in sacrifice. This false act attempts to do away with and belittle Christ's one sacrifice for sins forever.

> **By the which will we are sanctified through the offering of the body of Jesus Christ once for all. And every priest standeth daily ministering and offering oftentimes the same sacrifices, which can never take away sins: But this man, after he had offered one sacrifice for sins for ever, sat down on the right hand of God; From henceforth expecting till his enemies be made his footstool. For by one offering he hath perfected for ever them that are sanctified. (Hebrews 10:10-14)**

However, there were some overcomers in Thyatira. Christ had a believing remnant there. Harry Ironside wrote:

> *"The Lord gave Rome credit for a great deal that is good. Remember from the seventh century to the present there has been a great deal in the way of good works in the Roman Catholic church that cannot be overlooked. There have been Roman Catholic nuns and monks who have been ready to lay down their lives for the needy and the sick. Centuries before*

Luther, every hospital in western Europe was simply a Roman Catholic monastery or convent. The Lord does not forget all that. Where there is a bit of faith, His love takes note of it all. If there are hearts in the church of Rome that, amid the superstition, reach out to the blessed Lord Himself, He meets them in grace and demonstrates His love to them."

The Church at Thyatira was a cultural, contaminated, and compromising Church. It was the most corrupt of all seven Churches. In this letter we see what happens to a Church that compromises with the world and deteriorates into a culture centered, social club. Most Churches today are cultural, not Christian. They have dropped standards and convictions and have become accommodating to the moral standards of secularism. We see many Churches in our day that are the same way. Their main interest is in drawing a big crowd. To get their crowds they have brought in worldly music, drama teams and entertainers of all sorts. They have their crowds, but they do not have the presence and power of God. Compromise is a nasty devil to flirt with.

THE LORD'S CHARACTER

In the opening verse to the Church of Thyatira the Lord states several important facts concerning His character. Here we see *His Sovereignty*, *His Search* and *His Supremacy*.

His Sovereignty

And unto the angel of the church in Thyatira write; These things saith the Son of God, (Revelation 2:18a) Here it clearly stated that Jesus is **the Son of God.** He stresses His deity. This is God speaking! Jesus Christ was not a mere man. He was God manifested in human flesh. He is the Second Person of the Trinity incarnate. God Almighty looked down from Heaven and said:

This is my belo ved Son, in whom I am well pleased. (Matthew 3:17)

Paul said that Jesus was ...

> ... declared to be the Son of God with power, according to the spirit of holiness ... (Romans 1:4)

When Jesus was on earth, He was the incarnation of God. He was God in human flesh. Regardless of what the cults have to say, Jesus Christ is God.

His Search

... who hath his eyes like unto a flame of fire, (Revelation 2:18b) The eyes of fire represent the Lord's penetrating eyes that can search the hearts and minds of man. His flaming gaze can burn through all of the false outward appearances of man and see deep into his heart.

> **But the LORD said unto Samuel, Look not on his countenance, or on the height of his stature; because I have refused him: for the LORD seeth not as man seeth; for man looketh on the outward appearance, but the LORD looketh on the heart. (1 Samuel 16:7)**

God is not fooled by outer appearances; He sees the inward man. His eyes will search in judgment. They pierce and penetrate; they commend and condemn. There is no person that will escape the examination of his eyes of fire.

His Supremacy

... and his feet are like fine brass. (Revelation 2:18c) His **feet** speak of absolute authority and victory over His enemies.

> ... thou hast put all things under his feet: (Psalm 8:6)
>
> For he must reign, till he hath put all enemies under his feet. (1 Corinthians 15:25)
>
> Thou hast put all things in subjection under his feet. (Hebrews 2:8)

His feet **like fine brass** speak of judgment. We remember that the brazen altar in the Tabernacle was the place where the sin offering was sacrificed.

> **And he made the horns thereof on the four corners of it; the horns thereof were of the same: and he overlaid it with brass. (Exodus 38:2)**

The laver, also of brass, spoke of self-judgment. It was here the priests washed their hands and feet as they went in and out of the Holy Place. Brass in the Bible is many times seen as a symbol of judgment. The brazen serpent was the type of cross where Christ received the judgment of God for our sin.

> **And Moses made a serpent of brass, and put it upon a pole, and it came to pass, that if a serpent had bitten any man, when he beheld the serpent of brass, he lived. (Numbers 21:9)**
>
> **And as Moses lifted up the serpent in the wilderness, even so must the Son of man be lifted up: (John 3:14)**

The Lord Jesus Christ fulfilled the role of the brazen serpent when He suffered for our sin. However, His day of judgment is coming and when that day comes the Lord Jesus will be victorious overall.

THE LORD'S COMMENDATION

I know thy works, and charity, and service, and faith, and thy patience, and thy works; and the last to be more than the first. (Revelation 2:19) The Lord having just established Himself as a righteous Judge now gives His assessment of the work of this Church.

Their Performance

... works ... and service. (Revelation 2:19a) This was an active Church where some were serving God. True love always manifests itself in service. Service is a major aspect of the Christian life.

> **Looking for that blessed hope, and the glorious appearing of the great God and our Saviour Jesus Christ; Who gave himself for us, that he might redeem us from all iniquity, and purify unto himself a peculiar people, zealous of good works. (Titus 2:13-14)**
>
> **For we are his workmanship, created in Christ Jesus unto good works, which God hath before**

ordained that we should walk in them. (Ephesians 2:10)

Some in Thyatira were loyal to Him and His Church. A life of faithful service will pay great dividends when the Lord Jesus returns. Christ knew the heart of His faithful people.

Their Pleasure

Jesus commends them for their **charity. (Revelation 2:19b)** They were a loving Church. It was a pleasure for them to serve because they were motivated by a genuine love for Christ and others. Love is a verb. It is an action word. Love motivates us to serve others. When Jesus looked out over the multitudes of people

> .... he was moved with compassion on them, because they fainted, and were scattered abroad, as sheep having no shepherd. (Matthew 9:36)

Jesus was moved or motivated by His compassion and love for others. Anyone who has the Holy Spirit in them ought to manifest this kind of love.

> ... the love of God is shed abroad in our hearts by the Holy Ghost which is given unto us. (Romans 5:5b)

The Holy Spirit helps God's people to love others the way God loves us. There is no excuse for not caring for others.

All that being said, please let me point out that the devil has done a good job of confusing Christendom concerning Biblical love. True Christian love has become one of the most misunderstood teachings of our day. The love practiced and taught by most Christians today is nothing more than warm and fuzzy, blind ignorance. Preachers are handing out licenses to sin in the name of love. If a Christian takes any stand at all he is called a legalist and said to be unloving. Paul said:

> Let love be without dissimulation. Abhor that which is evil; cleave to that which is good. (Romans 12:9)

The word abhor means *"to render foul and to turn oneself away from."* As children of God we are to render foul and turn away from anything that is evil, whether in the world or in the church. Paul says, Let love be without dissimulation. The word dissimulation refers to the acting of a stage player and is the word from which we get our English word hypocrite. What Paul means is, *"if you claim to be a Christian, don't be a hypocrite and a stage player. If something is wrong, render it foul and turn away from it."* Let's be genuine believers rather than hypocrites.

Their Persuasion

... and faith... (Revelation 2:19c) Though the Church of Thyatira as a whole was compromising and corrupt, there was as small remnant that had remained faithful to the Lord Jesus. They were willing to step out on faith and follow the Lord.

> **But without faith it is impossible to please him: for he that cometh to God must believe that he is, and that he is a rewarder of them that diligently seek him. (Hebrews 11:6)**

This is fairly simple. Faith is belief in what God says. It is taking Him at His word. Without such faith it is impossible to please Him.

Their Patience

... and thy patience... (Revelation 2:19d) The word **patience** comes from *"hypomone"* and means *"to bear up under, to endure."* This is a graphic word that carries the idea of *"perseverance, endurance, fortitude, and persistence regardless of the circumstances."* This is the patience that enables us to stay by the stuff no matter what gets thrown at us. These believers endured the tough times and troubles they faced.

> *In his fifty-two years of serving Christ, John Wesley rode 280,000 miles on horseback. He preached 40,000 sermons. He learned 10 languages. He wrote 400 books. At age 83 he complained about the fact that his eyes would not hold up for him to write more than 15 hours a day. At age 86 he was concerned that his energy would not hold out for him to preach more than twice a day.*

I certainly would not agree with some of Wesley's doctrine, but I admire his endurance and diligence! Likewise, the faithful remnant of Thyatira didn't merely get involved, they stayed involved. Patience is needed if we are to be successful. Christ praises their patience and determination to continue steadfast in service. Jesus said:

... No man, having put his hand to the plow, and looking back, is fit for the kingdom of God. (Luke 9:62)

Paul was able to say ...

For I am now ready to be offered, and the time of my departure is at hand. I have fought a good fight, I have finished my course, I have kept the faith: (2 Timothy 4:6-7)

There were some in Thyatira were steadfast. They would not quit even in days of severe persecution and hardship. We need this kind of stalwart faithfulness today. Tragically we don't see so much of this kind of endurance in our day. The early Church was made up of men and women who had what it took to keep on the firing line. If we are going see God work, we will need Christians who resolve to continue steadfastly in His service. We need to get back to the *"Old Time Religion"* and stay by the stuff.

THE LORD'S CORRECTION

Notwithstanding I have a few things against thee... (Revelation 2:20a) Having commended the faithful remnant for their love and service, Jesus goes on to point out some problems that would prove to be deadly to Thyatira.

Concerning the Woman Preacher

... because thou sufferest that woman Jezebel, which calleth herself a prophetess... (Revelation 2:20b) The Lord revealed the dreadful corruption which had crept into the Church at Thyatira. Jesus used the wicked woman Jezebel, to symbolize the horrifying corruption and debauchery that had infiltrated the Church. Jezebel was a Zidonian princess who married king Ahab and led Israel into deep idolatry and paganism. Hence, Jezebel was responsible for establishing pagan worship in Israel. It was under Jezebel's influence that

> **... Ahab did more to provoke the LORD God of Israel to anger than all the kings of Israel that were before him. (1 Kings 16:33)**

Jesus uses Ahab and Jezebel's union as a picture to point out what was happening at Thyatira. In Ahab's time, Israel went into dark apostasy and served Baal, made groves for idolatrous worship and provoked the Lord to anger. Most of the apostasy and wickedness was initiated and enforced by Jezebel. God likens Thyatira to the days of Ahab and Jezebel. The Church's work is untrue, and her doctrine is false, for her teaching is turned over to Jezebel. Such is the Church that is involved with the pagan practices of false religion and this world. The church, with its rites, its forms and its ceremonies had formed an ungodly alliance with the pagan world.

Concerning The Woman's Platform

This woman was doing an evil work in the Church. She was given a place of prominence and influence and her doctrine was permeating the Church.

First, Her Platform. **... thou sufferest that woman Jezebel, which calleth herself a prophetess, to teach... (Revelation 2:20c)** Notice first of all that this woman **calleth herself a prophetess**. God didn't call her a prophetess; she took that title upon herself. Jezebel was self-styled, self-appointed, and self-serving teacher with no God-given authority whatsoever. The Church of Thyatira was guilty of a grave error. The word **sufferest** comes from "eao "and means "*to permit or allow.*" They were allowing Jezebel to teach in the Church. The name Jezebel tells us a lot about what was going on here. Jezebel introduced Baal worship into Israel, and thereby caused Israel to commit spiritual fornication. By giving her a teaching position, she had a platform to persuade others and lead them astray.

Second, Her Problem. The problem is that in a biblical New Testament Church, we must be careful about putting women in positions of teaching. While a woman can hold a teaching position, she is to only teach women and children. Under no circumstances is she permitted by God to teach men. This is by God's design.

> **But I suffer not a woman to teach, nor to usurp authority over the man, but to be in silence. For Adam was first formed, then Eve. And Adam was not deceived, but the woman being deceived was in the transgression. (1 Timothy 2:12-14)**

Remember, this was given to Paul by Divine inspiration. This is absolute truth and reveals to us God's reason for not allowing women to be teachers over men. The point God makes here is that women are more easily deceived than men. The Apostle Paul, when warning of apostate teachers, wrote ...

> **For of this sort are they which creep into houses, and lead captive silly women laden with sins, led away with divers lusts, Ever learning, and never able to come to the knowledge of the truth. (2 Timothy 3:6-7)**

The only way to see these passages is to look at them as God wrote them. God does not want women to be in a position where she establishes and promotes her doctrine.

> **Let your women keep silence in the churches: for it is not permitted unto them to speak; but they are commanded to be under obedience, as also saith the law. And if they will learn any thing, let them ask their husbands at home: for it is a shame for women to speak in the church. (1 Corinthians 14:34-35)**

It is clear that women are to are to learn in Church, but with silence. If she has a question, she is to ask her husband at home. Theodore Epp wrote:

> *It is apparent from other Scriptures, as well as from the immediate context of these verses, that wrong teaching was often injected into the assemblies of God's people because of some women who were easily brought under evil control.*

Many of the false doctrines of our day have women as their founders. A woman in the Bible originating a doctrine indicates something out of place. It is pictured in Matthew 13 where a woman hid leaven in the meal until the whole was leavened. The leaven was false doctrine that she introduced. Is it any wonder that under Jezebel's teaching there was spiritual fornication, idolatry, and image worship?

Tragically, many women have set themselves up as leaders and theologians and just as many men have been foolish enough to sit under them. In the New Testament Church, women are to teach only under the authority of the Pastor and are not to be in any position in the Church where they have authority or influence over men.

Third, <u>Her Perversion</u>. ... **and to seduce my servants to commit fornication... (Revelation 2:20d)** This woman's teaching was seen by God as seduction. This is a perverted woman propagating false doctrine. The word **seduce** comes from *"planao"* and means *"to lead astray."* Webster says ...

> *To draw aside from the path of rectitude and duty in any manner; to entice to evil; to lead astray; to tempt and lead to iniquity; to corrupt.*

In the last days, there will be a great increase of these seducing teachers.

> **But evil men and seducers shall wax worse and worse, deceiving, and being deceived. (2 Timothy 3:13)**
>
> **Now the Spirit speaketh expressly, that in the latter times some shall depart from the faith, giving heed to seducing spirits, and doctrines of devils; (1 Timothy 4:1)**

Just as Jezebel led Israel to commit spiritual fornication by worshipping Baal instead of the true God, this woman in Thyatira was leading the Church astray. The Church of Thyatira allowed her to teach false doctrine and seduce the Church causing them to commit spiritual adultery. Spiritual fornication is the act of spiritual unfaithfulness to the Lord.

> Ye adulterers and adulteresses, know ye not that the friendship of the world is enmity with God? whosoever therefore will be a friend of the world is the enemy of God. (James 4:4)

James addresses them as **adulterers and adulteresses**. Adultery is committed every time a Christian is unfaithful to the Lord. Thousands over the years have followed these false teachers into adultery and sin.

... and to eat things sacrificed unto idols. (Revelation 2:20e) This evil woman taught the Church to combine the practices of paganism and Christianity. The results of this is clear in many so-called Churches today.

THE LORD'S CONSISTENCY

God is consistent in His method of dealing with people. Those who repent find mercy. Those who do not repent face judgment.

Her Opportunity

And I gave her space to repent of her fornication... (Revelation 2:21a) This is grace! The wrath of God awaits Jezebel and her crowd, but before wrath, is an opportunity for Jezebel to repent. God gives Jezebel **space to repent**. The word **space** speaks of a period of time. God has given her a sufficient amount of time to repent. Even for the vilest of people, God's mercy allows for a space for repentance.

Her Obstinance

... and she repented not. (Revelation 2:21b) This is tragic! This seducer refuses the gracious opportunities God gives.

> Be not deceived; God is not mocked: for whatsoever a man soweth, that shall he also reap. (Galatians 6:7)

Apart from a repentant heart every person will face God and receive exactly what is coming to him. God's judgment will be righteous.

Her Outcome

Behold, I will cast her into a bed, and them that commit adultery with her into great tribulation, except they repent

of their deeds. (Revelation 2:22) Once the opportunity to repent comes to an end, only the wrath of God remains.

He, that being often reproved hardeneth his neck, shall suddenly be destroyed, and that without remedy. (Proverbs 29:1)

... into great tribulation. This is prophetically speaking of the great tribulation when the offspring of the Jezebellian Church will be dealt with and destroyed.

And I will kill her children with death; and all the churches shall know that I am he which searcheth the reins and hearts: and I will give unto every one of you according to your works. (Revelation 2:23) Notice that Jezebel's children will be judged. Those who are spawned by the adulterous relationship of the evil teacher will face certain death and those who have followed the doctrines of Jezebel will suffer the wrath of God when it arrives. Be warned, vengeance is coming!

THE LORD'S CHALLENGE

Our Lord recognizes those who have stood true. These had not fallen for Jezebel's heresy. Thank God there are always those who refuse to waver and waffle. They are the kind of believers who refuse to bow, no matter what.

The Remnant

... unto the rest in Thyatira, as many as have not this doctrine, and which have not known the depths of Satan... (Revelation 2:24a) In Thyatira there was a believing remnant who refused to follow the paganism and worldliness of the devil's Jezebel. They saw this woman for what she was, a wicked instrument of Satan. Praise God for His faithful servants who refused to follow the theological trends of the day but stayed true to their God instead.

The Relief

... I will put upon you none other burden. (Revelation 2:24b) In the midst of trial and tribulation our Lord and Saviour promises to protect them from having to deal with more than they could handle. Praise God for His mercy!

> There hath no temptation taken you but such as is common to man: but God is faithful, who will not suffer you to be tempted above that ye are able; but will with the temptation also make a way to escape, that ye may be able to bear it. (1 Corinthians 10:13)

May we, in these wicked times, be faithful to our Saviour. God honors and delivers those who have a desire to do right.

The Rapture

But that which ye have already hold fast till I come. (Revelation 2:25) Praise God! This verse is twofold: *First*, the Greek word *"krateo"* means *"to grasp, to retain."* The idea is that of keeping a firm grip on something. *Secondly*, they would have to hold on **till I come.** This tells us that Christianity will have to put up with this Jezebellian theology until Jesus returns. For those who reject the apostate doctrines of worldly Churches, there is a blessed hope. Jesus is coming back.

> Looking for that blessed hope, and the glorious appearing of the great God and our Saviour Jesus Christ. (Titus 2:13)

The promise of our Saviour's return is the **blessed hope**. The imminent rapture has been the hope of the Church through the ages. God's Word declares that Christians in Rome, Thessalonica, Corinth, Philippi, Ephesus, and Galatia were hopeful and waiting for the any moment return of the Lord Jesus Christ.

THE LORD'S CONQUERORS

There is an opportunity to rise above the deplorable conditions at Thyatira. Some will repent and be victorious, and some will not. There is a promise given here to the victors. Those who conquer will be rewarded.

The People Of Christ

And he that overcometh, and keepeth my works unto the end... (Revelation 2:26a) Christ speaks to a particular group of people. The word **overcometh** comes from the Greek *"nikao"* and means *"to subdue, conquer, overcome, prevail, get the* *victory."* God intends that every believer be an overcomer. Jesus never intended for Christians to be losers. We have the victory because Jesus Christ won it for us when He defeated death and crushed Satan's head on Cavalry. Sadly, many fail to overcome and Satan rules in their life. But praise God, some get the victory.

The Partnership With Christ

... to him will I give power over the nations: (Revelation 2:26b) This is not a blanket promise to every Christian. It is only to those who overcome. The overcomers will rule with Christ! The victorious Christian will share in Christ's rule. Great and glorious things are promised to the overcomer.

> **If we suffer, we shall also reign with him: (2 Timothy 2:12a)**

Faithful believers will rule with the Lord Jesus during the Millennium Kingdom when He sits on the throne of David. From Jerusalem, Jesus will rule the nations with a rod of iron for one thousand years.

The Power Of Christ

And he shall rule them with a rod of iron; as the vessels of a potter shall they be broken to shivers: even as I received of my Father. (Revelation 2:27) This speaks of Christ's authority to rule. The word **them** refers to the nations. The term **rule them with a rod of iron** is a specific reference to the Millennial reign of Christ. He will rule the nations with absolute authority. They will be **broken to shivers** or splinters. This will take place during the one thousand year Millennial reign that comes at the end of the Tribulation period. This is a right given by God the Father to God the Son.

> **I will declare the decree: the LORD hath said unto me, Thou art my Son; this day have I begotten thee. Ask of me, and I shall give thee the heathen for thine inheritance, and the uttermost parts of the earth for thy possession. Thou shalt break them with a rod of iron; thou shalt dash them in pieces like a potter's vessel. (Psalm 2:7-9)**

Thyatira: The Loose Church

As we look at the previous verses, we begin to get the picture.

> **Why do the heathen rage, and the people imagine a vain thing? The kings of the earth set themselves, and the rulers take counsel together, against the LORD, and against his anointed, saying, (Psalm 2:1-2)**

This describes a time when the kings of the earth gather and take counsel to fight against the Anointed of the Lord.

In Psalm two we see God's decree issued from Heaven right before the Lord Jesus will come to execute judgment on the unbelieving nations of the world who gathered for battle in the valley of Megiddo. This takes place just prior to the establishing of the Millennium when Christ will rule with absolute authority over the nations.

> **I saw in the night visions, and, behold, one like the Son of man came with the clouds of heaven, and came to the Ancient of days, and they brought him near before him. And there was given him dominion, and glory, and a kingdom, that all people, nations, and languages, should serve him: his dominion is an everlasting dominion, which shall not pass away, and his kingdom that which shall not be destroyed. (Daniel 7:13–14)**

> **Wherefore God also hath highly exalted him, and given him a name which is above every name: That at the name of Jesus every knee should bow, of things in heaven, and things in earth, and things under the earth; And that every tongue should confess that Jesus Christ is Lord, to the glory of God the Father. (Philippians 2:9–11)**

Jesus Christ is the Ruler and those believers who have been faithful and overcome the world will reign with Him. It is Jesus Christ who will rule with a **rod of iron**. We will have the privilege of serving during His reign.

The Presence Of Christ

I will give him the morning star. (Revelation 2:28) The morning star speaks of the precious presence of the Lord Jesus

Christ Himself. Jesus, who has given Himself to believers. Henry Morris said...

> *Jesus Christ Himself is "the bright and morning star" (Rev. 22:16) so that this promise assures His own presence as a gift to His people.*

At the end of the Revelation, we read ...

I Jesus have sent mine angel to testify unto you these things in the churches. I am the root and the offspring of David, and the bright and morning star. (Revelation 22:16)

The Lord Jesus clearly states that He is the **morning star**. Israel awaits the Sun of righteousness (Malachi 4:2). The Church age saints however, look for the Morning Star.

The Prodding Of Christ

He that hath an ear, let him hear what the Spirit saith unto the churches. (Revelation 2:29) Here again we see our Saviour's call for attention and obedience to His commands.

SARDIS: THE LIFELESS CHURCH
Revelation 3:1-6

The Church of Sardis—1517 to 1790. Sardis symbolizes the Church during the great reformation. Sardis means *"escaping ones or remnant."* This is a prophetic picture of the great reformation Church that escaped from the clutches and bonds of Rome. At this point in Church history, spiritual darkness covered the land. Only the so-called leaders had the Scriptures. Then with the invention of the printing press, the Word of God was put into the hands of the common man. Great truths were rediscovered and heresies were exposed. God's people were learning the Word of God. It was during this time that many came to Christ and the reformation began.

THE CHRIST OF THE CHURCH

And unto the angel of the church in Sardis write... (Revelation 3:1a) This is the Lord Jesus speaking here. He is walking amid the Churches assessing their works, whether good or bad. He sees and knows everything that is going on.

The Seven Spirits

These things saith he that hath the seven Spirits of God... (Revelation 3:1b) In chapter one we learned that **seven** is the biblical number of perfection and completeness. Of course, when Jesus speaks of the **seven Spirits of God,** He is not implying that there are actually seven Holy Spirits. Rather, it speaks of the sevenfold completeness and work of the Spirit. Isaiah lists the **seven Spirits** (Isaiah 11:2).

- The Spirit of the LORD,
- the Spirit of wisdom,
- the Spirit of understanding,

- the Spirit of counsel,
- the Spirit of might,
- the Spirit of knowledge,
- the Spirit of the fear of the LORD.

The seven Spirits could denote the sevenfold completeness of the Holy Spirit's work in and through believers.

The Seven Stars

... and the seven stars... (Revelation 3:1c) Back in chapter one (1:16, 1:20), we saw that these seven stars represent the pastors of the Churches to whom the seven letters are addressed. We noticed that the pastors are in Christ's right hand, the hand of power and authority. The stars bear light. Thus. the pastor's responsibility is to shine for Christ. He is to reflect the light of Christ to the people in his Church as well as to the world.

THE CONDITION OF THE CHURCH

Next Jesus speaks concerning the condition of the Sardis Church. We will notice in this letter that there is no commendation, Jesus has only condemnation for the Church of Sardis. When it comes time for judgment, we will receive an accurate assessment of our works from Christ.

The Reputation Of Their Church

... I know thy works, that thou hast a name that thou livest... (Revelation 3:1d) Jesus knew their works, the problem however, was that they weren't good works. They had a name for being alive and productive. Solomon said ...

> **A good name is rather to be chosen than great riches, and loving favour rather than silver and gold. (Proverbs 22:1)**

Names are important and we see that Sardis had a good name. They had a good reputation among men. However, a reputation is no good unless the reality is there to back it up.

The Reality Of Their Condition

... and art dead. (Revelation 3:1e) We notice that the Lord offers no approval to this Church, only criticism. The Lord Jesus

Sardis: The Lifeless Church

saw through the outward appearance of their activity. Christ's omniscient evaluation of things is often different from ours. He found Sardis to be a Church with a false profession. They were alive in name only. Like many Churches today, they have a lot of activity, but nothing is happening for God. Their works failed to measure up to their profession, hence, they were alive in name only. All they were really producing was **wood, hay** and **stubble (1 Corinthians 3:12).** The Church of Sardis was a morgue with a steeple. They were involved with all kinds of activity, but they were **dead.** We see plenty of this kind of activity among professing Christians today. They're as dead as a mummy and as cold as an iceberg. They meet, go through their form, run everything by the clock, to the minute, and then go home the same poor, empty, cold souls they were before they came to Church. What a sad thing to have Jesus pronounce a Church dead. We see Plans and Programs, but no Power. They were busy, but they lacked life. We live in the day of Super Churches, but if Christ were to evaluate their work, what would He find? Many churches today have a name, but they are dead.

THE CURE FOR THE CHURCH

The Lord gives Sardis some specific direction, that if heeded, would result in great blessings. There are four parts to this cure.

They Were to be Watching

Be watchful... **(Revelation 3:2a)** These instructions begin with the command to **be watchful.** Many are the dangers and pitfalls we face in this world. The word watchful comes from *"gregoreo"* carries the idea of *"staying awake, being vigilant, paying close attention."* Peter warned us to:

> **Be sober, be vigilant; because your adversary the devil, as a roaring lion, walketh about, seeking whom he may devour: (1 Peter 5:8)**

What a serious warning! The word **sober** means *"to be discreet and cautious"* and carries the idea of being *discerning.* The word **vigilant** means *"to be alert, awake and on the lookout."* Satan is always looking for opportunities to sow seeds of discontent, discord and false doctrine among God's people. Jesus spoke of Satan as an enemy who sowed weeds in with the wheat.

But while men slept, his enemy came and sowed tares among the wheat, and went his way. (Matthew 13:25)

Leonard Ravenhill said ...

Hell is burning while the Church sleeps.

We cannot afford to be sleeping when we ought to be watching and working. We are to be on the lookout and actually watching for a Satanic attack.

They Were to be Working

Strengthen the things which remain, that are ready to die: for I have not found thy works perfect before God. (Revelation 3:2b) We need to strengthen the things that remain. The word **strengthen** comes from *"steridzo"* and means *"to establish and set fast."* It carries the idea of setting something firmly in its place.

... that are ready to die... (Revelation 3:2c) Look at the danger here. The faithful remnant was still professing the Old Time Religion, but even it was **ready to die.** Unless we strengthen ourselves, we will die. There are some things that remain in these last days, but we need workers to strengthen them.

They Were to be Worthy

Remember therefore how thou hast received and heard, and hold fast, and repent... (Revelation 3:3a) Consider these words, **Remember therefore how thou hast received.** We need to remember what Jesus has done for us and walk worthy of Christ's sacrifice. Just the memory of what we were when Jesus saved us ought to cause us to hold fast and live for Him. We were lost and wretched, yet He loved us and took our place under the judgment of God.

But God commendeth his love toward us, in that, while we were yet sinners, Christ died for us. (Romans 5:8)

The command to **hold fast**. Paul instructed Timothy to:

> Hold fast the form of sound words, which thou hast heard of me, in faith and love which is in Christ Jesus. (2 Timothy 1:13)
>
> Seeing then that we have a great high priest, that is passed into the heavens, Jesus the Son of God, let us hold fast our profession. (Hebrews 4:14)
>
> Beloved, when I gave all diligence to write unto you of the common salvation, it was needful for me to write unto you, and exhort you that ye should earnestly contend for the faith which was once delivered unto the saints. (Jude 3)

Every Christian is commanded to hold fast and earnestly contend for the faith. There can be no letting up in God's work.

They Were to be Waiting

... If therefore thou shalt not watch, I will come on thee as a thief, and thou shalt not know what hour I will come upon thee. (Revelation 3:3b) The best is yet to come. Many are waiting for the next paycheck, party, retirement, or something else that is temporal. But,the Christian is waiting for God! These instructions begin with the command to **be watchful.** We are to be watching for His return. We are to be listening for the trump to sound and the cloud to appear. Of course, this speaks of the imminent return of Christ. The word *"imminent"* means *"impending"* and carries the idea of *"looming over."* Concerning the rapture, it means the Church could be caught out immediately, or at any moment. The Scriptures repeatedly admonish believers to watch, be ready and to expect it **at an hour when ye think not. (Luke 12:40)** This was the hope of the early Church. Even their popular greeting, **Maranatha (1 Corinthians 16:22),** set forth their belief in the imminent return of Christ for the church.

> For yourselves know perfectly that the day of the Lord so cometh as a thief in the night. (1 Thessalonians 5:2)

Jesus Christ will come as a **thief in the night.** That is, when no one expects Him. He is not going to announce His coming. For those who are blinded by sin, the Rapture will be a complete surprise to the world. Millions will suddenly be missing, and they will have no idea of what happened. However, for those who love His appearing and long for His coming, it will be a blessed delight. This prospect of an imminent rapture is referred to in Scripture as the believer's ...

... blessed hope. (Titus 2:13)

Someday the trump will sound, and Christ will catch us away to be with Him forever. The blessed hope is the most powerful incentive in the Word of God for the Christian to live a righteous and holy life.

THE CHRISTIANS OF THE CHURCH

Thou hast a few names even in Sardis which have not defiled their garments... (Revelation 3:4a) The Church of Sardis was sadly lacking in spiritual discernment, but there are **a few** who had held steadfast to the faith. Notice the word **few.** These were the faithful. There is a vast difference between making a profession of salvation and possessing salvation. In these last days, the emphasis is on numbers. About ninety percent of America claims to be Christian while all along becoming more and more enslaved to sin. This is the religion of those who make grace a license to sin. Most everyone is quick to proclaim their salvation, but God says there are actually only a **few** who are genuine believers.

The Remnant's Witness

The **few** that our Lord spoke of had not **defiled their garments. (Revelation 3:4b)** Their lifestyle was Christlike. Even in the midst of a wicked age, they had remained pure and holy unto the Lord. They hadn't dirtied the name of Christ. They were not involved in questionable things. Today, Christians have become so entangled in entertainment that they are of little or no good to the cause of Christ. Many Churches have become coffee shops and entertainment centers where rock music and drama dominate the program. The lost see professing Christendom as being no different than themselves.

Surely, we are living in the last days. The judgment of God is about to fall upon this pleasure drunken world. Because sin and iniquity abound, the love of many is waxing cold (Matthew 24:12). May we be like Moses who chose:

> **...rather to suffer affliction with the people of God, than to enjoy the pleasures of sin for a season. (Hebrews 11:25)**

Praise God for those who have not defiled their garments! Some have remained pure in a filthy world. As God's children we must learn to walk amidst the defilements of sin without becoming defiled ourselves.

The Remnant's Walk

... they shall walk with me in white: for they are worthy. (Revelation 3:4c) There was a faithful few in Sardis walked with God. He walks only with those who walk for Him.

> **Can two walk together, except they be agreed? (Amos 3:3)**

Paul said:

> **I ... beseech you that ye walk worthy of the vocation wherewith ye are called. (Ephesians 4:1)**

God expects Christians to live in a manner that depicts what God has done for them. God has prepared every believer for a victorious walk through this world.

THE CONQUERS OF THE CHURCH

This is a promise to the victors in the Church. For those who overcame the world and stood up for Christ. There was hope for them. As long as a person is alive, there is hope!

The Conquest

He that overcometh... (Revelation 3:5a) God expects His people to be overcomers. God does not save people so that they can be casualties on the battlefield. We are not victims, we are victors!

> **For whatsoever is born of God overcometh the world: and this is the victory that overcometh the world, even our faith. (1 John 5:4)**

The term *"defeated Christian"* is an oxymoron. One word contradicts the other. Theologically the words cannot be put together. In Christ we are:

> **... more than conquerors through him that loved us. (Romans 8:37)**

God's people are not to be defeated by that which Christ has already conquered. Look to Christ, conquer your problems, and overcome.

The Clothing

> **... the same shall be clothed in white raiment... (Revelation 3:5b)** This **white raiment** is the attire of the redeemed. This is the raiment that Christ's bride will wear.

> **Let us be glad and rejoice, and give honour to him: for the marriage of the Lamb is come, and his wife hath made herself ready. And to her was granted that she should be arrayed in fine linen, clean and white: for the fine linen is the righteousness of saints. (Revelation 19:7-8)**

The **white** symbolizes righteousness and purity. The Bride of Christ will be adorned in His righteousness (1 Corinthians 1:30, 2 Corinthians 5:21).

The Contract

> **... and I will not blot out his name out of the book of life... (Revelation 3:5c)** We must understand that this is not a threat, it is a promise. Some foolishly attempt to use this verse to support the false idea that a Christian's name can be blotted out of the Lamb's book of life. However, notice that it is not the Lamb's book of life, but the **book of life** that is referred to here. These are two different books. The *Book Of Life* is the book of physical life. The *Lamb's Book Of Life* is the book of eternal life.

The Book Of Life. The book of life contains the name of everyone who is born. It was the book of life that Moses referred to when he asked God to take his life.

Sardis: The Lifeless Church

> **And Moses returned unto the LORD, and said, Oh, this people have sinned a great sin, and have made them gods of gold. Yet now, if thou wilt forgive their sin--; and if not, blot me, I pray thee, out of thy book which thou hast written. (Exodus 32:31-32)**

Moses was asking God to kill him and remove his name from the book of the living. It was the Book of Life that David was speaking of:

> **Let them be blotted out of the book of the living, and not be written with the righteous. (Psalm 69:28)**

When a person dies, his or her name is removed from the book of physical life, but if saved it remains in the Lamb's book of life.

The Lamb's Book Of Life. When a person is born again his or her name is recorded in the Lamb's book of life. This is the book of eternal life. This is Heaven's registry or roll of the born again. Those whose names are written in the Lamb's book of life are guaranteed entry into Heaven.

> **And there shall in no wise enter into it any thing that defileth, neither whatsoever worketh abomination, or maketh a lie: but they which are written in the Lamb's book of life. (Revelation 21:27)**

When believers die, their name is blotted out of the physical book of life. However, once a person's name is recorded in the Lamb's book of life, it is there for eternity. If your name is written in the Lamb's book of life, it will never be blotted out.

The Confession

... but I will confess his name before my Father, and before his angels. (Revelation 3:5d) Jesus also assures them who are not ashamed of Him that He will confess their names before the Father in Heaven, for their faithful service and devotion to Him.

> **Whosoever therefore shall confess me before men, him will I confess also before my Father which is in heaven. (Matthew 10:32)**

Even at this very moment, Jesus pleading our case by the blood sprinkled mercy seat.

> **Who is he that condemneth? It is Christ that died, yea rather, that is risen again, who is even at the right hand of God, who also maketh intercession for us. (Romans 8:34)**

> **Wherefore he is able also to save them to the uttermost that come unto God by him, seeing he ever liveth to make intercession for them. (Hebrews 7:25)**

Obviously, there are some who Jesus will not confess before the Father. The point is, if we confess Him on earth, He will confess us before the Father in Heaven.

The Call

He that hath an ear, let him hear what the Spirit saith unto the churches. (Revelation 3:5-6) Again, Jesus issues a call to hear and obey. One of the problems of the day is that many people hear, but only a few actually do.

PHILADELPHIA: THE LOVING CHURCH
Revelation 3:7-13

Now we come to the Church of Philadelphia—1730 to 1900. It is the sixth of the seven letters to the churches of Asia Minor. Philadelphia represents the great Missionary period of Church history. The word **Philadelphia** means *"brotherly love."* During this time, the light of the Reformation had just about burned out, Christendom had become cold, formalistic and dead. The Lord at this time brought about a great revival. This revival centered largely within the United States, England, Scotland and Wales and was the beginning of the greatest Missionary movement of all times. God called men like Whitefield, Wesley,. Moody and many others to proclaim His Word. During this era, salvation through the shed Blood of Jesus Christ, along with the blessed hope of the believer was being preached everywhere. People were being saved and looking for the Saviour's return. God's people occupied themselves with the defense of the faith and preaching of the gospel. The Philadelphian Christians were given an open door of opportunity to take the gospel to the world. The Lord Jesus commends them for their faithfulness in doing so.

THE POSITION OVER THE CHURCH

The head of the Church is Jesus. He alone holds the position of absolute preeminence and authority.

> **And he is before all things, and by him all things consist. And he is the head of the body, the church: who is the beginning, the firstborn from the dead; that in all things he might have the preeminence. (Colossians 1:17-18)**

We live in a day and time when the word authority is not popular. There are many Churches that run on the authority of the board or some influential member. However, the true Church has Christ as its Head. In verse seven we learn several important facts about Christ.

Jesus Is Sinlessly Pure

These things saith he that is holy... (Revelation 3:7a) When Jesus speaks of Himself as being **holy**, He has been holy from eternity past. While on this earth, He came holy and remained holy from the hour of His birth! He was conceived by the Holy Ghost of God and was born of a virgin mother. Being born of a virgin, when He became man, He escaped the sin nature of fallen man. Therefore, Satan had no claim upon His soul, because He had no depraved nature or sin. He also lived a perfect sinless life as required by the law. What a Saviour! He is holy apart from forgiveness. He is holy without the need of the new birth. He is holy without the sanctifying power of God's Word. He is holy because He is God. In his commentary on Revelation, Dr. H. A. Ironside wrote:

> *"These words embody a challenge to separation from evil in life and error in doctrine. If we would walk in fellowship with the holy One we must remember the admonition, Be ye holy, for I am holy. (1 Peter 1:16) And if we would enjoy communion with Him who is the Truth, we must refuse Satan's lies, and love and live the truth ourselves. Hence it follows, as others have stated, that separation from evil is God's principle of unity. Not separation in a cold, pharisaic sense, but separation to Christ from that which is evil."*

As God, Christ is entirely holy, He is separated from sin and sinners. Christ identified with sinners in order to redeem them, but He never committed sin. If we are going to walk with Christ, we must walk on His terms.

> **But as he which hath called you is holy, so be ye holy in all manner of conversation; Because it is written, Be ye holy; for I am holy. (1 Peter 1:15-16)**
>
> **If we say that we have fellowship with him, and walk in darkness, we lie, and do not the truth. (1 John 1:6)**

Jesus is holy and true. He is perfectly righteous and to walk with Him one must also be righteous. For one to say that he is walking with God while living in habitual sin is to prove himself a liar.

> **I am come a light into the world, that whosoever believeth on me should not abide in darkness. (John 12:46)**

The Christian life is more than mere talk about Christ; we must also walk with Christ. The character of God will not allow compromise. Light is light and darkness is darkness. This is a principle of the Word of God.

> **Can two walk together, except they be agreed? (Amos 3:3)**

If we are going to walk and fellowship with God, we cannot walk in the ways of this world.

Jesus Is Supremely Principled

... he that is true... **(Revelation 3:7b)** Jesus Christ never deviates from His Word. He also works in accordance with His Word. The word **true** comes from *"alethinos"* It carries the idea of truth as opposed to a lie. Jesus said ...

> **I am ... the truth... (John 14:6)**

The Lord Jesus not only spoke absolute truth, but He is also Truth personified. Furthermore, He is the source of all truth.

Jesus Is Sovereignly Powerful

... he that hath the key of David... **(Revelation 3:7c)** Also we see what Jesus is, He **that hath the key of David**. Here Jesus is seen as having both authority and power. In the book of Luke, we see that Jesus is the legal heir to David's Throne.

> **And, behold, thou shalt conceive in thy womb, and bring forth a son, and shalt call his name JESUS. He shall be great, and shall be called the Son of the Highest: and the Lord God shall give unto him the throne of his father David. And he shall reign over the house of Jacob for ever, and of his kingdom there shall be no end. (Luke 1:31-33)**

In presenting Himself as He that hath the key of David, Jesus is proclaiming that He is the sole heir to the throne of David and will soon occupy that throne as King of kings and Lord of lords. The prophet Isaiah wrote of Christ:

> **And the key of the house of David will I lay upon his shoulder; so he shall open, and none shall shut, and he shall shut, and none shall open. And I will fasten him as a nail in a sure place; and he shall be for a glorious throne to his father's house. (Isaiah 22:22-23)**

He has the keys! He **openeth, and no man shutteth; and shutteth, and no man openeth. (Revelation 3:7d)** This further speaks of Jesus' Sovereign control. The one who has the key controls the door.! Oliver B. Greene said ...

> *No man can shut the door which is open to those who honor the Word of God and the precious name of Jesus.*

When we work according to God's plan and His power, He opens the doors of opportunity. Jesus can open doors that no one else can open. He can also shut doors.

THE PRAISE FOR THE CHURCH

Our Saviour lists five important facts about the Philadelphian Church. These five truths help us to understand why this was a great Church.

Exceptional In Their Service

I know thy works... (Revelation 3:8a) Notice the first two words, **I know.** Nothing escapes His knowledge. He knows every detail of everything. Nothing escapes His eye. Jesus referred to the omniscient mind of God when He said that even the very hairs of our head are numbered (Luke 12:7). The Lord knows exactly what is going on in Churches. This was a working Church. They were faithful with the opportunities God had given them. Now this is important! God never gives us greater opportunities, until we are faithful with that which we already have. Because of their faithfulness, He would open doors for them that no one could shut. Thus, the Church at Philadelphia represents the great missionary period of Church history which followed the great reformation period. Jesus promised to them and to us, an open door for service.

Enormous In Their Scope

... behold, I have set before thee an open door, and no man can shut it... (Revelation 3:8b) The Philadelphian Church had an open door. What a great potential these folks had. The Almighty had opened a door of opportunity for them. There is no doubt that Jesus was here speaking to them of the door of opportunity to take the gospel to a lost and dying world. Paul used this terminology concerning his commission and work.

> **For a great door and effectual is opened unto me, and there are many adversaries. (1 Corinthians 16:9)**

> **Furthermore, when I came to Troas to preach Christ's gospel, and a door was opened unto me of the Lord. (2 Corinthians 2:12)**

Paul in addressing the Colossian Church requested that they:

> **Continue in prayer, and watch in the same with thanksgiving; Withal praying also for us, that God would open unto us a door of utterance, to speak the mystery of Christ, for which I am also in bonds. (Colossians 4:2-3)**

When Jesus Christ opens a door for us, we must enter in. We must busy ourselves with His work, for the day will come when the door will be closed.

> **I must work the works of him that sent me, while it is day: the night cometh, when no man can work. (John 9:4)**

Christ has set before us an open door, and it remains open to this day. We must realize that the door of opportunity to preach the gospel carries with it great responsibility. May we remember as we serve Christ, He opens and shuts doors of service. Not only as individual Christians, but also as a local Church. It is not how strong we are and how we use our strength that will get the job done. Instead, it is realizing our weakness and His greatness. It is only by God's grace and power that, as we submit our weakness to Him, we can work. The Apostle Paul said ...

> **Therefore I take pleasure in infirmities, in reproaches, in necessities, in persecutions, in distresses for Christ's sake: for when I am weak, then am I strong. (2 Corinthians 12:10)**

We can have education available, the best of programs, great literature, and put on great evangelistic meetings, but apart from Christ opening the door of opportunity, we will fail most miserably.

Encouraged In Their Strength

... for thou hast a little strength... (Revelation 3:8c) Also, take notice that Christ said, **for thou hast a little strength.** Jesus is in no way speaking negatively here. In fact, the qualities Jesus is pointing out indicates just the opposite. Philadelphia was a stalwart, steadfast and striving Church. Their strength being referred to as **little** speaks to the number of people in the Church. However, though they were small in number, they were faithful with the opportunities the Lord had given them.

Established In The Scriptures

... and hast kept my word... (Revelation 3:8d) These five words give us the reason for their great success. They were grounded on principle. They knew, understood and followed the Word of God. No Church is successful where the people are not faithful to God's Word. Jesus answered

> **... Ye do err, not knowing the scriptures, (Matthew 22:29)**

In the Old Testament, God gave the prophet Hosea a serious warning ...

> **My people are destroyed for lack of knowledge: because thou hast rejected knowledge, I will also reject thee, that thou shalt be no priest to me: seeing thou hast forgotten the law of thy God, I will also forget thy children. (Hosea 4:6)**

Jesus said to the faithful at Philadelphia, **and hast kept my word**. The word **kept** comes from the Greek *"tereo"* and means *"to hold fast, to keep an eye on, to guard."* These Christians guarded and watched over the Word in the best way—they lived it. May God help us in this compromising age to stand for the Word of God.

Endured For The Saviour

... and hast not denied my name. (Revelation 3:8e) These people had remained true to Christ. Idols of pagan gods were everywhere. The area was engulfed in heathen worship. In the next verse Jesus speaks of **the synagogue of Satan**. The devil had afforded every opportunity for failure. There were numerous pagan gods they could have followed. However, they chose Christ and remained true to Him alone. Their faithfulness blessed the heart of the Lord.

THE PROBLEM IN THE CHURCH

Behold, I will make them of the synagogue of Satan, which say they are Jews, and are not, but do lie; behold, I will make them to come and worship before thy feet, and to know that I have loved thee. (Revelation 3:9) The **synagogue of Satan** probably refers to the Jews who were opposing the Church and denying the Messianic credentials of Jesus. The Jews opposed and persecuted, even unto death, those who accepted Christ as Messiah. God's people have suffered tremendously over the years, at the hand of established religion. However, keep in mind that none of the suffering has gone unnoticed by the all-seeing eye of the Omniscient Christ. The Lord Jesus Christ will vindicate his people.

Vengeance is mine, I will repay, saith the Lord. (Romans 12:19)

It is for certain that payday is coming! Keep in mind that those who reject Christ will one day have to acknowledge Him for Who He is.

Wherefore God also hath highly exalted him, and given him a name which is above every name:

> **That at the name of Jesus every knee should bow, of things in heaven, and things in earth, and things under the earth. (Philippians 2:9-10)**

This world hates Christ and His people. The religious crowd is no different. Many who are religious have no love for the true God of Heaven nor His children. Too many, Christians are seen as infidels. To others, Christians are nuts. Some peg Christians as hypocrites and so on. There may well be persecution in this world but rest assured that God knows all about it and He will settle the score.

THE PROMISE TO THE CHURCH

These Christians had been faithful to the Lord and His Word. Hence, the Lord Jesus gives them a wonderful promise concerning their future. God greatly rewards the overcomer. His people do indeed have a wonderful future. This is a promise of Deliverance and is based on their Dedication.

The Dedication To The Word

Because thou hast kept the word of my patience... (Revelation 3:10a) Again, we note that these believers were dedicated and loyal to God's Word. The word **patience** speaks of their endurance and perseverance under persecution. These Christians had kept the Word and stayed by the stuff. Every believer ought to desire to hear Christ say, thou hast kept the Word.

> **Therefore, my beloved brethren, be ye stedfast, unmoveable, always abounding in the work of the Lord, forasmuch as ye know that your labour is not in vain in the Lord. (1 Corinthians 15:58)**

The precious believers at Philadelphia were loyal to the Scriptures. The Word of God is under attack today like never before. Satan has cast doubt upon the old Book with the *"Yeah, hath God said?"* movement. The philosophy of doubt and destruction has been adopted by the modern-day translators who seem to be set on destroying the Word of God. The Bible is regularly attacked by liberals who deny its precious life changing truths. It is also being attacked and denied by professing believers who claim Christ with their lips but deny Him with their life. Christian, we must keep the Word. The faithful and true Christian loves the Word of God and obeys it.

The Delivery From The World

... I also will keep thee from the hour of temptation, which shall come upon all the world, to try them that dwell upon the earth. (Revelation 3:10b) The **hour of temptation** refers to the coming time of Tribulation spoken of by the prophet Daniel in chapter 9 of his book, by Jesus in Matthew 24-25, and by John in Revelation 6-19, which is to come upon the world at the end of the Church age. What a comforting promise to the Christian who is busy about the Lord's work. You will notice that the tribulation is not for the Church, but **to try them that dwell upon the earth.** H. A. Ironside said:

> *This is the Lord's own pledge to those who love His Name and seek to keep His Word. They will not be left down here to pass through the appalling tribulation that is just ahead of those who dwell upon the earth. This expression is found frequently in the book of Revelation. It does not simply mean those who live in the world. A careful reading of the various passages in which this peculiar term is found will make it clear that the earth-dwellers are in contrast to those whose citizenship is in Heaven.*

This is a precious promise for the believer. It is a reference to the blessed hope. God's children will be kept out of the tribulation that is yet to come upon the unbelieving world. Some wonderful day, just before the tribulation, He will rapture His people from this sin darkened earth.

THE PERSEVERANCE OF THE CHURCH

A Church that wants to serve Christ whole heartedly must be relentless and resolute. One of the great incentives for service is the realization that He is coming soon. Jesus is going to **come quickly,** and He is not running late. He is right on time. He will arrive just as He planned in eternity past. In this section, the Lord encourages His people to continue persevering for Him.

His Coming

Behold, I come quickly... (Revelation 3:11a) The use of the word **quickly** does not mean that He will come shortly or even within the lifetime of the Philadelphia believers. The word quickly comes from *"tachu"* and carries the idea of *prompt and swift*. Jesus is saying that when He comes for His people, the Rapture will unfold rapidly. When Jesus comes, He will come suddenly and without further announcement.

Jesus' return for His people is an event that is near and dear to His heart. Why is this precious truth not near and dear to the average Church member? Many today, even professing Christians, are not Heavenly minded, but worldly minded. They are not looking for Him and, sad to say, most do not even want Him to come back. However, the Spirit filled Christian _Looks_ for, _Longs_ for, and _Loves_ His appearing. God's children should be excited about the return of Jesus. There is a special reward for those who set their heart on the second coming.

> **Henceforth there is laid up for me a crown of righteousness, which the Lord, the righteous judge, shall give me at that day: and not to me only, but unto all them also that love his appearing. (2 Timothy 4:8)**

What a day that will be! All the trials and turmoil we have been through here on earth will amount to nothing once He appears.

His Caution

... hold that fast which thou hast, that no man take thy crown. (Revelation 3:11b) It is easy to get side-tracked and fall away. Put on the whole armor of God. Stand strong and fight the good fight of faith. We are on the winning side.

> **Look to yourselves, that we lose not those things which we have wrought, but that we receive a full reward. (2 John 1:8)**

It is a tragic possibility that we can lose the rewards we have earned. We must persevere. Just think of those wonderful words of Jesus...

> **Well done, thou good and faithful servant. thou hast been faithful over a few things, I will make thee ruler over many things: enter thou into the joy of thy lord. (Matthew 25:21)**

These words will be heard by all **who hold fast** till He returns.

Him that overcometh will I make a pillar in the temple of my God... (Revelation 3:12a) The overcomer will be honored by being a pillar in the heavenly temple. This is an eternal reward for faithfulness to Christ. Charles Ryrie comments:

> *"A promise that believers will be honored in the New Jerusalem, referring to the custom of honoring a magistrate by placing a pillar in his name, in one of the temples in Philadelphia."*

A **pillar** is a column designed to support and reinforce. Figuratively, the Bible uses this term for the Church.

> **But if I tarry long, that thou mayest know how thou oughtest to behave thyself in the house of God, which is the church of the living God, the pillar and ground of the truth. (1 Timothy 3:15)**

The promise here is that throughout eternity, the overcomer will be a pillar in the eternal Temple of God. God honors the faithful!

... and he shall go no more out: and I will write upon him the name of my God, and the name of the city of my God, which is new Jerusalem, which cometh down out of heaven from my God: and I will write upon him my new name. (Revelation 3:12) John mentions the New Jerusalem, the Holy City, that he describes in detail in chapter 21. He further speaks of a **new name**. In the last chapter of Revelation, John wrote:

> **And there shall be no more curse: but the throne of God and of the Lamb shall be in it; and his servants shall serve him; And they shall see**

his face; and his name shall be in their foreheads. (Revelation 22:3-4)

In that day we shall receive the name of Christ. These promises to the overcomer speak of stability, intimacy, and security in our relationship with Jesus Christ.

He that hath an ear, let him hear what the Spirit saith unto the churches. (Revelation 3:13) For the sixth time He repeats this command.

LAODICEA: THE LUKEWARM CHURCH
Revelation 3:14-22

The message to the Church at Laodicea—1900 to the end of the Church age. Laodicea represents the apostate Church of the last days. It speaks of the present stage of Church history. The name Laodicea comes from two Greek words, *"laos"* meaning *"people,"* and *"dika"* meaning *"rights."* The idea is the *"Rights of the People."* We hear a great deal of the same thing today. As we will see, the professing Christians of Laodicea were a self-sufficient, self-satisfied and self-serving people. They relied upon their riches and abilities and had need of nothing. They considered themselves to be self-sufficient. What a picture of the present-day. A large majority of professing Christians today are lukewarm and have judged themselves to be just fine.

THEIR CITY

Laodicea was located about forty miles east of Ephesus and eleven miles from the city of Colossae. There were three roads that crossed Asia Minor intersecting in Laodicea. Therefore, it was a busy commercial hub. This made Laodicea a wealthy city. In addition, Laodicea was a major exporter of fine black wool. This was not ordinary wool, but a beautiful, soft, shiny, raven black wool that was much in demand. Laodicea was also the home of a widely recognized school of medicine that was well-known for its eye salve. Hence, Laodicea was a very wealthy city of merchants, doctors, bankers and industry. Even the Church in Laodicea had declared themselves to have need of nothing. Yet, Jesus said to them ...

... thou art wretched, and miserable, and poor, and blind, and naked: (Revelation 3:17b)

Such is the overall condition of Christendom. There are fancy Church buildings, large denominations, elaborate programs, and much money, but the Church is poor. Many Churches have stored up great accounts in the banks of this world, but nothing in the bank of Heaven. Hence, Laodicea describes the general condition of professing Christendom just before the Rapture. You will notice in this letter that there is not one word of praise given to the Laodiceans. Our Saviour's silence in this area reflects the sad condition of this Church. As we said before, the name Laodicea means *"the rights of the people."* At Laodicea the people's opinions were more important than the God's Word. This is the case with today's apostate religion also. Most folks today ...

> **... will not endure sound doctrine; but after their own lusts shall they heap to themselves teachers, having itching ears. (2 Timothy 4:3)**

They are not interested in the Truth! Their opinions, preferences and manmade traditions are the only things that matter. Laodicea considered herself rich, but in the eyes of God she was poor. This is the church that Christ will vomit out. What a vivid illustration depicting how Christ feels about lukewarm religion. John R. Rice fitly called the Laodicean Church, *"The Church Members Who Make God Sick."* Laodicea is a fore view of churchianity in its final state of apostasy.

THEIR CHRIST

And unto the angel of the church of the Laodiceans write; These things saith the Amen, the faithful and true witness, the beginning of the creation of God. (Revelation 3:14) Our Lord begins this letter to the Laodicean Church with a description of Himself. Though with their life they denied Christ as their Lord, they will answer to Him none the less. There are three thoughts here.

Jesus Christ is the Final Word

...These things saith the Amen... (Revelation 3:14a) Our verse says that Christ is the **Amen.** The word **Amen** refers to something that is *"established and definite."* Noah Webster defines Amen this way:

> *"As a verb, it signifies to confirm, establish, verify; to trust, or give confidence; as a noun, truth, firmness, trust, confidence; as an adjective, firm,*

stable. In English, after the oriental manner, it is used at the beginning, but more generally at the end of declarations and prayers, in the sense of, be it firm, be it established."

Christ doesn't just teach the truth and proclaim the truth; He is Truth Himself.

Jesus saith unto him, I am the way, the truth, and the life: no man cometh unto the Father, but by me. (John 14:6)

Jesus is Truth personified! The word **amen** is used to guarantee a statement as being true. It affirms the validity of what is being said. This title speaks of Christ as the final word on matters of truth. To call Jesus the **Amen** is to say He is the personification of the truth of God.

Jesus Christ is the Faithful Word

Jesus is **the faithful and true witness... (Revelation 3:14b)** Jesus remains faithful amidst the unfaithfulness of his people. He is the true witness in contrast to the false witness and unfaithful conduct of the Laodiceans. In our day, the court systems are loaded down with crooked practices. Do not misunderstand me. There are some good men and women in our judicial system. However, there is also a lot of corruption. Crime is at an all-time high in the world and the lawyers are getting richer. Witnesses (many times false witnesses) are bought to testify, and criminals go free to peddle drugs, commit murder and rape again. However, every man has a **faithful and true witness** who will testify either for or against him. He is the Witness that will not be bought, bribed, or bashed. His testimony will be final and the sentence fair and just, according to the crime. What Jesus says is absolute truth. His witness will not be _Delayed_, _Diluted_, _Distorted_ or _Deluded_. That this will be a serious time begs the question, *"How will we fare when Jesus testifies about us?"*

Jesus is the Forever Word

... the beginning of the creation of God. (Revelation 3:14c) Some have stumbled at this verse and concluded that Jesus is a created being. However, this statement does not mean that

Christ was created by God, but that He is the Creator. The word **beginning** comes from the Greek *"arche"* and means *"source or origin."* Jesus Christ is the source of all creation. This world hates both Christ and His truth but they are not going to get rid of Him. The public schools and college classrooms are doing their best rid the world of absolute truth. They teach their erroneous evolutionary theory, promote their woke agenda, and anti-God ideology. Academia can babble forever and never prove their monkey theology. The day is coming when God's Word will preside in judgement over them. It is a fact that God's truth will stand for eternity.

> **The grass withereth, the flower fadeth: but the word of our God shall stand for ever. (Isaiah 40:8)**
>
> **Thy word is true from the beginning: and every one of thy righteous judgments endureth for ever. (Psalm 119:160)**
>
> **For the Lord is good; his mercy is everlasting; and his truth endureth to all generations. (Psalms 100:5)**
>
> **Heaven and earth shall pass away: but my words shall not pass away. (Mark 13:31)**
>
> **Being born again, not of corruptible seed, but of incorruptible, by the word of God, which liveth and abideth for ever. (1 Peter 1:23)**

Satan has been trying to destroy the Word of God since the garden. He hates the Bible, but he will never destroy it. It endures forever! Jesus Christ will have the final say! Those who have hated, ignored, and attempted to get rid of the Bible, but stand before it in the day of judgment.

> **He that rejecteth me, and receiveth not my words, hath one that judgeth him: the word that I have spoken, the same shall judge him in the last day. (John 12:48)**

Those who reject Christ will answer to Him. The lost will stand before Him in judgment. He is the Eternal, Almighty, Sovereign God of Glory. He is the one who said ...

Laodicea: The Lukewarm Church

Verily, verily, I say unto you, Before Abraham was, I am. (John 8:58)

... I am Alpha and Omega, the first and the last: (Revelation 1:11)

He is the eternal All in All. He is Everything. Hallelujah! He is God! When one takes up the Bible and examines the character of Christ, they discover the Divine. There is no way to look at the issue honestly and intelligently and fail to embrace the Divinity of the Lord Jesus Christ. What a Saviour!

THEIR CONDITION

Now Jesus moves on to the sad condition of the Laodicean Church. We will notice that there is no praise for this Church, only condemnation.

The Omniscient Christ

I know thy works... (Revelation 3:15a) The Lord knows indeed! Seven times Jesus has declared to these Churches, **I know thy works.** This is the omniscient Christ speaking. Omniscience is a divine attribute. Hence, the all-knowing God is speaking. It is a sobering thought that Jesus knows all about each of us. Nothing escapes His omniscient gaze.

The Offensive Condition

... that thou art neither cold nor hot: I would thou wert cold or hot. So then because thou art lukewarm, and neither cold nor hot... (Revelation 3:15b-16a) Our Lord goes right to the root of the problem. The most difficult people in this world to deal with are those who are indifferent. The Laodiceans were such people. They were neither cold nor hot. James W. Knox explains the significance of our Lord's terminology:

> *"The implications of this statement would have been immediately apparent to every believer with a Laodicean background. They knew that in Hierapolis, six miles away, the water from the hot springs had a real medicinal value. They also knew that in Colosse, ten miles away, the pure cold water was most refreshing. They knew their own water in Laodicea was*

notorious throughout the province. Ducted through closed conduits and over aqueducts from five miles south, it was lukewarm and totally unpalatable, even nauseous to drink. A normal reaction was to spit it out."

Our Lord used the water situation of Laodicea to illustrate the people's spiritual condition. When used metaphorically, the word **cold** describes the lack of zeal and enthusiasm. The word **hot** comes from *"zestos"* and means *"to boil, to be fervent."* Metaphorically it speaks of zeal and fervency. The Laodiceans were **neither cold nor hot.** If they were **cold**, they would at least be uncomfortable enough that maybe they would move toward the fire, but not this crowd. On the other hand, if they were **hot**, they would be on fire for God.

The Lord loves sold-out servants. The Laodiceans, however, were **lukewarm.** They were compromising fence straddlers. The tragedy is that they were comfortable in their sickening condition. They were living in the comfort zone. The word **lukewarm** comes from *"chliaros"* and means *"to be tepid."* Tepid water is not refreshing or satisfying. **Lukewarm** is the most horrible condition anyone could be in. In the spiritual sense, lukewarmness is a picture of indifference, compromise, and apathy. Someone has said that lukewarmness is *"a yawn in the face of Almighty God."* It is a condition that says, *"Lord I'm saved, thank you for the fire escape, but I am bored with you now."* This is indeed an appropriate picture of the spiritual apathy of today's Churches. All around this world, sitting in Church pews are people who hear sermon after sermon and go on as though the Word of God means nothing to them. They are a Church going people and yet, they have no sense of the horrible condition they are in. They live with no <u>Concern</u>, no <u>Conviction</u>, no <u>Contrition</u> and no <u>Conversion</u>. They are half-hearted and putrid. They are like the people Jesus was talking about when He said ...

> **This people draweth nigh unto me with their mouth, and honoureth me with their lips; but their heart is far from me. (Matthew 15:8)**

These professing Christians are self-serving, self-satisfied, self-sufficient, and self-secure, and they are proud of it. Keep in mind that these were mostly lost church members to whom Jesus was speaking. They were people who gave lip service to the things of God but had no heart in their worship.

The Outcome Confirmed

... I will spue thee out of my mouth. (Revelation 3:16) The word **spue** comes from the Greek *"emeo"* and literally means *"to emit or vomit."* The medical procedure of giving someone an emetic solution comes from the word. An emetic solution is usually made up of strong salt water, dry mustard and ipecac. Its purpose is to cause vomiting, especially after the ingestion of poison. The Laodicean's spiritual apathy and lack of enthusiasm was nauseating to Christ. Christ was sickened by their lukewarmness. It is sickening for professing believers to live in such a half-hearted manner. Their condition was so nauseating to Christ that He threatens to spew them out of His mouth.

THEIR CONDEMNATION

The Laodicean's represent the kind of Christians that make God sick. Jesus was nauseated by their lethargic condition, self-righteous attitude and haughty opinion of themselves. This all led to their ultimate condemnation. In verse 17, the Lord Jesus pointedly describes the details of their situation.

Their Foolish Contentment

Because thou sayest, I am rich, and increased with goods, and have need of nothing... (Revelation 3:17a) The Laodiceans were rich and well to do people. As far as they were concerned, they needed no help from man or from God. They were a people much like Americans today. They believed that money could buy anything. They were trusting in their wealth.

> **Riches profit not in the day of wrath: (Proverbs 11:4)**
>
> **He that trusteth in his riches shall fall: (Proverbs 11:28)**
>
> **But they that will be rich fall into temptation and a snare, and into many foolish and hurtful lusts,**

> which drown men in destruction and perdition. (1 Timothy 6:9)

The Faithful and True Witness now steps forward and testifies. He rejects their lukewarm *"I'm OK and you're OK"* philosophy. He answers their proud boasting with the straight and startling words.

Their Fatal Condition

... and knowest not that thou art wretched, and miserable, and poor, and blind, and naked: (Revelation 3:17b) Notice the phrase, **and knowest not.** This is spiritual ignorance. They were tragically blind and completely oblivious to their condition. What a sad state to be in. Jesus confronts their lukewarm and apathetic attitude head on! Here Jesus uses five words to describe their true condition.

First, they were <u>Sinfully Wicked</u>. They were **wretched. (Revelation 3:17c)** Regardless of their high opinion of themselves, Christ assured them that they were **wretched**. The word **wretched** comes from the Greek *"talaipros"* and means *"to be afflicted."* They thought they were okay, but they were afflicted with sinfulness. This is man's problem.

> **For all have sinned, and come short of the glory of God; (Romans 3:23)**

The Laodiceans were afflicted with the worst possible condition. They were righteous and okay in their own eyes, but in the eyes of God, they were exceedingly sinful and fell far short.

Second, they were <u>Sadly Miserable</u>. They were **miserable. (Revelation 3:17d)** Our Lord now identifies them as **miserable**. The word miserable carries the idea of pitiable. These people had everything in this life but were completely unprepared for the next life. The Lord Jesus pitied these people. What a strike against this self-righteous social club. A man without Christ is a miserable man! Oh, they laughed, played, and had a good time. They enjoyed the **pleasures of sin** for a season, but seasons soon change, and bad weather comes.

> **But she that liveth in pleasure is dead while she liveth. (1 Timothy 5:6)**

Laodicea: The Lukewarm Church

Yes, they had a heartbeat, they moved and enjoyed the pleasures of this wicked world, but it would be short lived. The Laodiceans were miserable in their souls and had no real or lasting happiness, but they did not know it.

Third, they were *Spiritually Bankrupt*. They were **poor. (Revelation 3:17e)** This Church was made up of wealthy people who assumed that it **had need of nothing** when in reality they were spiritually bankrupt. Paul said:

> **Charge them that are rich in this world, that they be not highminded, nor trust in uncertain riches, but in the living God, who giveth us richly all things to enjoy. (1 Timothy 6.17)**

The lukewarm Laodiceans were trusting their uncertain riches. The Bible clearly states...

> **So is he that layeth up treasure for himself, and is not rich toward God. (Luke 12:2)**

The Laodiceans had fashionable clothes, beautiful houses, an abundance of money, the best of food and extravagant lifestyles, but they stood before God as bankrupt beggars without any hope of salvation. This well describes the sad state of many today.

Fourth, they were *Scripturally Blind*. They were **blind. (Revelation 3:17f)** So far as the things of God, they were blind—spiritually blind. They were blind to the reality of their true condition. These were natural men with no spiritual sight.

> **But the natural man receiveth not the things of the Spirit of God: for they are foolishness unto him: neither can he know them, because they are spiritually discerned. (1 Corinthians 2:14)**

These self-centered, self-righteous Church members were miserably **blind** concerning their own needs. They suffered from the worst kind of blindness—spiritual blindness.

Fifth, they were *Shamefully Bare*. **... naked. (Revelation 3:17g)** Though beautifully and fashionably clothed, they stood **naked** in their sin before Jesus Christ. Laodicea was known for its cloth and the clothing industry. A good amount of their wealth came from this industry. Christ made it clear to them that their expensive and elaborate clothing would not cover them in the day of judgment. They were well clothed, but spiritually naked. Christ spoke of such people.

> **Ye are they which justify yourselves before men; but God knoweth your hearts: for that which is highly esteemed among men is abomination in the sight of God. (Luke 16:15)**

These miserable people were proud, self-righteous, lost religionists. They had boasted that they had **need of nothing**, but God found them to be liars.

THEIR COUNSEL

I counsel thee to buy of me gold tried in the fire, that thou mayest be rich; and white raiment, that thou mayest be clothed, and that the shame of thy nakedness do not appear; and anoint thine eyes with eyesalve, that thou mayest see. (Revelation 3:18) The Faithful and True Witness offers this worldly and worthless Church solid counsel. His counsel involves three things.

Their Virtue

... buy of me gold tried in the fire, that thou mayest be rich... (Revelation 3:18a) The Laodiceans were proud of their riches, but Christ counsels them to buy of His true riches. Gold is a symbol of righteousness and purity and here speaks of real riches. The idea is that of genuine riches as opposed to the possessions of this world, that they were trusting in. Jesus said:

> **So is he that layeth up treasure for himself, and is not rich toward God. (Luke 12:21)**

They boasted of their riches, but in reality, they were spiritually bankrupt. The Laodiceans were rich with this world's goods and had nothing laid up for eternity. They were like the rich man of whom Jesus spoke in the book of Luke. God said to him

> **... Thou fool, this night thy soul shall be required of thee: then whose shall those things be, which thou hast provided? (Luke 12:20)**

This is the story of a man who had accumulated great wealth and possessions but died without God. He urges them to buy **gold tried in the fire**. This speaks of refined and purified gold. Peter used this same illustration.

> **That the trial of your faith, being much more precious than of gold that perisheth, though it be tried with fire, might be found unto praise and honour and glory at the appearing of Jesus Christ: (1 Peter 1:7)**

The self-righteous Laodiceans needed a different kind of righteousness. They needed to be genuinely purified and saved.

Their Vesture

... and white raiment, that thou mayest be clothed, and that the shame of thy nakedness do not appear... (Revelation 3:18b) The Lord counsels them concerning their much needed clothing. Their need was **white raiment.** They were well clothed in the eyes of the world, but in the eyes of God they were naked. The world's fashion would not do. They needed **white raiment** to enter into the presence of God. The white raiment speaks of Christ's imputed righteousness.

> **For he hath made him to be sin for us, who knew no sin; that we might be made the righteousness of God in him. (2 Corinthians 5:21)**

As we noted before, Laodicea was a fashion center, known for its clothing industry. Yet, these Church going people were spiritually naked before God. As opposed to their own filthy rags of self-righteousness, they were to trust in Christ's imputed righteousness.

Their Vision

... and anoint thine eyes with eyesalve, that thou mayest see. (Revelation 3:18c) Christ now informs them that they also need spiritual sight. Laodicea was also known for its famous medical school that specialized in the treatment of diseased eyes. However, they needed a different kind of medicine. They suffered from the worst kind of blindness. They could not see spiritually. When it comes to the things of God, only the Spirit of

God can make them known to man's sin darkened heart. The Laodiceans were much like many of today's professing Christians. All they could see was their own agenda. They were focused on earthly things. They were religious, but blind concerning the things of God. This of course speaks of spiritual illumination.

> **But the natural man receiveth not the things of the Spirit of God: for they are foolishness unto him: neither can he know them, because they are spiritually discerned. (1 Corinthians 2:14)**

The Church has never had better trained preachers or more brilliant intellects than today. There are thousands of Bible colleges and institutes across the land. Many thousands of books are pouring off the presses daily. Christian radio broadcasts number in the thousands. The internet is flourishing with preachers and teachers. Tragically many are dangerous and apostate. There are home Bible studies and Bible conferences, and yet, we've never had more spiritual blindness than in these last days. How desperately we need spiritual discernment!

THEIR CORRECTION

As many as I love, I rebuke and chasten: be zealous therefore, and repent. (Revelation 3:19) In this verse, the Lord reveals some details concerning their correction. They were in a situation that needed correction. The Lord always has a solution for man's failure.

The Compassion

As many as I love... (Revelation 3:19a) Even though this letter contains the sharpest rebuke of the seven letters, it also reveals Christ's love and compassion for people. This is a comforting statement that reveals the tremendous hope that lies in the Saviour. God's grace is always available. William R. Newell, in his commentary on *Revelation*, spoke of this love as the ...

> *Astonishing love of the Savior! Loving even the lukewarm! Loving an assembly that has really no heart for Him!*

Laodicea: The Lukewarm Church

Astonishing indeed that the Holy God of Heaven could love sinful man in such a way. Donald Grey Barnhouse wrote:

> *"Yet upon a church that has sunk as low as Laodicea, the risen Lord still showers His love. He is standing there, the faithful and true Witness, counseling them, calling them away from their self-styled riches, pleading with them to repent, promising to supply every need. He holds before them the wonderful promise of fellowship and closes with the amazing promise that in one step they can go from the Laodicean state to His very throne. How great is the grace of God!"*

This is God's holy and pure love. The Bible makes it very clear that ...

God is love. (1 John 4:8, 16)

This kind of love is a Divine attribute of God. This is in no way the warm and fuzzy sentimental love as practiced by sinful man. The problem with man's love is that it is limited and conditional. Man, too often fails to balance God's love with His other attributes. God's love must be balanced with His Holiness, Righteousness, Justice and Judgment.

The Correction

... I rebuke... (Revelation 3:19b) The word **rebuke** comes from *"elencho"* and means *"to confute, admonish, tell a fault, rebuke."* It carries the idea of refuting and correcting something to be false. This would have been tough for the Laodiceans to swallow. However, Christ rebuked them because it was necessary. Rebuke is for our good. Rebuke corrects us and helps to get on the right track, but only if we are humble enough to respond correctly to the rebuke. That is why God has given Pastors the authority to rebuke.

Preach the word; be instant in season, out of season; reprove, rebuke, exhort with all longsuffering and doctrine. (2 Timothy 4:2)

People don't like to be rebuked, but it is part of the Christian life. Pride too often gets in the way of listening to Christ.

However, Christ is rebuking the Laodiceans for their own good. This is rebuke that is coming from One who loves them. He wants them to correct the error of their way.

The Chastening

... and chasten... (Revelation 3:19c) This is another misunderstood truth of Scripture. Many believers are so fooled by man's standard of love that they have no idea that true love corrects and chastens. God's chastisement is for a purpose. It is His desire that we would see sin as He does. He wants His people to come to the realization of our sin and repent. Chastisement is a product of God's love. Because God loves us, He will chastise us when we fall into sin.

First, <u>Chastisement Has To Do With Our Heritage</u>. **Thou shalt also consider in thine heart, that, as a man chasteneth his son, so the Lord thy God chasteneth thee. (Deuteronomy 8:5)** A Christian belongs to the family of God and He is our Father. We have a wonderful heritage. The plans that God has for His children are far beyond our wildest imaginations. He wants His very best for us. Therefore, He chastens His children.

> **For whom the LORD loveth he correcteth; even as a father the son in whom he delighteth. (Proverbs 3:12)**

If God did not love us, He wouldn't chastise us. His chastisement proves His love for us. In fact, if a professing believer lives in sin without being chastised, he is probably not a genuine believer. God's love and chastisement go hand in hand.

> **For whom the Lord loveth he chasteneth, and scourgeth every son whom he receiveth. If ye endure chastening, God dealeth with you as with sons; for what son is he whom the father chasteneth not? But if ye be without chastisement, whereof all are partakers, then are ye bastards, and not sons. (Hebrews 12:6-8)**

God spells this out in no uncertain terms. One who professes to be a Christian, but continues in sin **without chastisement**, is not God's child. The word **bastards** is used here to describe such people. The word bastards comes from *"nothos"* and speaks of an *"illegitimate son."* The idea is that they have no claim to spiritual sonship.

Second, <u>Chastisement Has To Do With Our Hope</u>. **Chasten thy son while there is hope, and let not thy soul spare for his crying. (Proverbs 19:18)** God's chastening shows that there is still hope for us. A father scripturally chastises his children because he has a hope that they will turn out right. He corrects and chastens his children so that they will know what is wrong and what is right. Every decent and serious parent has this hope for their child. By the same token, God is Holy and demands our holiness.

Third, <u>Chastisement Has To Do With Our Holiness</u>. **... for our profit, that we might be partakers of his holiness. Now no chastening for the present seemeth to be joyous, but grievous: nevertheless afterward it yieldeth the peaceable fruit of righteousness unto them which are exercised thereby. (Hebrews 12:10-11)** Yes, God chastises His erring children. If we receive the chastening of the Lord with the right attitude, we will experience the fruit of righteousness in our lives. His chastisement is for our betterment. We are told that **it yieldeth the peaceable fruit of righteousness.** It is better that we be chastened rather than condemned.

> But when we are judged, we are chastened of the Lord, that we should not be condemned with the world. (1 Corinthians 11:32)

Chastening is always for our good and when we respond correctly, we are saved from a more severe judgment. We can then enjoy fellowship with God. Christ's chastisement upon the Laodiceans was for the purpose of getting their attention and turning them to Himself.

The Change

... be zealous therefore, and repent. (Revelation 3:19d) The word zealous means *"to boil or burn."* Christ is calling for zeal on their part. The zealousness of which Christ spoke stands in stark contrast to their lukewarmness. Christ was telling them to get on fire for God. He was tired of their fake, halfhearted and hopeless religion. Their religion wasn't doing them or Christ's work any good and it made Him sick.

The Conviction

... and repent. (Revelation 3:19d) The word **repent** comes from *"metanoeo"* and basically means *"to change one's mind."* The word *"meta"* means *"to change after,"* *"noeo"* means "to perceive." Hence, the word **repent** literally means *"to perceive afterwards."* This implies a change of mind which comes after thinking about something. This is the point at which sinful man comes to the realization of his sinful condition. He changes his mind about his sin and about God. This is when he comprehends the truth, receives the truth and turns to Christ. Paul described it as

... repentance toward God, and faith toward our Lord Jesus Christ. (Acts 20:21)

All a person needs to do to be saved is in this verse. One must simply repent toward God and put his or her faith in the Lord Jesus Christ.

THEIR CURE

A great opportunity is given to the Laodicean Church. He extends His grace. Christ is still available if they will only openly respond to His call.

The Presence Of Christ

Behold, I stand at the door... (Revelation 3:20a) Here stands the loving Christ at their very door. Imagine Jesus coming to the Church house and finding the door shut. Why would He stay? Why would He make His presence know? What an awful place to attend Church. I have heard of the Open Door Church, but this is the Closed Door Church. It is a Church that has locked Christ out! It is a sad situation when Christ is present but locked out of the Church!

The Proof Of A Crime

... and knock... (Revelation 3:20b) Here is one of the saddest pictures in Scripture. Remember, this Church represents the condition of Christianity at the end of the Church age. Jesus is here seen on the outside and knocking at the door of this Church in an attempt to gain entry. This is a perfect word picture of religious America. What is clearly seen here is the unwanted Christ locked out of the Church. In his commentary on *Revelation*, Oliver B. Greene said:

> *Here we have a true display of the grace of God, even when the church has stooped to the lowest degree and has pushed the Lord Jesus out.*

How sad that Jesus should be on the outside and knocking at the door of the very Church that is supposed to love Him. Though it sounds awful this is the major crime of today's religionists. Because of their selfish and wicked motives, along with their lack of love for God, many churches have locked Christ out. They are rich and increased with goods and have need of nothing, not even Christ. Oh yes, their bank accounts are full. They have beautiful stained-glass windows, plush carpets, padded pews, and elaborate steeples! They meet to sing hymns and go through the motions of worship. Isn't it an amazing thing how churches can operate without Christ's involvement? Tragedy of tragedies! Paul spoke of those who have ...

... a form of godliness, but denying the power thereof: from such turn away. (2 Timothy 3:5)

Masses of people regularly have Church services, but know nothing of Christ's presence, Christ is not in the service. Rather, He is locked out. God have mercy on such a Church. This is indeed a sad state of affairs for any outfit claiming to be Christian. The Church age began with Him in the midst of the churches and ends with Him locked out of the Church. He is locked out of many Churches today.

The Possibility Of Companionship

... if any man hear my voice, and open the door, I will come in to him, and will sup with him, and he with me. (Revelation 3:20c) This is the invitation of restoration and fellowship. Notice the personal responsibility here. Jesus says, **... if any man hear my voice, and open the door.** We must accept

His invitation and open the door. Christ will never force His way into a Church. He does, however, stand at the door asking to be let in.

The Promise Of Caste

To him that overcometh will I grant to sit with me in my throne, even as I also overcame, and am set down with my Father in his throne. (Revelation 3:21) To those who overcome, open the door to Christ and prevail in the Christian life, Christ promises an eternal and lofty position. We must follow Christ's example in this matter. Christ is now seated on the Father's throne. It was by humbling Himself and being obedient, even unto death.

> **And being found in fashion as a man, he humbled himself, and became obedient unto death, even the death of the cross. Wherefore God also hath highly exalted him, and given him a name which is above every name: That at the name of Jesus every knee should bow, of things in heaven, and things in earth, and things under the earth; And that every tongue should confess that Jesus Christ is Lord, to the glory of God the Father. (Philippians 2:8-11)**

If we follow His example, we will humble ourselves and surrender our life to Him. Are you a Laodicean? Have you locked Christ out? Won't you open the door now?

THE RAPTURE
Revelation 4:1

After this I looked, and, behold, a door was opened in heaven: and the first voice which I heard was as it were of a trumpet talking with me; which said, Come up hither, and I will show thee things which must be hereafter. **(Revelation 4:1)** This verse parallels with 1 Thessalonians chapter four. It perfectly pictures the Rapture of God's people away from earth before the Tribulation begins.

> **For the Lord himself shall descend from heaven with a shout, with the voice of the archangel, and with the trump of God: and the dead in Christ shall rise first: Then we which are alive and remain shall be caught up together with them in the clouds, to meet the Lord in the air: and so shall we ever be with the Lord. (1 Thessalonians 4:16-17)**

The Rapture is the next great event in the redemptive plan and purpose of God. What a wonderful subject—the Rapture of God's people. The Devil hates the doctrine of the imminent pre-tribulation rapture. The return of Christ in the Rapture is one of the Christian's great incentives to live a holy life. The Rapture is also the great **blessed hope** of the Christian. However, there are many who scoff at the idea of an any moment rapture. Satan has confused the minds of multitudes concerning this great doctrine of the rapture. Their unbelief is to be expected in these last days. Peter warned us that in the last days there would be those who would reject and ridicule the idea of the Lord's coming.

> **Knowing this first, that there shall come in the last days scoffers, walking after their own lusts, And saying, Where is the promise of his coming? for since the fathers fell asleep, all things continue as they were from the beginning of the creation. For this they willingly are ignorant of, that by the**

word of God the heavens were of old, and the earth standing out of the water and in the water (2 Peter 3:3-5)

The Apostle. They have made a conscious choice to reject the truth of Christ's return. Let's consider several facts about the rapture.

THE POSITIONS ON THE RAPTURE

The Rapture is one of the most exciting and encouraging events in the Bible. It is the believer's blessed hope. The Scriptures have quite a bit to say about the removal of Christ's bride and the awful time of tribulation to follow. Like many other precious doctrines of God's Word, man has done a good job of confusing the teaching of the rapture.

There are several theories concerning the rapture. New books are flowing from presses daily. There are those who teach that the Church will go into part of the tribulation. Others hold the view that God's people must endure all of God's wrath. Yet another group teaches that only part of the Church will be raptured, and that carnal and disobedient Christians will be punished in the tribulation. It seems that you can ask ten different people about the Rapture and get eleven different opinions. However, God has not left His people in the dark concerning this great event. We will briefly look at the varying positions and then examine what the Bible says about the rapture.

The Pre-tribulation Rapture

Pre-tribulationists hold that the Church will be raptured before the tribulation period begins. This is the only view that is consistent with the doctrine of imminence (meaning that Christ can come at any moment) as taught in God's Word. The imminent rapture has been the hope of the Church down through the ages. The Word of God declares that Christians in Rome, Corinth, Thessalonica, Philippi, Ephesus, and Galatia were hopeful and waiting for the any moment return of Jesus Christ. The **Bible** is clear that there is a distinction between the imminent return of Christ for His people and His coming in

The Rapture

wrath (1 Corinthians 15:50-58; 1 Thessalonians 1:9-10; 2:19; 4:13-18; 2 Thessalonians 2:1; Titus 2:13; 1 John 3:2-3).

The Mid-tribulation Rapture

Mid-tribulationists ignore the doctrine of imminency and teach that the Rapture will take place at the midpoint of the Tribulation period. They teach that none of the events of the first three and one half years of the tribulation are connected with God's wrath. However, a careful reading of Revelation chapter six shows the opposite to be true.

> **And the kings of the earth, and the great men, and the rich men, and the chief captains, and the mighty men, and every bondman, and every free man, hid themselves in the dens and in the rocks of the mountains; And said to the mountains and rocks, Fall on us, and hide us from the face of him that sitteth on the throne, and from the wrath of the Lamb: For the great day of his wrath is come; and who shall be able to stand. (Revelation 6:15-17)**

This passage is clear—it is the wrath of the Lamb, and He is the One who opened the seals that brought the judgments.

The Post-tribulation Rapture

Post-tribulationists believe that the Church will have to endure the entire tribulation period and that the Rapture takes place right before the second coming of Christ. They ignore the fact that God has promised to deliver His people from His wrath. Post tribulationists ignore the dispensational distinctions between Israel and the Church. This is a common problem among those who attempt to put the Church in the tribulation.

The Partial Rapture

There is also a partial rapture view which teaches that only the faithful Christians will be raptured before the Tribulation, and those who have not been so faithful will be punished by going through the tribulation. This view is promoted by Robert Govett, G. H. Lang, and others. These and others go so far as to teach that the disobedient children of God will be cast into outer darkness to be punished. This view is really nothing more than a protestant purgatory.

The Pre-wrath Rapture

The pre-wrath is a new view position within the past 25 years or so by Marvin Rosenthal, a former pre-tribulationist and director of Friends of Israel, who, at the urging of a friend, reexamined his pre-tribulation views. As a result, he came up with the pre-wrath theory. This view is also pushed and promoted by Robert Van Kampen who has authored several books on the subject. The pre-wrath position is nothing more than a rehashed and warmed up mid-tribulation position. The pre-wrath teaches that the Rapture will take place five and a half years into the Tribulation. There are several problems with the pre-wrath position, here are a few observations:

- It is doubtful that God waited until 1990 to reveal His plan of prophecy. Rosenthal's pre-wrath plan is a new doctrine, never before taught in the history of the Church. It is indeed a dangerous thing to start coming up with new doctrine after two thousand years of Church history. Learned men and Holy Spirit-filled preachers down through the years have held to the imminent return of Christ. Such men as M. R. DeHaan, Oliver B. Greene, Clarence Larkin, William L. Pettingill, C. I. Scofield, Arno C. Gaebelein, Charles Ryrie, John Walvoord and numerous others have faithfully preached and served the Lord and have had a great impact concerning the work of Christ, without the need for a new doctrine concerning the rapture.

- Rosenthal makes much of looking for signs. Let us remember that the Lord's coming is compared to a thief in the night. For yourselves know perfectly that the day of the Lord so cometh as a thief in the night. (1 Thessalonians 5:2) A thief does not call ahead and announce his coming to break into your house. He does not give you signs. He comes suddenly, does his work and he is gone. The Church is not to be looking for red heifers, temples, or wars. Jesus said, A wicked and adulterous generation seeketh after a sign; and there shall no sign be given unto it, but the sign of the prophet Jonas. And he left them and departed. (Matthew 16:4) We are not looking for signs, we are looking for our Saviour. We are to be looking for that blessed hope and the glorious appearing of the Lord and Saviour Jesus Christ. (Titus 2:13), who will come as a thief in the night. (1 Thessalonians 5:2), to catch His bride away.

- Rosenthal attempts to avoid the true meaning of immanency. He redefines imminence and makes a big fuss about *"expectancy."* Those who deny the imminent return of Christ rob God's people of the incentive to watch for their Lord. It is only the pre-tribulation interpretation views the coming of Christ as imminent. All other views reject the imminent return of Christ. The imminence of His coming is what gives the message of the Rapture its strength. It is the certainty of His return and the uncertainty of the time that gives His people the incentive to stay pure, do His work, watch and occupy until He comes.

- Rosenthal constantly takes passages out of context in an attempt to prove his theory. In failing to recognize the difference between Israel and the Church, Rosenthal consistently misapplies Scripture. This is a common problem with those who fail in rightly dividing the word of truth. (2 Timothy 2:15)

The bottom line is that the Bible teaches the rapture, not the rupture. While men have their theories, the Bible states its facts.

And to wait for his Son from heaven, whom he raised from the dead, even Jesus, which delivered us from the wrath to come. (1 Thessalonians 1:10)

... For God hath not appointed us to wrath, but to obtain salvation by our Lord Jesus Christ. (1 Thessalonians 5:9)

Any teaching that puts the Church into tribulation and under the penal wrath of God misses the whole purpose of the Rapture and the tribulation.

THE PICTURE OF THE RAPTURE

Here in Revelation chapter four the dispensation of the Church is over, His bride has been caught up to Heaven and the day of the Lord has been ushered in.

> **After this I looked, and, behold, a door was opened in heaven: and the first voice which I heard was as it were of a trumpet talking with me; which said, Come up hither, and I will show thee things which must be hereafter. (Revelation 4:1)**

William R. Newell points out that:

> *Daniel, the prophet, saw the same glorious sight (Daniel 7): the Ancient of Days enthroned, and 'One like unto a son of man brought near before him' and given 'dominion, and glory, and a kingdom, that all the peoples, and languages should serve him.*

Notice John said, **After this.** John is commanded to write about the things which are to take place after the things **which are**, that is, after the church age. The phrase **after this** is not hard to understand. It is clear from these words that something has ended, and John obviously begins a new division here, **The things that are to be hereafter.** Chapter 4:1 is a transition verse from the **things which are** to the **things which must be hereafter.** This is the same terminology John used for future things in verse nineteen of chapter one. The first division, chapter one, lasted a short time; the second division has lasted two thousand years so far. Here John is transported into the throne room and from where he stands the Church age has passed. John does not mention the Church between chapters six and eighteen. The Church is not seen again until she returns with Christ in chapter nineteen. The phrase **after this,** is positive proof that what takes place from this point on, must take place after the events of chapters two and three has come to an end.

The Rapture

John looked and a **door was opened in Heaven.** The open door speaks of Christ who is the door to Heaven. Jesus is the way into Heaven.

> **I am the door: by me if any man enter in, he shall be saved, and shall go in and out, and find pasture. (John 10:9)**

John saw a door opened in Heaven, and a voice said **come up hither.** What the Apostle John experienced here is representative of what will happen to all living Christians someday. This is the clear teaching of the Word of God and the view held by the greatest of Bible Scholars and teachers. Consider the writings of just a few of them. Lehman Strauss, in his book on Revelation says this:

> *I see in these words one of the briefest, yet one of the clearest statements on the Rapture of the Church. It is symbolic of the fulfillment of the believer's 'blessed hope.' Our Lord promised that He would keep His own from the hour of trial that is to come upon the whole world. (3:10) Thus we see in the Apostle John a representative figure of those who will be 'caught up' to meet the Lord in the air and be with Him forever.*

Oliver B. Greene wrote:

> *After this. (after the Church has run its course and all things concerning the Church have been fulfilled) I looked . . . and behold, a door was opened in heaven. John 10:9 tells us that Jesus is that door. After His resurrection He ascended to Heaven, and called John. (in the spirit) up to where He is. He opened the door and John stepped into Heaven to witness the events that were to follow. This is a true picture of the Rapture. John experienced in the spirit what we will literally experience when the Rapture takes place. (I Thess. 4:14-18) .... When the Rapture occurs, the trumpet will sound, and the voice of the archangel will call the saints up. Jesus will not come to this earth when He comes in the Rapture ... the saints will be*

caught up to meet Him in the air; but when He comes in judgment, He will come to the earth, and will stand on the Mount of Olives. (Zech. 14:4)

M. R. DeHaan wrote:

> We have in this passage the Rapture of the Church, the catching away in that dark Laodicean Age of those who had not been carried away by the world's false hopes of a man-made millennium and Utopia. The time is at hand, and although we would not attempt to set any dates for the coming of the Lord, for we know that no man knows the day nor the hour of His appearing, we are confident that the day is near at hand. Of one fact we are absolutely confident: today, this moment, we are nearer the coming of the Lord than we have ever been before. One of these days, He will come ... John, having beheld the last phase of professing Christendom, typified by Laodicea, says, 'after this I looked.' The next event on God's program we confidently believe to be the Rapture of the church.

H. A. Ironside wrote:

> I believe that we must understand the Rapture of 1 Thessalonians 4:16-17 as transpiring between Revelation 3 and 4. The apostle is the symbol of this rapture. He sees the door opened in Heaven. His attention is turned from earth to glory. He is caught up in spirit, and far above all the mists of this world he sees a throne set in Heaven and someone sitting on it.

I. M. Haldeman, wrote:

> Without previous warning John is caught up to Heaven at the sound of a trumpet-like voice. John is a representative of the true Church, those who have Christ in them the hope of glory. Like John the Church without previous warning and at any time will be caught up at the sound of a trumpet and a voice into Heaven. The Twenty-four elders symbolize the Church in Heaven as a body of enthroned priests waiting for

The Rapture

the hour of the kingdom and the exercise of their priestly function.

J. A. Seiss, wrote:

I have said that this open door in heaven, and this calling up of the Apocalyptic seer through that door into heaven, indicate to us the manner in which Christ intends to fulfill His promise to keep certain of His saints 'out of the hour of temptation,' and by what means it is that those who 'watch and pray always' shall 'escape' the dreadful sorrows with which the present world, in its last years, will be visited. Those of them that sleep in their graves, shall be recalled from among the dead; and those of them who shall be found living at the time, 'shall be changed, in a moment, in the twinkling of an eye;' and both classes 'shall be caught up together in the clouds, to meet the Lord in the air.' The same voice which John heard, even 'the voice as of a trumpet,' whether dead or living, they shall hear, saying to them, 'Come up Hither.' And there shall attend it a change and transfer as sudden and miraculous as in his case.

The list of quotes could go on and on. Over the years great Bible teachers like Clarence Larkin, C. I. Scofield, John Walvoord, J. Dwight Pentecost, John Phillips and countless others recognize the Rapture of the Church here in Revelation 4:1. When we compare John's experience to the rapture, the fact that the Rapture does occur here is hardly deniable.

- Heaven's door is opened to receive the Church at the time of the Rapture (1 Thessalonians 4:16-18).
- There is a voice like a trumpet (1 Thessalonians 4:16; 1 Corinthians 15:52).
- It happens imminently and suddenly (1 Corinthians 15:52).
- It transpires at the end of the church age (Revelation 2-3).

- John, the raptured saint, is immediately in Heaven's throne room (Revelation 4:2).
- The next thing concerning earth is God's judgment (Revelation 6-18).
- The Church is not seen in Revelation 6-18 which describes the Tribulation Period.

Revelation 4:1-2 is without a doubt the Rapture of the Church. The Scripture establishes beyond any doubt that those who are saved will someday be raptured away to spend eternity with the Lord Jesus Christ. We do not know when this will be, but we do know that it will happen in God's timing. In a day and hour known only to God, the trumpet will sound, and God's people will be caught up!

THE PERSON OF THE RAPTURE

There are those who teach that the second coming of Christ is fulfilled in a person's life at the moment that he becomes saved. They teach that every time a soul is born again into the Kingdom of God, their salvation is the fulfillment of the second coming for that individual. However, if we study and rightly divide the word of God, we learn that such an interpretation will not do. The Bible teaches beyond any shadow of a doubt that the second coming of Christ will be a literal, visible and personal return. Jesus said ...

> **In my Father's house are many mansions: if it were not so, I would have told you. I go to prepare a place for you. And if I go and prepare a place for you, I will come again, and receive you unto myself; that where I am, there ye may be also. (John 14:2-3)**

In this reference to the Rapture Jesus unmistakably and clearly stated that He would return personally for His people. This truth is also taught in the book of Acts, where Luke gives us the account of Jesus' ascension back to Heaven.

> **Until the day in which he was taken up, after that he through the Holy Ghost had given**

> commandments unto the apostles whom he had chosen: To whom also he showed himself alive after his passion by many infallible proofs, being seen of them forty days, and speaking of the things pertaining to the kingdom of God. (Acts 1:2-3)

We learn that after His resurrection, Jesus spent forty days with His disciples. During this time, He taught them things pertaining to the Kingdom of God. Then, He assures them of the promise Holy Spirit and power of God for the ministry.

> But ye shall receive power, after that the Holy Ghost is come upon you: and ye shall be witnesses unto me both in Jerusalem, and in all Judaea, and in Samaria, and unto the uttermost part of the earth. (Acts 1:8)

Now, notice what happens next!

> And when he had spoken these things, while they beheld, he was taken up; and a cloud received him out of their sight. (Acts 1:9)

Now take notice of the fact that the Lord Jesus Christ literally, bodily, and visibly ascended into Heaven. That is important. Next the Bible says:

> And while they looked stedfastly toward heaven as he went up, behold, two men stood by them in white apparel; Which also said, Ye men of Galilee, why stand ye gazing up into heaven? this same Jesus, which is taken up from you into heaven, shall so come in like manner as ye have seen him go into heaven. (Acts 1:10-11)

There is only one way to interpret this passage. Just as surely as Jesus was literally and visibly taken up into Heaven, He will literally return to this earth. Just as there was a literal and visible ascension, there will be a literal and visible return of our Lord Jesus Christ. It cannot be otherwise. Paul tells us in unmistakable language that Jesus will return personally.

> For the Lord himself shall descend from heaven with a shout, with the voice of the archangel, and

> with the trump of God; and the dead in Christ shall rise first; Then we which are alive and remain shall be caught up together with them in the clouds, to meet the Lord in the air: and so shall we ever be with the Lord. (1 Thessalonians 4:16-17)

Notice that text clearly states that the **Lord himself shall descend.** Our Lord will return literally and visibly and summon His people with a shout like a trumpet blast. The grave of every saint will give up it's dead and those still living at that time will be caught up with Christ to ever be with Him. This is the Word of God speaking!

THE PROMISE OF THE RAPTURE

Revelation 4:1-2 perfectly parallels the Rapture passage given by Paul in First Thessalonians 4:13-18. What a comforting passage to every child of God. It means that if Christ should come in our day, we, like John on the Isle of Patmos, would also see the door open in Heaven, and we too would hear His voice like a trumpet saying, **Come up hither.** The Rapture of the Christian is indeed our wonderful and blessed hope. In other words, every true child of God should be waiting and looking for this event to happen today, and it can take place at any moment. Are you anticipating Christ's return? Are you looking for the Rapture today?

> **Looking for that blessed hope, and the glorious appearing of the great God and our Saviour Jesus Christ. (Titus 2:13)**

Now there is no doubt that the doctrine of the Rapture is clearly taught in the Bible. In fact, the Rapture is a major Bible doctrine. This will be a great day for the Christian. Every Spirit filled child of God longs and looks for this great event to take place.

THE PERVERSION OF THE RAPTURE

The Word of God is absolute truth and therefore, it is the principal source of all truth and our final authority concerning doctrine and practice. There are too many people who are letting men's books determine their positions and doctrine, rather than studying the Bible for themselves. While there is nothing wrong with reading good books, we must let the Bible be our final authority. The Word of God stands like a tower above the latest best sellers on eschatology. It must be remembered that the most important factor in understanding the Scriptures is the Holy Spirit's leading and teaching us. Jesus called Him the **Spirit of truth**:

> **Howbeit when he, the Spirit of truth, is come, he will guide you into all truth: for he shall not speak of himself; but whatsoever he shall hear, that shall he speak: and he will show you things to come. (John 16:13)**

Isn't it interesting that Jesus said, **He will show you things to come.** To understand Bible truth, one must be willing to accept the Spirit's leading and the Word of God as the final authority. This is so even when one's favorite author is wrong. Of course, people are going to disagree. But tone thing is clear! God's Word is the final authority. Our Lord has promised that the believer will have the ability to study and understand the Word of God, including the doctrine of **things to come,** because of the Holy Spirit's ministry in his life.

One of the biggest mistakes made by Bible students is failing to distinguish between the nation of Israel and the Church. This is a serious blunder that confuses the interpretation of Scripture. It is often made by those who teach that the Christian is going into the coming Tribulation Period. This is a major perversion of truth. It is an affront to the blessed hope.

> **Looking for that blessed hope, and the glorious appearing of the great God and our Saviour Jesus Christ; (Titus 2:13)**

Notice Who we are to be looking for. We are looking for Jesus, not the antichrist. In failing to see the separation of God's dealing with the Church and Israel, many miss the comfort and purpose of the rapture. Paul wrote:

Study to show thyself approved unto God, a workman that needeth not to be ashamed, rightly dividing the word of truth. (2 Timothy 2:15)

This is key to understanding God's Word. **Rightly dividing the Word of truth** is one of the major principles of Biblical interpretation. If we don't get this right, our doctrine won't be right. The term **rightly dividing** speaks of the dispensations of the Bible. Here we see that a workman must divide the Word and not only divide, but **rightly** divide. The command to rightly divide the Word of God comes directly from Almighty God Himself, and it is the Christian's responsibility to carry it out. The term *"rightly divide"* means *"to cut straight."* The workman is to cut a straight line through the Word of God, making proper distinctions between various subjects, such as salvation and stewardship, Israel and the Church, law and grace, rapture and revelation and other great truths of the Bible.

Those who fail to rightly divide God's Word will also fail to reach the proper interpretation and conclusion. Many false doctrines have been the result of failing to **rightly divide** the Word of God. There must be sound hermeneutical principle applied to Bible study. If we follow this principle of rightly dividing the Word and compare the Olivet Discourse of Christ with the Rapture of the Church, we can see that they describe two different events.

In Matthew 24 and 25 our Lord was answering the disciples' questions and discussing events that will take place on earth during the time of Tribulation. In verse 8 of chapter 24, the phrase **beginning of sorrows** is clearly a symbol of the tribulation period. The Church is not the focus of Matthew 24 and 25. Keep in mind that the implications and environment of the Olivet discourse are strictly Jewish. Jesus spoke of Judea (24:16), the Sabbath (24:20) and the prophecies of Daniel concerning the Jewish people (24:15). To apply the Olivet Discourse to the nation of Israel is simply to follow the basic rules of hermeneutics. On the other hand, to apply this to the Church, is to fail in ...

The Rapture

> **... rightly dividing the word of truth. (2 Timothy 2:15)**

Comparing the events of the Rapture in 1 Thessalonians, with the events of the Olivet discourse in Matthew 24-25, we see that they simply do not line up together. That's because one is for Israel and the other for the Church.

OLIVET DISCOURSE	THE RAPTURE
The Nation Israel	The Church
False Christ's & Prophets	Christ Himself
Focus Is On The Nations	Focus Is On Heaven
Famines & Hunger	The Marriage Supper
Pestilences & Disease	No More Sickness
Earthquakes & Turmoil	Eternal Peace
Sorrow & Mourning	Comfort & Joy

The events of the Olivet discourse and those of the Rapture in no way coincide with one another. However, if we compare the Olivet discourse with the beginning of the tribulation period, the two match perfectly. We know from honest, contextual Bible study that the tribulation begins in Revelation, chapter six, when the Lamb of God begins to open the seals. Surely this is the wrath of God as it is clearly stated.

> **For the great day of his wrath is come; and who shall be able to stand. (Revelation 6:17)**

This is Jesus, the Lamb, beginning to pour out His wrath upon an unbelieving world. We can clearly see the truth of the pre-tribulation rapture here. Notice also how the seal judgments correspond perfectly with the events of the Olivet discourse.

MATTHEW 24	REVELATION 6
False Christ. (5)	First Seal. (1-2)
Wars. (6-7)	Second Seal. (3-4)
Famine. (7)	Third Seal. (5-6)
Pestilence. (7)	Fourth Seal. (7-8)
Kingdom preaching. (14)	Fifth Seal. (9)
Martyrdom. (9)	Fifth Seal. (9-10)
Earthquakes. (7)	Sixth Seal. (12)

No amount of theological sleight of hand can stuff the Church into the tribulation. It is obvious that the Rapture and the Olivet discourse are two different events, that are designed to deal with two different people, at two different times.

THE PRIORITY OF THE RAPTURE

Concerning this matter of the rapture, we will study and rightly divide, letting the Word of God be our final authority. The Rapture involves a two-fold priority. The first priority of the Rapture is to *deliver* God's people from the wrath to come. When we study this subject in the Bible, we learn that the purpose of the Rapture is designed by God to deliver His (Church age) people from the wrath that He is going to pour out on the lost

The Rapture

world and Israel. My friend, you mark it down, God will deliver His blood-bought, redeemed people from the wrath to come. God has promised that He will deliver His Church and we can take Him at His word.

> **Because thou hast kept the word of my patience, I also will keep thee from the hour of temptation, which shall come upon all the world, to try them that dwell upon the earth. (Revelation 3:10)**

Over and over, again and again, the Bible teaches that the Christian is not appointed unto wrath.

> **For God hath not appointed us to wrath, but to obtain salvation by our Lord Jesus Christ. (1 Thessalonians 5:9)**

God has promised to deliver His people from the tribulation, as we are not appointed to His wrath. The seven-year Tribulation period will certainly be the outpouring of God's wrath upon the world. The fact that God raptured Enoch (a type of the Church) before the flood, and then rescued Lot before raining fire down and destroying Sodom, sets a Biblical precedent for the truth that God delivers His children before He pours out His wrath. The Rapture is the New Testament believer's means of deliverance from God's wrath. Those who are born again are exempt from ever suffering God's wrath. This is our **blessed hope.** The Tribulation begins with the breaking of the first seal when the first horseman of the Apocalypse rides. This first horseman is easily identified as the antichrist. In that same chapter it is clear that the tribulation has begun. Speaking of Jesus Christ as the Lamb is clearly stated:

> **For the great day of his wrath is come; and who shall be able to stand? (Revelation 6:17)**

Many try to put the Church into the Tribulation and end up chopping the book of Revelation up like hash. However, if we follow the book of Revelation, in the chronological order in which God gave it to us, it is clear that the tribulation period begins in chapter six and runs through chapter eighteen. The Church is seen in Heaven during this time. The tribulation period is described in Scripture by such terms as:

> ... the day of the LORD. (Amos 5:18)
> ... time of Jacob's trouble. (Jeremiah 30:7)
> ... hour of temptation. (Revelation 3:10)
> ... great day of his wrath. (Revelation 6:17)

God's children do not look for wrath, but rapture. We were saved from God's wrath.

> **And to wait for his Son from heaven, whom he raised from the dead, even Jesus, which delivered us from the wrath to come. (1 Thessalonians 1:10)**

The second priority of the Rapture is to *deal* with the nation of Israel. According to the Bible, the Church age must come to an end before God will once again deal with Israel. The Church will not be involved in Jacob's trouble, as the Scriptures are clear that God will not deal with Israel again until He is finished with the Church.

> **For I would not, brethren, that ye should be ignorant of this mystery, lest ye should be wise in your own conceits; that blindness in part is happened to Israel, until the fulness of the Gentiles be come in. (Romans 11:25)**

The phrase **fulness of the Gentiles** speaks of the completion of the Church. The end of the Church age is necessary for God to deal with Israel as a nation. The tribulation period is the time of Jacob's trouble, not the Church's trouble. Jeremiah describes the tribulation and then writes:

> **Alas! for that day is great, so that none is like it: it is even the time of Jacob's trouble; but he shall be saved out of it. (Jeremiah 30:7)**

Dr. H. A. Ironside identified this time of Jacob's trouble as being for Israel, He wrote:

> *After the church has been caught away to Heaven at the close of this dispensation, the Jews will be deceived into accepting the claims of a blasphemous impostor claiming to be the Messiah. It is he who is going to place the abomination that causes desolation.*

He will demand that all men worship the image that he sets up; thus, the scene of the plain of Dura will be reenacted. In that day, as in the past, a remnant among the Jews will refuse to believe his claims or to obey his voice. This will be the signal for the breaking out of the great tribulation, 'the time of Jacob's trouble'. (Jeremiah 30:7)

God says what He means and means what He says. The tribulation is Jacob's trouble. Hence, it is Israel's, trouble. The Church is having her persecution now but will be delivered from the wrath to come.

For God hath not appointed us to wrath, but to obtain salvation by our Lord Jesus Christ, (1 Thessalonians 5:9)

Because thou hast kept the word of my patience, I also will keep thee from the hour of temptation, which shall come upon all the world, to try them that dwell upon the earth. (Revelation 3:10)

A thorough study of the Seventy Weeks Of Daniel clearly shows that the Church cannot and will not be involved in the tribulation.

Seventy weeks are determined upon thy people and upon thy holy city, to finish the transgression, and to make an end of sins, and to make reconciliation for iniquity, and to bring in everlasting righteousness, and to seal up the vision and prophecy, and to anoint the most Holy. Know therefore and understand, that from the going forth of the commandment to restore and to build Jerusalem unto the Messiah the Prince shall be seven weeks, and threescore and two weeks: the street shall be built again, and the wall, even in troublous times. And after threescore and two weeks shall Messiah be cut off, but not for himself: and the people of the prince that shall come shall destroy the city and the sanctuary; and the end thereof shall be with a flood, and unto the end of

> the war desolations are determined. And he shall confirm the covenant with many for one week: and in the midst of the week he shall cause the sacrifice and the oblation to cease, and for the overspreading of abominations he shall make it desolate, even until the consummation, and that determined shall be poured upon the desolate. (Daniel 9:24-27)

Make special note here that the 70 weeks are determined upon...

> ... thy people and upon thy holy city. (Daniel 9:24)

It goes without saying that the Holy City is Jerusalem (Nehemiah 11:1, Isaiah 52:1). It is an established fact that Jerusalem is God's city. The place where He has chosen to put His name.

> ... in Jerusalem, the city which I have chosen me to put my name there. (1 Kings 11:36)

> ... in Jerusalem, the city which the LORD did choose out of all the tribes of Israel, to put his name there. And his mother's name was Naamah an Ammonitess. (1 Kings 14:21)

Jerusalem is God's city, but just who is **thy people,** referring to in this passage? The Bible gives us the clear answer.

> And whiles I was speaking, and praying, and confessing my sin and the sin of my people Israel, and presenting my supplication before the LORD my God for the holy mountain of my God. (Daniel 9:20)

We see here that the time set apart is for the purpose of dealing with Israel and not the Church. The laws of Bible interpretation prohibit trying to put the Church into a passage that the Holy Spirit has clearly stated refers to Israel.

This is the meaning of the **seventy weeks.** The **weeks** here, is a generic term that literally means seven. The word "weeks" could apply to days, weeks, months, or years. Literally, Daniel was saying that seventy sevens were determined upon Israel.

The Rapture

We can easily see from the context that Daniel is dealing with years (Daniel 9:2). God has determined that He will take 70 weeks of years or 490 years to bring this prophecy to pass with Israel. This entire period of 490 years is related only to Israel, (the Jews) and to the holy city of Jerusalem. We note also that the 70 weeks, or sevens of years, are divided into three main periods. The first division involves 7 weeks of years, for a total of 49 years. The second division contains 62 weeks of years for a total of 434 years. The first 7 weeks and 62 weeks totaling 69 weeks have been fulfilled. We learn that at the end of the first 69 weeks the Messiah would be cut off. This happened when Jesus Christ died on the cross. He came unto His own and His own received Him not. When Israel rejected their Messiah and crucified Him, God set Israel aside temporarily for the purpose of calling out a bride—the Church. The third division is 1 week for a total of 7 years. This is the concluding week of God's dealings with Israel and is the tribulation period. These seven years of tribulation are divided into two 3½ year periods. The first 3½ years are called:

... the beginning of sorrows. (Matthew 24:8)

The last 3½ years are called the:

... great tribulation... (Matthew 24:21),

This is the event known in Scripture as the ...

... time of Jacob's trouble. (Jeremiah 30:7)

Again, we must note that the entire 70th week of Daniel, the whole week of years, is connected to the nation of Israel—not the Church.

The 69th week of Daniel ended with the death of Jesus Christ upon Calvary's cross. It was at this time that the Messiah was **cut-off. (Daniel 9:26)** We are now living in that undetermined space of time between the 69th and the 70th week known as the Church Age. But when the Rapture takes place, the remaining 70th week of Daniel will start. During this time of the Church age, God is not dealing with Israel as a nation. However, He is not finished with them.

> **For I would not, brethren, that ye should be ignorant of this mystery, lest ye should be wise in your own conceits; that blindness in part is happened to Israel, until the fulness of the Gentiles be come in. And so all Israel shall be saved: as it is written, There shall come out of Sion the Deliverer, and shall turn away ungodliness from Jacob. (Romans 11:25-26)**

Once the **fullness of the Gentiles** (the Church) is completed, Christ will rapture His bride out of this world and the last week, (7 years), of Daniel's 70 weeks, (490 years), will begin. Anyone who studies and rightly divides the Word of God, (2 Timothy 2:15), will conclude that the tribulation is for Israel. The whole seven-year tribulation period has nothing to do with the Church! This entire seven-year period known as the seventieth week of Daniel, (Daniel 9:24-27), is designed by God Almighty to deal with the nation of Israel.

THE PROGRAM OF THE RAPTURE

The pre-tribulation rapture is based upon the Bible's doctrine of the imminent return of Christ. The word imminent means *"impending or looming."* Concerning the rapture, it means that the Church can be caught out of this world at any moment. The Scriptures continually admonish believers to watch, be ready, and to expect His return at a time when we think not. This imminent return was the hope of the early Church. Their popular greeting, **Maranatha** (1 Corinthians 16:22), expressed their belief in the imminent return of Christ. Paul wrote:

> **For our conversation is in heaven; from whence also we look for the Saviour, the Lord Jesus Christ. (Philippians 3:20)**

Looking is in the present tense. Paul was looking for Christ's return Paul. He wasn't looking for signs and wonders, red heifers, the rebuilding of the Temple, or some other sign. Jesus said ...

> **An evil and adulterous generation seeketh after a sign. (Matthew 12:39)**

The Rapture

The Christian's watch is for the imminent return of Jesus Christ. We are not looking for the antichrist, but for the Christ. The Bible teaching of imminence rules out anything except a pre-tribulation rapture. All other tribulation views, (mid, post, and pre-wrath), are out of line with the clear Bible teaching of the imminent return. As we said before, those who deny the imminent return of Christ robs God's people of the incentive to work and watch for their Saviour. The imminence of His coming is what gives the message of the Rapture its strength. It is the certainty of His return and the uncertainty of the times that gives God's people the incentive to stay pure and do His work until He comes.

THE PROOF OF THE RAPTURE

There is plenty of support for the pre-tribulation rapture. There are many proofs that the believer will not go through the tribulation. Here we reiterate a few of them along with some we have not mentioned thus far.

God's Own Outline Of Revelation

The God-given divisions of the book of Revelation are proof that the Church will not enter into the tribulation. In chapter 1:19 John is given the Divine outline to this book.

> **Write the things which thou hast seen, and the things which are, and the things which shall be hereafter; (Revelation 1:19)**

First, John was told to write, **The things which thou hast seen.** This is not a hard phrase to understand. John was told to write what he had seen. You will notice the past tense. This was the Patmos vision, a description of the risen Lord in His glory (Chapter 1).

Second, he was to write, **The things which are...** This refers to the Church Age (Chapters 2-3). These seven churches represent the succession of seven different periods of Church history, from the beginning of the Church to the second coming of Christ, with one being dominant. The entire view of Church history is laid out here in the description of these seven churches, in a most wonderful way. Looking back over Church history we can see this to be the case. In fact, we can look at these seven Churches as a prophetic chart of the entire history of the Church.

Third, John was instructed to write, **The things which shall be hereafter...** The things that will take place after the Christians are taken out of the world, the outpouring of God's wrath during the seven-year tribulation, the re-gathering of the nation of Israel, the Millennial Kingdom, and the eternal state. (Chap 4-22)

According To The Clear Teaching Of Scripture The Rapture Must Take Place Before The Tribulation

That the Bible teaches the imminent return of Christ cannot be disputed. In fact, the next great event on God's prophetic calendar is the Rapture of the Church. To teach that the antichrist must come and that the Church enters into the tribulation before Christ comes, is contrary to, and destroys the doctrine of imminency. If the Church must go into the tribulation period, this means the Lord cannot come at any moment. It also forces the Christian to be looking for the antichrist instead of Christ. Their teaching makes the coming of the antichrist imminent, but not the coming of our Christ—the Bridegroom. If the antichrist is coming first, it is futile to be looking for the coming of our Lord. To teach that the Church must enter the tribulation is to destroy the doctrine of the imminent return of Christ and the blessed hope of the Church.

No Penal Wrath For The Believer

Although we have already covered this point, we will mention it again. The Bible teaches that the tribulation is an awful and terrible time of God's wrath and judgment. We know that the tribulation period will be 7 years. (Daniel 9:27) The Bible expressly states that the Christian is not appointed unto wrath.

> **For God hath not appointed us to wrath, but to obtain salvation by our Lord Jesus Christ. (1 Thessalonians 5:9)**

The Rapture

God has promised to deliver His people from the tribulation as we are not appointed to His wrath. The Tribulation will certainly be the outpouring of God's wrath upon the world (Revelation 6:16-17). I am confident that Jesus Christ has no intention of throwing His bride to the antichrist.

Biblical Typology lends support to the Pre-tribulation Rapture Position

God has established a pattern of removing His people before judgment. John himself is a good picture of the Rapture. John is representative of the Church, and he is invited to **come up hither** just before the tribulation begins. (Revelation 4:1-2)

We do not build doctrine on types alone. However, when the type clearly teaches truth that is revealed in Scripture, we must look at it. We see the truth of deliverance from the wrath to come in the lives of those who stand out as types of the Church. Enoch was providently removed from the outpouring of God's judgment. (Genesis 5:24) Enoch is a type of believer who walks with God and is delivered before the storm.

> **And Enoch walked with God: and he was not; for God took him. (Genesis 5:24)**

Enoch never saw death because God raptured him before the flood. Noah, on the other hand, is a type of Israel, who will be dealt with and preserved through the storm.

God delivered Lot before He sent Judgment upon Sodom. (Genesis 18:23-25; 19:22) God said to Lot:

> **Haste thee, escape thither; for I cannot do any thing till thou be come thither. Therefore the name of the city was called Zoar. (Genesis 19:22)**

The judgment upon wicked Sodom was delayed until Lot was safely removed. *God* does not destroy the righteous with the wicked. God's very purpose in the Rapture is to deliver His people from His wrath.

> **And to wait for his Son from heaven, whom he raised from the dead, even Jesus, which delivered us from the wrath to come. (1 Thessalonians 1:10)**

> **For God hath not appointed us to wrath, but to obtain salvation by our Lord Jesus Christ, (1 Thessalonians 5:9)**

The believer has been delivered from God's wrath. It is impossible for the believer to fall under the penal judgment of the Lord.

The Spirit And Church Missing From Earth

The Church is not mentioned even once during the detailed description of the events of the seven-year tribulation period between chapters six and eighteen. The Church leaves in Revelation 4:1 and is not seen on earth again until she returns as the bride of Christ at the end of the tribulation period. It is interesting that there are sixteen references to the Church in the first three chapters of Revelation. However, chapters six through eighteen, which cover the Tribulation period, do not mention the Church even once. The next time we see the Church is in chapter nineteen after the seven-year tribulation period has ended. The Church is then seen as the Bride of Christ, coming back to earth with Jesus Christ.

Seven times in the book of Revelation, the Lord Jesus Christ spoke to the local Churches of Asia Minor:

> **He that hath an ear, let him hear what the Spirit saith unto the churches. (Revelation 2:7, 2:11, 2:17, 2:29, 3:6, 3:13, 3:22)**

However, during the tribulation period, when this admonition is given, He says:

> **If any man have an ear, let him hear. (Revelation 13:9)**

Notice the two things that are missing here—the Spirit and the Church. The Church will not be on earth at that time and the Spirit will not work the same way in the tribulation as He does during the Church age.

> **For the mystery of iniquity doth already work: only he who now letteth will let, until he be taken out of the way. (2 Thessalonians 2:7)**

The Rapture

The words **letteth** and **let** simply mean to hold down or restrain. They speak of a restraining power. In the context of 2 Thessalonians, they are referring to that which is holding back the appearance of the antichrist. Although we live in days of apostasy and the **mystery of iniquity doth already work,** it is being restrained and held down. It will not become full blown during the Church age. There are a variety of ideas about who or what this restrainer is. Many have speculated that this restrainer is Michael, (Rosenthal's invention), or the Roman government. However, when we compare Scripture with Scripture and rightly divide the Word of truth the answer becomes obvious. Without a doubt it is that the One who **letteth** or restrains full-blown apostasy and the antichrist is the Holy Spirit, whose ministry it is to restrain sin. (Genesis 6:3).

God is the only one with the power to control Satan. We see Satan restrained by God from doing as he desired with Job. The Spirit of God came at Pentecost to indwell and empower the believer to live in victory and perform the work of Christ during the Church age. When the Rapture takes place, the Church and the Holy Spirit will be removed and there will be no restraints left. The lights of the world and the salt of the earth will have been removed. The Spirit-indwelled Church must be removed before the antichrist can rise. Dr. Donald Grey Barnhouse, commented on the Holy Spirit's removal:

> *Well, what is keeping the antichrist from putting in his appearance on the world stage? You are! You and every other member of the body of Christ on earth. The presence of the church of Jesus Christ is the restraining force that refuses to allow the man of lawlessness to be revealed. True, it is the Holy Spirit who is the real restrainer. But as both 1 Corinthians 3:16 and 6:19 teach, the Holy Spirit indwells the believer. The believer's body is the temple of the Spirit of God. Put all believers together then, with the Holy Spirit indwelling each of us, and you have a formidable restraining force.*
>
> *For when the church is removed at the rapture, the Holy Spirit goes with the church insofar as His*

restraining power is concerned. His work in this age of grace will be ended. Henceforth, during the Great Tribulation, the Holy Spirit will still be here on earth, of course-for how can you get rid of God? —but He will not be indwelling believers as He does now. Rather, he will revert to His Old Testament ministry of coming upon special people.

As far as the ministry of the Holy Spirit is concerned, He will leave with the Church at the rapture. Once the Church is raptured and the Spirit is no longer here to restrain the forces of evil, a floodtide of apostasy will sweep in and the antichrist will gain control and this world will be overrun with wickedness.

During the tribulation period He will be dealing with the nation of Israel, and we learn from the Old Testament that He dealt differently with them than He does the Church. They were not indwelt with the Spirit in the Old Testament. He came upon God's people to anoint and empower them for a specific calling, but they were not indwelt. In the Old Testament economy, the Spirit would come and go from a person. Of Saul the Bible says:

But the Spirit of the LORD departed from Saul. (1 Samuel 16:14)

The same is true of Samson, (Judges 16:20), as well as others. However, in the New Testament the Holy Spirit works in a new way with God's people. Pay careful attention to the words of Christ.

And I will pray the Father, and he shall give you another Comforter, that he may abide with you for ever; Even the Spirit of truth; whom the world cannot receive, because it seeth him not, neither knoweth him: but ye know him; for he dwelleth with you, and shall be in you. (John 14:16-17)

You will notice two ways here in which the Holy Spirit works differently during the Church age.

- Jesus said **that he may abide with you for ever.**
- **He dwelleth with you, and shall be in you.**

These phrases, **for ever** and **in you** are strictly New Testament truths concerning the Spirit's relationship with the believer. In the Old Testament the Holy Spirit did not permanently indwell believers.

THE PROSPECT OF THE RAPTURE

John heard the trump of God and said, **immediately I was in the spirit: and, behold, a throne was set in heaven. (Revelation 4:2a)** Notice the terminology John uses here. He said, **immediately.** The Rapture will be instantaneous. What John experienced here in the Book of Revelation; every child of God will literally experience when the Rapture takes place. What a day that will be! The Rapture, according to Scripture, is the believer's **blessed hope.** Paul wrote:

> **Looking for that blessed hope, and the glorious appearing of the great God and our Saviour Jesus Christ. (Titus 2:13)**

The unsaved live as if there is no God. Before salvation we were going our own way. God wasn't even on our minds. The Bible says:

> **... there is none that seeketh after God. (Romans 3:11b)**

The last thing this world wants is for Jesus Christ to return. However, once we are saved and begin to live for God the blessed hope becomes the desire of our heart. The Rapture is the great **blessed hope** of the Christian. Someday the trump will sound, and Christ will catch us away to be with Him forever. We can see from the context that the blessed hope is a powerful incentive for the Christian to live a righteous and holy life. Like John we ought to say:

> **Amen. Even so, come, Lord Jesus... (Revelation 22:20a)**

We are looking for Christ. He is coming and His coming is imminent. This great truth ought to be the heart prayer of every Christian. In the book of Revelation, John spoke about the city of God, the eternal dwelling place of His children.

> And I saw a new heaven and a new earth: for the first heaven and the first earth were passed away; and there was no more sea. And I John saw the holy city, new Jerusalem, coming down from God out of heaven, prepared as a bride adorned for her husband. And I heard a great voice out of heaven saying, Behold, the tabernacle of God is with men, and he will dwell with them, and they shall be his people, and God himself shall be with them, and be their God. And God shall wipe away all tears from their eyes; and there shall be no more death, neither sorrow, nor crying, neither shall there be any more pain: for the former things are passed away ... And I saw no temple therein: for the Lord God Almighty and the Lamb are the temple of it. And the city had no need of the sun, neither of the moon, to shine in it: for the glory of God did lighten it, and the Lamb is the light thereof .... And there shall in no wise enter into it any thing that defileth, neither whatsoever worketh abomination, or maketh a lie: but they which are written in the Lamb's book of life. (Revelation 21:1-4, 22-23, 27)

John describes Heaven by focusing on several things that will be missing from the Heavenly city. Heaven is a place that words can never adequately describe. It is a wonderful place prepared for the redeemed of the Lord. It is a place where there will be no more _Separation_, no more _Sorrow_, no more _Suffering_, no more _Sin_. Hallelujah! What a hope! What a joy to be headed for that wonderful place called Heaven. God's people have a wonderful and glorious future!

THE PURITY OF THE RAPTURE

God requires that His children live holy and righteous in this present world. Christian purity is important to our Saviour. Paul spoke of a ...

> ... holiness, without which no man shall see the Lord: (Hebrews 12:14)

Peter says ...

> **But as he which hath called you is holy, so be ye holy in all manner of conversation; (1 Peter 1:15)**

The imminent return of Jesus Christ motivates the believer to live a holy life and promotes the purity and separation of the Church from the world. Christians too often lose sight of Christ's come and grow and indifferent to the things of God. When the any moment return of Christ is ignored, people become lax in their living.

> **Beloved, now are we the sons of God, and it doth not yet appear what we shall be: but we know that, when he shall appear, we shall be like him; for we shall see him as he is. And every man that hath this hope in him purifieth himself, even as he is pure. (1 John 3:2-3)**

The Apostle John is speaking of the coming of the Lord and the glorification of the believer. This is the believer's blessed hope. We are told that ...

> **... every man that hath this hope in him purifieth himself, (1 John 3:3b)**

The Rapture motivates us to live pure and separated lives for the Lord. Certainly, believers want to be living right when Jesus appears. Speaking of this passage, the late John Linton wrote:

> *That is a natural result of belief in Christ's at-any-moment coming. If to love the Lord's appearing led to careless living, to coldness of heart toward God and the saving of men, one could understand why some Christians would not love it. But when this truth helps us live a separated life, gives earnestness to our prayers, urgency to our preaching, and keeps our passion for souls warm and alive, then I love this truth for its salutary effect and marvel that any other Christian would not as fervently love it.*

Every man that hath this hope! What hope? The return of Christ—the rapture! The Christian who is expecting the any moment return of Christ will be a committed Christian. The

Christian's duty is to live at all times the way he would want his Saviour to find him living when He comes back in the rapture. Jesus Christ asked the question:

> **...when the Son of man cometh, shall he find faith on the earth? (Luke 18:8)**

The faithful Christian commits his life to living and watching for the return of his Saviour. God's Word clearly teaches the imminent return of Jesus Christ. He may return at any moment—that is the blessed hope that Paul spoke of!

> **For the grace of God that bringeth salvation hath appeared to all men, Teaching us that, denying ungodliness and worldly lusts, we should live soberly, righteously, and godly, in this present world; Looking for that blessed hope, and the glorious appearing of the great God and our Saviour Jesus Christ. (Titus 2:11-13)**

We are not looking for the antichrist—we are looking for Christ! Jesus is our focus. There is no greater incentive to living a sanctified life than the imminent return of Christ. Dr. R. A. Torrey said:

> *"The imminent return of our Lord is the greatest Bible argument for a pure, unselfish, devoted, unworldly, active life of service."*

The child of God who understands and anticipates the any moment return of Christ will be serious about living in the power of the indwelling Holy Spirit. He will seek to please the Lord Jesus with his life. Our Lord Jesus Christ believed in and taught an imminent return. In the book of Luke, He gave a parable that taught the importance of being ready for an any moment return.

> **But and if that servant say in his heart, My lord delayeth his coming; and shall begin to beat the menservants and maidens, and to eat and drink, and to be drunken; The lord of that servant will come in a day when he looketh not for him, and at an hour when he is not aware, and will cut him in**

sunder, and will appoint him his portion with the unbelievers. (Luke 12:45-46)

Jesus is talking to a mixture of people here, including unbelievers, faithless believers, and believers who were not well informed about the Lord's coming and His will. However, they all had one thing in common. They were not expecting the Master's return and, as a result, were not living as they ought to been. They were living as if they had plenty of time. Many today are living as if Jesus is not coming back. Perhaps they are looking for some sign or maybe they just don't believe in the imminent return. Hence, they are fiddling about wasting their time on the world. But Jesus said:

The lord of that servant will come in a day when he looketh not for him, and at an hour when he is not aware.

Many are saying today, just as the wicked and unfaithful steward, **My Lord delayeth his coming. (Luke 12:45)** No wonder there are so many defeated and discouraged Christians today. They are not looking forward to the rapture. They have no blessed hope. They have lost sight of God's best and are seeing only the world's worst. They are anticipating the revelation of the antichrist instead of the Rapture of Christ. The British Bible expositor, G. Campbell Morgan wrote:

> *"I never lay my head upon the pillow without thinking that maybe before the morning breaks, the final morning may have dawned. I never begin my work in the morning without thinking that perhaps He may interrupt my work and begin His own."*

We are not looking for death, we are looking for Heaven. We are looking for Jesus. The pre-tribulation is the promise of our Lord to His people.

Because thou hast kept the word of my patience, I also will keep thee from the hour of temptation, which shall come upon all the world, to try them that dwell upon the earth. (Revelation 3:10)

The Revelation Of Jesus Christ

The New Testament is consistent in teaching that the return of Christ might occur at any moment. The Church will not go through any part of this seven-year Tribulation. Revelation chapters 4 and 5 fully describe the Rapture of the Church which will occur before the Tribulation. Chapters six through nineteen then deal with the Tribulation. Not once is the Church mentioned in these chapters. Throughout Scripture the believer is constantly admonished to be ready for an any moment return of Christ in the Rapture.

> **Be patient therefore, brethren, unto the coming of the Lord. Behold, the husbandman waiteth for the precious fruit of the earth, and hath long patience for it, until he receive the early and latter rain. Be ye also patient; stablish your hearts: for the coming of the Lord draweth nigh. Grudge not one against another, brethren, lest ye be condemned: behold, the judge standeth before the door. (James 5:7-9)**
>
> **But the end of all things is at hand: be ye therefore sober, and watch unto prayer. (1 Peter 4:7)**
>
> **And let us consider one another to provoke unto love and to good works: Not forsaking the assembling of ourselves together, as the manner of some is; but exhorting one another: and so much the more, as ye see the day approaching. (Hebrews 10:24-25)**

HEAVEN'S THRONE ROOM
Revelation 4:2-11

At this point the Church age has run its course, the Rapture has taken place, and the child of God is in Heaven's Throne Room. Please think about that! After the Rapture we will gather in the very dwelling place of the Almighty—the home of our great God.

THE SOVEREIGNTY ON THE THRONE

And immediately I was in the spirit: and, behold, a throne was set in heaven, and one sat on the throne. And he that sat was to look upon like a jasper and a sardine stone: and there was a rainbow round about the throne, in sight like unto an emerald... (Revelation 4:2-3a) Heaven in this passage speaks of the very dwelling place of God. Yes, this is where God resides! You will remember that Paul speaks of having been caught up into the third heaven, where he heard words which were unlawful for man to speak.

> **It is not expedient for me doubtless to glory. I will come to visions and revelations of the Lord. I knew a man in Christ above fourteen years ago, (whether in the body, I cannot tell; or whether out of the body, I cannot tell: God knoweth;) such an one caught up to the third heaven. And I knew such a man, (whether in the body, or out of the body, I cannot tell: God knoweth;) How that he was caught up into paradise, and heard unspeakable words, which it is not lawful for a man to utter. (2 Corinthians 12:1-4)**

The atmospheric heavens immediately above the earth, are also spoken of as heaven, but the heaven referred to here is without a doubt the highest heaven, above all principality and power, where God's throne is located. John's attention was drawn to the One who occupies the throne. It is Almighty God Who occupies this throne. He is the One whom Isaiah saw upon the throne, when the Seraphim's cried:

... Holy, holy, holy... (Isaiah 6:3)

He who sat upon the throne was to look upon like a **Jasper** and a **Sardine Stone.** Oliver B. Greene wrote:

> *The Jasper and the Sardine (or Sardius) stones are mentioned in the list of precious stones set in the breastplate of the high priest (Exodus 28:17-20). Please read these Scriptures, for time and space will not permit me to give you the text of all the references used in this study. These same stones also are mentioned among those describing the glory of the king of Tyre (Ezekiel 28:13). We find them mentioned again in the description of the Holy City, the New Jerusalem (Revelation 21:19,20).*
>
> *The HOLY SPIRIT uses these two stones to symbolize the brilliant glory and unsurpassed splendor of the Lord GOD insofar as His glory can be displayed and symbolized to mortal man. The brilliance of the Jasper stone symbolizes the pure holiness of GOD, and the deep red of the Sardius symbolizes the Blood atonement demanded by GOD for the remission of sins.*

These stones are very suggestive. The **Jasper** is a clear stone like a diamond, while the Sardine is blood red like a ruby. A Jasper, therefore, suggests the clear majestic, shining and matchless glory of God. And since the **Sardine Stone** is blood red, it reminds us of the cross and the redemptive character of Christ in shedding His blood to make atonement for the sins of the world. It was God the Father Who sent His Son to pay the price of sin.

THE SCENE AROUND THE THRONE

... And there was a rainbow round about the throne, in sight like unto an emerald. (Revelation 4:3b) The rainbow reminds us of the unchanging mercy of God. In judgment He will remember mercy as He promised (Genesis 9:13-17). The rainbow is symbolic of God's desire and purpose to bestow His grace upon man. Usually, a rainbow appears after a storm; here it appears before the storm. The rainbow is the evidence of God's grace during the pouring out of judgment upon the earth. David said:

> **Justice and judgment are the habitation of thy throne: mercy and truth shall go before thy face. (Psalm 89:14)**

This earth is about to see the most devastating judgment ever poured out by God, but even during times of justice and judgment, He offers mercy and forgiveness for those who will repent. The rainbow speaks of calm and sunshine after the storm. Notice that the rainbow is **... in sight like unto an emerald.** The **emerald** is green, a color that speaks of new life and new beginnings.

> **And he that sat upon the throne said, Behold, I make all things new. (Revelation 21:5)**

In the end God will sit upon the throne and make all things new. There will be a recreation of the earth and it will be restored to its previous perfect state.

THE SAINTS ABOUT THE THRONE

And round about the throne were four and twenty seats: and upon the seats I saw four and twenty elders sitting, clothed in white raiment; and they had on their heads crowns of gold. (Revelation 4:4) The number twenty-four suggests the twenty-four orders or courses into which David divided the Priesthood. (1 Chronicles 24 and 25) The twenty-four elders represent the redeemed saints of the Church age in the same way that the twenty-four elders of the Old Testament represented the complete body of Priests. These four and twenty elders are symbolic of all the family of the redeemed. The children of God are described as sharing God's throne, clothed in the white garments, and crowns of gold. Here the saints are enthroned in glory with their Lord and Saviour.

THE SOUNDS FROM THE THRONE

And out of the throne proceeded lightnings and thunderings and voices: and there were seven lamps of fire burning before the throne, which are the seven Spirits of God. **(Revelation 4:5)** The **lightnings and thunderings** depict the displays of Divine power and presence. We see this thunder at Sinai when He gave Moses the law.

> **And it came to pass on the third day in the morning, that there were thunders and lightnings, and a thick cloud upon the mount, and the voice of the trumpet exceeding loud; so that all the people that was in the camp trembled. And Moses brought forth the people out of the camp to meet with God; and they stood at the nether part of the mount. And mount Sinai was altogether on a smoke, because the LORD descended upon it in fire: and the smoke thereof ascended as the smoke of a furnace, and the whole mount quaked greatly. (Exodus 19:16–18)**

The **lightnings** and **thunderings** are also associated with divine judgment and retribution. This is a sign that the awful storm of God's wrath is about to strike! We see this in the account of God sending judgment upon unbelieving Egypt.

> **And Moses stretched forth his rod toward heaven: and the LORD sent thunder and hail, and the fire ran along upon the ground; and the LORD rained hail upon the land of Egypt. So there was hail, and fire mingled with the hail, very grievous, such as there was none like it in all the land of Egypt since it became a nation. (Exodus 9:23-24)**

Also, when our Lord smote the Philistines in Samuel's day there was the sound of mighty thundering.

> **And as Samuel was offering up the burnt offering, the Philistines drew near to battle against Israel: but the LORD thundered with a great thunder on that day upon the Philistines, and**

discomfited them; and they were smitten before Israel. (1 Samuel 7:10)

The thunder and lightning are warnings that the storm of God's wrath is coming! Many today do not like to see this side of God. They like to thing of Him as a God of love and that He is, but He is also a God of righteousness, justice, and judgment.

THE SEA BEFORE THE THRONE

And before the throne there was a sea of glass like unto crystal… (Revelation 4:6a) This is an analogy to the laver in the Tabernacle. (Exodus 30:18-21), where the priests cleansed themselves before entering the place of worship. Sometimes water is used symbolically in the Bible. Jesus said:

Now ye are clean through the word which I have spoken unto you. (John 15:3)

Speaking of the Church, Jesus said:

That he might sanctify and cleanse it with the washing of water by the word, (Ephesians 5:26)

God's Word has great cleansing power. The water in the brass laver of the Tabernacle therefore pictures the Word of God, as the priest used it to wash himself before entering into the presence of God. When we are saved, we are forgiven and justified. Our standing with God is just as if we have never sinned. However, because we have the old nature and live in a wicked world we often succumb to sin. It is then that the Holy Spirit uses the Word of God to show us that we need cleansing. We must then go before God for forgiveness and when we do, we have the promise that…

If we confess our sins, he is faithful and just to forgive us our sins, and to cleanse us from all unrighteousness. (1 John 1:9)

In Heaven the sea of glass is not of water as in the tabernacle of old. It is a sea of glass like unto crystal—it is solid. That being the case, the sea of glass before the throne takes on a wonderful meaning. The cleansing of the saint is not needed after he is home with the Lord. Pure at last from the filth of sin, the redeemed will stand on the sea of glass before the throne. Never again will we have to go before Him and ask forgiveness. Never again will we fail Him. This sea of glass, solid as crystal, symbolizes the fixed state of holiness and purity that every child of God awaits.

THE SIGHT IN THE MIDST OF THE THRONE

We now come to a scene around the throne of God where we find four living creatures. These creatures are very interesting and are found several times in the Word of God.

The Cherubim

... and in the midst of the throne, and round about the throne, were four beasts full of eyes before and behind. (Revelation 4:6b) These beasts are angelic beings. The prophet Ezekiel saw similar creatures (Ezekiel 1:4-14; 10:1-22). He described these four creatures as cherubim.

> **This is the living creature that I saw under the God of Israel by the river of Chebar; and I knew that they were the cherubims. (Ezekiel 10:20)**

The cherubim are an order of heavenly beings that are often mentioned in the Word of God (Genesis 3:23-24; Exodus 25:18-22; 37:7-9, Exodus 26:1, 31; 36:8, 35, I Kings 6:23-28; 8:6-7; II Chronicles 3:10-13; 5:7-8, Revelation 4:6; 5:6; 14:3). These creatures are somewhat like the seraphim that Isaiah saw.

> **Above it stood the seraphims: each one had six wings; with twain he covered his face, and with twain he covered his feet, and with twain he did fly. And one cried unto another, and said, Holy, holy, holy, is the LORD of hosts: the whole earth is full of his glory. (Isaiah 6:2–3)**

The first mention in Scripture of the cherubim is found back in the book of Genesis. After Adam and Eve sinned, God drove them out of the garden and placed cherubim at the entrance to keep them from returning, lest they eat of the tree of life and live forever in their sinful state.

> So he drove out the man; and he placed at the east of the garden of Eden Cherubims, and a flaming sword which turned every way, to keep the way of the tree of life. (Genesis 3:24)

These Cherubim are a special order of angelic beings assigned to the throne of God.

> The LORD reigneth; let the people tremble: he sitteth between the cherubims; let the earth be moved. (Psalm 99:1)

> O LORD of hosts, God of Israel, that dwellest between the cherubims, thou art the God, even thou alone, of all the kingdoms of the earth: thou hast made heaven and earth. (Isaiah 37:16)

Other mentions of cherubim are ...

- They covered the mercy seat in the Tabernacle (Exodus 25:18-22; 37:7-9).
- We find them guarding the holy of holies in the Tabernacle (Exodus 26:1, 31; 36:8, 35).
- Guarding Solomon's temple (1 Kings 6:23-28; 8:6-7; 2 Chronicles 3:10-13; 5:7-8).
- Surrounding the throne of God (Revelation 4:6; 5:6; 14:3).

We are told that God. These four living creatures carry out a very specific purpose. In the Word of God, we see cherubim closely associated with God's power, holiness, and glory. They are intricately connected to the throne of God which suggests that their work is to carry out divine purposes. The most thorough description of cherubim is in Ezekiel 1:4-14; 10:1-22.

The Characteristics

And the first beast was like a lion, and the second beast like a calf, and the third beast had a face as a man, and the fourth beast was like a flying eagle. (Revelation 4:7) We are given several characteristics of these beasts. The *first* beast had a face as a **lion**. The lion denotes majesty and power among the animal kingdom. The lion is the king of all the beasts, whose great strength and majesty carry out the plan and purpose of God with majestic dignity.

> **The lion hath roared, who will not fear? the Lord GOD hath spoken, who can but prophesy. (Amos 3:8)**

The *second* beast John saw was like a **calf** or an ox. The cow, whether a calf or an ox, being a beast of burden and labor, denotes humility and patience. This symbol speaks of these angelic beings who are servants of God.

The *third* beast John saw had the **face of a man**. Man being the highest of God's creation, implies reason and intelligence. These beings have the intelligence to perform their task.

The *fourth* beast was a **flying eagle**. The eagle is the wisest and fastest of all birds. He flies the highest, is keenest of sight and is swift of action. So, these beings also have the swiftness of a flying eagle. Above all, their main purpose is to praise God. They have perfect wisdom and render unceasing worship and service for the Heavenly Father.

And the four beasts had each of them six wings about him; (Revelation 4:8a) Having **six wings** they are swift and rapid in their movement. These angelic beings stand ready at a moment's notice to carry out God's will and purpose.

... and they were full of eyes within: (Revelation 4:8b) The creatures are **full of eyes** implying that they have full knowledge and understanding. Nothing is hidden from them.

THE SINGING AROUND THE THRONE

As we come to this point, we see a marvelous worship scene taking place in Heaven right after the Rapture and just before God's judgement is poured out. This worship scene is full of energy and excitement. Keep in mind that the experience John records in chapters 4 and 5 will literally be realized by all of God's people when we get to Heaven.

The Continuance Of The Praise

... and they rest not day and night, saying, Holy, holy, holy, Lord God Almighty, which was, and is, and is to come.

(Revelation 4:8b) Notice the perpetual worship taking place here. These creatures **rest not day and night.** They sing **Holy, holy, holy.** These cherubim sing praises and worship the holy God of Heaven

> **Exalt the LORD our God, and worship at his holy hill; for the LORD our God is holy. (Psalm 99:9)**
>
> **Who shall not fear thee, O Lord, and glorify thy name? for thou only art holy: for all nations shall come and worship before thee; for thy judgments are made manifest. (Revelation 15:4)**

These creatures never stop praising God. Heaven is a place where the Lamb of God will be constantly praised and exalted. Jesus is the central theme of Heaven's worship. The praise offered by the four beasts is like that of the seraphim in Isaiah's vision which cried ...

> **... Holy, holy, holy, is the LORD of hosts: (Isaiah 6:3)**

However, in Revelation, they not only praised the holiness of God, but also the fact that He is the **Lord God Almighty, which was, and is, and is to come.** He is praised for being the Omnipotent and eternal God. He is the All-powerful Almighty God of eternity. He is preparing to execute and inflict judgment upon the world and its inhabitants during the Tribulation Period.

The Cause Of The Praise

And when those beasts give glory and honour and thanks to him that sat on the throne, who liveth for ever and ever, The four and twenty elders fall down before him that sat on the throne, and worship him that liveth for ever and ever, (Revelation 4:9-10a) Of course, the cause for all the praise is that God is worthy. These twenty-four elders prostrate themselves **before him that sat on the throne.** They worship Him in the beauty of holiness.

> **Give unto the LORD the glory due unto his name; worship the LORD in the beauty of holiness. (Psalm 29:2)**

This is the very throne of God. Though many reject the idea of a Sovereign God, it is true nevertheless that God is in control and rules in the affairs of men.

> **The LORD hath prepared his throne in the heavens; and his kingdom ruleth over all. (Psalm 103:19)**

The elders join in worshiping the King of kings. At this time there will be no sin to hinder the believers' fellowship with his Saviour. This will be worship in the beauty of holiness.

The Certainty Of The Praise

... and cast their crowns before the throne, saying, Thou art worthy, O Lord, to receive glory and honour and power: (Revelation 4:10b-11a) The twenty-four elders, representative of Church age saints who cast their crowns before the throne. These crowns are earned by the believer for his faithfulness and service. As the saints cast their crowns at the Saviour's feet, they cry **Thou art worthy, O Lord.** By casting their crowns before the throne, they are acknowledging that they owe their victory to the One who sits on the throne.

The Creation Of The Praise

... for thou hast created all things, and for thy pleasure they are and were created. (Revelation 4:11b) Notice that the worship here is based on the fact that God created all things for His pleasure. Earlier they worshiped God for His *Attributes*, now they worship Him in *Adoration*. They acknowledge the fact God is the Creator of the universe. Everything belongs to Him was designed for His pleasure.

> **The earth is the LORD'S, and the fulness thereof; the world, and they that dwell therein. (Psalm 24:1)**

Back in Genesis we find that God created the earth and man. God gave Adam dominion over the earth. However, Adam fell into sin and judgment fell upon man and creation. Adam he lost his dominion over the earth. It fell into Satan's hand and has been on a downward spiral ever since. But the day is coming when Jesus reclaims the earth, and it will return to what God intended it to be. While groaning and travailing in pain creation itself has long awaited this moment.

> **For the creature was made subject to vanity, not willingly, but by reason of him who hath subjected the same in hope, Because the creature itself also shall be delivered from the bondage of corruption into the glorious liberty of the children of God. For we know that the whole creation groaneth and travaileth in pain together until now. And not only they, but ourselves also, which have the firstfruits of the Spirit, even we ourselves groan within ourselves, waiting for the adoption, to wit, the redemption of our body. (Romans 8:20-23)**

Both man and earth are waiting for that day when everyone and everything will return to glorifying God without interruption or end. Even the ungodly will bow their knees and acknowledge Christ.

> **Wherefore God also hath highly exalted him, and given him a name which is above every name: That at the name of Jesus every knee should bow, of things in heaven, and things in earth, and things under the earth; And that every tongue should confess that Jesus Christ is Lord, to the glory of God the Father. (Philippians 2:9-11)**

Christ will receive the glory due His name. We ought to take this precious truth to heart. There is no greater activity that man can involve himself in than the worship of God.

> **For the LORD is great, and greatly to be praised ... (Psalm 96:4)**
>
> **Praise him for his mighty acts: praise him according to his excellent greatness. (Psalm 150:2)**
>
> **Let every thing that hath breath praise the LORD... (Psalm 150:6)**
>
> **My praise shall be of thee in the great congregation. (Psalm 22:25)**

Heaven will be a place of praise and worship. In fact, it will be a place of perpetual worship. We should be praising Him now, but we are really going to cut loose when we get to Heaven. What a day that will be when all His redeemed fall down before Him and cast their crowns at His feet, singing:

Thou art worthy, O Lord, to receive glory and honour and power: for thou hast created all things, and for thy pleasure they are and were created.

Worship is the outward expression of an inward affection. We are not to wait till we get to Heaven to worship. Worship is to be the habitual practice of every believer.

WORTHY IS THE LAMB
Revelation 5:1-10

In this section, John sees some of the most majestic sights of Heaven along with the preparations for the most devastating judgment to ever hit earth. John is completely absorbed into the vision of the Lord and the worship and the imminent judgement that is about to take place. This throne room scene parallels the vision that Daniel the prophet saw many years earlier.

> **I beheld till the thrones were cast down, and the Ancient of days did sit, whose garment was white as snow, and the hair of his head like the pure wool: his throne was like the fiery flame, and his wheels as burning fire. (Daniel 7:9)**

However, Daniel was instructed to **shut up the words, and seal the book**. His vision was not to be revealed at that time.

> **But thou, O Daniel, shut up the words, and seal the book, even to the time of the end: many shall run to and fro, and knowledge shall be increased ... And I heard, but I understood not: then said I, O my Lord, what shall be the end of these things? And he said, Go thy way, Daniel: for the words are closed up and sealed till the time of the end. (Daniel 12:4, 8-9)**

In the book of Revelation, we see that the prophetic words are no longer **closed up**. John sees the sealed scroll and a search is launched to find the One Who is worthy to break the seals and open the scroll. The seven-sealed book is basically the record of the things which shall be hereafter (Revelation 1:19).

THE SETTING

Let's keep in mind that this is a worship scene taking place in Heaven just after the rapture. Heaven will be a place of continual worship. Folks who don't like Church will be out of place before the throne. Heaven will be a place of perpetual praise. There is no greater or more important activity for man to be involved in than the worship of God.

For the LORD is great, and greatly to be praised ... (Psalm 96:4)

Praise him for his mighty acts: praise him according to his excellent greatness. (Psalm 150:2)

Let every thing that hath breath praise the LORD... (Psalm 150:6)

Its sad to hear people grumble about having to go to Church and sit through an hour-long service. What are they going to do if they make it Heaven and find it to be a place of eternal worship?

THE SCROLL

And I saw in the right hand of him that sat on the throne a book written within and on the backside, sealed with seven seals. (Revelation 5:1) John saw the throne, and in the right hand of the One who sat upon it, was a book written within and on the backside and sealed with seven seals. The book which John saw was not a book like we are familiar with today, but rather, it was a scroll such as that used by the ancient Hebrews. It was common in Bible times for a person in authority to seal an important document so that its contents could not be seen or altered. Such documents were sealed with wax and could only be opened by a qualified person.

In chapter six we will see that the removing of the seals to open this scroll enacts the judgments of God upon earth in order to bring about the return of Christ as King of the earth. This scroll, sealed and in the hand of God, contains the title deed of earth. Dominion over the earth was once given to Adam.

And God said, Let us make man in our image, after our likeness: and let them have dominion over the fish of the sea, and over the fowl of the air, and over the cattle, and over all the earth, and over every creeping thing that creepeth upon the earth. (Genesis 1:26)

When God placed Adam in the garden of Eden, He brought all created things to him and he named them all, showing His headship and dominion under God. Through sin he lost his dominion over the earth. Dominion is now held by Satan. The Bible calls him:

> **... the god of this world. (2 Corinthians 4:4)**

In the law given through Moses, if a man lost his possession, his near of kin had the privilege of redeeming it back again.

> **Either his uncle, or his uncle's son, may redeem him, or any that is nigh of kin unto him of his family may redeem him; or if he be able, he may redeem himself. (Leviticus 25:49)**

Jeremiah teaches this same truth.

> **And Jeremiah said, The word of the LORD came unto me, saying, Behold, Hanameel the son of Shallum thine uncle shall come unto thee, saying, Buy thee my field that is in Anathoth: for the right of redemption is thine to buy it. So Hanameel mine uncle's son came to me in the court of the prison according to the word of the LORD, and said unto me, Buy my field, I pray thee, that is in Anathoth, which is in the country of Benjamin: for the right of inheritance is thine, and the redemption is thine; buy it for thyself. Then I knew that this was the word of the LORD. (Jeremiah 32:6-8)**

This all speaks of the kinsman redeemer in the physical realm. However, the same truth is seen in the spiritual realm also. Man is a lost sinner. Through Adam's fall death and judgment have passed upon him, and he has no ability to redeem himself. Therefore, someone else must redeem him. The redeemer must be a near kinsman, for no one else has any right to redeem. To have the right to redeem fallen man, he must be a near kinsman, like Boaz in the book of Ruth, near to us by birth and by mercy. He must also have the wherewithal to pay the redemptive price. No stranger has a right of redemption. However, the Son of God became man in order to be our near Kinsman.

> **But when the fulness of the time was come, God sent forth his Son, made of a woman, made under the law. (Galatians 4:4)**

Jesus, by becoming man became our Kinsman Redeemer, that by death He might redeem us from the slavery of sin. Praise God for the contents of the scroll—the title deed to the earth. Adam lost it through sin. Jesus redeemed it with His blood on Calvary's cross and now He is about to take possession of that which He has purchased. The finished work of Christ not only guarantees the redemption of the sinner, but also everything else that Adam lost in the fall—including world dominion.

> **For we know that the whole creation groaneth and travaileth in pain together until now. And not only they, but ourselves also, which have the firstfruits of the Spirit, even we ourselves groan within ourselves, waiting for the adoption, to wit, the redemption of our body. (Romans 8:22-23)**

Satan has no real authority of his own, but he does have usurped authority. The God of Heaven is the God of all. He alone is supreme in authority. He delegated authority to Adam to have dominion over the world. Adam, however, lost his dominion when he sinned. Satan now has usurped authority. Thus, Satan is now the ...

> **... god of this world. (2 Corinthians 4:4)**

The Devil holds only a temporary dominion. He is already a defeated foe. We can be assured that his usurped authority will last only until Christ comes back in supreme authority and power.

THE SEARCH

Coming to the next three verses, we find a great search about to take place. The scroll must be opened, but not just anyone may open it.

The Desire In The Search

And I saw a strong angel proclaiming with a loud voice, Who is worthy to open the book, and to loose the seals

thereof? (Revelation 5:2) The word strong comes from *"ischyros"* and means *"mighty, forceful and valiant."* Though very powerful this angel did not take the scroll from God. Instead, he looked for One who was **worthy**. The desire is to locate the One **Who is worthy to open the book**. The word **worthy** comes from *"axios"* conveys the idea of a set balances or scales. In Bible times scales worked by counterbalancing a product with a weight. For instance, when a five-pound weight balanced with a sack of grain, you knew that there was five pounds of grain in the sack. The idea of the word **worthy** in our text it that of measuring up. Not just anyone could open the scroll. It had to be One who was worthy. Even the strong angel did not measure up to the task. The issue here is the worth of the person loosening the seals and opening the scroll. Once someone begins to open the scroll, then the Tribulation Period will begin. We will study this in more detail a bit later.

The Delay In The Search

And no man in heaven, nor in earth, neither under the earth, was able to open the book, neither to look thereon. (Revelation 5:3) Now, here is God the Father on the throne with the scroll in His hand. John is weeping because no one could be found who was worthy to open the scroll. Notice the three realms searched:

In **heaven** (angelic realm).

In **earth** (human realm).

Under the earth (demonic realm).

Things seemed hopeless to John. The situation was desperate. At this point no one was found who had the authority to break the seals of the scroll. If no one was found, it would be a great tragedy for the creation would have to remain in a cursed state.

The Despondency In The Search

And I wept much, because no man was found worthy to open and to read the book, neither to look thereon. (Revelation 5:4) No one in God's creation could be found who was worthy to take the deed from the Almighty and open it. The Apostle **wept much**. John fully understood the significance of the scroll and the ramifications of what he saw. To the brokenhearted Apostle, it seemed the scroll's contents would remain hidden.

THE SAVIOUR

In the midst of his misery and mourning, John receives some comforting words from one of the elders. There was indeed One who was worthy to release the seals and open the scroll. In this section the **elders** offer a unique description of our Lord. The Lord Jesus is described as a *Prevailing Lion* and a *Powerful Lamb*. These two titles are the credentials of the Messiah who is to rule the earth.

A Prevailing Lion

And one of the elders saith unto me, Weep not: behold, the Lion of the tribe of Juda, the Root of David, hath prevailed to open the book, and to loose the seven seals thereof. (Revelation 5:5) And then one of the elders said, **weep not**. Theis is good news! Someone has been found Who has the authority and power to reclaim that which was lost through Adam's transgression. Sovereign dominion belongs to Jesus Christ, the King of kings and the Lord of lords. The world had rejected and crucified Him; God raised Him from the dead and took Him to Heaven to be at His right hand. He is no longer despised, rejected, spit upon, and crowned with thorns. Instead, He is exalted! He is high and lifted up in the open courts of glory. All the hosts of Heaven worship and praise Him. He steps forth in all of His Majesty and Might to take the title deed, loose the seals and unleash His wrath upon a wicked and Christ denying world. Dear believer weep not, Jesus is still on the throne of Heaven.

Jesus is depicted as the **Lion of the tribe of Juda. (Revelation 5:5b)** The Lion reminds us of the Supreme, Majestic, and Kingly character of our Lord Jesus Christ. Jacob said:

> **Judah is a lion's whelp: from the prey, my son, thou art gone up: he stooped down, he couched as a lion, and as an old lion; who shall rouse him up? The sceptre shall not depart from Judah, nor a lawgiver from between his feet, until Shiloh come;**

and unto him shall the gathering of the people be. (Genesis 49:9-10)

The **tribe of Judah** was one of Israel's prominent tribes Judah is the royal tribe from which the scepter was not to depart until Shiloh came, and Shiloh means the one who brings peace. It is a reference to Jesus Christ who will bring peace to Jerusalem at last. The New Testament confirms and establishes the fact that Jesus Christ is out of the tribe of Judah.

For it is evident that our Lord sprang out of Juda. (Hebrews 7:14)

We are further told that:

All things were made by him; and without him was not any thing made that was made. (John 1:3)

For by him were all things created, that are in heaven, and that are in earth, visible and invisible, whether they be thrones, or dominions, or principalities, or powers: all things were created by him, and for him: And he is before all things, and by him all things consist. (Colossians 1:16-17)

He is the heir of all things and as such, He is the only one who is worthy to redeem the earth from its curse, and to rule and reign in righteousness over all creation.

I will overturn, overturn, overturn, it: and it shall be no more, until he come whose right it is; and I will give it him. (Ezekiel 21:27)

Notice here that the word **overturn** is used three times consecutively. This draws attention to the fact that the kingdom of Judah would be overthrown and exist no more until the coming of Him whose right it is to have it.

... the Root of David. (Revelation 5:5c) The Lord Jesus Christ is the rightful heir to the Davidic Covenant.

And thine house and thy kingdom shall be established for ever before thee: thy throne shall be established for ever. (2 Samuel 7:16)

> And there shall come forth a rod out of the stem of Jesse, and a Branch shall grow out of his roots: (Isaiah 11:1)
>
> 1 The book of the generation of Jesus Christ, the son of David, the son of Abraham. (Matthew 1:1)
>
> I Jesus have sent mine angel to testify unto you these things in the churches. I am the root and the offspring of David, and the bright and morning star. (Revelation 22:16)

The One on the throne is the root of David— the rightful heir of that throne. Therefore, He has every right to take the scroll and loose the seals thereof.

... hath prevailed to open the book. (Revelation 5:5b) The word **prevailed** is powerful. It comes from *"nikaō"* and means *"to subdue, conquer, overcome, to get the victory."* By His acceptable sacrifice on Calvary, Jesus prevailed! God the Father accepted His atoning sacrifice. By His shed blood He paid the price demanded by God for man's sin.

A Powerful Lamb

And I beheld, and, lo, in the midst of the throne and of the four beasts, and in the midst of the elders, stood a Lamb as it had been slain, having seven horns and seven eyes, which are the seven Spirits of God sent forth into all the earth. (Revelation 5:6) John saw a Lamb standing in the midst of the throne and of the four beasts along the elders. One of the Lamb's main characteristics is that it was as if **it had been slain**. There are a great many people who will accept the earthly Jesus. They will acknowledge that His teachings are helpful. They are willing to acknowledge that He was a great man and a good teacher. However, they fall short of accepting Him as God's sacrifice for their sins. My friend, the good life of Jesus Christ can save no man. It is not His life which saves us, but His death in our place. It is by the shedding of His precious blood.

We also see that this Lamb has **seven horns** and **seven eyes.** As we have already seen, the number **seven** speaks of completeness and perfection. Horns in the Word of God speak of strength, power, and authority to conquer the enemy.

> **The adversaries of the LORD shall be broken to pieces; out of heaven shall he thunder upon them: the LORD shall judge the ends of the earth; and he shall give strength unto his king, and exalt the horn of his anointed. (1 Samuel 2:10)**
>
> **God came from Teman, and the Holy One from mount Paran. Selah. His glory covered the heavens, and the earth was full of his praise. And his brightness was as the light; he had horns coming out of his hand: and there was the hiding of his power. (Habakkuk 3:3–4)**

Here we see the fullness of the strength and power that belongs to the Lamb of God.

The **seven eyes** show the completeness of His perception and intelligence. He is omniscient. Nothing or no one escapes the gaze of God. We Bible tells us that the eyes of the Lord:

> **... run to and fro through the whole earth. (Zechariah 4:10)**
>
> **For the ways of man are before the eyes of the LORD, and he pondereth all his goings. (Proverbs 5:21)**
>
> **The eyes of the LORD are in every place, beholding the evil and the good. (Proverbs 15:3)**

Let no one think he will escape the all-seeing eye of Christ. We may be able to hide our sin from the eyes of man, but there is nothing that is hidden from the Lord Jesus. He sees all, He knows all, and He will judge all.

And he came and took the book out of the right hand of him that sat upon the throne. (Revelation 5:7) The Lion of Judah, the Lamb of God steps forward and takes the scroll out of the right hand on the One who has just manifested Himself in their presence. Jesus stepped up to the throne and took the book and by doing so claimed the authority which no one else could claim. The scene is one of authority and majesty. Christ steps forward to reclaim that which was lost Adam's sin. As we learned earlier Christ will exercise full authority and redeem everything from the curse of sin. Adam, by his sin, lost everything to the usurper; Christ, by His perfection, regains all that was lost (Romans 8:21-23).

THE SINGING

Great joy is seen in Heaven's Throne Room when the announcement is made that One Who is worthy has been found. Worship explodes as everyone begins to praise the Lord! This was not one of those cut and dried Church services that begins and 11 o'clock sharp and ends at 12 o'clock dull. Do not think for one minute that this is not an exciting event. In an instant we are moved from silence to shouting. The elders are shouting with a loud voice, the angels are singing, and the harpers are strumming. This is an exciting worship that glorifies the Lord Jesus.

The Song Was Different

And they sung a new song, (Revelation 5:9a) Here we see the redeemed of the Lord singing a **new song**, which only they can sing. That is significant. This is a new song for a new creature.

> **Therefore if any man be in Christ, he is a new creature: old things are passed away; behold, all things are become new. (2 Corinthians 5:17)**

There is no place for worldly music in the life of a believer. The old flesh continues to desire the wicked music, but the new creature needs godly music This was a new song—it was different.

> **Sing unto him a new song ... (Psalms 33:3)**

> **And he hath put a new song in my mouth ... (Psalms 40:3)**

> **O sing unto the LORD a new song ... (Psalms 96:1, Psalms 98:1)**

> **I will sing a new song unto thee, O God ... (Psalms 144:9)**

Praise ye the LORD. Sing unto the LORD a new song ... (Psalms 149:1)

As believers we sing a new song. God's people can sing in a way that pleases and praises the Lord. We can sing about His salvation, His grace, His blood, His comfort, His power, His coming again, etc. There is so much for a Christian to sing about. Let's just be sure that our song glorifies Him.

The Sacrifice Was Discerned

... saying, Thou art worthy to take the book, and to open the seals thereof: (Revelation 5:9b) This song starts with the acclamation that Jesus is **worthy**. In Heaven it will be all about Jesus. The redeemed will sing about His worthiness. it is always about the Lord. As Charles Keen said...

This is not now, nor has it ever been about us. It is about Christ.

May God help us to pattern our worship services after what we see here. Jesus is the only One who is preeminent and worthy. Not the preach, not the singer, not the drama team—Jesus only should be exalted in worship.

... for thou wast slain, and hast redeemed us to God by thy blood out of every kindred, and tongue, and people, and nation; And hast made us unto our God kings and priests: and we shall reign on the earth. (Revelation 5:9c-10) It is noted that the Lamb **wast slain**. Let me say again that Salvation and atonement are only by the **blood** of the Lamb (Ephesians 2:13, Hebrews 9:22; 1 Peter 1:2, 19; Leviticus 17:11). When John the Baptist saw Jesus for the first time He said:

Behold the Lamb of God, which taketh away the sin of the world. (John 1:29)

The Lord Jesus Christ did not come simply to live a good life. He did live a good and sinless life, but He came to die a sacrifice for fallen mankind. In our text His appearance is like a Lamb as if it had been slain. This Lamb, the Lord Jesus Christ, bears the marks of His sacrifice. The mark of the world's rejection and His payment for our sin is still evident upon Him. The scars that He received on earth; He will bear for all eternity. Our Saviour has the same body in Heaven that He had when He said to Thomas,

> **Reach hither thy finger, and behold my hands; and reach hither thy hand, and thrust it into my side: and be not faithless, but believing. (John 20:27)**

He is the only One who bears the marks of this world in His resurrected body, for our scars will be left behind. Each of His children will have a glorious, immortal, resurrected body in glory. It is by His death that He reconciled us to God. It was the blood which God passed over, when He smote the Egyptians, and saved Israel. (Exodus 12:13) Some seven hundred years before Christ's death, the prophet Isaiah said:

> **He was oppressed, and he was afflicted, yet he opened not his mouth: he is brought as a lamb to the slaughter, and as a sheep before her shearers is dumb, so he openeth not his mouth. (Isaiah 53:7)**

What a Saviour we are blessed with. Without the blood of Christ there would be no salvation. Praise God for the Blood of Christ!

> **Forasmuch as ye know that ye were not redeemed with corruptible things, as silver and gold, from your vain conversation received by tradition from your fathers But with the precious blood of Christ, as of a lamb without blemish and without spot. (1 Pet 1:18-19)**

In Heaven the redeemed will have full knowledge to understand in a greater way the preciousness of Christ's sacrifice. The redeemed sing **hast redeemed us to God by thy blood.** We have something to sing about. This is about Jesus the Messiah Who conquered death and the devil. He died upon Calvary's cross shedding His blood as an atonement for lost humanity. He was buried and rose victoriously on the third day. That which was lost by Adam, Jesus paid the redemptive price and purchased back. He alone has the legal authority to take the scroll and loose its seven seals. When Christ removes the first seal, the Tribulation Period will commence and seven years later it will conclude with His return to sit one the Throne of David and rule the world.

The Singing Was Dynamic

And I beheld, and I heard the voice of many angels round about the throne and the beasts and the elders: and the number of them was ten thousand times ten thousand, and thousands of thousands; (Revelation 5:11) What a choir! What a tremendous seen of worship! The angels of Heaven along with the redeemed of the ages singing before God. The voices of **ten thousand times ten thousand, and thousands of thousands** burst into song and praise. This was not the depressing, dead and dry moaning that we hear so much of in fundamentalism today. The idea that music has to be <u>Slowed Down</u>, <u>Sucked Dry</u>, <u>Shot Dead</u>, and <u>Sound Depressed</u> before it can be used in Church is foreign to Scripture Sometimes you have to sling your coat off, loosen your tie and let'er rip. Music does not have to be dead to glorify God.

The Saviour Was Declared

Saying with a loud voice, Worthy is the Lamb that was slain to receive power, and riches, and wisdom, and strength, and honour, and glory, and blessing. And every creature which is in heaven, and on the earth, and under the earth, and such as are in the sea, and all that are in them, heard I saying, Blessing, and honour, and glory, and power, be unto him that sitteth upon the throne, and unto the Lamb for ever and ever. (Revelation 5:12-13) Notice the word **loud**. Not only was this service loud, it was lively. The angels along with every Christian in Heaven, under **the earth, and such as are in the sea** will sound out in praise. All creation will flood Heaven with praise and glory.

And the four beasts said, Amen. And the four and twenty elders fell down and worshipped him that liveth for ever and ever. (Revelation 5:14) Heaven is going to be a place of praise and worship. Notice the elders worship Him who lives **for ever and ever.** True worship involves eternity. A lot of folks miss out on real worship because they have no vision of eternal things. They are so stuck in the here and now that they are not enjoying the benefits of salvation. It all about another _Day_, another _Deal_ and another _Dollar_. In Heaven it is going to be all about spend eternity with the precious Lamb of God.

What a joyful time when all the Blood-bought children of God fall down before Christ and give praise and honor to the He who paid the price for our salvation. The Bible has a great deal to say about worshipping God.

> **Let every thing that hath breath praise the LORD. Praise ye the LORD. (Psalm 150:6)**
>
> **That ye may with one mind and one mouth glorify God, even the Father of our Lord Jesus Christ. (Romans 15:6)**
>
> **For ye are bought with a price: therefore glorify God in your body, and in your spirit, which are God's. (1 Corinthians 6:20)**

Worship is the outward expression of an inward affection. How sad that so many fail to show love for the Saviour.

> **Praise ye the LORD. Praise, O ye servants of the LORD, praise the name of the LORD. Blessed be the name of the LORD from this time forth and for evermore. From the rising of the sun unto the going down of the same the LORD'S name is to be praised. The LORD is high above all nations, and his glory above the heavens. (Psalm 113:1-4)**

THE WRATH OF THE LAMB
Revelation 6:1-17

This present age, the Church age, will end and judgment will begin. The wrath of God will be poured upon the world, Israel, and apostate Christendom. Chapters six through nineteen of Revelation covers the seven years known as the Tribulation Period. It is referred to in the Bible as Daniel's Seventieth Week, (Daniel 9:20-27), and Jacob's Trouble, (Jeremiah 30:7), and the wrath to come, (1 Thessalonians 1:10). As stated previously, there is absolutely no mention of the Church on earth during these seven years. This period of time is set aside by God to deal with the nation of Israel. The emphasis is on the Jew from here on out. Like Enoch, the family of God, which is His own, will be caught up before the judgments of God are poured out on the world. Like Noah's house, the faithful remnant of Israel will be sealed (Revelation 7) and pass safely through the tribulation. Dr. W. A. Criswell said:

> *"This is not a pretty picture. But God is the Lord of truth, and He writes here things as they are, as they will be."*

For three and one-half years antichrist will be God's scourge of Judah who wickedly rejected their Messiah and received another who came in his own name.

> **I am come in my Father's name, and ye receive me not: if another shall come in his own name, him ye will receive. (John 5:43)**

The house of David and to the inhabitants of Jerusalem will be tried and purified as silver (Zechariah 13:9; Malachi 3:2-4). This will be a time of severe judgment and their chastisement will be so severe that their blood will flow like a river through the streets (Revelation 14:20). It should be noted that Revelation 6-7 parallels with Matthew 24. Both passages speak of the same event.

MATTHEW 24:4-14	REVELATION 6-7
False Christ's (4-5)	The Rider on the White Horse (1-2)
Wars and Rumors of Wars (6-7)	The Rider on the Red Horse (3-4)
Famines & Earthquakes (7b)	The Rider on the Black Horse (5-6)
Famines & Pestilence (7)	The Rider on the Pale Horse (7-8)
Persecution & Martyrdom (9-10)	Martyrs (9-11)
Earthquakes & Worldwide Catastrophes (7)	Terror (12-17)
Worldwide Preaching of the Gospel (v. 14)	Ministry of the 144,000 (7:1-8)

The opening of the seven seal judgments by the Lamb of God will begin the Tribulation Period. Everything from Revelation chapter 6 through chapter 7 describes the Tribulation Period. These judgments are providential in character— they produce wars, famine, pestilences, and death. This is a riveting scene of judgement where Christ takes possession of the world.

THE FIRST SEAL

We now come to the opening of the first four seals. What a dramatic scene! The seals are represented by what has become known as the *"four horsemen of the Apocalypse."* Most of those

The Wrath Of The Lamb

who write novels and produce movies have no real idea of the meaning of these for horseman.

The Seal Removed

And I saw when the Lamb opened one of the seals, (Revelation 6:1a) The Lamb of God, Jesus Christ, the One Who has been counted worthy, now opens the first seal and the Tribulation Period begins at once. There is a great pouring out of God's wrath upon the earth. This is His judgment on evil and the beginning of His plan to fully restore the nation of Israel to her homeland.

The Sound Rumbling

... and I heard, the noise of thunder, one of the four beasts saying, Come and see. (Revelation 6:1b) When the seal is broken there is a great sound **as it were the noise of thunder**. We say earlier that thunder is sometimes a display of divine power and presence. The thunder is an indicator that God is about to begin His judgment.

The Sight Revealed

And I saw, and behold a white horse: and he that sat on him had a bow; and a crown was given unto him: and he went forth conquering, and to conquer. (Revelation 6:2) With the opening of this seal the first horseman begins to ride. The average person in Bible times rode donkeys and camels and other beasts. Horses, however, were ridden primarily by soldiers. In the Old Testament, horsemen were symbols of war and judgment.

> **The horse is prepared against the day of battle: but safety is of the LORD. (Proverbs 21:31)**

We see the same thought back in the book of Ezekiel.

> **By reason of the abundance of his horses their dust shall cover thee: thy walls shall shake at the noise of the horsemen, and of the wheels, and of the chariots, when he shall enter into thy gates, as men enter into a city wherein is made a breach. With the hoofs of his horses shall he tread down all thy streets: he shall slay thy people by the sword,**

and thy strong garrisons shall go down to the ground. (Ezekiel 26:10-11)

In Zechariah 6:1-8, we have a picture of horses and chariots **which go forth from standing before the Lord of all the earth.** Also see Jeremiah 46:1-10, and Joel 2:3-11. These horsemen are released when Jesus breaks the seals—it is a Divine act! This is the ...

... the wrath of the Lamb: For the great day of his wrath is come; and who shall be able to stand. (Revelation 6:16-17)

These four horsemen are the judgment of God on this unbelieving world. In his classic book on the Apocalypse, Joseph Seiss says:

In these four different horses and horsemen, we are to see four different forms of the coming forth of the judicial power of God upon the inhabitants of the earth, looking to the breaking up of the dominion of wickedness, the punishment and casting out of transgression and the consummation of that long pending revolution, whose accomplishment is at once the fulfillment of all prophecy and all prayer.

Some claim that this white horse rider is Jesus Christ. Nothing could be further from the truth. Christ has many distinguishing marks to identify Him when He comes in power. His appearance is given in Revelation 19:14.

- He also is on a white horse.
- In righteousness He doth judge and make war.
- He is called Faithful and True.
- On His head are many crowns.
- His vesture is dipped in blood.
- His name is called The Word of God.
- The armies of heaven follow Him.

In comparing these two riders we see that they are two different people with two different purposes. The rider here in chapter six is carrying a bow. When our Lord comes, He comes with a sword.

> **Gird thy sword upon thy thigh, O most mighty, with thy glory and thy majesty. And in thy majesty ride prosperously because of truth and meekness and righteousness; and thy right hand shall teach thee terrible things. (Psalm 45:3-4)**

When Christ appears, He comes to judge and make war in righteousness. This rider of chapter six comes **conquering and to conquer.** Christ has the armies of heaven with Him, this one has to do with the armies of earth. Who then is this white horse rider who is disguised as our Lord, who has a bow and a crown and who goes forth **conquering and to conquer?** This is the antichrist, Satan's imitation of our Lord Jesus Christ. He is Satan's substitute. Paul warns the Church of false apostles and deceitful workers transforming themselves into apostles of Christ. For instance, he declares:

> **It is no marvel for Satan himself is transformed into an angel of light. Therefore it is no great thing if his ministers also be transformed as the ministers of righteousness whose end shall be according to their works. (2 Corinthians 11:14-15)**

This rider is the antichrist, who through deceit lures Israel and apostate Christendom into an alliance and sets up a false peace on earth.

> **For many shall come in my name, saying, I am Christ; and shall deceive many. (Matthew 24:5)**

Christ came as God's representative to **seek and to save that which was lost. (Luke 19:10)** and spread the soul-saving gospel throughout the earth. This rider is the devil's representative, going in opposition to the Gospel to fill the earth with his deceit and false religion. This white horse rider is:

> **... the prince that shall come, (Daniel 9:26)**

> ... that man of sin, Who opposeth and exalteth himself above all that is called God, or that is worshipped; so that he as God sitteth in the temple of God, shewing himself that he is God. (2 Thessalonians 2:3-4)

He is the one who will reign during the tribulation period. He is the anti-Christ. He will come into power peaceably and get his kingdom by deception. The Jews will enter into a covenant with the antichrist for seven years; but in the midst of the week of years, (after 3½ years), he will break his covenant with God's chosen people. He will reveal his true character when, in pride and arrogance, he sets himself up in the Temple and arrogantly demands to be worshipped as the God of Heaven.

THE SECOND SEAL

Now we come to the red horse and his rider. As we have previously said, these horses symbolize the going forth of God's judgment against the wicked. While there are various and sundry ideas given as to who this red horse represents, the symbolism seems clear.

The Call To Attention

And when he had opened the second seal, I heard the second beast say, Come and see. (Revelation 6:3) The second beast is the calf (Revelation 4:7). As was the case with the first beast, the second beast cried **Come and see.** The word **see** comes from *"blepo"* and has the connotation of perception. This was to be more than a haphazard glance. John was to see this with seriousness and discern the meaning of it. We too are to study and rightly divide the Word of Truth (2 Timothy 2:15).

The Color Of The Animal

And there went out another horse that was red: (Revelation 6:4a) It is significant that this second horse is red. Red is symbolic of war and bloodshed. This red horse rider depicts the slaughter and spilling of blood that will take place during the Tribulation Period.

> And the winepress was trodden without the city, and blood came out of the winepress, even unto the horse bridles, by the space of a thousand and six hundred furlongs. (Revelation 14:20)

The word **red** comes from the Greek *"pyrros"* and means *"fire-like, flame-colored."* This speaks of the savagery of warfare. It denotes the pain and suffering of war. There will be worldwide warfare specifically during the last half of the Tribulation Period which is the Great Tribulation.

The Combat And Aggression

> ... and power was given to him that sat thereon to take peace from the earth, and that they should kill one another: and there was given unto him a great sword. (Revelation 6:4b)

Keep in mind that the Tribulation Period will be a time of **wars and rumours of wars: (Matthew 24:6)** There should be no doubt whatsoever as to the meaning of this red horse rider. The very wording of our text indicates that since the horse is red and power **was given to him that sat thereon to take peace from the earth**, that the going forth of the red horse and his rider could represent nothing else but war! The Bible teaches very clearly that world-wide war is coming. This is confirmed by Daniel's prophecy.

> There shall be a time of trouble such as never was since there was a nation even to that same time. (Daniel 12:1)

Jesus was the greatest prophet of all times. In His Olivet discourse He said:

> For nation shall rise against nation, and kingdom against kingdom: and there shall be famine and pestilences and earthquakes, in divers places. All these are the beginning of sorrows ... For then shall be great tribulation such as was not since the beginning of the world to this time, no, nor ever shall be. And except those days should be shortened there should no flesh be saved; but for the elect's sake those days shall be shortened. (Matthew 24:7-8, 22)

We hear a lot about peace today. We have peace accords and peace talks, but no peace. The cry of our day is peace, peace, peace, but God has declared:

> **For when they shall say, Peace and safety; then sudden destruction cometh upon them, as travail upon a woman with child; and they shall not escape. (1 Thessalonians 5:3)**

Also see Jeremiah 25:27-33 in connection with world-wide war and judgment. This old world is headed for serious trouble. Yet, they cry peace and safety as sudden destruction is imminent (1 Thessalonians 5:3). Man will never bring peace to the world. Only when King Jesus returns will there be peace.

THE THIRD SEAL

The **third beast** announces the opening of the third seal with the same invitation as the first two, **come and see**.

The Scales

And when he had opened the third seal, I heard the third beast say, Come and see. And I beheld, and lo a black horse; and he that sat on him had a pair of balances in his hand. (Revelation 6:5) The fact that the rider on the black horse has **a pair of balances** in his hand indicates that a time of famine and rationing will come upon the world. The food being weighed is a mark of dearth. This will follow the conditions which will come to pass under the opening of the second seal. War often results in famine and hunger. These will be dire times. In the Bible, black is the color of famine.

> **Their visage is blacker than a coal; they are not known in the streets: their skin cleaveth to their bones; it is withered, it is become like a stick. They that be slain with the sword are better than they that be slain with hunger: for these pine away, stricken through for want of the fruits of the field. (Lamentations 4:8-9)**
>
> **Our skin was black like an oven because of the terrible famine. (Lamentations 5:10)**

One of the common effects of war is that it always results in shortages of food and high prices! Many will die because of famine during this black horse judgment.

The Scarcity

And I heard a voice in the midst of the four beasts say, A measure of wheat for a penny, and three measures of barley for a penny; and see thou hurt not the oil and the wine. (Revelation 6:6) The shortage of food and high Inflation will know no limits during these times. A measure (one quart) of wheat will be sold for a penny; and three measures of barley at the same price. One quart of wheat, or three quarts of barley will cost a day's wage.

> **Take thou also unto thee wheat, and barley, and beans, and lentiles, and millet, and fitches, and put them in one vessel, and make thee bread thereof, according to the number of the days that thou shalt lie upon thy side, three hundred and ninety days shalt thou eat thereof. And thy meat which thou shalt eat shall be by weight, twenty shekels a day: from time to time shalt thou eat it. Thou shalt drink also water by measure, the sixth part of an hin: from time to time shalt thou drink. (Ezekiel 4:9-11)**

The rider says **hurt not the oil and the wine. (Revelation 6:6b)** The oil and wine will be luxuries that only the rich could afford. They will survive for a while because of their money. However, their sorrows are sure to come later, for they will not escape unpunished. James spoke of the payday of the rich.

> **Go to now, ye rich men, weep and howl for your miseries that shall come upon you. Your riches are corrupted, and your garments are motheaten. Your gold and silver is cankered; and the rust of them shall be a witness against you, and shall eat your flesh as it were fire. Ye have heaped treasure together for the last days. Behold, the hire of the labourers who have reaped down your fields, which is of you kept back by fraud, crieth: and the cries of them which have reaped are entered into**

the ears of the Lord of sabaoth. Ye have lived in pleasure on the earth, and been wanton; ye have nourished your hearts, as in a day of slaughter. (James 5:1-5)

James is not condemning people for being rich. Rather he is dealing with those who's possessions to become their god. God does not mind His people being wealthy if their wealth does not keep them from their responsibility to Him. The problem is that most men make gods of their wealth. God's judgment will be one event that the rich will not be able to buy themselves out of.

THE FOURTH SEAL

With the opening of the fourth seal that under the ongoing judgments, conditions will continue to grow worse and worse.

The Death

And when he had opened the fourth seal, I heard the voice of the fourth beast say, Come and see. And I looked, and behold a pale horse: and his name that sat on him was Death, (Revelation 6:7-8a) The word **pale** comes from "*chloros.*" It is the word from which we get the English "*chlorine.*" It means greenish and is the color of a rotting corpse which often has a greenish tint. The first three horsemen were unnamed, but this one is named **Death**. Death always follows war and famine.

The Damnation

... and Hell followed with him. (Revelation 6:8b) Notice that Hell rides with him to swallow up its victims. The death of unbelievers always results in eternity in Hell. In his commentary on Revelation, the late Herbert Lockyer said ...

> *... the corpse-like color of the horse is in keeping with the rider. Death and Hell are inseparable companions, and they now act together in judgment, dividing the spoil. Hell, as a consort and companion, receives those whom Death cuts off.*

For the unsaved this will be a time of unprecedented misery. Imagine living through the warfare and enduring famine only to die and go to Hell. In our scene Death takes the body and Hell follows to take the soul. Hell is in fact, the second death.

The Devastation

... And power was given unto them over the fourth part of the earth, to kill with sword, and with hunger, and with death, and with the beasts of the earth. (Revelation 6:8c) This is an eye-opening statement. To kill a fourth part of the population is a sobering thought. The population of the world today (2020) is nearly eight billion. A fourth part would be nearly two billion people dead. Oliver B. Greene comments ...

> *The bloody sword in the hand of the rider of the second horse will not be withdrawn until the divinely appointed task is finished. Hunger will not be withdrawn until its deadly work and painful death has come to completion. Many times hunger brings a much more painful death than the sword. Pestilence will reap its harvest-and last, but by no means least, the beasts of the earth will rush in upon the poor victims, to finish the ghastly destruction of the enemies of Jesus Christ!*

Never in the history of mabn has the world seen such plagues and catastrophes as there will be in the Great Tribulation.

THE FIFTH SEAL

Here the scene shifts from earth to heaven and John sees a vision of a martyred remnant with the opening of the fifth seal.

The Place

And when he had opened the fifth seal, I saw under the altar ... (Revelation 6:9a) The place mentioned is under the altar. In the Old Testament when the priest sacrificed an animal, the blood was poured out at the base of the brazen altar (Exodus 29:12; Leviticus 4:7, 5, 9, 18, 25, 30). The imagery implies that these martyr's lives were given sacrificially to the glory of God.

The People

... the souls of them that were slain for the word of God, and for the testimony which they held. (Revelation 6:9b) These are martyrs of the tribulation. These who were slain because of the Word of God and for their testimony are martyrs of the Tribulation Period. They are tribulation saints. They are the first to seal their testimony with their life's blood under antichrist's rule. The Church age saints will have been raptured. However, through the evangelistic efforts of the 144,000, many will turn to Christ and be saved. Jesus warned about the persecution during this time:

> **Then shall they deliver you up to be afflicted, and shall kill you: and ye shall be hated of all nations for my name's sake. (Matthew 24:9)**

The Tribulation Period will bring wide-spread persecution upon these believers. Jesus warned of this very truth.

The Petition

And they cried with a loud voice, saying, How long, O Lord, holy and true, dost thou not judge and avenge our blood on them that dwell on the earth? (Revelation 6:10) The Martyrs requested of God that justice be carried out. Their prayer was quite different from the one Stephen offered when he was martyred.

> **And he kneeled down, and cried with a loud voice, Lord, lay not this sin to their charge. And when he had said this, he fell asleep. (Acts 7:60)**

Stephen died praying for the forgiveness of his murderers. However, this prayer of the martyrs under the altar is more like the imprecatory of the Old Testament. That is because the tribulation is a different dispensation—it is characterized by the spirit of the law when God is once again dealing with the Jew. Stephen's prayer for the pardon of his murderers was appropriate in a time of grace. But when grace has run its course and judgment comes, prayers for divine retribution are appropriate.

The Promise

And white robes were given unto every one of them; and it was said unto them, that they should rest yet for a little season, until their fellowservants also and their brethren, that should be killed as they were, should be fulfilled.

(Revelation 6:11) The **white robes** that were given to them stand as a symbol of purity and holiness. The Lord gave ear to their prayers, and He answered them with words of the assurance that in a little season everything would be taken care of. We can be sure that vengeance will be carried out! However, it will be in God's timing.

> **Vengeance is mine, I will repay... (Romans 12:19)**

Notice that the instruction given them was that **they should rest yet for a little season**. How comforting it is to know that death of the child of God brings his soul to a place of rest in the presence and protection of Jesus Christ. This life is often one of labor and burden. But there is coming a day when we can lay our burdens down and enter into the presence of our Lord; not only into His presence, but if we have been faithful in this life, we will enter into His joy.

> **His lord said unto him, Well done, good and faithful servant; thou hast been faithful over a few things, I will make thee ruler over many things: enter thou into the joy of thy lord. (Matthew 25:23)**

Because the martyrs served with their life. Here we see that they will have a prominent place in the affairs of the Millennium. Serving God pays great dividends. Of these the Bible says:

> **They lived and reigned with Christ a thousand years. (Revelation 20:4)**

Sincere service to God pays great dividends. Even if one loses the temporal things of this world, he enjoys the eternal things of God.

THE SIXTH SEAL

With the opening of the sixth seal, we come upon a terrible and terrifying scene. When this seal is removed there is no word of warning as when the other seals were broken. Judgment falls immediately and without notice. God did the same with Pharaoh when he refused to heed His warnings and judgments. However,

The Revelation Of Jesus Christ

this sixth seal is not just another earthquake, but a shaking of the entire universe. Henry Morris comments:

> "While the inhabitants of the earth are still suffering under the famines, plagues and violence of the earlier seal judgments, a great physical cataclysm will suddenly strike. For the first time in history, a global earthquake will convulse the earth, accompanied by tremendous volcanic eruptions, spewing vast quantities of dust particles into the upper atmosphere, turning the appearance of the sun into darkness and the moon blood-red."

This will be the most devastating disaster known to man. The sun, moon, stars, atmosphere, and earth are all affected, even to the point that the mountains and islands are moved out of their places.

The Shaking Of The Earth

When the sixth seal was broken ... **there was a great earthquake. (Revelation 6:12a)** Many times in the Bible earthquakes occurred during God's judgment and presence. When God came down on Mt. Sinai, at the giving of the law (Exodus 19:18). The same is true of Elijah Mt. Horeb (1 Kings 19:11). When Jesus died on the cross, the earth did quake, and the rocks rent. (Matthew 27:51) Jesus told of these coming judgments while He was here on earth.

> **For nation shall rise against nation, and kingdom against kingdom: and there shall be famines, and pestilences, and earthquakes, in divers places. (Matthew 24:7)**

The Word of God stands in perfect harmony. The Prophet Haggai, under inspiration of the Holy Spirit prophesied of these events many years before Jesus.

> **For thus saith the LORD of hosts; Yet once, it is a little while, and I will shake the heavens, and the earth, and the sea, and the dry land; And I will shake all nations, and the desire of all nations shall**

come: and I will fill this house with glory, saith the LORD of hosts. (Haggai 2:6-7)

The Prophet Joel also warned of God's coming judgment.

> **The earth shall quake before them; the heavens shall tremble: the sun and the moon shall be dark, and the stars shall withdraw their shining: And the LORD shall utter his voice before his army: for his camp is very great: for he is strong that executeth his word: for the day of the LORD is great and very terrible; and who can abide it? (Joel 2:10-11)**

Christ Himself warned of massive earthquakes during the tribulation.

> **For nation shall rise against nation, and kingdom against kingdom: and there shall be famines, and pestilences, and earthquakes, in divers places. (Matthew 24:7)**

All of the earthquakes, tsunamis and disasters that this world has experienced thus far will seem minuscule compared to the devastation and destruction of the wrath of the Lamb. The earthquake in out text will be so catastrophic that it will be in a class of its own.

The Sun Blackened

... and the sun became black as sackcloth of hair. (Revelation 6:12b) The sun, which hid its face when Jesus was crucified, becomes **black as sackcloth of hair** In the tribulation. God turned Egypt into darkness before His final judgment. (Exodus 10:21-23). The prophet Isaiah warned:

> **Behold, the day of the LORD cometh, cruel both with wrath and fierce anger, to lay the land desolate: and he shall destroy the sinners thereof out of it. For the stars of heaven and the constellations thereof shall not give their light: the sun shall be darkened in his going forth, and the moon shall not cause her light to shine. (Isaiah 13:9-10)**

This is the first of several earthquakes that we find throughout the Tribulation Period (Revelation 8:5; 11:13, 19;

16:18). It seems that God is giving Satan and his kingdom a foretaste of the darkness which for him and his cohorts will be forever.

The Stars Falling

And the stars of heaven fell unto the earth, even as a fig tree casteth her untimely figs, when she is shaken of a mighty wind. (Revelation 6:13) During this awful time of judgment the stars will fall from Heaven like the rotten fruit of a fig tree beaten by the fierce wind of a storm. Again, this is the fulfillment of Isaiah's prophecy (Isaiah 13:9-13).

The Separation Of Mountains and Islands

And the heaven departed as a scroll when it is rolled together; and every mountain and island were moved out of their places. (Revelation 6:14) The heavens part as a scroll when it is rolled open and every **mountain and island were moved out of their places.** This is an earthquake of greater severity than has ever been known. We have seen the geographical changes which can be wrought by an earthquake. We hear of earthquakes regularly in America and around the world. In earthquakes that have already happened, great cities have been destroyed and mountains have crumbled right into the sea. However, all that this world has seen is nothing in comparison with the great and terrible day of the Lord, when He unleashes His fierce anger and righteous wrath upon this unbelieving world.

The Saddest Prayer Meeting Ever

And the kings of the earth, and the great men, and the rich men, and the chief captains, and the mighty men, and every bondman, and every free man, hid themselves in the dens and in the rocks of the mountains; And said to the mountains and rocks, Fall on us, and hide us from the face of him that sitteth on the throne, and from the wrath of the Lamb: (Revelation 6:15-16) Imagine the utter shock and fear that will grip the heart of wicked men when these judgments fall. Notice the classes of ungodly men who are dealt with when

Christ pours out His judgment upon the nations and punishes them for their wickedness.

- The **kings**. (all rulers) of the earth will fear.
- The **great**. (powerful) of the earth will fear.
- The **rich** of the earth will fear.
- The **chief captains**. The military leaders of the earth will fear.
- The **mighty** of the earth will fear.
- The **bondman**. (slaves) of the earth will fear.
- The **free man** of the earth will fear.

This is an awful time of wrath, and no one shall escape.

> **And I will punish the world for their evil, and the wicked for their iniquity; and I will cause the arrogancy of the proud to cease, and will lay low the haughtiness of the terrible. (Isaiah 13:11)**

This very event is prophesied in various other places in God's Word.

> **Howl ye; for the day of the lord is at hand; it shall come as a destruction from the Almighty ... and they shall be afraid: pangs and sorrows shall take hold of them; they shall be in pain as a woman that travaileth: they shall be amazed one at another; their faces shall be as flames. (Isaiah 13:6-8)**

> **The great day of the lord is near, it is near, and hasteth greatly, even the voice of the day of the lord: the mighty man shall cry there bitterly. (Zephaniah 1:14)**

> **Blow ye the trumpet in Zion, and sound an alarm in my holy mountain: let all the inhabitants of the land tremble: for the day of the lord cometh, for it is nigh at hand. (Joel 2:1)**

> **The high places also of Aven, the sin of Israel, shall be destroyed: the thorn and the thistle shall come up on their altars; and they shall say to the**

> mountains, Cover us; and to the hills, Fall on us. (Hosea 10:8)

> Then shall they begin to say to the mountains, Fall on us; and to the hills, cover us. (Luke 23: 30)

This is that awful and terrible day known in God's word as **The Day of the Lord.** There will be no escape from it.

> **How shall we escape, if we neglect so great salvation. (Hebrews 2:3)**

In his commentary on the book of Thessalonians, John Walvoord writes of this day:

> *"The Day of the Lord is a period of time in which God will deal with wicked men directly and dramatically in fearful judgment. Today a man may be a blasphemer of God, an atheist, can denounce God and teach bad doctrine. Seemingly God does nothing about it. But the day designated in Scripture as 'the day of the Lord' is coming when God will punish human sin, and He will deal in wrath and in judgment with a Christ-rejecting world. One thing we are sure of, that God in His own way will bring every soul into judgment."*

And said to the mountains and rocks, Fall on us, and hide us from the face of him that sitteth on the throne, and from the wrath of the Lamb: (Revelation 6:16) This will be a day so dreadful that even the greatest, (in the sense that the world sees greatness), will run into the mountains and cry for the mountains and rocks to fall upon them and kill them; obviously not knowing that they will only go from horror and terror on earth to eternal horror and terror in Hell.

THE SEALING OF THE 144,000
Revelation 7:1-17

As we come to this section, we see judgment cease for a short period. In the last few verses of chapter six we saw the opening of the sixth seal, but we do not find the opening of the seventh seal until we come to chapter eight. Therefore, chapter seven is a parenthetical passage between the sixth and seventh seals. Here we will see a pause in the judgments hat are being inflicted upon the earth and its inhabitants. The pause is for the sealing of 144,000 Jewish evangelists for their protection. He seals 12,000 witnesses from each of the 12 tribes of Israel. They will comprise a force of 144,000 Jewish witnesses sealed for His service. These sealed missionaries will go forth and preach the gospel during the Tribulation Period. They will be protected and delivered from the devil and from the enemies of God. The antichrist will not be able to destroy Jewish missionaries or their work. Their enemies will be many, but their work will be effective.

THE SUSPENDED JUDGMENT

Here we see four angels dispatched to temporarily bring a halt to the outpouring of God's wrath that is being inflicted upon the earth and its inhabitants during the Tribulation Period.

Their Position

And after these things I saw four angels standing on the four corners of the earth, (Revelation 7:1a) This scene opens with a view of four angels standing on the four corners of the earth. The phrase **four corners** do not even remotely refer to a flat earth, a disproven notion that even some in our day hold to. Rather it is an expression for four directions of the earth — North, South, East and West. We see that God's judgment will come from all directions on earth. The Tribulation Period will not be judgement upon a particular region or country, rather God will pour out is wrath globally. The Tribulation will bring worldwide judgement upon the ungodly.

Their Power

... holding the four winds of the earth, that the wind should not blow on the earth, nor on the sea, nor on any tree. (Revelation 7:1b) These angels were **holding the four winds of the earth.** The holding back of the winds speaks of the calm before the storm. These angels were given great power and authority was over the elements. God's judgment will come from all directions. He will with the world globally. These angels were sent to restrain the four winds. The blowing of the **four winds** is symbolic of the infliction of Divine wrath. The four angels protect the earth, the sea and the trees. However, all these will be affected in the upcoming trumpet judgments (Revelation 8:7-8).

Their Purpose

And I saw another angel ascending from the east, having the seal of the living God: and he cried with a loud voice to the four angels, to whom it was given to hurt the earth and the sea, Saying, Hurt not the earth, neither the sea, nor the trees, (Revelation 7:2-3a) An angel tells four angels who have the authority to execute judgment to halt that judgment for a short time. It is specially mentioned that this angel is seen ascending from the East. The tabernacle was pitched toward the East and the royal tribe of Judah faced the East. The star which announced the birth of Christ was in the East, and it was from the East that the wise men came searching for Him who was King of the Jews. The glory of the Lord departed from Israel by the east side of the city (Ezekiel 11:23). Our Lord was led out of Jerusalem by way of the east gate. When the glory of the God of Israel returns, it is by the way of the East (Ezekiel 43:2, Matthew 24:27). The angel's message was **Hurt not the earth, neither the sea, nor the trees.** Thus, the ongoing judgment of God is put on hold.

The Priority

... till we have sealed the servants of our God in their foreheads. (Revelation 7:3b) The priority of the angels is to

The Sealing Of The 144,000

seal the servants of God. The seal speaks of protection and permanency. In this present dispensation God seals the believer with the Holy Spirit (Ephesians 1:13; 4:30; 2 Corinthians 1:22). This seal identifies Christians as God's own property. The seal guarantees our safe arrival to our eternal destination.

In the following verses we see that 12,000 from each of the twelve tribes of Israel will be sealed and protected by God. John Phillips points out ...

> *This sudden stillness is so that the 144,000 can be sealed. God said to delinquent Lot, "I cannot do anything till thou be come thither" (Gen. 19:22). Just so, God will not allow the Great Tribulation to develop until He has secured and sealed a remnant of believing Jews. The*

We have here the wonderful truth of God's keeping grace and protecting power over His own. God actually puts His judgment on temporary hold, to seal His faithful remnant. We know from other passages of Scripture that angels look after the wellbeing of God's children (1 Kings 19:5, Psalm 35:5; Psalm 91:11-12; Daniel 6:22) and are to be associated with Christ in His second coming and judgment (Matthew 25:31; Matthew 13:30; 41-42). These Angels are referred to as...

... the reapers. (Matthew 13:30, 39)

They will have the important responsibility of protecting and looking after the safety and welfare of those who are to be saved through the Great Tribulation Period.

We find in the following chapter, as the angels sound their trumpets, judgment falls upon the earth. Another angel ascending from the east, cries with a loud voice and bids them to stay their hand till these servants of God receive His mark on their foreheads. There will be great and fearful judgments and calamities during which these 144,000 evangelists will be spared, and the days will be shortened. Otherwise, will ...

... no flesh be saved. (Matthew 24:22)

What a devastating time of judgment! The Lord however, watches over His own to protect and deliver them from danger.

He puts them in a place of safety so that none can be plucked out of His hands (John 10:27-29). This is the assurance of the great keeping power of God.

THE SEALED JEWS

And I heard the number of them which were sealed: and there were sealed an hundred and forty and four thousand of all the tribes of the children of Israel. (Revelation 7:4) These 144,000 as we can clearly see are Jews. There is no reason to spiritualize this passage. The context is clear! They are Jews and the number is not symbolic—there are 144,000 of them. Let's take just a moment to dispel the foolish notion that these 144,000 are the Jehovah's Witnesses. For years, the Jehovah Witnesses claimed that they were the 144,000 spoken of here, claiming that only an elite group will actually go to heaven. Everyone else will live for eternity in paradise here on earth. Their interpretation, however, ran into a big problem when their members grew beyond 144,000. Hence, they manipulated and further contorted their interpretation to adjust to their circumstances. They then begin to teach that there was an earthly band of 144,000. They claimed there was an additional heavenly band of 144,000. Now they have grown beyond 288,000 and have again adjusted their doctrine to meet their situation. Now they now claim a third category known as the servant band.

From the context we see that these twelve tribes are Israelites. They are Jews—not Jehovah's Witnesses. Before the manifestation of the Beast these servants of God receive His seal upon them. The seal will be for their protection as they go about preaching the Gospel. These 144,00 Jewish evangelists will be sealed and protected by the power and ministry of the Holy Spirit.

You will remember that the Holy Spirit has been removed with the Church (2 Thessalonians 2:7), but only so far as His indwelling ministry is concerned. The Church dispensation has ended. The indwelling ministry of the Spirit was special only to this (the Church), dispensation. God is again dealing with the

The Sealing Of The 144,000

Jews and through the Holy Spirit, will deal with them the same way that He did in the Old Testament. The Old Testament saints were not indwelt with the Holy Spirit. He came upon God's people to anoint and empower them for a specific calling, but they were not indwelt. The sealing of the Christian is by the Holy Spirit Himself, as an:

> ... **earnest of our inheritance. (Ephesians 1:13, 14)**

We are sealed:

> ... **unto the day of redemption. (Ephesians 4:30)**

It is God's inward and outward evidence of Salvation, of Safety, and Security. The Christian has the mark of God upon his heart. These redeemed ones of the 7th chapter of Revelation belong to another class. They have God's mark outwardly. This sealing is a manifest token and is spoken of as a mark in their foreheads. When we look at the meaning of the names of the tribes and their order of sealing, they present to us a great spiritual lesson.

In the names of the following tribes, we notice that two tribes are missing, and another added. *First*, the Tribes of Dan and Ephraim are missing. Perhaps because they were the first to lead their people into idolatry. Dan is described as a serpent lying by the way.

> **Dan shall be a serpent by the way, an adder in the path, that biteth the horse heels, so that his rider shall fall backward. (Genesis 49:17)**

The tribes of Dan were associated with Jeroboam in setting up golden calves to be worshipped. One of these was set up in the tribe of Dan, and the other at Bethel (1 Kings 12:25-30) and at Shiloh. (Judges 18:30–31).

Second, the Tribe of Manasseh is included. Manasseh was Joseph's firstborn son. He was Ephraim's brother. Ephraim's association with idolatry disqualified him and he was replaced by Manasseh.

JUDAH is the ruling aristocratic tribe. This is the tribe of King David and of Jesus. Judah means confession or praise of God, and this will be fulfilled when our Lord visits Israel again. It will lead to both confession and praise.

REUBEN means viewing the Son, and this blessing comes only as they acknowledge the Lord Jesus as the Son of God and their Messiah.

GAD means a company or a troop and the prophecy concerning him says, Gad, a troop shall overcome him: but he shall overcome at the last. Gad overcame and is numbered with God in the tribulation.

ASER means happy or blessed. **Out of Aser, his bread shall be fat and he shall yield royal dainties. (Genesis 49:20)** God's blessing to Abraham will be carried out (Genesis 12:2, 3).

NEPTHALIM means wrestling. This shows the spirit of Jacob, the father, who wrestled all night with the Lord and only gave in when his thigh, the place of natural strength, was broken. He would not let God go, however, without a blessing, and his name was changed to Israel. As he went on his way the next day, **the sun...rose upon him**. And so, the Sun of Righteousness is going to rise upon Israel after her long night of wrestling against God.

MANASSEH is the next tribe sealed, and the word means one who causes to forget. What a picture to us of God's Grace to His people.

> **For Israel hath not been forsaken, nor Judah of his God of the Lord of hosts; though their land was filled with sin against the Holy One of Israel. (Jeremiah 51:5)**

God will yet open a fountain for the house of David, (Zechariah 13:1). He will bring them into their own land and cause them to forget their sorrows through their restoration and the blessings which He will bring upon them.

SIMEON means hearing or obeying and speaks of the hearing ear and the obeying heart of God's delivered people. God will cleanse them from all their idols and filthiness when he takes

The Sealing Of The 144,000

them out from all countries and brings them into His own land, (Ezekiel 36:23-30), and they will not defile themselves anymore.

> **... so shall they be my people and I will be their God. (Ezekiel 37:23)**

LEVI means associate, joining or cleaving to. Levi, one of the worst of the tribes by nature, was made the Lord's own inheritance and His priestly tribe by grace. They are here seen cleaving to Him in the time of the great tribulation and the persecution of the Beast.

ISSACHAR means hire or reward, and it tells us of the blessed reward of those who are brought into the millennial kingdom, which has been spoken of by the prophets since the world began.

ZABULON means a home or dwelling place. The nation will indeed be at home and in their dwelling place (Amos 9:15).

JOSEPH means added and the prophecy is:

> **Joseph is a fruitful bough, even a fruitful bough by a well; whose branches run over the wall: The archers have sorely grieved him, and shot at him, and hated him: But his bow abode in strength, and the arms of his hands were made strong by the hands of the mighty God of Jacob;. (from thence is the shepherd, the stone of Israel:) (Genesis 49:22-24)**

To all of God's grace in the past will be added the blessing which He has in store in the future.

BENJAMIN means the son of the right hand. His promise is that he:

> **... should devour the prey and divide the spoil. (Genesis 49:27)**

As Israel carried away the spoil of Egypt when they were delivered, so God is yet to give them the spoil of the nations and make them the channel through whom the nations of the world are to be blessed.

John Phillips sums up the protection and purpose of sealing the 144,000.

Those sealed will go unscathed through the Great Tribulation. They will be a perpetual thorn in the side of the Beast and a constant reminder to the devil that, while millions may bow to his will, God still has him on a leash and says to him, 'Thus far and no farther.' The mobilized armies of the earth will not be able to touch a hair of the heads of these sealed ones. The concentration camps and torture chambers of the Beast's fearful inquisition will leave them unscathed. The fire will not kindle upon them, nor will the smell of smoke be on their garments. The floods will not be able to drown them ... The seal of God rests upon them, and they are saved and secured, come what may. They will be a living proof to the devil that not only is his secular power strictly limited by divine decree, but in the end he cannot win. If he cannot conquer these, then he cannot possibly win in the end. No matter how many millions he liquidates in his insane rage, he is obviously under the control of God.

The sealing of these tribes shows how dear His brethren of the flesh are to Him, even as Joseph's brethren, though they had delivered Joseph up to death. The Apostle Paul speaks of himself as one born out of due time, or before the due time for Israel's national conversion and turn to the Lord. These sealed ones are the first fruits of the Jewish nation.

THE SAVED MULTITUDE

After this I beheld, and, lo, a great multitude, which no man could number, of all nations, and kindreds, and people, and tongues, stood before the throne, and before the Lamb... (Revelation 7:9a) A **great multitude** of all nations, kindreds, and tongues are those saved through the faithful testimony of the sealed remnant who will preach the gospel of the kingdom during the Great Tribulation (Revelation 7:13-14).

The Sealing Of The 144,000

And this gospel of the kingdom shall be preached in all the world for a witness unto all nations; and then shall the end come. (Matthew 24:14)

They stand **clothed with white robes. (Revelation 7:9b)** This multitude will be made up of the martyrs of the sixth chapter to whom **white robes** are given. No doubt this company includes:

their fellow servants also and their brethren that should be killed as they were. (Revelation 6:11)

This numberless host no doubt includes all of the martyred servants of the tribulation, and the greatness of the multitude shows to what extent the antichrist will be permitted to prevail against the saints of God and overcome them.

I beheld, and the same horn made war with the saints, and prevailed against them; (Daniel 7:21)

... and palms in their hands; (Revelation 7:9c) They are raised from the dead and lifted to the throne of Heaven. What joy. Palms are an emblem of joy and victory! This reminds us of the feast of Tabernacles, which we find in Nehemiah's day was a time of:

... great gladness... (Nehemiah. 8:14-18)

They have gone through the tribulation and are now celebrating their deliverance by the blood of the Lamb, with palms in their hand. The feast of Tabernacles was celebrated as a sign of joy and victory for deliverance from Egypt. During this feast they had to use branches of palm trees. (Leviticus 23:40-43) Here in Revelation the palms represent their deliverance from the tribulation. They have gained the victory over the beast. It is the victory of faith, for:

... this is the victory that overcometh the world, even our faith. (1 John 5:4)

Therefore are they before the throne of God, and serve him day and night in his temple: and he that sitteth on the throne shall dwell among them. (Revelation 7:15) These tribulation saints have a place of high honor. They stand **before the throne of God.** Their ministry is that of ceaseless praise, but when the battle is over and Christ's glorious kingdom is established in the earth, this redeemed company is given prominent place in the affairs of state. They live and reign with Christ for a thousand years (Revelation 20:4). The awful experiences of the tribulation will forever be in the past.

THE STILL BEFORE THE STORM
Revelation 8:1-6

This section begins where Revelation six left off with the opening of the seals resuming. Here we witness the breaking of the seventh seal. Hence, the eighth chapter takes up a new series of devastating judgments and continues where the sixth seal left off in chapter six. Out of the seventh seal comes the seven trumpet judgments and the seven vial judgments. Dr. Oliver B. Greene said ...

The seven seal includes all that happens during the sounding of the seven trumpets, and also the pouring out of the seven vials, and extends down to the time when the Millennium is ushered in

This will be a series of judgments far more severe than the seven seals. This is a climatic event where we see the wrath of God continuing to increase and intensify until the end of the Tribulation.

THE SILENCE

And when he had opened the seventh seal, there was silence in heaven about the space of half an hour. (Revelation 8:1) Imagine such a silence! When the Lamb of God breaks the seventh seal there is **silence in heaven about the space of half an hour.** The opening of the seventh seal is a climactic moment with a chilling and eerie silence. This silence is in the anticipation of God's Judgment grips their souls.

But the LORD is in his holy temple: let all the earth keep silence before him. (Habakkuk 2:20)

Bear in mind that the redeemed and the angels do not know the content of that book. Only God knows what is in the book.

When the seventh seal is broken and the book is about to be opened, the angels and the redeemed stand silent with awe, amazement, and anticipation of what is coming next. Dr. H. A. Ironside said ...

> *He will judge according to the holiness of His character and the righteousness of His throne. The seventh seal introduces the final drama of the Great Tribulation. No wonder there is silence in Heaven for half an hour before that seal is broken!"*

Can you imagine a perfect silence lasting a half hour? Not a single sound! It will be a time of great importance and intense anticipation. In his commentary on the book Revelation, C. A. Coates makes an interesting comment on this silence:

> *The opening of the seventh seal is followed by silence in the heavens about half an hour. It is something like the 'Selahs' which we find in the Psalms; a solemn pause indicating the momentous character of the subject in hand and its demand for the quiet consideration of heaven.*

The saints and angels are still and silent. There is no voice from God. The whole earth is overwhelmed. Lehman Strauss points out ...

> *Now "half an hour" is not a long period of time when one is engaged in some pleasantry, but thirty minutes of intense suspense can be well-nigh nerve shattering.*

This will be a long thirty minutes. These seven angels are seen standing before God waiting for their orders. All of Heaven waits to see what is next. And what could be the meaning of this silence?

Be still and know that I am God. (Psalm 46:10)
But the LORD is in his holy temple: let all the earth keep silence before him. (Habakkuk 2:20)

> Be silent, O all flesh, before the LORD: for he is raised up out of his holy habitation. (Zechariah 2:13)
>
> Hold thy peace at the presence of the Lord GOD: for the day of the LORD is at hand: (Zephaniah 1:7a)

Without a doubt this eerie silence was in anticipation of the dreadful judgment of God that would come when the seven trumpets sounded. There is great alarm and concern here.

THE SCENE

And I saw the seven angels which stood before God; and to them were given seven trumpets. (Revelation 8:2) The **seven angels** received the trumpets from God in preparation for judgment. They took their place and prepared to sound. Notice that these angels **stood before God.** They stand in an appointed place, prepared to do God's bidding. Jesus taught that the Angels would play a significant role in the end time judgement on the world (Matthew chapters 13, 16, 24, 25).

> **The Son of man shall send forth his angels, and they shall gather out of his kingdom all things that offend, and them which do iniquity; (Matthew 13:41)**
>
> **So shall it be at the end of the world: the angels shall come forth, and sever the wicked from among the just, (Matthew 13:49)**
>
> **For the Son of man shall come in the glory of his Father with his angels; and then he shall reward every man according to his works. (Matthew 16:27)**

We also see that **seven trumpets** are given to these angels who are associated with the Lamb, and when they begin to sound their trumpets, terrible judgments will follow. Earlier we saw that in the Tribulation Period there are three series of sevens: the seven seals, the seven trumpets, and the seven vials. All of these contain the plagues that God will pour out upon the earth in the time of the Tribulation Period. In the Bible trumpets are used as an alarm concerning war:

> **And if ye go to war in your land against the enemy that oppresseth you, then ye shall blow an alarm with the trumpets; (Numbers 10:9a)**
>
> **My bowels, my bowels! I am pained at my very heart; my heart maketh a noise in me; I cannot hold my peace, because thou hast heard, O my soul, the sound of the trumpet, the alarm of war. (Jeremiah 4:19)**

The Bible declares our Lord to be a man of war (Exodus 15:3). The great battle day of the Lord is drawing nigh, and these angels are about to sound the alarm. Trumpets are also associated with the overthrow of the ungodly, as in the overthrow of the wicked city of Jericho. So here the sound of the trumpets is associated with the overthrow of Anti-Christ, his armies, as well as the destruction of Babylon.

THE SUPPLICATION

And another angel came and stood at the altar having a golden censer... (Revelation 8:3a) The priest of the Old Testament used censers to carry hot coals from the brazen altar to the altar of incense. This messenger could well be the Lord Jesus Christ Who is our Great High Priest. Oliver B. Greene wrote:

> *The service rendered by the other angel at the altar proves that it could be none other than the Lord Jesus Christ, the High Priest. Both the brazen and the golden altars are mentioned here. No ordinary creature could add to the prayers of the saints. The action of this other angel is of a mediatorial nature ... One who is between the suffering, praying saints on earth and their God. There is "one Mediator between God and men, the man Christ Jesus" (I Tim. 2:5). Therefore, we conclude that this angel could be none other than the Lord Jesus Himself.*

Jesus Christ perfectly fulfilled the Old Testament type of the High Priest and his Tabernacle functions. Here we see the Lord Jesus, our Great High Priest in the Heavenly Holy of Holies carrying out His work of intercession before the God the Father.

The Fragrance

... having a golden censer; and there was given unto him much incense, that he should offer it with the prayers of all saints upon the golden altar which was before the throne. (Revelation 8:3b) Here in we have our Lord in His High Priestly work (Hebrews 4:14-16; 6:20-7:28; 13:15), offering **incense ... with the prayers of all saints.** The censer is usually mentioned in connection with the High Priest, (Leviticus 16:12; Hebrews 9:4).

And the smoke of the incense, which came with the prayers of the saints, ascended up before God out of the angel's hand. (Revelation 8:4) We see the prayer of the saints, like the smoke of incense **ascended up before God out of the angel's hand.** This further indicates that this angel was none other than the Lord Jesus Christ — our eternal High Priest. The Psalmist said:

> **Let my prayer be set forth before thee as incense; and the lifting up of my hands as the evening sacrifice. (Psalm 141:2)**

The Lord God hears the cry of His people in their distress.

> **And the LORD said, I have surely seen the affliction of my people which are in Egypt, and have heard their cry... (Exodus 3:7a)**

The **prayers of all saints (v.4)** no doubt refers to the imprecatory prayers of the tribulation saints (those saved during the tribulation).

The Fire

And the angel took the censer, and filled it with fire of the altar, and cast it into the earth: and there were voices, and thunderings, and lightnings, and an earthquake. (Revelation 8:5) The intercession of saints is presented before God and then **the angel took the censer, and filled it with fire of the altar,**

and cast it into the earth. The angel first offered these coals as incense before God and then threw them on the earth. Henry Morris points out that, the same censer which had brought the prayers up to heaven, now carries fire from heaven to the earth. Here we see the prayers of the saints rise into the presence of God. Out of the imprecatory prayers of God's people come these trumpet judgments. God does avenge His people.

> **Dearly beloved, avenge not yourselves, but rather give place unto wrath: for it is written, Vengeance is mine; I will repay, saith the Lord. (Romans 12:19)**

Haters of God and persecutors of saints might think they have the upper hand, but God will avenge. God's people must pray and leave matters in God's hands. God is well able to handle it with our enemies.

THE FIRST FOUR TRUMPET JUDGMENTS
Revelation 8:7-13

In this passage of Scripture, our Lord Jesus Christ begins to answer the prayers of the saints we read about earlier. Their prayers are answered in the punishment of the unbelieving. This, in the remainder of chapter 8 we are introduced to the first four trumpet judgments. The first four trumpet judgments fall on creation and the last three on mankind. You will remember that after the opening of the sixth seal there was a cessation of events and the four angels holding the four winds of the earth were commanded not to blow on the earth, nor on the sea, nor on any tree. But the calm is about to end, and the storm of judgment continues.

THE SUDDEN SCORCHING

When the Angel blows this first trumpet the calm in the storm will be broken and the outpouring of God's wrath will be greatly increased upon the earth and its guilty, godless inhabitants. God still punishes sin. Those who have chosen evil will be righteously and severely judged for their deeds.

The Disturbance

The first angel sounded, and there followed hail and fire mingled with blood, and they were cast upon the earth: (Revelation 8:7a) Here we see the first angel step out and blast his trumpet and immediately God's judgment begins to fall. In the Word of God, hail is often associated with divine judgment (Exodus 9:13-25; Job 38:22-23; Psalms 105:32; Isaiah 28:2; Haggai 2:17). The same is true of fire (Genesis 19:24; Psalms 11:6; Ezekiel 38:22). Now, we should remember that the purpose of this great book is to reveal the truth, not to hide it. Keep in mind that even symbolic passages have meaning and application. Whenever symbols are used in the Book of Revelation, the fact that they are symbols is always clearly indicated within the text of the passage. Therefore, we do not need to be in doubt about the meaning. In the passage now before us, no symbolism is indicated. Therefore, the only safe thing for us to do is to accept any passage as literal. Such is always the case unless a symbolic meaning is clearly indicated.

Relying upon this solid principal of interpretation we are compelled to believe that when the first angel sounds his trumpet there will come upon the earth a great storm of **hail and fire mingled with blood**, exactly as stated in our text. It should not be difficult to believe this fact especially if we believe the Word of God. Revelation is not a book to be spiritualized and allegorized. We can take this literally. This is not the first time this sort of judgment has occurred. A similar event took place in Egypt under Moses and Aaron, who were sent of God to deliver the children of Israel from Egyptian bondage. This is confirmed in the book of Exodus.

> **And Moses stretched forth his rod toward heaven: and the LORD sent thunder and hail, and the fire ran along upon the ground; and the LORD rained hail upon the land of Egypt. So there was hail, and fire mingled with the hail, very grievous, such as there was none like it in all the land of Egypt since it became a nation. And the hail smote throughout all the land of Egypt all that was in the field, both man and beast; and the hail smote every herb of the field, and brake every tree of the field. (Exodus 9:23-25)**

The only difference between what happened in Egypt and that which is to take place at the sounding of the first trumpet, is that blood will be added to the hail and fire. But we do not need to wonder at this since the prophet Joel said:

> **And I will show wonders in the heavens and in the earth, blood, and fire, and pillars of smoke. The sun shall be turned into darkness, and the**

moon into blood, before the great and the terrible day of the LORD come. (Joel 2:30-31)

Imagine being lost and missing the rapture. To be left behind to face such severe judgment. What a tragedy!

The Desolation

... and the third part of trees was burnt up, and all green grass was burnt up. (Revelation 8:7b) As a result of this judgment, one third of the trees will be burnt up and all the green grass will be destroyed. This judgment will result in a horrifying desolation. Think about the forest fires, the orchards, the timber lands, the grain fields wasted, and all the pasture lands burnt up. Famine and economic ruin will engulf the world and millions of people will be affected. We have seen what these things can do on a local level, but just think of the devastation, destruction and dearth that will occur world-wide during these awful times.

THE STORMY SEA

And the second angel sounded, and as it were a great mountain burning with fire was cast into the sea: and the third part of the sea became blood; And the third part of the creatures which were in the sea, and had life, died; and the third part of the ships were destroyed. (Revelation 8:8-9) Those who delight in mocking God ought to seriously consider His coming wrath in passages such as this one. These are real catastrophic events that will be hurled at this sin darkened earth by the Almighty. As our attention is drawn to this stormy sea, we notice two things:

The Disaster In The Sea

And the second angel sounded, and as it were a great mountain burning with fire was cast into the sea: and the third part of the sea became blood; And the third part of the creatures which were in the sea, and had life, died... (Revelation 8:8-9a) Something which had the appearance of a great mountain burning with fire was cast into the sea. In the judgment of Egypt God struck a death blow at the Egyptians and their false gods, by turning their waters into blood.

> **And Moses and Aaron did so, as the LORD commanded; and he lifted up the rod, and smote the waters that were in the river, in the sight of Pharaoh, and in the sight of his servants; and all the waters that were in the river were turned to blood. And the fish that was in the river died; and the river stank, and the Egyptians could not drink of the water of the river; and there was blood throughout all the land of Egypt. (Exodus 7:20-21)**

This is a strike against one of man's major food sources. We also have the added testimony of Zephaniah concerning the fact that God will destroy the fish of the sea.

> **I will consume man and beast; I will consume the fowls of the heaven, and the fishes of the sea, and the stumbling blocks with the wicked, and I will cut off man from off the land, saith the Lord. (Zephaniah 1:3)**

With the second seal, the fishing trade will take a major hit. People all around the world will be affected by a shortage of seafood! Fish have always been an important food source for man. Imagine therefore, if you can, what it is going to be like when God destroys at least one third of the fish and other seafoods that are in the ocean.

The Destruction Of The Ships

... and the third part of the ships were destroyed. (Revelation 8:9b) One third of the ships of the sea will be destroyed. This is no small matter. The consequences of this will be devastating to the whole world. Just think what it is going to mean when that many ships are destroyed! We thought it was awful when one great ship, like the Titanic, struck an iceberg and went to the bottom of the sea, with all the lives lost, and not to mention all the wealth lost. This will include oil tankers that bring oil to western countries from the Middle East. But imagine, if you can what a massive loss of human life, what a tremendous loss of material goods, and the loss in dollars it will mean when the second trumpet sounds and one third of all the ships at sea are destroyed at one time. Just think about the interruption to the chain of supply. It will affect the traffic between the nations, the oil, the food, and merchandise of all kinds. This judgment will disrupt world trade and result in financial disaster as well.

THE SOUR STAR

And the third angel sounded, and there fell a great star from heaven, burning as it were a lamp, and it fell upon the third part of the rivers, and upon the fountains of waters; And the name of the star is called Wormwood: and the third part of the waters became wormwood; and many men died of the waters, because they were made bitter. (Revelation 8:10-11) We are told that **there fell a great star from heaven.** The word **great** comes from *"megas"* and denotes that which is exceedingly large. With the sounding of the third trumpet the fresh water is affected. A **third part of the rivers and the fountains of waters** will be poisoned and be as bitter as **wormwood**. Wormwood is a plant that is native to Israel and Northern Africa and has a strong bitter taste. Thus, the metaphorical use of the plant in our text. The bitter waters will cause the death **many**. These will be horrible times. This was prophesied by Jeremiah.

> **And the LORD saith, Because they have forsaken my law which I set before them, and have not obeyed my voice, neither walked therein; But have walked after the imagination of their own heart, and after Baalim, which their fathers taught them: Therefore thus saith the LORD of hosts, the God of Israel; Behold, I will feed them, even this people, with wormwood, and give them water of gall to drink. (Jeremiah 9:13-15)**

We are told that wormwood is bitter which, when it is used freely, produces convulsions, paralysis, and death! Just think of what it is going to mean when men thirst for water and find, to their horror and to their own hurt and to their complete undoing, that the waters have become suddenly bitter and are unfit and unsafe to drink. There is no question, but that many will die because they will innocently drink of these waters, and others will die from thirst because all sources of healthy water will have been cut off.

THE SMITTEN SUN

And the fourth angel sounded, and the third part of the sun was smitten, and the third part of the moon, and the third part of the stars; so as the third part of them was darkened, and the day shone not for a third part of it, and the night likewise. (Revelation 8:12) The fourth trumpet affects the sun, moon, and stars. With the sounding of the first three trumpets, the trees and vegetation, the sea and the fish, the ships of the sea, as well as fresh water were greatly affected. The first three trumpet judgments effected the earth. But the sounding of the fourth trumpet effects the heavens above. Judgment is falling with full force and fast. The sorrows of the ungodly are multiplied upon them.

A third part of the day becomes as night, and a third part of the night has neither moon nor stars to lighten the darkness. The cycle of day and night as we know it today will be changed. The twenty-four-hour cycle that we are accustomed to will be shortened to a sixteen-hour cycle, as a result of this fourth trumpet. The Prophet Joel wrote:

> **The earth shall quake before them; the heavens shall tremble: the sun and the moon shall be dark, and the stars shall withdraw their shining. (Joel 2:10)**

Jesus warned of these days as well.

> **And there shall be signs in the sun, and in the moon, and in the stars; and upon the earth distress of nations, with perplexity; the sea and the waves roaring. (Luke 21:25)**
>
> **Immediately after the tribulation of those days shall the sun be darkened, and the moon shall not give her light, and the stars shall fall from heaven, and the powers of the heavens shall be shaken:**

> And then shall appear the sign of the Son of man in heaven: and then shall all the tribes of the earth mourn, and they shall see the Son of man coming in the clouds of heaven with power and great glory. And he shall send his angels with a great sound of a trumpet, and they shall gather together his elect from the four winds, from one end of heaven to the other. (Matthew 24:29–31)

Men have long trampled underfoot the goodness and grace of God. They have spurned His Word and rejected His grace. Instead of repenting and being saved they have rejected the Holy God. What a tragedy! Now there is no hope—no escape. Payday is coming.

> Because I have called, and ye refused; I have stretched out my hand, and no man regarded; But ye have set at nought all my counsel, and would none of my reproof: I also will laugh at your calamity; I will mock when your fear cometh. (Proverbs 1:24-26)

God has called all men to salvation. In grace, He calls for repentance. In addition to calling them, He stretches out His hand to sinful man. The Bible says, **no man regarded.** The word **regarded** means *"to give heed, incline, listen."* Sinful and hard-hearted men do not heed God's warning. They reject His offer of wisdom and salvation. They will not heed the warnings and reproofs of the Word of God.

> For that they hated knowledge, and did not choose the fear of the LORD: They would none of my counsel: they despised all my reproof. (Proverbs 1:29-30)

There are many down through the years who snubbed God and rejected His counsel only to end up in Hell. They are those who simply hated and rejected the truth until God turned them over to their own way. Judgment is inevitable for those who refuse to accept God's way.

> And I beheld, and heard an angel flying through the midst of heaven, saying with a loud voice, Woe, woe, woe, to the

inhabiters of the earth by reason of the other voices of the trumpet of the three angels, which are yet to sound! (Revelation 8:13) At this point, an angel flies through Heaven announcing woes concerning the three remaining judgments. This angel issues a solemn warning to all the men of the earth that the coming three trumpets that are yet to sound will be more terrible than anything thus far.

THE DAY ALL HELL BREAKS LOOSE
Revelation 9:1-11

In the closing verse of the last chapter, we saw an angel flying in the heavens crying with a loud voice, Woe, woe, woe. These three woes pronounced upon the inhabitants of the earth by reason of the trumpets of the three angels which are yet to sound. With the sounding of these last three trumpets will come a greater and a more severe judgment than any of the first four that have already been sounded. This will be one of the most terrifying and dreadful events to ever take place on the earth. This passage tells us that the very pit of Hell will be opened, and hordes of demons released upon man. The torment and misery that ensues will surpass anything that this world has ever experienced.

THEIR DELIVERY

And the fifth angel sounded, and I saw a star fall from heaven unto the earth: and to him was given the key of the bottomless pit. (Revelation 9:1) This is another verse that men have interpreted in various ways. However, we will draw our comments from the verse itself. John saw a star fall from heaven, but it is certain that this is not to mean a literal star. Notice three things:

1. The pronouns **him** and **he** are used in reference to this star. Thus, this star has a human personality. This is a personal being.
2. A key is given to the star. The star takes possession of the key.
3. The star uses the key to open the bottomless pit. He has power over the realm of demons.

We have already learned in chapter 1:20 that a star was used as a symbol of an angel. This **star** is an angel to whom was given authority to open the bottomless pit. This is more than likely none other than Satan himself. Satan is referred to as one who fell from Heaven. When Satan rebelled against God, he was thrown down to the earth.

> **How art thou fallen from heaven, O Lucifer, son of the morning! How art thou cut down to the ground, which didst weaken the nations! (Isaiah 14:12)**

Satan has fallen from Heaven and he above all would want this pit opened. He allows it for the purpose of judgment on the wicked and Christ rejecting world. Their path in life has been after Satan, now he is used to inflict punishment and doom upon them.

THEIR DWELLING

And he opened the bottomless pit ... (Revelation 9:2a) God is in full control. He allows Satan to open the pit to unleash further judgment upon the inhabitants of the earth. The bottomless pit is the place of torment where the fallen angels are held. This is hell's prison house. It is the place where the angels who followed Satan in his rebellion against God are chained in darkness

> **And the angels which kept not their first estate, but left their own habitation, he hath reserved in everlasting chains under darkness unto the judgment of the great day. (Jude 6)**
>
> **For if God spared not the angels that sinned, but cast them down to hell, and delivered them into chains of darkness, to be reserved unto judgment; (2 Peter 2:4)**

Demons hate the pit but know that they will all eventually end up there. In Luke, the demons asked Jesus not to send them to the pit.

And they besought him that he would not command them to go out into the deep. (Luke 8:31)

This corresponds with their request that He not torment them, in Luke 8:28. John Phillips comments:

> *"Picture what the world would be like if we were to open the doors of all the penitentiaries of earth and set free the world's most vicious and violent criminals, giving them full reign to practice their infamies upon mankind. Something worse than that lies in store for the world. Satan, cast out of heaven, is now permitted to summon to his aid the most diabolical fiends in the abyss to act as his agents in bringing mankind to the footstool of the Beast."*

We have heard the expression *"Hell on earth."* Those who make such a statement do not even began to comprehend what Hell is like. However, Hell on earth is just what it will be like when Hell's prison house is opened, and the demons allowed to flood this earth.

THEIR DARKNESS

What we see here comes from the brimstone and blackness of Hell. That which lurks in the depth of darkness will be released to invade the earth.

The Ascending Of Smoke

And he opened the bottomless pit; and there arose a smoke out of the pit, as the smoke of a great furnace; and the sun and the air were darkened by reason of the smoke of the pit. (Revelation 9:2) This bottomless pit is the place we know as Hell. It is a place of fire and smoke; so much so that when Hell is opened the smoke that ascends darkens the sun and the air above the earth. Hell is an awful place of judgment and torment.

Many foolishly deny the existence of Hell. When Hell is mentioned today, it is generally ridiculed, as if the whole idea of Hell were so old-fashioned that only the ignorant could really believe in such a place. The Lord Jesus dogmatically stated of the rich man who died lost ...

> **And in hell he lift up his eyes, being in torments, (Luke 16:23)**

Many are they who foolishly deny the existence of Hell. However, their unbelief and denial does not do away with the fact of Hell. The tragic results are the same for everyone who dies without Christ.

> **And in hell he lift up his eyes, being in torments, (Luke 16:23a)**

Man's unbelief does not thwart the truth of Scripture. In our text we see the opening of the pit, yes, with literal darkness following. All the awful darkness of Hell will accompany these demons as they go forth throughout the earth. We live in a day of great spiritual darkness, but just think of what it will be like when these demons are released from Hell. Evil lurks in the dark. Wicked men love spiritual darkness.

> **And this is the condemnation, that light is come into the world, and men loved darkness rather than light, because their deeds were evil. (John 3:19)**

One of the reasons for the spiritual decline in America is increased demon activity in these last days. However, keep in mind that this is not only spiritual darkness, but a literal darkness.

The Analogy Of Scorpions

And there came out of the smoke locusts upon the earth: and unto them was given power, as the scorpions of the earth have power. (Revelation 9:3) These demons are compared to locusts. The analogy here is that of destruction and devastation. Locusts devour crops, grass, and leaves. Swarms of locusts have been known to cause food shortages and famine. Locusts come in great swarms and destroy everything in their path (Exodus 10:12-17). It is obvious from their description that these are not locusts as we know them. Rather, these creatures are vicious demons such as the human eye has never seen before in all human history. John does not say that these demons were scorpions but that they have the power of a scorpion. Their dominion is over unsaved people of the Tribulation Period. Everyone in all the earth except for the 144,00, will be tormented by these demon creatures.

THEIR DOMINION

And it was commanded them that they should not hurt the grass of the earth, neither any green thing, neither any tree; but only those men which have not the seal of God in their foreheads. (Revelation 9:4) Locusts normally eat green foliage, but these attack people. They are not allowed to kill men, but they are to torment them. Imagine the horror that will grip the heart of the lost as demon creatures attack and torment. They have power to sting and inflict torment upon the people. There will be no relief from the anguish and agony. Even suicide is not an option. Only the 144,000 sealed Jews are exempt from their vicious attack.

We serve a merciful God. He is the God of Heaven who loves all men and would have all come to repentance (2 Peter 3:9). Salvation is God's heart desire for all men, but we must realize that He is also a God of judgment. The liberals and modernists delight in focusing on the love of God and yes**:**

God is love. (1 John 4:8)

All of us can be thankful that God is love. It was His great love that moved God to sacrifice His only begotten Son for the sin of lost man (John 3:16; Romans 5:8). Over and over throughout the Word of God His love is declared. However, God is also ...

... a consuming fire. (Deuteronomy 9:3; Hebrews 12:29)

No one will ignore the conditions of the Tribulation Period. These demons hurt not any green thing; they only torment the inhabitants of the earth. These demons will attack and severely punish all who have not the seal of God upon their foreheads. The 144,000 who received the seal of God will not be harmed. However, everyone else will be tormented for five horrible months by these demons. The judgment of God awaits those who reject His grace and mercy, here God turns them over to Satan for their punishment.

THEIR DURATION

And to them it was given that they should not kill them, but that they should be tormented five months: and their torment was as the torment of a scorpion, when he striketh a man. (Revelation 9:5) These will have a sting like a scorpion's and will invade the earth for five months. These locusts represent the judgment of Almighty God upon a wicked world. God has given to them the power to torment man for five full months. Nothing can stop them. There will be no reprieve. This is God's judgment!

THEIR DESTRUCTION

And in those days shall men seek death, and shall not find it; and shall desire to die, and death shall flee from them. (Revelation 9:6) These demons will not be allowed to kill people, only torment them. The inhabitants of the earth will be tormented to the extent that they will seek death but be unable to find it. Think about the horror of this truth! Five months of anguish and torment. Five months of scorpion like demons. People will **seek death ... and shall desire to die.** People will attempt to take their own lives to escape the horrendous suffering caused by these demons, but they will not die. There will be no escape from the torment until God says. What a contrast to the grace of God that makes man long for and enjoy life. Christ always offers life eternal, but it is Satan who deals in death.

THEIR DESCRIPTION

And the shapes of the locusts were like unto horses prepared unto battle; and on their heads were as it were crowns like gold, and their faces were as the faces of men. And they had hair as the hair of women, and their teeth were as the teeth of lions. And they had breastplates, as it were

breastplates of iron; and the sound of their wings was as the sound of chariots of many horses running to battle. And they had tails like unto scorpions, and there were stings in their tails: and their power was to hurt men five months. **(Revelation 9:7-10)** There is an eight-fold description given of these demon locusts.

The locusts were like unto horses prepared unto battle... (Revelation 9:7a) These are not literal horses but are **like unto** horses. They resemble horses **prepared unto battle.** Horses and chariots in the Word are a sign of judgment, (Jeremiah 46:1-10, Joel 2:3-11). In Zechariah 6:1-8, we have a picture of horses and chariots which go forth from standing before the Lord.

> **And I turned, and lifted up mine eyes, and looked, and, behold, there came four chariots out from between two mountains; and the mountains were mountains of brass. In the first chariot were red horses; and in the second chariot black horses; And in the third chariot white horses; and in the fourth chariot grisled and bay horses. Then I answered and said unto the angel that talked with me, What are these, my lord? And the angel answered and said unto me, These are the four spirits of the heavens, which go forth from standing before the Lord of all the earth. The black horses which are therein go forth into the north country; and the white go forth after them; and the grisled go forth toward the south country. And the bay went forth, and sought to go that they might walk to and fro through the earth: and he said, Get you hence, walk to and fro through the earth. So they walked to and fro through the earth. Then cried he upon me, and spake unto me, saying, Behold, these that go toward the north country have quieted my spirit in the north country. (Zechariah 6:1–8)**

Joel says:

> **The appearance of them is as the appearance of horses; and as horsemen, so shall they run. (Joel 2:4)**

And on their heads were as it were crowns like gold... (Revelation 9:7b) A crown speaks of authority, their authority. God has granted these demons full reign to carry out their torturous mission. The crown also speaks of victory in their purpose. In other words, the demons will be successful in their mission.

And their faces were as the faces of men. (Revelation 9:7c) The faces of men probably speak of intelligence. Man is the most intelligent of God's creation.

And they had hair as the hair of women. (Revelation 9:8a) Notice that it specifically states that their hair is like **as the hair of a woman.** This means that it was long hair.

> **Doth not even nature itself teach you, that, if a man have long hair, it is a shame unto him? But if a woman have long hair, it is a glory to her: for her hair is given her for a covering. (1 Corinthians 11:14-15)**

That these demonic creatures have long hair suggests a two-fold meaning. First, the long hair speaks of glory on a woman. It refers to the seductive power of these demons to lure their victims. Second, long hair on a man is a shame and speaks of rebellion. Absalom is a good example of such rebellion. (2 Samuel 14:26) Absalom went on to lead a rebellious life, to the point that he rose up against his own father, but ended up dead himself, hung by his long hair in an oak tree. (Samuel 18) So, the long hair suggests the rebellious, self-serving nature of demonic creatures.

... and their teeth teeth were as the teeth of lions. (Revelation 9:8b) The teeth as lions speaks of their relentless cruelty. This shows how ferocious they truly are. They are vicious! They rip and tear the flesh of men, like lions. They have a violent and unquenchable thirst for prey as a hungry lion would have.

Be sober, be vigilant; because your adversary the devil, as a roaring lion, walketh about, seeking whom he may devour: (1 Peter 5:8)

And they had breastplates, as it were breastplates of iron... (Revelation 9:9a) They are a protected and resistless enemy. That they have **breastplates of iron** implies that they are resistant and protected from destruction. Neither power and technologies nor fighting forces of man will be able to overcome this painful and torturous army.

And the sound of their wings was as the sound of chariots of many horses running to battle. (Revelation 9:9b) The sound will be great and cause extraordinary confusion and chaos. Their victims will be overrun with the most horrible terror and fear.

Like the noise of chariots on the tops of mountains shall they leap, like the noise of a flame of fire that devoureth the stubble, as a strong people set in battle array. (Joel 2:5)

The fact that they have wings also implies great speed and suggests the impossibility of escaping their attack.

And they had tails like unto scorpions, and there were stings in their tails. (Revelation 9:10) The demonic locusts will have stinging tails like scorpions. This speaks of the demonic torture that wicked men will have to endure during the tribulation. This is just one of God's judgments during the tribulation period. Just imagine the horror of having to deal with these hellish horsemen with no place of escape.

THEIR DIRECTOR

And they had a king over them, which is the angel of the bottomless pit, whose name in the Hebrew tongue is Abaddon, but in the Greek tongue hath his name Apollyon. (Revelation 9:11) Unlike regular locusts (Proverbs 30:27), these demonic locusts have a **king over them.** The ruler over these demons is the angel of the bottomless pit, the Devil himself. The king is named in the Hebrew **Abaddon** and in the Greek **Apollyon.** Both names mean destroyer. Destruction will be the desire and work of these locusts during their five months of Hell on earth. These locusts, therefore, will not be an unorganized mass of creatures, such as ordinary locusts who ravage and destroy without restraint, but they will carry on their work under the leadership of their king—the master destroyer, Satan himself.

My friend, the day is coming when all Hell will be turned loose upon this earth. The bottomless pit, which is the dwelling place of all the demons, is going to be opened. Will you be here, or will you call upon Christ now?

HELL'S HIDEOUS HORSEMAN
Revelation 9:13-21

Now we come to the sixth trumpet judgment. This is the second of the three woes pronounced upon the world. The sixth angel is commanded to lose four other angels who have been bound in the Euphrates River. Unlike the demons from the bottomless pit who could torment, but not destroy, these angels are instructed to take the lives of one-third of the world's population. These hideous horsemen are allowed to target human life. As the Almighty's judgment continues to fall the chaos and suffering on earth continues to increase.

THE SCENE IN HEAVEN

And the sixth angel sounded, and I heard a voice from the four horns of the golden altar which is before God. (Revelation 9:13) As the sixth trumpet sounds, John hears a voice coming from the four horns of the golden altar which is in the presence of God. This is the same altar we saw in chapter eight—the altar of incense which stands before the throne in Heaven. The voice, without a doubt, is the voice of the Lord. This verse is easily understood when compared with the Old Testament scriptures that describe the use of the altar. We know that, according to the book of Hebrews, the Tabernacle which Moses built, with its altar and other articles of furniture, was made after the pattern of the true Tabernacle in the Heavenlies.

On the Day of Atonement, the blood of the sacrificed animals was put on the four horns of the altar (Leviticus 4:7-18, 16:18-19). God's judgments are directly linked with God's the place of atonement. The altar reminds us of the shed blood of Jesus. Paul warned about severe judgment for those who reject the blood sacrifice for their atonement. Many reject the message of Christ's blood atonement.

> **He that despised Moses' law died without mercy under two or three witnesses: Of how much sorer punishment, suppose ye, shall he be thought worthy, who hath trodden under foot the Son of God, and hath counted the blood of the covenant, wherewith he was sanctified, an unholy thing, and hath done despite unto the Spirit of grace? (Hebrews 10:28-29)**

Keep in mind that the altar is a place of mercy where sacrifice can be made for sinners. No one who rejects the blood can be saved. It is the place where guilty men receive grace and mercy from the Lord. The voice came from the four horns, which is a place of mercy. This reminds us that God is still a God of grace and mercy—even in times of severe judgment.

THE SORROW ON EARTH

The sorrow that man experiences in the Tribulation Period will be unparalleled to anything in history. The inhabitants of this world will be devastated.

The Angels

Saying to the sixth angel which had the trumpet, Loose the four angels which are bound in the great river Euphrates. (Revelation 9:14) Now orders are given to the angel with the sixth trumpets to lose four angels which are bound in the great River Euphrates. The Euphrates River is one of the ancient rivers of the Bible and of the Middle East. It is a river of some 1,800 miles long. Between the Nile River and the great River lies the land God promised to Abraham (Genesis 15:18).

This is in the area of the garden of Eden that we read about in the book of Genesis. This is where Satan first began his evil work of sin and destruction and brought misery upon man. The great Bible expositor, J. A. Seiss wrote:

> *"It was in this locality that the powers of evil made their first attempts against the human race. It was in this locality that the first murder was committed. It was in this region that the great apostasies, both before and after the flood, had their centers. It was in*

this region that Israel's most oppressive enemies resided, and that the Jews were compelled to drag out the long and weary years of their great captivity. It was in this region that the great oppressive world powers took their commencement. It is the region where all this world's beginnings were made — where man first saw the light, first sinned, fell from his first estate, was banished from Paradise, and introduced all earth's miseries—where Satan first alighted upon our planet, won his first triumphs, and first set his foul agencies against man in operation. The Euphrates itself is one of the primeval rivers, and the only one we know of that remains. And there, where guilt came into the place of innocence, and Babylon supplanted Eden, and hell sent up its Upas instead of the Tree of Life, and death came in upon the children of men, these four fallen sons of light, with their evil hosts, rave in the bonds, imposed in mercy, but, at the appointed hour, in wrath to be relaxed, that earth's blaspheming millions may feel what shall then have been so richly merited."

Yes, the place of man's first rebellion against God is the heartland of final judgments upon this world. It all began here, and the great prophetic events of the future will center around this place—this is where sin and evil will come to an end.

The Euphrates River is in the same area where everything began. No doubt these four angels are fallen angels of some sort who kept not their first estate and therefore were bound. It is clearly seen that these are angels of destruction. These four angels will serve as the instruments of God in His divine judgment upon the wicked.

The Awfulness

The Bible says that the, **the four angels were loosed, which were prepared for an hour, and a day, and a month, and for a year, for to slay the third part of men. (Revelation 9:15)** The population of earth is presently 7.9 billion souls. In our study of

Revelation, we have seen one-fourth of this number die under the pale horse rider (Chapter 6:8). Thus, at this point in time, earth's population is about 2 billion. Now an additional one-third will die as these four fallen angels are released. These four angels are **prepared for an hour, and a day, and a month, and for a year.** They have evidently been bound as a protection to the human race, but will now be permitted, for a season, to carry out their evil purposes. God is working exactly as He planned.

The Army

And the number of the army of the horsemen were two hundred thousand thousand: and I heard the number of them. (Revelation 9:16) As soon as the four angels are released, an army of hellish horseman appears on the scene. Their purpose will be to kill a third part of mankind. Remember that with the fifth trumpet, the first woe brought Hell's locusts upon men making them wish they could die, but death evaded them. However, in this judgment untold numbers will die. Men stand powerless against these demonic horsemen. Note the description of this demonic army.

The Amount

... two hundred thousand thousand... (Revelation 9:16) of them. There is no need to explain this number away as if it were some symbolic mystery. We must pay close attention to the wording of Scripture. John said, **And the number of the army of the horsemen were two hundred thousand thousand.** John affirms the size of this army to the exact number, then he says, **and I heard the number of them.** This is a literal army of 200 million soldiers. There has been great debate about who this army is. Some Bible students are of the opinion that this is a human army. However, the description given leaves no doubt that this is a supernatural army. Clarence Larkin comments:

> *That these Four Angels who were bound at the river Euphrates, were bad angels is seen from the fact that they were bound, and that they are the leaders or commanders of an army of 200,000,000 men is a*

supernatural army. It is not composed of ordinary men and horses.

Dr. Henry Morris wrote:

> Like the scorpion-locusts under the preceding trumpet, this will be a demonic legion of nightmarish animals indwelt by evil spirits, hitherto bound up in the Euphrates with their four evil overlords. It must be that these frightful horses and horsemen are demon-possessed creatures whose bodies are specially created by God for the awful judgment which they are thereby enabled to inflict upon mankind. Their bodies are real physical bodies, capable of generating physical fire and brimstone and causing the physical death of those men and women whom they attack. This suggests that the bodies are specially created right at the time of the release of the unclean spirits from their prison, and are then immediately taken over by the ascending spirits.
>
> Like a great storm, they spread forth from their pit, raging over the earth to take vengeance on mankind, whom they regard as responsible for their miserable circumstances. No longer constrained as they once were by the need of some kind of physical body wherewith to enslave men, they now are able to use their newly-secured bodies to destroy men.
>
> No doubt all this sounds fantastic and impossible, so commentators have invented all sorts of figurative meanings to apply to these deadly horses. But these are not the first fire-breathing animals the earth has seen. Ancient nations everywhere describe fire-breathing dragons which formerly existed on earth, and the Bible describes at least one such creature, called leviathan (Job 41:19-21). There are many indications that these dragons were actually dinosaurs, and the fossil evidence does show structures on at least some dinosaurs that could well

have served as mixing chambers for flammable chemicals that could be expelled in the form of fire and smoke. John is merely describing what he actually saw.

Hindson points out that this army is as large as the entire population of America and Russia. The size alone is astronomical! There has never been anything like it. Like the locusts of the first woe, these are more demons unleashed on wicked man.

The Armor

The riders wore **breastplates of fire, and of jacinth, and brimstone. (Revelation 9:17a)** This speaks of their appearance. In ancient days breastplates were used to protect soldiers from the weapons of their enemies. The breastplates imply that these demon horsemen will be greatly protected. The **fire** (red), **jacinth** (blue), and **brimstone** (yellow) further imply that this army is from Hell.

The Appearance

We are told that **the heads of the horses were as the heads of lions. And out of their mouths issued fire and smoke and brimstone. (Revelation 9:17b)** Again, the horses speak of war. These creatures had unrelenting power and determination. Like the locusts previously, this speaks of their relentless cruelty.

The **heads of lions** are picturesque. Lions are savage beasts strike fear in the heart of all who come in contact with them. They are merciless and terrifying creatures known as the king of the beasts. The heads of lions speak of the horsemen's violent and unquenchable thirst for prey. Like hungry lions they go forth with persistence and power to devour and destroy.

Fire, **smoke**, and **brimstone** are their main weapons. These are all products of Hell and it will seem like Hell on the earth when these hideous creatures are turned loose upon the wicked.

Their Attack

By these three was the third part of men killed, by the fire, and by the smoke, and by the brimstone, which issued out of their mouths. (Revelation 9:18) Remember that with the opening of the fourth seal, one fourth of the population of the earth was killed. Herbert Lockyer said:

> *These elements out of the mouths of the horses will give the godless a foretaste of the agony of the lake of fire. Belching forth hellish fumes, the horses will manifest diabolic pleasure in their task.*

Here with the sounding of the sixth trumpet another one third is killed. When we add just these two judgments together, over one-half of the world's population is dead. Add to that number the millions of who died from the other plagues and judgments, and we begin to see the devastation of the people of this earth.

THE STUBBORNNESS OF MAN

And the rest of the men which were not killed by these plagues yet repented not of the works of their hands, that they should not worship devils, and idols of gold, and silver, and brass, and stone, and of wood: which neither can see, nor hear, nor walk: Neither repented they of their murders, nor of their sorceries, nor of their fornication, nor of their thefts. (Revelation 9:20-21) Wickedness knows no boundaries. Jeremiah said:

> **The heart is deceitful above all things, and desperately wicked: who can know it? (Jeremiah 17:9)**

This awful prophecy reveals to us the depth to which unbelieving depravity can take a man. Dr. John Philips wrote:

> *There is a lack of repentance man ward. John tells us, 'Neither repented they of their murders, nor of their sorceries, nor of their fornication, nor of their thefts.' What a picture of a crime oriented culture! Man has finally arrived at his goal--a government and culture in which permissiveness is the accepted norm and where all kinds of deviation and misbehavior are applauded and encouraged, a government presided*

> over by a fascinating but foul individual called the man of sin. (2 Th. 2:3)

Just think about it! The wicked have passed through the six seal judgments. They have heard the gospel preached. They have just come through the shocking disasters of the six trumpet judgments. Yet they **repented not.** They refuse to turn from their wicked ways and seek God. Oh! How stubborn and wicked man can be. What a picture of the way sin hardens the heart.

> **He, that being often reproved hardeneth his neck, shall suddenly be destroyed, and that without remedy. (Proverbs 29:1)**

Five characteristics are specially mentioned, showing the corrupt and immoral condition of society in the end times. We are no doubt seeing the precursor to these things in our own day.

The wicked **repented not of the works of their hands, that they should not worship devils, and idols of gold, and silver, and brass, and stone, and of wood: which neither can see, nor hear, nor walk. (Revelation 9:20)** When the sixth trumpet sounds devil worship will be at an all-time high. Please take note of how we are clearly told that the use and worship of idols is a demonic and devil-driven act. No wonder God's people are so seriously warned about idols.

> **Little children, keep yourselves from idols. (1 John 5:21)**

God's way of deliverance through the blood of Jesus will be rejected and there will be open idol worship. It is hard to believe that men worship the devil, but they do. Paul said:

> **But I say, that the things which the Gentiles sacrifice, they sacrifice to devils, and not to God: and I would not that ye should have fellowship with devils. Ye cannot drink the cup of the Lord, and the cup of devils: ye cannot be partakers of the Lord's table, and of the table of devils. (1 Cor. 10:20-21)**

Today we easily see Satan getting the world ready for the manifestation of the man of sin, the wicked one, (2 Thess. 2:7) and the heading up of iniquity as in the days of Noah.

Neither repented they of their murders... (Revelation 9:21a) Man places little value on human life, unless it is his own. Violence and bloodshed have increased, and murder has actually become big business, with over 4,000 babies murdered every day in America. May we remember that life is sacred to God and man will answer to Him. (Genesis 9:6) Remember all the martyrs that John saw in Heaven? These are all believers slaughtered by the antichrist and his followers. The martyrs were so many that the Bible says, **no man could number. (Revelation 7:9)** While we see a blatant disregard for human life now, it will be much worse during the tribulation.

Nor of their sorceries... (Revelation 9:21b) The word for **sorceries** is the Greek word *"pharmakeia."* It is the word from which the English word *"pharmacy"* is derived. It is a word that has to do with dealing and dabbling with drugs. It involves dealing with witchcraft, magical arts, potions, and incantations. In this context it would include all forms of sorcery including astrology, palm reading, seances, fortune telling, crystals, and other forms of witchcraft. God has again and again warned His people against familiar spirits, enchanters, witches, magicians, sorcerers, etc. In the days when Jesus was on earth these demons, called wicked and unclean spirits, were abundant, and sought for embodiment in men. They were manifest in Paul's day:

> **Then certain of the vagabond Jews, exorcists, took upon them to call over them which had evil spirits the name of the Lord Jesus, saying, We adjure you by Jesus whom Paul preacheth. And there were seven sons of one Sceva, a Jew, and chief of the priests, which did so. And the evil spirit answered and said, Jesus I know, and Paul I know; but who are ye? And the man in whom the evil spirit was leaped on them, and overcame them,**

> **and prevailed against them, so that they fled out of that house naked and wounded. (Acts 19:13-16)**

The same is also very real in our own day. Sad to say, even Christians are dabbling in demonism. (Astrology, Hypnotism, Rock music, etc.) The whole thing is contrary to the Word of God and makes people a prey to Satan's power and deceit.

Nor of their fornication... (Revelation 9:21c) The tribulation will be a time when the laws of God mean nothing to people. Sexual sin will engulf the world. We are now seeing attempts to redefine and restructure the family after that of the world. Even now the practice of free love and easy divorce abound. *"Can't make it in marriage—just quit." "Unwanted pregnancy—get an abortion."* Physical fornication is a picture of the spiritual fornication that is a major problem in this world today.

> **Ye adulterers and adulteresses, know ye not that the friendship of the world is enmity with God? whosoever therefore will be a friend of the world is the enemy of God. (James 4:4)**

Nor of their thefts. (Revelation 9:21d) Stealing is a worldwide problem already. Thieving, robbery and burglary run rampant. Young people are being killed on our streets for nothing more than a jacket or a boom box. Even now in our country we see children and teenagers as well as adults filling the courts and jails of our land because of shoplifting. But, during the tribulation it will be much worse, if one could imagine that.

Surely, the picture of the world during the time of the great tribulation is exceedingly dark. The world will not be converted as many claim, but will be given over to demon worship, idolatry, and spiritism. They will be steeped in licentiousness and sin. It will be a world filled with violence and bloodshed. Surely anyone looking out upon the world today with its outbursts of war, strikes, overflowing prisons, divorces, and pleasure-mad men cannot help realizing that we are fast approaching the awful tribulation period. The Bible proves itself true over and over (Jeremiah 17:9).

TIME NO LONGER
Revelation 10:1-11

Chapter 10:1-11:13 forms another parenthetical passage that lies between the sixth and seventh trumpets. Two of the terrible woes have been carried out and one is coming soon. The parenthetical passage shows us some things that are happening between the second and third woe. So far, we have seen the terror of the six trumpet judgments with one more trumpet yet to sound to complete these seven particular judgments. These events will further devastate the earth and those that therein at that time.

THE DESCENDING ANGEL

And I saw another mighty angel come down from heaven, clothed with a cloud; and a rainbow was upon his head, and his face was as it were the Sun, and his feet as pillars of fire. (Revelation 10:1) John introduces another angel that is different from the seven blowing the trumpets. The first thing we notice in this chapter is John's vision shifts from heaven to earth when he sees a messenger from Heaven. Thus, our attention is drawn first, to the **mighty angel** which John saw come down from Heaven. This is not an ordinary angel by any means. The angel is described in the first verse. There are many expositors who believe this Mighty Angel to be Christ (Oliver B. Greene, William Pettingill, M. R. DeHaan, H. A. Ironside, Dr. Henry Morris). Along with the angel's description, in chapter 11:3, He refers to the two witnesses as **my two witnesses.** There are seven things about this Angel that helps us discern his identity:

1. This Angel is mighty.
2. This Angel came down from Heaven.
3. This Angel is clothed with a cloud.
4. The face of this Angel is like the sun.

5. The feet of this Angel are as pillars of fire.
6. He has in His hand a little book open.
7. He stands with one foot on the land and one on the sea- denoting universal ownership and authority.

This certainly supports the view that this Angel is none other than our Lord Jesus Christ. Keep in mind that the word angel is used of men, of spirit beings, and of Deity. It sometimes speaks more of a title than of a nature. And keep in mind that Jesus is described in Scripture as the Angel of the Lord. From the description given here, it is plainly evident that this was no ordinary angel; for he is described as a **mighty angel.**

There is a striking resemblance between the description of this **mighty angel** and the glorified Christ described in chapter one of Revelation. From the description and the symbolism used here it is evident that the angel referred to was not an ordinary created angel, but none other than the Lord Jesus Christ Himself. In the Old Testament Jesus often appeared as the ...

> Angel of God (Genesis 21:17, 31:11; Exodus 14:19; Judges 6:20).

Therefore, we can conclude that there is no problem whatsoever in believing that the Angel referred to here is none other than the Lord Jesus Christ.

THE DAZZLING APPEARANCE

This mighty angel is ... **clothed with a cloud; and a rainbow was upon his head, and his face was as it were the sun, and his feet as pillars of fire. (Revelation 10:1)** What a sight! There are several truths to be learned in this passage. Here we see here a four-fold description of this mighty angel.

His Clothing

We see Him descending and **clothed with a cloud. (Revelation 10:1b)** In Scripture clouds are associated with the presence and majesty of the Almighty. The cloud was of old, the garment of Divine presence. We are told of God that:

> He maketh the clouds His chariot. (Psalm 104:3)

The Lord led Israel by day in:
> ... a pillar of a cloud. (Exodus 13:21)

When Israel murmured:
> ... the glory of the LORD appeared in the cloud. (Exodus 16:10)

At Sinai He descended in:
> ... a thick cloud. (Exodus 19:9,16)

When the tables of stone were renewed to replace the broken ones:
> The LORD descended in the cloud. (Exodus 34:4-5)

When the tabernacle was completed:
> ... a cloud covered the tent of the congregation, and the glory of the LORD filled the tabernacle. (Exodus 40:34)

This cloud was called the:
> ... cloud of the LORD. (Exodus 40:38)

God had said:
> ... I will appear in the cloud upon the mercy seat. (Leviticus 16:2)

On the Mount Of Transfiguration:
> A bright cloud overshadowed them: and behold a voice out of the cloud, which said, This is My beloved Son, in whom I am well pleased; hear ye Him. (Matthew 17:5)

Also, when Christ ascended into Heaven, we are told that:
> ... a cloud received Him. (Acts 1:9)

Of His second coming we read:
> They shall see the Son of Man coming in a cloud with power and great glory. (Luke 21:27)
> Behold, He cometh with clouds. (Revelation 1:7)

For man's protection, God veils Himself in the clouds when appearing before sinful men who cannot, in their present condition, look upon His unveiled glory. Being clothed with a cloud denotes His majesty. The day, however, is coming when all His children will see Him as He is—in His glorified state (1 John 3:1-3). What a day that will be!

His Covenant

... a rainbow was upon his head... (Revelation 10:1c) We have already studied about the rainbow in chapter four. Rainbow is a reminder that He is a God who keeps His covenants (Genesis 9:12-17). There we saw a rainbow round about the Throne that was in Heaven. The presence of the rainbow upon the head of this Mighty Angel shows that He is associated with the Throne of God. As we have already learned, the rainbow is a sign or symbol of God's grace and mercy. The rainbow shines brightest against the darkest clouds, and no matter how severe the storm, the rainbow reminds us of the fact that God will remember mercy in the midst of judgment. Even during the outpouring of His wrath, He will still save anyone who will call upon and receive His offer of salvation. The rainbow is a reminder that God keeps His Word.

His Countenance

And his face was as it were the sun... (Revelation 10:1d) The face of this Mighty Angel was like the sun. The idea here is that this angel's face shines with the glory of God. John had before said of Him:

> **... as the sun shineth in his strength. (Revelation 1:16)**

When Peter, James and John saw Him in His glory on the Mount of Transfiguration:

> **His face did shine as the sun. (Matthew 17:2)**

His appearance to Saul of Tarsus was:

> **... above the brightness of the sun. (Acts 26:13)**

The prophet Malachi speaks of Him as **the Sun of righteousness,** yet to arise with healing in His wings. (Malachi

4:2). Dr. Henry Morris in his book, The Revelation Record states that *the glory of the sun is a picture of the glory of Jesus Christ who is the light of the world (John 8:12).* As the bright shining sun scatters the darkness, so does this angel's face shine into the dark corners of man's existence. Nothing will escape His penetrating look.

His Condemnation

And his feet as pillars of fire. (Revelation 10:1e) Earlier His feet had been spoken of as **fine brass** burning in a furnace (Revelation 1:15). We saw back there that the brass symbolizes judgment and indicates that by judgment He will take possession of all that was lost due to sin and wickedness will be put away. Thus, His feet **as pillars of fire** indicate he is come to execute judgment

THE DEFINITE AUTHORITY

We know that because of man's sin the earth was cursed, and Satan came into temporary possession of the earth. Satan is looked upon as ...

... the god of this world. (2 Corinthians 4:4)

However, his is a usurped authority and will not last long. In this passage we see the Lord Jesus Christ laying claim to that which Satan has tried to take. Notice two things concerning Christ's authority.

His Claim

And He had in His hand a little book open: and He set His right foot upon the sea, and his left foot upon the earth. (Revelation 10:2) As He descends from heaven, He does a significant thing. We have already seen the seven sealed Book back in chapter five. In our study of that portion of Revelation we found that the seven sealed book was a book of redemption. In other words, this book represented the title deed of the universe which was forfeited by Adam when he sinned back in the Garden of Eden, and which was to be recovered by the Lion of the Tribe of Judah, the root of David, who also was found worthy to lose the seven seals and open the book. This **little book** comprised the impending mission of the Lord Jesus Christ. Jesus holds the title deed to the world, and He is in the process of repossessing the world from Satan.

Notice that this Mighty Angel came down with the open book in His hand and set His right foot on the sea and His left foot upon the earth. This is very significant. Jesus Christ is about to take possession of what is rightfully His.

Our Lord steps out of Heaven onto the earth and sea. His right foot is placed upon the sea and His left upon the earth. This is a sign of taking possession and ownership. He is officially claiming the sea and earth as His. This is a declaration that He is about to redeem creation. This truth is seen in God's dealing with Abraham concerning His promise to give the land of Canaan to him and his descendants. God told Abraham to:

> **Arise, walk through the land in the length of it and in the breadth of it; for I will give it unto thee. (Genesis 13:17)**

When Joshua was preparing to claim the promised land, he was assured that:

> **Every place that the sole of your foot shall tread upon, that have I given unto you, as I said unto Moses. (Joshua 1:3)**

We know that:

> **The earth is the LORD'S, and the fulness thereof; the world, and they that dwell therein. (Psalm 24:1)**

All of it belongs to Him by right of creation.

> **All things were made by Him, and without Him was not anything made that was made. (John 1:3)**

Satan loses! By this act of setting His feet upon the land and the sea, The Sovereign Creator is laying claim to that which is rightly His.

His Cry

Now we are told that He **cried with a loud voice as when a lion roareth. (Revelation 10:3)** This is the mighty and majestic voice of our God. It is a voice that is vividly described in Scripture. (Psalm 29:1-11) He cries with a voice like a lion, the king of beasts, and He is indeed **the Lion of the tribe of Judah.** Jeremiah prophesied this event (Jeremiah 25:29–31).

And when he had cried, seven thunders uttered their voices. And when the seven thunders had uttered their voices, I was about to write: and I heard a voice from heaven saying unto me, Seal up those things which the seven thunders uttered, and write them not. (Revelation 10:3b-4) Heaven immediately responds to the voice. The seven thunders are no doubt the voice of God the Father. Thunder is clearly a type of God's voice in judgment.

> **... the LORD thundered with a great thunder on that day upon the Philistines, and discomfited them; and they were smitten before Israel. (1 Samuel 7:10b)**

The Psalmist wrote:

> **The LORD also thundered in the heavens, and the Highest gave his voice; hail stones and coals of fire. (Psalm 18:13)**

When God the Father spoke to Jesus on earth the people who heard it thought that it was thunder (John 12:28-29). The mighty voice of God us deafening. Job said:

> **God thundereth marvellously with his voice; (Job 37:5)**

No doubt the Lion's roar had something to do with Divine judgment. However, as John was about to write what the thunder had uttered, he was expressly forbidden to do so. To this day the words are unwritten and unknown. There are some things that we are not allowed to know (Deuteronomy 29:29). The Apostle Paul saw things that were unlawful for him to utter on earth. (2 Corinthians 12:4).

THE DREADFUL ANNOUNCEMENT

The Lord Jesus Christ raises his hand up towards heaven and swears an oath in the name of our God the Father Who created the heaven, the sea, and the earth and everything in between them, that God will wait no longer. Here we see that time has run out for the world. There will be no further delay in God's plans to judge the world.

The Dominating Angel

And the angel which I saw stand upon the sea and upon the earth lifted up his hand to heaven, (Revelation 10:5) The Angels position of standing emphasizes His sovereignty and dominion over all creation. The act of lifting up His hand to Heaven signals that He is about to take an oath.

> **Yet have I set my king upon my holy hill of Zion. I will declare the decree: the LORD hath said unto me, Thou art my Son; this day have I begotten thee. Ask of me, and I shall give thee the heathen for thine inheritance, and the uttermost parts of the earth for thy possession. (Psalm 2:6-8)**

God is going to take back what is rightfully His The angel had his right foot on the sea and his left foot on the land indicating His authoritative right of over the earth.

The Dreadful Announcement

And sware by him that liveth for ever and ever, who created heaven, and the things that therein are, and the earth, and the things that therein are, and the sea, and the things which are therein, that there should be time no longer: (Revelation 10:6) Now this Mighty Angel, the Lord Jesus Christ, makes a startling announcement. He lifts His hand to heaven and declares that **there should be time no longer.** The word time carries the idea of delay. God in His grace and mercy has been delaying His judgments giving lost sinners time to be saved.

> **The Lord is not slack concerning his promise, as some men count slackness; but is longsuffering to us-ward, not willing that any should perish, but that all should come to repentance. (2 Peter 3:9)**

The day is coming when there will no more delay in judgment and the carrying out of God's purposes. This is a most solemn time. At this point, the angel swears that there will be no further delay in God's judgment upon the world.

The Divine Anger

But in the days of the voice of the seventh angel, when he shall begin to sound, the mystery of God should be finished, as he hath declared to his servants the prophets. (Revelation 10:7) Here we see the sequence of the order of events when the purposes of God will be accomplished. We are told that it will take place **in the days of the voice of the seventh angel.** The announcement of the seventh trumpet judgment lead to the outpouring of the seven vials of divine wrath upon the earth and its inhabitants. The fulfillment of all the divine purposes of God are at hand.

THE DIRECT ASSIGNMENT

And the voice which I heard from heaven spake unto me again, and said, Go and take the little book which is open in the hand of the angel which standeth upon the sea and upon the earth. And I went unto the angel, and said unto him, Give me the little book. And he said unto me, Take it, and eat it up; and it shall make thy belly bitter, but it shall be in thy mouth sweet as honey. (Revelation 10:8-9) The voice of God came again to John instructing him to go and take the scroll from the angel. John obeyed immediately, (immediately is the best way to obey when God speaks). When John received the scroll, he received further orders as well.

Take it, and eat it up; and it shall make thy belly bitter, but it shall be in thy mouth sweet as honey. And I took the little book out of the angel's hand, and ate it up; and it was in my mouth sweet as honey: and as soon as I had eaten it, my belly was bitter. And he said unto me, Thou must prophesy again before many peoples, and nations, and tongues, and kings. (Revelation 10:9b-11) John was told to eat this book. Of course, this was not literal eating, but a mental assessment and learning, concerning the contents of the scroll.

> **How sweet are thy words unto my taste! yea, sweeter than honey to my mouth! Through thy precepts I get understanding: therefore I hate every false way. (Psalm 119:103-104)**

When John did **eat** the book, it was both bitter and sweet. Remember that this book is the title deed to the universe. It contains the conditions and judgments of Christ that will be carried out when He reclaims His creation. As with Ezekiel (Ezekiel 3:1-5), when John had meditated upon the contents of this scroll there was a sweetness about it. There will be a sweetness of the Lord in His glory when He takes possession of earth and puts things back as they were. However, in John's case, there was bitterness associated with God's judgment.

THE TEMPLE MEASURED
Revelation 11:1-2

It has been almost two-thousand years since the Jews have had a Temple in which to sacrifice and worship. It is the prayer and desire of every orthodox Jew to see the Temple rebuilt and Jewish worship restored.

At least three temples have been built in Jerusalem and destroyed. Solomon built one as described in 1 King chapter 8. This one was destroyed by Nebuchadnezzar around 583 B.C. After the Babylonian captivity, some of the Jews returned to Jerusalem and built the second Temple under Zerubbabel's leadership. This Temple was later destroyed by Antiochus Epiphanes.

During Christ's time on earth, Herod's temple was standing, but later was destroyed by Titus of Rome in 70 A.D. All that is left of the temple today are the lower three rows of stones known as the wailing wall. This is where orthodox Jews meet and pray regularly for the coming of their Messiah and the rebuilding of their Temple.

Since A. D. 691 the Temple site has been occupied by the Islamic Mosque known as the Dome of the Rock. Muslims erroneously believe this to be the place where Mohammed ascended to heaven on the winged horse. However, this is the place where the future Temple will be built. We know that the temple will be rebuilt, and the sacrificial system of Jewish worship restored during the first half of the tribulation period. Make no mistake about it, the Temple will be built in Jerusalem, the Holy City of Good. God is not finished with the Jewish people, as some erroneously teach. The seven years of the Tribulation Period will be a time of God's renewal of the nation of Israel.

It is possible that we could Temple rebuilt before the Rapture of the Church. It is also possible that the Temple could be built at the beginning of the Tribulation. The Word of God tells us that the antichrist will sign a seven-year peace treaty with Israel at the beginning of the Tribulation period.

> **And he shall confirm the covenant with many for one week: and in the midst of the week he shall cause the sacrifice and the oblation to cease, and for the overspreading of abominations he shall make it desolate, even until the consummation, and that determined shall be poured upon the desolate. (Daniel 9:27)**

This section opens with John's first mention of the temple which will be rebuilt before or early in the first part of the Tribulation Period. According to Daniel the Jews will be permitted to offer sacrifices in the temple for the first half of the Tribulation Period. Everything will look good for three and a half years. Then in the middle if the Tribulation the antichrist will set himself up as God in the Temple and demand to be worshiped (Matthew 24:15; Mark 13:14; 2 Thessalonians 2:4). At the same time, Gentile forces will tread Jerusalem under foot (Psalm 55:9-11; Isaiah 63:18; Joel 3:2-5).

It should also be noted that the second half of the Tribulation Period begins here. God is preparing to pour out His judgment and reclaim that which is His. The Word of God Is clear that all of this is going to take place. Oliver B. Greene says ...

> *In this chapter, God is about to take possession of what belongs to Him. The earth is the Lord's, it was created by Him and for Him-but it has been under Satanic control for six thousand years. God gave Adam dominion over all creation and made him dictator of the universe, but he sold out to the devil. God gave Adam a command which he deliberately disobeyed, thereby losing everything God had entrusted to him. One of these glorious days the second Adam (Christ) will redeem all that the first Adam lost, including the earth and all creation.*

The Temple Measured

The measuring of the Temple is an act that denotes a spiritual assessment. Mark it down! The Temple will be rebuilt in Jerusalem by the Jews sometime around the Rapture of the Church. It will be built where the Mosque of Omar now stands. God will evaluate the Temple as He prepares to begin the second half of the Tribulation Period. Chapter 11 focuses on the nation of Israel as references are made concerning the Millennial Temple of God, to the altar, to the worshippers, to the outer courtyard, to the Holy City of Jerusalem, and the two prophets. This reminds us that the Tribulation Period does not pertain to the Church, but to Israel.

THE COMMAND

And there was given me a reed like unto a rod: and the angel stood, saying, Rise, and measure the temple of God, and the altar, and them that worship therein. (Revelation 11:1) John is now instructed to take a reed and measure the temple. He is also instructed to measure the altar and the place where the people worship. A similar measuring rod was used by the Prophet Ezekiel.

> **And he brought me thither, and, behold, there was a man, whose appearance was like the appearance of brass, with a line of flax in his hand, and a measuring reed; and he stood in the gate. And the man said unto me, Son of man, behold with thine eyes, and hear with thine ears, and set thine heart upon all that I shall shew thee; for to the intent that I might shew them unto thee art thou brought hither: declare all that thou seest to the house of Israel. And behold a wall on the outside of the house round about, and in the man's hand a measuring reed of six cubits long by the cubit and an hand breadth: so he measured the breadth of the building, one reed; and the height, one reed. (Ezekiel 40:3-5)**

The Temple, the Altar, the worshippers, and the Court referred to in this passage, do not refer to the Church, but rather to the rebuilding of the Jewish Temple in Jerusalem. We have no problem recognizing that we are on Jewish ground. A new survey is about to be conducted. A measuring reed is seen. This is like a rod, which also carries with it the thought of correction.

> **I will cause you to pass under the rod, and I will bring you into the bond of the covenant. And I will purge out from among you the rebels and them that transgress against me: I will bring them forth out of the country where they sojourn, and they shall not enter into the land of Israel; and ye shall know that I am the Lord. (Ezekiel 20:37-38)**

Rise, and measure the temple of God, and the altar, and them that worship therein. (Revelation 11:1b) This temple of God here is a literal one, with an altar and worshippers. It shows the nation of Israel gathered back into their own land, the temple rebuilt, their altar set up, and worship reinstated. You say, "Preacher, the mosque of Omar now sits on the Temple mound." I agree. However, it won't stand there much longer. The day is coming when God will miraculously remove the mosque and His Temple will be rebuilt. The Jews will once again worship in their Temple in Jerusalem. However, they will be interrupted by the antichrist.

> **Let no man deceive you by any means: for that day shall not come, except there come a falling away first, and that man of sin be revealed, the son of perdition; (2 Thessalonians 2:3)**

Trying days are before them, for in this temple is to be the abomination of desolation.

> **When ye therefore shall see the abomination of desolation, spoken of by Daniel the prophet, stand in the holy place, (whoso readeth, let him understand:) (Matthew 24:15)**

During the Tribulation antichrist will take possession of the temple, claiming to be God, he will demand to be worshiped. He is driven by Satan and desperately desires the worship that belongs only to God.

THE COURT

But the court which is without the temple leave out, and measure it not; for it is given unto the Gentiles... (Revelation 11:2a) John was to take a measuring reed and measure the temple, altar and those that worship there. Henry Morris says,

> *This measurement of the temple and its worshipers is obviously a spiritual evaluation.*

The outer court of this temple was to be left out. The reason for this is given, **for it is given unto the Gentiles.** Notice that these verses speak of Jews and Gentiles. Let's keep in mind that the whole idea of the Temple is strictly Jewish. Again, the Church is not mentioned because the tribulation has nothing to do with the Church.

THE CONTEMPT

And the holy city shall they tread under foot forty and two months. (Revelation 11:2b) How plain and significant the language of Scripture! The place is identified as **the holy city**. There can be no doubt as to which city is meant. It is Jerusalem—God's city.

> **Awake, awake; put on thy strength, O Zion; put on thy beautiful garments, O Jerusalem, the holy city. (Isaiah 52:1)**
>
> **Many of the saints which slept arose and came up out of their graves after His resurrection and went into the holy city. (Matthew 27:52-53)**

Now **forty and two months** are three and one-half years. We know that the Tribulation Period is a seven-year span of time. The **forty and two months** is the length of the Great Tribulation. This is to be taken literally. It is forty-two months of thirty days each. The Tribulation Period is divided into two parts. The last three and one-half years is referred to by the Lord Jesus as the Great Tribulation

For then shall be great tribulation, such as was not since the beginning of the world to this time, no, nor ever shall be. (Matthew 24:21)

The destruction of this Temple will take place in the middle of the Tribulation. This time known as the Great Tribulation will only last for the forty-two-month period and culminate with the Second Coming of Christ in His Glory.

Also, in the book of Ezekiel, we find a great deal of information concerning God's people and the Millennial Temple. From chapter forty thru forty-eight of Ezekiel, there are plans and specifications for the rebuilding of the Temple in Jerusalem.

THE TWO WITNESSES
Revelation 11:3-14

In this section, we are at the mid-point of the Tribulation Period. God introduces us to His two witnesses. The antichrist has just entered the temple and sat on the throne of God and proclaimed himself to be God. He is the one who ...

> **Who opposeth and exalteth himself above all that is called God, or that is worshipped; so that he as God sitteth in the temple of God, shewing himself that he is God. (2 Thessalonians 2:4)**

Daniel refers to this as the abomination of desolation and the Antichrist just committed it.

> **And he shall confirm the covenant with many for one week: and in the midst of the week he shall cause the sacrifice and the oblation to cease, and for the overspreading of abominations he shall make it desolate, even until the consummation, and that determined shall be poured upon the desolate. (Daniel 9:27)**

> **And arms shall stand on his part, and they shall pollute the sanctuary of strength, and shall take away the daily sacrifice, and they shall place the abomination that maketh desolate. (Daniel 11:31)**

> **And from the time that the daily sacrifice shall be taken away, and the abomination that maketh desolate set up, there shall be a thousand two hundred and ninety days. (Daniel 12:11)**

The two witnesses go forth preaching the Word of God during these troublous times. Some have presented these tow witness as symbolic figures, but we will see that they are not symbolic but two actual men who are God's sent messengers. We are dealing with the Jews in this passage. Jewish law required that at least two witnesses give evidence in cases concerning matters of law, religion, and the dealings of men with one another.

> **One witness shall not rise up against a man for any iniquity, or for any sin, in any sin that he sinneth: at the mouth of two witnesses, or at the mouth of three witnesses, shall the matter be established. (Deuteronomy 19:15)**

You will recall that there were two angels at the tomb of Jesus the morning of His resurrection (John 20:12). There were two men who appeared to the disciples at the Lord's ascension (Acts 1:9-10). When witnessing, Jesus sent the seventy out two by two (Luke 10:1). Likewise, during the Tribulation Period God will send two witnesses to prophesy 1,260 days. We notice several truths concerning these two witnesses.

THEIR PERSONALITY

Two witnesses now appear on the scene. The attempt to identify these witnesses have resulted in a great deal of confusion and speculation. There are all sorts of ideas about these witnesses. Someone has said that Calvin and Luther are in view here. Some have attempted to explain these two witnesses as law and grace, the Old and New Testaments, and various other strange interpretations. However, we will see that they are not symbolic. God refers to them as **my two witnesses.** These are two living witnesses that will be sent by God for witness and preach the gospel.

THEIR PERSONAGE

And I will give power unto my two witnesses, (Revelation 11:3a) Again, we do not look at these two men symbolically. These are real men who are alive and minister during the Tribulation Period. They speak, they have mouths, they preach, they are heard and hated, they have bodies, and they die. There is no way to refer to these two as anything other than two actual witnesses. We notice from the beginning that God calls these men **my two witnesses.**

The Two Witnesses

The word **power** speaks of God's authority and Divine enabling. These men have been enabled by God to witnesses on the earth. They will be given great authority to do whatever is necessary in their ministry. They will have power over nature and Satan and his followers can do nothing to stop them until they are finished. They are as blazing lights shining in the darkness of the world. They are God's witnesses who go forth and preach during the Great Tribulation. These witnesses have a single purpose. They have been given the power of God to preach the Word.

THEIR PROPHECY

... and they shall prophesy a thousand two hundred and threescore days, clothed in sackcloth. These are the two olive trees, and the two candlesticks standing before the God of the earth. (Revelation 11:3b-4) These two witnesses will come on the scene and prophesy for **a thousand two hundred and threescore days** [1260 days, 42 months]. They will be dressed in sackcloth. Sackcloth is a sign of mourning and grief. They are grieved because of the reign of the Antichrist and the wickedness of the people.

According to the Jewish calendar this is exactly a three and one-half years. This will be the last half of the Tribulation period. The first half will be a time of false peace. The antichrist will lead the world. It will be a time of peace and prosperity. As we saw earlier, in the middle of the seven years, the antichrist will enter into the Temple and demand to be worshipped as God. This is what Jesus called the ...

... abomination of desolation. (Matthew 24:15)

The temple will be desecrated and defiled at this point. Hence, the wrath of God will be kindle and the temple destroyed. This will take place at the beginning of the Great Tribulation.

For then shall be great tribulation, such as was not since the beginning of the world to this time, no, nor ever shall be. (Matthew 24:21)

This will be a time of fierce judgment upon this world. Mark it down! There is coming a day when God will unleash His wrath and fury and execute His relentless judgment upon the unbelieving world.

THEIR POWER

As we saw in verse 3, God gives these two witnesses remarkable power. Not only will these men have the power to witness for the Lord during the last half of the Tribulation Period, they will also have the authority to impose judgment and vengeance upon those who harm them.

Their Indignation

And if any man will hurt them, fire proceedeth out of their mouth, and devoureth their enemies: and if any man will hurt them, he must in this manner be killed. (Revelation 11:5) These two witnesses have been given great supernatural power from God. Remember, they will be prophesying during times of great hostility towards Israel. The antichrist will be raging and persecuting God's people with full force. As these two witnesses preach the gospel, great numbers of people will turn to Christ. Thus, they will become target of Satan and the antichrist. Anyone who harms them will be destroyed by fire.

Their Identification

These have power to shut heaven, that it rain not in the days of their prophecy: and have power over waters to turn them to blood, and to smite the earth with all plagues, as often as they will. (Revelation 11:6) The power that these two men display says a lot about their identity. There is much discussion as to who the two witnesses are. Some say they are Elijah and Enoch. They base their view on (Hebrews 9:27).

... It is appointed unto men once to die.

This leads them to conclude that since Enoch and Elijah were the only two men to leave this world without dying, they must be the two witnesses. This is faulty reasoning. May I remind you that at the Rapture of the Church a great multitude will ascend to Heaven without dying (1 Thessalonians 4:16-17). Nothing about

The Two Witnesses

these two witnesses has anything to do with whether or not these two men have ever died or whether they entered Heaven without death. Death is not the issue. The issue here is that these men are God's witnesses to and against the Jewish people in the last half of the tribulation.

> **One witness shall not rise up against a man for any iniquity, or for any sin, in any sin that he sinneth: at the mouth of two witnesses, or at the mouth of three witnesses, shall the matter be established. (Deuteronomy 19:15)**

According to Jewish law God sends two witnesses to His people during the tribulation period. These witnesses preach the gospel and have the supernatural power of God to smite the earth with plagues as in the days of Moses and to call down fire as Elijah did. The two witnesses deal in fire and blood, the characteristics of Elijah (2 King 1:7-14, James 5:17-18), and Moses. (Exodus 7:20; 8:1; 12:29).

One of the witnesses' identities can easily be discerned from Scripture. This witness is Elijah. In the book of Malachi, we learn that Elijah's ministry will bring many to Christ during the Tribulation Period.

> **Behold, I will send you Elijah the prophet before the coming of the great and dreadful day of the LORD: And he shall turn the heart of the fathers to the children, and the heart of the children to their fathers, lest I come and smite the earth with a curse. (Malachi 4:5–6)**

So, one of the witnesses is certainly Elijah. The second witness is Moses. It was Moses whom God used to lead Israel out of their worst physical bondage and Elijah that God used to deliver them from a time of great spiritual bondage. Here during the tribulation, God will once again use these two men to deliver Israel, but this time, once and for all. Moses and Elijah are connected with the second coming of Christ on the Mount of transfiguration (Matthew 17:1-5 and 2 Peter 1:10-19). These two witnesses are Moses and Elijah returned to earth to witness during the Great Tribulation period.

These two witnesses will be missionaries on the streets of Jerusalem for **a thousand two hundred and threescore days.** For three and a half years these prophets of God will preach the Gospel bringing many Jewish people to Christ.

THEIR PERSECUTION

These two preachers will face intense persecution during their ministry. They are disliked, despised, and detested.

The Completion Of Their Mission

And when they shall have finished their testimony, (Revelation 11:7a) The two witnesses were faithful to the finish. Regardless of all the persecution, troubles, and resistance, they **finished their testimony.** These men finished well! They fulfilled the work for which they were called. Like the Apostle Paul they could say ...

> I have fought a good fight, I have finished my course, I have kept the faith: (2 Timothy 4:7)

What an example of what God expects from every believer. Every Christian ought to have a sincere desire to fulfill their calling. There are too many professing believers who start well, but do not finish well. Let's finish our course!

The Culprit In Their Murder

... the beast that ascendeth out of the bottomless pit shall make war against them, and shall overcome them, and kill them. (Revelation 11:7b) As we come to the midpoint of the tribulation period, we see these two faithful witnesses come to the end of their ministry. For 3½ years they have faithfully persevered, preached, and prevailed with the power of God. No man has been able to overcome them, but now the Beast has come upon the scene. This Beast is the antichrist, the head of the revived Roman Empire. He has entered into the Temple of God and declared that he is God and demanded to be worshipped as God thus desecrating the Templar. Though these witnesses are hated with a vengeance, no power on earth or in Hell can touch them until they have finished their testimony. Nothing or no one will be able to harm these witnesses until they have completed their work. When we are obedient unto the call of God, He will preserve us in our work.

The Contempt Of Their Mockery

And their dead bodies shall lie in the street of the great city, which spiritually is called Sodom and Egypt, where also our Lord was crucified. (Revelation 11:8a) These two witnesses were disrespected and dishonored even after their death. Leaving a body lie without burial was the greatest contempt that could be expressed in Bible times.

... of the great city, which spiritually is called Sodom and Egypt, (Revelation 11:8b) The character and spiritual condition of the city of Jerusalem is distinctly described by the terms **Sodom and Egypt.** Both of these places were centers of unbelief and wickedness, and both were abominations to God.

... where also our Lord was crucified. (Revelation 11:8c) In the city of Jerusalem, **where our Lord was crucified,** the dead bodies of these two witnesses will lie in the street. Prophets and preachers through the years have faced the most awful treatment. Jesus said:

> **O Jerusalem, Jerusalem, which killest the prophets, and stonest them that are sent unto thee... (Luke 13:34a)**

These two witnesses lie dead in the streets and are even deprived of a burial. David had prophesied this very event:

> **The dead bodies of thy servants have they given to be meat unto the fowls of the heaven, the flesh of thy saints unto the beasts of the earth. Their blood have they shed like water round about Jerusalem; and there was none to bury them. (Psalm 79:23)**

For three and one-half days, a day for every year of their testimony, they are refused even a decent burial, and lay in the streets of Jerusalem, where their enemies can see and rejoice over their death. It is the mark of the vicious hatred of their enemies. By decree of the Mosaic law, even criminals were to be buried the same day they were executed.

> And if a man have committed a sin worthy of death, and he be to be put to death, and thou hang him on a tree: His body shall not remain all night upon the tree, but thou shalt in any wise bury him that day; (for he that is hanged is accursed of God;) that thy land be not defiled, which the LORD thy God giveth thee for an inheritance. (Deuteronomy 21:22-23)

The way these preachers were treated in life and death reveals the utter hated of the world for God's people. Jesus warned:

> If the world hate you, ye know that it hated me before it hated you. (John 15:18)

The word **world** comes from *"kosmos"* and speaks of the unbelieving world system that is opposed to God and His people. The word **hate** comes from *"miseo"* and carries the idea of extreme animosity. It is a hatred that results in bitter hostility.

The Celebration Of Madness

And they that dwell upon the earth shall rejoice over them, and make merry, and shall send gifts one to another; because these two prophets tormented them that dwelt on the earth. (Revelation 11:10) Something is seriously wrong when the world celebrates the murder of good people. The wicked people to whom these two preachers were sent hated them with a passion. Now they are dead, and the world celebrates as if it is a great victory. These wicked people will actually throw a party and exchange gifts in honor of the Beast who defeated these tribulation preachers. This world has no love for the Christian. The Lord Jesus said:

> If the world hate you, ye know that it hated me before it hated you. If ye were of the world, the world would love his own: but because ye are not of the world, but I have chosen you out of the world, therefore the world hateth you. (John 15:18-19)

Standing for God and staying by the truth is not always easy and oft time results in persecution. Notice that they are not harmed until they finish their testimony. God will not let anything interfere with their work as long as they stay in His will. What a comfort and encouragement to stand for the truth at any cost. The fastest way to stir things up is to stand by Jesus. The world hates Christ and they will hate those who stand with Him.

THEIR PREVAILING

After three and a half days a great miracle takes place the two faithful witnesses prevail. It looked as though all hope was gone, but God lifted them up and the victory was theirs. God always delivers His people.

The Resurrection

And after three days and an half the Spirit of life from God entered into them, and they stood upon their feet; (Revelation 11:11a) The deceived world presumes that they have won the victory. The bodies of their enemies lie in the street and a celebration is in progress. However, after 3½ days God will pour life back into their bodies and resurrect them. This great miracle that will take place before the unbelieving eyes of the world.

While they're watching the dead bodies and rejoicing because they're dead, the **Spirit of life from God entered into them** and there is a resurrection and a rapture. Imagine the looks on the faces of their enemies as the **spirit of life** enters into them and empowers them to stand up on their feet.

The Reaction

... and great fear fell upon them which saw them. (Revelation 11:11b) The party is over! As the world looked on, great fear fell upon them. In a moment's time the wicked went from a worldwide party to deep and gripping fear the next. Terror struck their hearts as the two prophets stood up and were raptured back to Heaven.

The Rapture

And they heard a great voice from heaven saying unto them, Come up hither. And they ascended up to heaven in a cloud; and their enemies beheld them. (Revelation 11:12)

God calls His faithful witnesses back to Heaven. As they ascend to heaven their enemies watch in amazement and fear. Their apparent victory crashes into defeat.

The Retribution

And the same hour was there a great earthquake, and the tenth part of the city fell, and in the earthquake were slain of men seven thousand: and the remnant were affrighted, and gave glory to the God of heaven. (Revelation 11:13) As the two witnesses disappear into a cloud a powerful earthquake hits the city The parties stop, and cries of terror take the place of laughter. There is no more gift giving and making merry. They are left without anything to rejoice over. They had failed to accept the message of God's redeeming grace. Not only have they rejected the message, but they have murdered the messengers. They must now face the God whom they have rejected.

> **It is a fearful thing to fall into the hands of the living God. (Hebrews 10:31)**

The wicked go on day by day as if they can get away with it, but payday is coming. Every man will answer directly to God.

The second woe is past; and, behold, the third woe cometh quickly. (Revelation 11:14) This **second woe** began with the sixth trumpet judgment and at this point is **past**. The **third woe** will come in the seventh trumpet judgment.

THE THIRD WOE
Revelation 11:15-19

The sounding of the seventh trumpet pronounces judgment that covers and continues throughout the last three and a half years of the Tribulation Period. In other words, the message of the seventh trumpet covers all that transpires during the last half of the tribulation, right up to the great and long-awaited event of the second coming of Jesus Christ. Jesus spoke of this time as the great tribulation.

> **For then shall be great tribulation, such as was not since the beginning of the world to this time, no, nor ever shall be. (Matthew 24:21)**

These three and a half years will be a time of the most severe and intense persecution of Jewish and Gentile believers. Many will be put to death for their faith by the forces of the anti-Christ

THE ANNOUNCEMENT OF HEAVEN

And the seventh angel sounded; and there were great voices in heaven, saying, The kingdoms of this world are become the kingdoms of our Lord, and of his Christ; and he shall reign for ever and ever. (Revelation 11:15) When the seventh angel sounds his trumpet, the loud and clear announcement is made that God will now overthrow the kingdoms of the world and establish in its place His everlasting kingdom. The Lord is taking back what rightfully belongs to Him.

> **The earth is the LORD'S, and the fulness thereof; the world, and they that dwell therein. (Psalm 24:1)**

A complete transfer of the Lordship will take place during the last half of the tribulation. Up to now God has been ignored and His Sovereign right to rule has been rejected by fallen man and the antichrist. However, all of that is about to come to an end.

Since the fall of man Satan has ruled this world. Keep in mind that Satan's authority is usurped. However, the kingdoms of this world now belong to Satan. He is the driving force behind the evil word system. Satan is called:

> ... the god of this world... (2 Corinthians 4:4)

Jesus called him the:

> ... prince of this world. (John 12:31; 14:30; 16:11)

Satan's dominion is a usurped one and it is about to come to an end. God is allowing Satan to have his own rule. But his rule will not last. The prophets of old spoke of this world being conquered by the coming Messiah.

> **And in the days of these kings shall the God of heaven set up a kingdom, which shall never be destroyed: and the kingdom shall not be left to other people, but it shall break in pieces and consume all these kingdoms, and it shall stand for ever. (Daniel 2:44)**
>
> **And there was given him dominion, and glory, and a kingdom, that all people, nations, and languages, should serve him: his dominion is an everlasting dominion, which shall not pass away, and his kingdom that which shall not be destroyed. (Daniel 7:14)**
>
> **And the LORD shall be king over all the earth: in that day shall there be one LORD, and his name one. (Zechariah 14:9)**

Paul spoke of this day as well.

> **Wherefore God also hath highly exalted him, and given him a name which is above every name: That at the name of Jesus every knee should bow, of things in heaven, and things in earth, and things under the earth; And that every tongue should confess that Jesus Christ is Lord, to the glory of God the Father. (Philippians 2:9-11)**

Man may think he is in charge and the Devil may act like the ruler of this world; however, it is only temporary. God is going to take back what rightfully belongs to Him.

The earth is the LORD'S, and the fulness thereof; the world, and they that dwell therein. (Psalm 24:1)

Although the transfer of Lordship is announced here, it does not happen immediately. Let us bear in mind the fact that when God determines a thing it is as though it were already done. All that transpires during the last half of the tribulation results in the change of authority from Satan to Jesus Christ. We will see all this come to fruition in chapters 20 and 21.

The kingdoms of this world are become the kingdoms of our Lord, and of his Christ; What a breathtaking proclamation! God has taken back His creation and the Lord Jesus shall reign forever and forever.

THE ADORATION OF THE ELDERS

And the four and twenty elders, which sat before God on their seats, fell upon their faces, and worshipped God, Saying, We give thee thanks, O Lord God Almighty, which art, and wast, and art to come; because thou hast taken to thee thy great power, and hast reigned. (Revelation 11:16-17) As this wonderful announcement is made the elders begin to sing songs of thanksgiving, adoration, and victory to Almighty God for His sovereign action in reclaiming the world and establishing His righteous reign. This will be a time of great joy in Heaven. This will be worshiped at its best. Take note of the three tenses referring to the Lord in verse 17. He was God, He is God, and this same God, our Lord Jesus Christ, is coming again to this earth to rule.

THE ANGER OF THE NATIONS

And the nations were angry, and thy wrath is come, and the time of the dead, that they should be judged, and that thou shouldest give reward unto thy servants the prophets, and to the saints, and them that fear thy name, small and

great; and shouldest destroy them which destroy the earth. (Revelation 11:18)** This ungodly world system and its people are angry with God. The things that result in rejoicing in Heaven stir up anger on earth. The anger of the world has increased in its intensity until they now boldly declare war against God even imagining that they can defeat Him.

Their attitude appears to be the same as the one Jesus gave in one of His parables.

But his citizens hated him, and sent a message after him, saying, We will not have this man to reign over us. (Luke 19:14)

The world wants nothing to do with Jesus. What a contrast! While Heaven rejoices in God's reign, the nations of the world express their anger. This depraved world is never happy with the things of God. They love darkness because their deeds are evil (John 3:19).

THE ARK OF HIS TESTAMENT

And the temple of God was opened in heaven, and there was seen in his temple the ark of his testament: and there were lightnings, and voices, and thunderings, and an earthquake, and great hail. (Revelation 11:19) The fact that we see the Temple and the Ark assures us that we are on Jewish ground. The Church has no temple. God is dealing with the Jews during the tribulation. This Ark is very significant in this scene. There are five names for the Ark in scripture.

1. *The Ark Of The Covenant* (Numbers 10:33). The ark of the covenant contained the Law of God. For there was a tabernacle made; the first, wherein was the candlestick, and the table, and the showbread; which is called the sanctuary. And after the second veil, the tabernacle which is called the Holiest of all; Which had the golden censer, and the Ark of the Covenant overlaid roundabout with gold, wherein was the golden pot that had manna, and Aaron's rod that budded, and the tables of the covenant. (Hebrews 9:2-4) The law was the schoolmaster (Galatians

3:24) designed by God to show Israel their need of Christ. The tables of the covenant show that the Ark is associated with God's purpose and plan for Israel.

2. *The Ark of the Testimony*. (Exodus 25:22) Let's keep in mind that the mercy seat was the lid that covered the Ark. This is where the High Priest would sprinkle the blood on the day of atonement. It speaks of the fact that man is separated from God and can meet with Him only by merit of sacrificial blood. The Ark speaks of the fact that God is getting ready to meet with His people.
3. *The Ark of God* (1 Samuel 3:3). It is clearly identified as the Ark of God. It is His Ark—not man's.
4. *The Ark Of Thy Strength* (Psalm 132:8). This speaks of power of God, along with all the miracles and works associated with the Ark.
5. *The Holy Ark* (2 Chronicles 35:3). The Ark was holy because it was a place where God dwelt in His Shekinah glory.

The tabernacle in the wilderness and its furniture. (Including the Ark) was patterned after their heavenly counterparts.

And look that thou make them after their pattern, which was shewed thee in the mount. (Exodus 25:40)

The Ark of the Covenant seen here in Heaven is probably the same one Moses saw and from which he patterned the one he had built for the tabernacle. As we have already learned, the Ark contained the tables of the law—God's covenant with Israel which they failed to keep. However, God is faithful to keep His covenant. The Ark in the heavenly temple speaks of the covenant of God with Israel that can never be broken.

Now the LORD had said unto Abram, Get thee out of thy country, and from thy kindred, and from thy father's house, unto a land that I will show thee: And I will make of thee a great nation, and I will bless thee, and make thy name great;

and thou shalt be a blessing: And I will bless them that bless thee, and curse him that curseth thee: and in thee shall all families of the earth be blessed. (Genesis 12:1-3)

God is ever so faithful. Even in this present dispensation and speaking of the relationship of Christ to His people the Bible says:

If we believe not, yet he abideth faithful: he cannot deny himself. (2 Timothy 2:13)

Though we, even as God's children often fail, He **abideth faithful**.

Also seen and heard are **lightnings, and voices, and thunderings, and an earthquake, and great hail.** These all speak of the continuing judgments of God that will be poured out against the wicked in bringing their kingdoms to an end.

WAR IN HEAVEN
Revelation 12:1-17

The details in this passage of the clothing and appearance of the sun-clad woman reminds us of Jacob, Rachel, and their eleven sons as they appeared in Joseph's dream (Genesis 37:9). There are several details to take note of here.

THE SUN-CLAD WOMAN

As God continues to unveil the details of His prophetic program, we see a great conflict taking place. This is the conflict of the ages. The great conflict between God and Satan is in view here.

The Importance Inferred

Many are the ideas and teachings of men concerning this passage. The importance of this passage cannot be overstated. Concerning the significance of this chapter, Dr. Harry A. Ironside wrote:

> *If the interpreters are wrong as to the woman and the man-child, it necessarily follows that they will be wrong as to many things connected with them.*

Hence, we must be careful as we study this passage. We must rightly divide and compare Scripture with Scripture if we are going to reach the correct interpretation.

The Inaccurate Interpretations

So, who does this woman represent? There are many ideas. Because of the hordes of false interpretations, we must begin by looking at who this woman is not.

First, this woman does not represent the Church. Some teach that she represents the Church of Jesus Christ. However, the simple context of the passage disproves such a notion. According to our text, the woman gave birth to a child and that child is

Jesus Christ. This of course rules out the Church as the Church did not give birth to the Lord Jesus Christ. It was the exact opposite—Jesus founded the New Testament Church. Also, as we have already learned that the church is not on earth during this time. She has been raptured and is now with her Lord in Heaven. There are only two classes of people on earth during the tribulation—the Jews and the Gentiles.

Secondly, this woman does not represent the Virgin Mary. The Roman Catholic Church teaches that this woman represents the Virgin Mary whom they say ascended into Heaven. This interpretation can in no way be substantiated by the Word of God. There is absolutely no scripture to support the view that the Virgin Mary ascended into Heaven.

Thirdly, this woman does not represent Mary Baker Patterson Glover Eddy. Mrs. Eddy was the founder of the corrupt Christian Science cult. She taught that this symbol was a prophecy of her, and the man-child represented the Christian Science religion that she founded, and that the great red dragon was the mortal mind struggling to destroy her new religion. Christian Science denies the fundamentals of the faith and leads millions into Hell. This passage has nothing to do with Eddy and her religion.

Many are the absurdities of false teachers who desire to claim a Bible basis for their existence. However, their claims do not hold up under the examination of God's Word.

The Illustrative Character

And there appeared a great wonder in heaven; (Revelation 12:1a) The Apostle John said, **there appeared a great wonder.** A **wonder** is something unusual. It is something that goes beyond the realm of nature. We notice that this is no ordinary wonder, but a **great** wonder. It Oliver B. Greene commented ...

> *The adjective "GREAT" is used five times in chapter 12—which is indeed a GREAT chapter!*

should be noted that this is not a literal woman. The word **wonder** comes from *"semeion"* and speaks of *"a token or a sign."* A sign is a symbol, of what God is about to reveal. John is speaking symbolically here. The symbolism is meant to teach who she is. This sign is a symbol, of what God is about to reveal. So, who is she? As we dig in a little deeper, her identity becomes clear.

The Israel Connection

... a woman clothed with the sun, and the moon under her feet, and upon her head a crown of twelve stars: (Revelation 12:1b) The symbolism in this verse helps us to identify this sun clad woman. The figure of a woman is frequently used as a symbol of religion. Jezebel represents paganism and idolatrous worship.

> **Notwithstanding I have a few things against thee, because thou sufferest that woman Jezebel, which calleth herself a prophetess, to teach and to seduce my servants to commit fornication, and to eat things sacrificed unto idols. (Revelation 2:20)**

> **And it came to pass, as if it had been a light thing for him to walk in the sins of Jeroboam the son of Nebat, that he took to wife Jezebel the daughter of Ethbaal king of the Zidonians, and went and served Baal, and worshipped him. (1 Kings 16:31)**

The Bride of Christ represents the true Church (Revelation 19). The sun-clad woman also represents a religion. Notice this woman is clothed with the **sun**. The **moon** is under her feet and her **crown** is made up of **twelve stars**. This is quite revealing. In Joseph's dream the Sun and the Moon and the eleven Stars are mentioned prophetically concerning Joseph and the future of Israel.

> **And he dreamed yet another dream, and told it his brethren and said, Behold, I have dreamed a dream more; and, behold, the Sun and the Moon and the eleven stars made obeisance to me. And he told it to his father, and to his brethren; and his father rebuked him, and said unto him What is this dream that thou hast dreamed? Shall I and thy mother, and thy brethren indeed come to bow down ourselves to see to the earth? And His**

brethren envied him; but his father observed the saying. (Genesis 37:9-11)

We see eleven stars and Joseph himself was the twelfth. There is no doubt that the woman of Revelation 12 is the nation of Israel. William R. Newell said:

> *The splendor and fulness of governmental authority on earth, belong, by God's sovereign appointment, to Israel: and the restoring of the kingdom to Israel, under Christ, is the subject before us in this part of the Revelation.*

Notice that this woman, Israel, is seen here as being with child, travailing in birth, and in constant pain to be delivered. This is a picture of the nation Israel, from the call of Abraham to the birth of Christ, who was constantly expecting the birth of the Messiah. In the Old Testament, Israel is many times compared to a woman and at times a woman in travail (Isaiah 66:5-12; Jeremiah 3:6-10; Micah 4:10; 5:2-3). There is no question, but that the woman refers to the nation of Israel. Thus, the twelve stars speak of Joseph and his eleven brothers, the twelve patriarchs of the twelve tribes of Israel.

The Incarnate Christ

And she being with child cried, travailing in birth, and pained to be delivered. (Revelation 12:2) This woman was experiencing labor pains and about to give birth. Israel is the woman who birthed Jesus in His first coming (Romans 9:5). A few verses later we will see that the **man child** she delivers is in fact the Lord Jesus Christ — the incarnate Son of God.

THE SATANIC DRAGON

In the following verses we see another wonder in heaven. We learn that this wonder speaks of none other than Satan.

The Red Dragon

And there appeared another wonder in heaven; and behold a great red dragon, having seven heads and ten horns, and seven crowns upon his heads. (Revelation 12:3) This time it is a great red dragon with seven heads, ten horns and seven crowns upon his heads. The word **wonder** denotes that this is not a literal dragon, but a sign or a symbol.

The **seven heads and ten horns** identify him with the beast of Daniel 7 and Revelation 13:1. This beast is none other than Satan himself (Revelation 12:9). He is the adversary of the woman and stands ready to devour her child as soon as He is born. The identification of this dragon is no problem.

> **And he laid hold on the dragon, that old serpent, which is the Devil, and Satan, and bound him a thousand years, (Revelation 20:2)**

John expressly identifies the dragon as **the Devil, and Satan**. He is the archenemy of God and His people. Satan could not devour Christ, so now he seeks to devour God's people.

> **Be sober, be vigilant; because your adversary the devil, as a roaring lion, walketh about, seeking whom he may devour: (1 Peter 5:8)**

What a graphic description of our enemy! The picture is of a lion on the prowl. He is hungry, merciless, and vicious. He is bloodthirsty and looking for anything he can find to rip apart and devour. His hostility and ravenous ways will reach its height in the Tribulation Period.

The Ruinous Draw

And his tail drew the third part of the stars of heaven, and did cast them to the earth. (Revelation 12:4) The stars which he drew from heaven and cast to the earth are the angels who followed him when he rebelled and attempted to take the throne of God. It was this rebellion against God that resulted in Satan and a third of the angels being cast out of God's Heaven (Ezekiel 28:12-17; Jude 6; 2 Peter 2:4).

The Resolute Desire

... and the dragon stood before the woman which was ready to be delivered, for to devour her child as soon as it was born. (Revelation 12:4b) Here Satan is seen standing before the women awaiting the birth of Christ with a resolute determination to destroy Him as soon as He is born. Down through the ages, ever since Genesis 3:15, the Devil has been set on destroying the Messiah.

- He first tried to destroy the seed of the Messiah in the Garden of Eden. He brought about the fall of man thinking that he had corrupted people. But God is a redeemer! He stepped in and saved Adam and Eve.
- Later he corrupted the whole world and God judged the world with a flood. The Devil thought for sure he had destroyed the seed at that time. However, righteous Noah and his family survived the flood by God's grace.
- A little later the Devil tried to thwart God's plan with getting Abraham to father a child with Sarah's hand maiden. Abraham thought God would accept Ishmael as the son of promise. However, God rejected Ishmael. God performed an amazing miracle and Sarah had a child at the age of ninety. God brought His plan to fruition and Isaac was born just as He had planned.
- The great promise of Genesis 3:15 was fulfilled when Jesus was born. Satan had King Herod ready to devour the Christ child. Satan used Herod to attempt to destroy God's Messiah when ordered the death all male children 2 years old and under. However, God intervened and Satan's attempts were defeated. (Matthew 2:13-18).
- Again, Satan's last-ditch effort to destroy the Saviour was when he led evil men to crucify Christ. But Gods stepped in and used the cross as an altar to sacrifice His Son for the sines of the world. When they rolled the stone over the grave, Satan thought he had finally won. But Jesus rose three days and is alive forever more.

Satan is a great enemy of God and His people. Believers have a very formidable enemy. Satan and his demon forces are ever on the attack.

THE SOVEREIGN CHILD

Verses five and six give us yet another wonder. As the red dragon stands by, the man child is born. His desire was to devour the child. Throughout the years of the Old Testament Satan launched attempts to destroy the messianic line and ruin God's plan to redeem the lost. We notice in this section ...

The Delivery Accomplished

And she brought forth a man child, who was to rule all nations with a rod of iron: (Revelation 12:5a) Who is this man child? The prophecy of His reign with a rod of iron helps us to identify Who He is. Of the Jesus the Bible prophecies:

> **Thou shalt break them with a rod of iron; thou shalt dash them in pieces like a potter's vessel. (Psalm 2:9)**

We see this again, when the Lord Jesus Christ returns in glory at the end of the Tribulation Period with His bride.

> **And out of his mouth goeth a sharp sword, that with it he should smite the nations: and he shall rule them with a rod of iron: and he treadeth the winepress of the fierceness and wrath of Almighty God. (Revelation 19:15)**

It is obvious that this male child is the Lord Jesus Christ. David L. Cooper said ...

> *The correct interpretation which is demanded by all the facts is that this woman signifies Israel. It was the Hebrew race that produced the Christ, the man child. Isaiah sang "Unto us a child is born, unto us a son is given" (Isa. 9:6). We therefore conclude that this man child who is to rule the nations with a rod of iron is the Christ, the Messiah of Israel.*

The only person who is said to rule all nations with a rod of iron is Jesus Christ. (Psalm 2:8-9; Revelation 19:15) And of course the only person ever caught up to the throne of God was Christ. (Luke 24:51; Acts 1:9-11) Therefore, the male child of the woman Israel is Jesus Christ, the Messiah of Israel.

The Dazzling Ascension

... and her child was caught up unto God, and to his throne. (Revelation 12:5b) The woman, Israel, brought forth a male child **who was to rule all nations with a rod of iron; and her child was caught up unto God, and to his throne.** This is a reference to the glorious ascension of the Lord Jesus, which marked the completion of His earthly ministry.

> **And when he had spoken these things, while they beheld, he was taken up; and a cloud received him out of their sight. And while they looked stedfastly toward heaven as he went up, behold, two men stood by them in white apparel; (Acts 1:9-10)**

Christ, after His resurrection ascended into the Heavens to be seated at the right hand of the Father. He now sits upon the throne of God. Today, as our Great High Priest He intercedes for us. This is Christ's great ministry during the Church age.

The Divine Asylum

And the woman fled into the wilderness, where she hath a place prepared of God, that they should feed her there a thousand two hundred and threescore days. (Revelation 12:6) This speaks of the time after the Church is raptured and the first three and one-half years of the Tribulation have come to a close, when God will sovereignly protect Israel from being annihilated by the antichrist. The Almighty has always sustained Israel down through the ages and will continue to keep them even in the time of the Great Tribulation Period.

THE STRIFE OF WAR

As Satan stood by to devour the man child a great war erupted in the heavens. This is a war between good and evil, between the forces of God and the forces of Satan. This conflict occurs at the midpoint of the Tribulation Period.

The Enemy Opposition

And there was war in heaven: Michael and his angels fought against the dragon; and the dragon fought and his angels, (Revelation 12:7) Between the Tribulation and the Great Tribulation there will be all out war in the heavenly realm. We

War In Heaven

want to keep in mind that there are three heavens. You will recall how the Apostle Paul testified that he was ...

> **... caught up to the third heaven. (2 Corinthians 12:2)**

The first heaven is where the birds and the clouds are. The second heaven is where the stars and moon are. The third heaven is God's home. The devil and all of his angels are loose in the first and second heavens. The heavens referred to here is probably the atmosphere, the sky and starry heavens where the prince of the power of the air rules.

The Enemy Overwhelmed

And prevailed not; (Revelation 12:8a) Satan did not prevail against **Michael and his angels.** Satan and his demons will not win this war. Though he has won many battles over the years, he loses the war. Michael and his angels defeat the Devil and his angels.

The Enemy Ousted

... neither was their place found any more in heaven. And the great dragon was cast out, that old serpent, called the Devil, and Satan, which deceiveth the whole world: he was cast out into the earth, and his angels were cast out with him. (Revelation 12:8b-9) The term **dragon** identifies the devil as the wild beast that he is. He is identified as the power and force behind the antichrist and the False Prophet. As we see from Scripture, Satan's career is a short one. In the beginning Satan was the most beautiful and powerful of God's creations. (Ezekiel 28:12-17)

> Son of man, take up a lamentation upon the king of Tyrus, and say unto him, Thus saith the Lord GOD; Thou sealest up the sum, full of wisdom, and perfect in beauty. Thou hast been in Eden the garden of God; every precious stone was thy covering, the sardius, topaz, and the diamond, the beryl, the onyx, and the jasper, the sapphire, the emerald, and the carbuncle, and gold: the workmanship of thy tabrets and of thy pipes was prepared in thee in the day that thou wast

> created. Thou art the anointed cherub that covereth; and I have set thee so: thou wast upon the holy mountain of God; thou hast walked up and down in the midst of the stones of fire. Thou wast perfect in thy ways from the day that thou wast created, till iniquity was found in thee. By the multitude of thy merchandise they have filled the midst of thee with violence, and thou hast sinned: therefore I will cast thee as profane out of the mountain of God: and I will destroy thee, O covering cherub, from the midst of the stones of fire. Thine heart was lifted up because of thy beauty, thou hast corrupted thy wisdom by reason of thy brightness: I will cast thee to the ground, I will lay thee before kings, that they may behold thee. (Ezekiel 28:12-17)

God created Satan as one of the most beautiful creatures to ever live. Sin, however, destroyed him. When he was lifted up in pride and fell, he was cast out from the highest Heaven to the earth which he now occupies as the prince of the power of the air and the god of this world.

And the great dragon was cast out. Though Satan had fallen from his majestic position in the angelic system, he still has some sort of access to Heaven (Job 1:6-12; 2:1-6). The time, however, will come when God will cast Satan out of Heaven once for all. This is the battle that is described in these verses. God will use Michael and his angels to carry out His will and Satan and his hordes of demons will be fully and finally cast out of Heaven.

The Enemy Overcome

Now a great and welcome announcement is made from Heaven declaring Satan's fall and coming demise. There is a sevenfold application to be made here.

The Proclamation. **And I heard a loud voice saying in heaven, Now is come salvation, and strength, and the kingdom of our God, and the power of his Christ: (Revelation 12:10a)** There is a tremendous proclamation of victory announced. There is a great anticipation of the coming of the millennial Kingdom. The news causes people to break out into praise to God. They sing of Christ's wonderful salvation. They shout about God's strength and omnipotence in crushing the power of Satan. They pronounce that the kingdom of our God has come, and the millennial reign of Christ begun.

The Perpetrator. **... for the accuser of our brethren is cast down, which accused them before our God day and night. (Revelation 12:10b)** Notice that Satan is called the **accuser** of the brethren. By **day and night,** he slandered and railed against God's people. It seems clear that Satan now has access into the presence of God. He enters into the presence of God in order that he may accuse the brethren. This is seen in the case of Job, who he accused before God several times. We see the same truth in the book of Zechariah.

> **And he shewed me Joshua the high priest standing before the angel of the LORD, and Satan standing at his right hand to resist him. And the LORD said unto Satan, The LORD rebuke thee, O Satan; even the LORD that hath chosen Jerusalem rebuke thee: is not this a brand plucked out of the fire? (Zechariah 3:1-2)**

No wonder John calls him **the accuser of the brethren.** He constantly attempts to move the hand of God against us. However, he fails!

The Perseverance. **And they overcame him by the blood of the Lamb, (Revelation 12:11a)** You will notice that **they overcame him by the blood of the Lamb.** Oh! How Satan hates the blood of Christ. When he accuses us before the throne, Jesus, our great High Priest, pleads our case. He points to the mercy seat where the blood is applied. Because of the blood we constantly stand righteous before Him and the devil is proved to be a false accuser. The same thing is true here in the tribulation period. My friend, It's Still The Blood!

The Profession. **... and by the word of their testimony; (Revelation 12:11b)** Their profession of faith in the Lord Jesus Christ was a great source of strength. This was the message they proclaimed—it was their testimony.

Their Passion. ... **and they loved not their lives unto the death. (Revelation 12:11c)** The driving force behind these believers was not their life, but their Lord. They loved the Lord Jesus more than their very life. There is a great reward for those who are willing to give their life for the Lord Jesus.

> **... be thou faithful unto death, and I will give thee a crown of life. (Revelation 2:10)**

Many down through the ages have given their lives for the Lord and His gospel. They were determined to remain true even if it cost them their lives.

The Praise. **Therefore rejoice, ye heavens, and ye that dwell in them. (Revelation 12:12a)** The word **rejoice** comes from *"euphraino"* and means *"to be made glad."* Many will be made glad when Satan is cast down and defeated. The Millennial Reign is beginning here. This will be a time of great rejoicing and jubilation.

The Peril. ... **Woe to the inhabiters of the earth and of the sea! for the devil is come down unto you, having great wrath, because he knoweth that he hath but a short time. (Revelation 12:12b)** That which resulted in great rejoicing among the saints of God, is the reason for the sorrow among those who are lost. Those who inhabit the earth at this time will face unparalleled anguish and tribulation.

> **Alas! for that day is great, so that none is like it: it is even the time of Jacob's trouble; but he shall be saved out of it. (Jeremiah 30:7)**
>
> **That day is a day of wrath, a day of trouble and distress, a day of wasteness and desolation, a day of darkness and gloominess, a day of clouds and thick darkness, (Zephaniah 1:15)**

The Apostle says, **for the devil is come down unto you.** The world, already suffering under the fierce wrath of the Almighty, will now be subjected to the **great wrath** of Satan who punishes t world in the most unmanageable and vicious ways. Satan is furious because **because he knoweth that he hath but a short time.** Satan knows that his reign will soon come to an end. He is furious because he knows that soon he's going to be put into the bottomless pit when Jesus comes in power and great glory (Revelation 19).

THE SATANIC WRATH

Here we come to a more detailed account of the woman's flight into the wilderness that was mentioned back in verse 6. We see ...

The Persecution

And when the dragon saw that he was cast unto the earth, he persecuted the woman which brought forth the man child. (Revelation 12:13) When Satan and his cohorts are removed from the heavens, he has no place to go but the earth. During this time, he will launch his greatest attack upon Israel. The word **persecuted** comes from *"dioko"* and means *"to pursue, to follow after, to persecute, to pursue with repeated acts of hostility."* Satan will attack Israel with everything he has.

The Provision

And to the woman were given two wings of a great eagle, that she might fly into the wilderness, into her place, where she is nourished for a time, and times, and half a time, from the face of the serpent. (Revelation 12:14) God will personally step in on behalf of the Jews and provided the Jews with a means of escape as well as a place of refuge. Here we see that Israel will be divinely nourished and cared for during the Great Tribulation Period. The woman escapes Satan's wrath by means of the **two wings of a great eagle**. This is an interesting figure of speech. In the Word of God, eagles' wings are a type of God's protection (Exodus 19:4; Deuteronomy 32:11-12).

We are told that she escapes into the wilderness. Where this wilderness is, we do not know. However, we do know that the Lord will preserve the Jewish nation until Christ returns in His glory. Hosea prophesied:

> **Therefore, behold, I will allure her, and bring her into the wilderness, and speak comfortably unto her. (Hosea 2:14)**

The Almighty will sovereignly care for His chosen people during the Great Tribulation Period.

The Pursuit

And the serpent cast out of his mouth water as a flood after the woman, that he might cause her to be carried away of the flood. (Revelation 12:15) Satan will attempt to overcome Israel with an army likened unto a **flood**. This flood of soldiers is likely sent by antichrist. Satan is still determined to exterminate the nation of Israel.

The Protection

And the earth helped the woman, and the earth opened her mouth, and swallowed up the flood which the dragon cast out of his mouth. (Revelation 12:16) God moved upon nature and supernaturally delivered Israel from her enemies. He caused the earth to open and swallow the armies that pursued His people.

The Pique

And the dragon was wroth with the woman, and went to make war with the remnant of her seed, which keep the commandments of God, and have the testimony of Jesus Christ. (Revelation 12:17) The word **wroth** comes from *"orgizō"* and means *"to be angry, to provoke or enrage, to become exasperated."* Satan was furious and burning up with anger. He is still determined **to make war with the remnant of her seed.** Satan is determined to devour Israel.

THE RISE OF THE ANTICHRIST
Revelation 13:1-10

In this section we find Satan furious, fuming, and ferocious. Having been cast to the earth he **knoweth that he hath but a short time. (Revelation 12:12)** He launches his greatest effort to retain his rule over the world. During the times of confusion, chaos and conflict that will prevail in the tribulation, the world will long for a leader who can offer a solution for the turmoil. Satan will meet the world's desire with his own antichrist and the false prophet. These men empowered by Satan will come and they will be openly accepted by the masses of that day. We learn in Scripture that there are three characters who will play major roles in Satan's plans during the Tribulation Period.

1. The First Beast Out Of The Bottomless Pit—Satan.
2. The Second Beast Out Of The Sea—antichrist.
3. The Third Beast Out Of The Earth—False Prophet.

Here we are introduced to the satanic trinity. This satanic trinity is Satan's counterfeit of the Holy Trinity.

1. The place occupied by God the father is held by Satan.
2. The place held by Christ is assumed by the second Beast.
3. The ministry of the Holy Spirit is discharged by the False Prophet.

Satan is an imitator. In his commentary, *Exploring Revelation*, John Phillips says ...

> *Here is Satan's imitation of the incarnation. He conjures up a man, a beast, who bears all the characteristics of Satan himself. Whatever Satan is in his person, his nature, and his personality, so is*

the Beast. He is the visible expression of the invisible devil

Satan's objective is to form a one world confederation headed up by the antichrist and promoted by the false prophet. His plan is to unite the unbelieving world in a final conflict against Christ. Even in our day, the world is shaping up, both politically and religiously, for the appearing and acceptance of the antichrist.

HIS PEOPLE

And I stood upon the sand of the sea, and saw a beast rise up out of the sea... (Revelation 13:1a) The waves and churning of the **sea** speaks of the unrest and agitation among the people. In the Word of God, the **sand** of the sea is representative of a great multitude of people. God told Abraham that He would multiply his seed as the sands of the sea.

> **That in blessing I will bless thee, and in multiplying I will multiply thy seed as the stars of the heaven, and as the sand which is upon the sea shore; and thy seed shall possess the gate of his enemies. (Genesis 22:17)**

Later in the book of Revelation, John refers to God's army as being ...

> **... as sands of the sea. (Revelation 20:8)**

The symbolic language here speaks of an innumerable multitude — great masses of people Sand stands for the multitudes and the sea stands for trouble and turmoil among the great masses of people.

> **But the wicked are like the troubled sea, when it cannot rest, whose waters cast up mire and dirt. There is no peace, saith my God, to the wicked. (Isaiah 57:20-21)**

The beast rising up out of the sea is a leader who rises up from among the people. This beast represents the head of the Revived Roman Empire. The old Roman Empire became modern Europe. During the Tribulation, ten nations from Europe will form the Revived Roman Empire. Rome will be the capital of this Empire (Revelation 17-18).

HIS PARTNERSHIP

This beast will have **seven heads and ten horns, and upon his horns ten crowns, (Revelation 13:1b)** The seven heads represent the seven mountains on which the harlot woman sits (Revelation 17:1-9). The ten horns represent kingdoms (Revelation 17:12). The ten crowns represent the ten kings of the ten-nation federation or the United States of Europe. All this was prophesied in the book of Daniel.

> **And the ten horns out of this kingdom are ten kings that shall arise: and another shall rise after them; and he shall be diverse from the first, and he shall subdue three kings. (Daniel 7:24)**

Keep in mind that Revelation 13 is actually the explanation of Daniel 7. These ten kings will give their power and authority to the antichrist during the Tribulation Period (17:12-13).

... and upon his heads the name of blasphemy. (Revelation 13:1c) We know that the anti-christ will be a great blasphemer. During the Tribulation Period he is described as one ...

> **Who opposeth and exalteth himself above all that is called God, or that is worshipped; so that he as God sitteth in the temple of God, shewing himself that he is God. (2 Thessalonians 2:4)**

The anti-Christ will blaspheme the name of God by proclaiming himself to be god and demanding to be worshipped as God. This was Satan's desire when he attempted to exalt himself about God.

> **For thou hast said in thine heart, I will ascend into heaven, I will exalt my throne above the stars of God: I will sit also upon the mount of the congregation, in the sides of the north: I will ascend above the heights of the clouds; I will be like the most High. (Isaiah 14:13–14)**

Satan's great ambition is to be above the Most High God. This desire will be one of the driving forces behind his evil. This will be Satan ultimate attempt to be worshipped. This event was prophesied by Daniel and referred to as the abomination of desolation.

HIS PROFILE

And the beast which I saw was like unto a leopard, and his feet were as the feet of a bear, and his mouth as the mouth of a lion... (Revelation 13:2a) This description of the beast is the same as in Daniel 7. Daniel saw a lion, a bear, a leopard, and the fourth beast he could not describe. Here, John saw the same three creatures, but notice that they are in reverse order. Daniel was looking forward and he saw the kingdoms of the world as they were to be after him. John was looking back, and he saw these kingdoms as they had been. The little horn of Daniel 7:8 is now the first beast, the antichrist in this thirteenth chapter of Revelation. A study of Daniel reveals that the wild beasts represent different world kingdoms—Babylon, Medo-Persia, Greece, and Rome. Notice that here in Revelation 13 the four have become one beast, showing that a confederacy of the kingdoms has taken place. There is little doubt that since the same symbols are given to Rome (seven heads and ten horns in Revelation 17) this beast out of the sea represents the antichrist—the head of the revived Roman Empire of the Last Days.

HIS POWER

And the dragon gave him his power, and his seat, and great authority. And I saw one of his heads as it were wounded to death; and his deadly wound was healed: and all the world wondered after the beast. (Revelation 13:2-3) The antichrist will be a man with supernatural power, but his power will come from Satan. It is important to realize that we have symbolic language here. John explains the seven heads in chapter 17 and the mountains, and speaks of the seven kings, implying that the mountains are symbolic of kingdoms. Here in chapter 13, we see that one of the seven heads (kingdoms) received a mortal wound and died. In other words, this government fell. John Walvoord comments:

> *The wounding of one of the heads seems instead to be in reference to the fact that the Roman Empire as such, seemingly died and is now going to be revived. It is significant that one of the heads is wounded to death but that the beast itself is not said to be dead. It is questionable whether Satan has the power to restore to life one who has died, even though his power is great. Far more probable is the explanation that this is the revived Roman Empire in view.*

The head that was wounded as it were dead refers to the political death of the Roman empire. However, Satan will resurrect this kingdom during the tribulation. Rome fell in A. D. 476. At this time Rome is an insignificant power, but it will rise again to world power under the leadership of the antichrist after the Rapture of the Church. A ten-nation confederacy from Europe will form the Revived Roman Empire.

HIS PRAISE

And they worshipped the dragon which gave power unto the beast: and they worshipped the beast, saying, Who is like unto the beast? who is able to make war with him? ... And all that dwell upon the earth shall worship him, whose names are not written in the book of life of the Lamb slain from the foundation of the world. (Revelation 13:4, 8) The previous verses say that the world **worshipped** and **wondered after the beast.** Oliver B. Greene said ...

> *With the exception of those who have believed and been redeemed through the testimony of the 144,000 and the two witnesses of chapter 11, the masses will fall down and receive the Beast as their messiah, and joyfully line up to receive his mark in their forehead or in their right hand. They will be*

> *sent strong delusion; they will believe the lie. Read II Thessalonians 2:8-12.*

It is hard to believe that the world could stoop so low and be so deceived as to knowingly worship Satan, but it does. Satan's great desire is to be praised and worshipped as God. (Isaiah 14:13) The antichrist's power will be great. He will defy the very God of Heaven and blaspheme His name. As a result of his work the wicked and unsaved people of this world will be duped. People will be so captivated by his works and powers that they will willingly accept him as God and worship him. Their anthem of praise will be **Who is like unto the beast? who is able to make war with him?**

HIS PRIDE

And there was given unto him a mouth speaking great things and blasphemies; and power was given unto him to continue forty and two months. And he opened his mouth in blasphemy against God, to blaspheme his name, and his tabernacle, and them that dwell in heaven. (Revelation 13:5-6) The character of this dictator is described by Daniel as fierce (8:23), self-willed and self-exalting (11:36), and proud (11:37). The New Testament calls him the **antichrist. (1 John 2:18)** and the **man of sin ... the son of perdition. (2 Thessalonians 2:3)** All that the antichrist is, stems from satanic power and pride. The pride of Satan runs in veins of the antichrist. Pride was born in the heart of Satan. (Isaiah 14:12-18) Pride was Satan's downfall and this antichrist being empowered and driven by Satan has plenty of the same. So prideful is he that he openly blasphemes God. Daniel said:

> **And he shall speak great words against the most High. (Daniel 7:25)**

Paul spoke of him as one:

> **Who opposeth and exalteth himself above all that is called God, or that is worshipped; so that he as God sitteth in the temple of God, showing himself that he is God. (2 Thessalonians 2:4)**

The prideful and abominable acts of the antichrist will result in God's final judgment and utter desolation.

> **The fear of the LORD is to hate evil: pride, and arrogancy, and the evil way, and the froward mouth, do I hate. (Proverbs 8:13)**

God will not tolerate pride. Satan's pride brought him down and will bring his antichrist down as well.

> **A man's pride shall bring him low... (Proverbs 29:23)**
>
> **The LORD will destroy the house of the proud ... (Proverbs 15:25)**

The arrogance of the antichrist will be met with the power and judgment of the Almighty. Finally, and fittingly, his rule will end in complete destruction.

HIS PROGRAM

And it was given unto him to make war with the saints, and to overcome them: and power was given him over all kindreds, and tongues, and nations. And all that dwell upon the earth shall worship him, whose names are not written in the book of life of the Lamb slain from the foundation of the world. If any man have an ear, let him hear. He that leadeth into captivity shall go into captivity: he that killeth with the sword must be killed with the sword. Here is the patience and the faith of the saints. (Revelation 13:7-10) It is hard sometimes to digest the fact that God allows persecution and even death to be imposed on Hid children. We are told that **it was given unto him to make war with the saints.** John Phillips Commented ...

> *The age-old mystery of the suffering of the saints is again brought into focus. It was given unto him to make war with the saints and to overcome them, just as it was given unto Herod to imprison and behead John the Baptist, just as it was given to Satan to persecute Job, and just as it was given to Pilate to pass sentence of death upon Jesus.*

The antichrist unleashes his fury upon God's people. He makes **war with the saints.** He hates God's people. He makes war and slaughters the saints. These martyred saints are probably referred to in chapter 6 when the martyrs were told to wait for a little season until their fellow servants be killed in like manner.

With God's people murdered and gone the antichrist becomes the world's dictator. He is the head of **all kindreds, and tongues, and nations. And all that dwell upon the earth shall worship him, whose names are not written in the book of life of the Lamb slain from the foundation of the world.** Daniel prophesied that this beast would:

> **... devour the whole earth, and shall tread it down, and break it in pieces. (Daniel 7:23)**

However, we learn from our current text that the extent of the antichrist's reign is limited to the ungodly world. By the will of God, His people are martyred and enter Heaven triumphantly. Satan may be allowed to have a believer's physical life, but he can never take our eternal life.

THE COMING WORLD FALSE PROPHET
Revelation 13:11-18

Here in this passage, we come to the second beast of this chapter. He is the beast out of the earth — the false prophet. He will be the antichrist's representative and enforcer during the Tribulation Period. He is the third person of the satanic trinity. He will be the religious leader of the Revived Roman Empire. We will study this in detail we come to chapters 17 and 18. Now, looking at the characteristics of the false prophet we see ...

HIS DESCRIPTION

And I beheld another beast coming up out of the earth; and he had two horns like a lamb, and he spake as a dragon. (Revelation 13:11) This beast is easily identified as **the false prophet, (Revelation 16:13; 19:20; 20:10)**, who ministers in connection with the first beast, as his prophet or spokesman. Notice that this beast **had two horns like a lamb.** He has two horns like a lamb but speaks as a dragon. Horns speak of power and authority, while the lamb speaks of meekness. However, his general appearance is deceptive. This religious leader will appear to be a lamb— he will come across as one of God's sheep. His lamb-like appearance and meekness are only an outward appearance and hide true character. He will be deceptive and destructive. He will speak as **a dragon.** The dragon has already been identified as Satan.

> **And the great dragon was cast out, that old serpent, called the Devil, and Satan, which deceiveth the whole world: he was cast out into the earth, and his angels were cast out with him. (Revelation 12:9)**

Outwardly this beast will appear innocent, meek, attractive, and harmless. But inwardly he is as vicious as a dragon. This false prophet will be powerful in his appearance and speech. He will be a great deceiver and motivator. He will multitude into Satan's grasp. He will work under the authority and with the power of Satan, as does the first beast.

HIS DEEDS

And he exerciseth all the power of the first beast before him, and causeth the earth and them which dwell therein to worship the first beast, whose deadly wound was healed. (Revelation 13:12) The second beast will be a representative of the first beast by acting as his prophet. The chief objective of the false prophet is to attract men's attention and point them to the Antichrist. This is a satanic counterfeit of the Holy Spirit's ministry in pointing people to Christ. Just as the Holy Spirit came to bear witness to the Lord Jesus, (John 15:26), the false prophet will be devoted to bearing witness to the second beast, the antichrist. His supreme purpose will be to lead in the worship and promotion of the first beast. In his commentary on the book of Revelation, Oliver B. Greene wrote:

> Keep in mind that these two Beasts work together- political and religious. The first will be the leader of the most powerful united kingdom that has ever been on this earth. He will be the most colossal ruler—the boldest, most blasphemous ruler who ever lived upon the face of this earth. The second Beast will have no royal authority outside of Palestine; therefore, he uses the power and prestige of the political Beast to bring about his diabolical design to get all the peoples of earth to bow down to Rome and worship the great Beast who was wounded unto death but now has miraculously come alive. The second Beast will have no military power of his own. Military power will be turned over to the first Beast by the dragon-the devil. The second Beast is much worse than the first. He influences men religiously and leads them into the vilest blasphemy and idolatry. He demands men to

worship him. He sits in the temple in Jerusalem and announces publicly that he is God Almighty.

The first beast is a political leader, while this second beast is a religious leader. Lehman Strauss commented ...

> *This second beast is the false prophet who works to support the Antichrist. He is an administrator of the affairs of Satan. As a means of impressing the people favorably, he performs miracles. This is a means of accomplishing his purposes. He substantiates his claims by demonstrating supernatural control over the forces of nature.*

This second is the head of the coming one world church; the ecumenical monster that we see forming in our very day. He will draw untold thousand to join the one world religious system. This movement will come to its climax during the Tribulation Period. This false prophet will also be directly involved in the persecution of tribulation saints.

HIS DECEPTION

The Tribulation Period will be a time of great deception. The world will be especially vulnerable to his deception during the Tribulation for they will have been sent strong delusion that they should believe the lie (2 Thessalonians 2:11). Thus, the antichrist's false prophet will deceive millions to pledge allegiance to the antichrist and even worship him. Of this false prophet we see ...

His Miracles

And he doeth great wonders, so that he maketh fire come down from heaven on the earth in the sight of men, (Revelation 13:13) This false prophet is going to perform great wonders. So great will be his wonders and miracles that he will call fire down and give life unto the image of the beast, so that the idol itself will speak. He will put on a good show and display great power, even calling fire down from Heaven as Elijah did. Paul said ...

> **And no marvel; for Satan himself is transformed into an angel of light. (2 Corinthians 11:14)**

Don't make the mistake of thinking something is of God just because it seems to look good. Jesus warned that this day would come.

> **For there shall arise false Christs, and false prophets, and shall show great signs and wonders; insomuch that, if it were possible, they shall deceive the very elect. (Matthew 24:24)**

Satan is powerful with the ability to deceive he is a great imitator, and he will do anything within his power to deceive man. For one thing, the antichrist and the false prophet will be miracle workers.

> **Even him, whose coming is after the working of Satan with all power and signs and lying wonders, And with all deceivableness of unrighteousness in them that perish; because they received not the love of the truth, that they might be saved. (2 Thessalonians 2:9-10)**

It is important for us to realize that the performance of miracles is not proof that the one working the miracles is from God. The so-called miracle worker could be from Satan. Remember that Satan is a great deceiver. He is a liar and an imitator. J. A Seiss wrote of Satan and his false signs:

> *"Miracles have ever been the chief evidence of the presence of what is worshipful and Divine. It is by these especially that men's faith is begotten and controlled. It is by seeing and experiencing what is manifestly above and beyond all natural human power, and what cannot be accounted for on natural principles, that the human mind is forced to a conviction of the presence of some great and worshipful potency superior to Nature. And this arch-prophet of falsehood knows well how needful and mighty is the force of miracles to establish his credit, and to secure belief in his claims. The religion*

of God is a religion of miracles, and to make his infernal deception appear the only true and rightful religion he needs to mimic and counterfeit all that supernaturalism on which the true faith reposes. To this, therefore, he sets himself, and becomes one of the greatest workers of signs and wonders the earth has ever seen. Nor need we be surprised at this. There is a supernatural power which is against God and truth, as well as one for God and truth. A miracle, simply as a work of wonder, is not necessarily of God. There has always been a devilish supernaturalism in the world running alongside of the supernaturalism of Divine grace and salvation."

Satan can appear as an angel of light making evil look good. He is a great deceiver. That fact that Satan can imitate supernatural signs is clear from the Word of God. We find this to be true in the case of Jannes and Jambres, the magicians in Pharaoh's court.

Now as Jannes and Jambres withstood Moses, so do these also resist the truth: men of corrupt minds, reprobate concerning the faith. (2 Timothy 3:8)

These were corrupt men with corrupt minds who resisted the truth. It is sad when truth is available, but men reject it. Many in our day will gladly follow a lie before they will the truth. They will believe Jannes and Jambres before they will believe Jesus. This is the downfall of deception. When Paul spoke of Jannes and Jambres, he was drawing from the book of Exodus.

Then Pharaoh also called the wise men and the sorcerers: now the magicians of Egypt, they also did in like manner with their enchantments. For they cast down every man his rod, and they became serpents: but Aaron's rod swallowed up their rods ... And the magicians of Egypt did so with their enchantments: and Pharaoh's heart was

hardened, neither did he hearken unto them; as the LORD had said. (Exodus 7:11-12, 22)

By satanic power Jannes and Jambres were able to imitate the miracles God did through Moses and Aaron, thereby further deceiving Pharaoh. Likewise, the false prophet will appear as an angel of light and deceive millions during the Tribulation Period. Sadly, people who reject God's call usually end up being deceived and following whatever else comes along.

His Mandate

And deceiveth them that dwell on the earth by the means of those miracles which he had power to do in the sight of the beast; saying to them that dwell on the earth, that they should make an image to the beast, which had the wound by a sword, and did live. (Revelation 13:14) By way of his great wonders the false prophet will deceive untold millions into worshipping the antichrist. The false prophet will instruct people to **make an image to the beast.** He will lead people away from the true God to worship the antichrist and tragically many will follow him.

His Murder

And he had power to give life unto the image of the beast, that the image of the beast should both speak, and cause that as many as would not worship the image of the beast should be killed. (Revelation 13:15) Anyone who will not worship the antichrist will be **killed.** If one chooses to worship God, he will pay with his life. We are fortunate in America to have the freedom to worship our God. However, such will not be the case in the under the reign of the antichrist. At this time Religious Liberty will be a thing of the past. All men—murderers, thieves, drunkards, religionists, agnostics, and atheists will be forced to worship the antichrist; they will either by choice or by compulsion. And we are told that as many as will not worship the image of the beast will be killed.

HIS DEMAND

As we will come to this point, we find that men will be forced to make a decision whether or not to follow the antichrist. The line will be drawn. It will be Christ and Heaven or the antichrist and Hell. Likewise, in our day men must choose Heaven or Hell. To reject Christ and His Heaven is to automatically choose Hell.

The Duress Stated

And he causeth all, both small and great, rich and poor, free and bond, to receive a mark in their right hand, or in their foreheads: (Revelation 13:16) Notice that the false prophet **causeth** the people to take the **mark** of the beast. The mark here is a counterfeit of the mark that God placed on the 144,000 for protection. We learn here that when the antichrist reigns, he will have world-wide control over the necessities of life. In order to enforce his demands and to assure the allegiance of the people, he will literally mark them on their right hand or on their foreheads with the mark of the beast.

The Dictating Seen

And that no man might buy or sell, save he that had the mark, or the name of the beast, or the number of his name. (Revelation 13:17) The false prophet will control the economy worldwide. No one will be able to buy or sell unless he has the mark of the beast. Without the mark no one will be able to buy food, medicine, clothes, or any of the necessities of life. Those who take the mark and identify with the antichrist will be allowed to buy. Anyone who refuses to take the mark of the beast will either be executed or starve to death. Many Tribulation saints will die because they refuse to accept the mark.

The Discernment Sought

Here is wisdom. Let him that hath understanding count the number of the beast: for it is the number of a man; and his number is Six hundred threescore and six. (Revelation 13:18) In biblical numerology six is the number of man while seven is the number of completeness. Six falls short of seven just as man always falls short of God's requirement. The number six is connected to man throughout the Scriptures. Adam was created on the sixth day. Man was given six days to labor. Goliath, a type of physical strength, stood six cubits and a span high. Solomon's income in gold was 666 talents a year. Nebuchadnezzar's image was sixty cubits tall and six cubits broad. The beast is the pinnacle of human ability and pomp, his number being 666. He falls far short of the perfect God he is trying to imitate. The tragedy is that in his attempt to be worshipped he will drag millions into Hell with him.

VICTORY ON THE MOUNTAIN
Revelation 14:1-5

In chapter thirteen we saw those who followed after the Beast and False prophet. However, in chapter fourteen we see many who remain faithful to the Lord Jesus. This chapter continues the parenthetic revelation that began back in chapter 12. John is allowed to see more of what transpires in Heaven and on earth during the Tribulation Period. Here we see the contrast between God's people and those who receive the mark of the beast. On earth the beast enjoys the worship of his deceived followers. In heaven, on Mount Zion the faithful people of God enjoy the presence of the Lord Jesus Christ. The beast's followers are sealed with his mark and enjoy only a temporal safety on earth. Bear in mind that the rewards of Satan are only temporal. But the 144,000 are sealed by God with His Divine seal and are secure for eternity. It is tragic that so many people are sacrificing the eternal on the altar of the temporal.

THEIR PLACE

This incredible scene takes place on mount Sion. The following five verses introduce what will take place with the 144,000 during the Great Tribulation.

The Sight Of The Master

And I looked, and, lo, a Lamb ... (Revelation 14:1a) We note that the Lamb begins with a capital L. It is a title that belongs solely to the Lamb of God, the Lord Jesus Christ. John sees the Lamb of God— the Lord Jesus standing on Mount Sion. The word **Lamb** appears twenty-eight times in Revelation as a title for Christ. You will remember that back in chapter 5 we saw the ...

... Lamb as it had been slain, (Revelation 5:6)

When John the Baptist saw Jesus, he said ...

> **... Behold the Lamb of God, which taketh away the sin of the world. (John 1:29)**

Notice that John identified Christ as **the** Lamb, not a lamb. The use of the definite article **the** shows that John viewed Christ as the long-awaited Messiah. By referring to Jesus as **the Lamb of God,** John was saying that Christ was the Supreme Lamb—the Lamb Who would fulfill every Old Testament type and His blood completely satisfy once and forever, the righteous requirements of God. Jesus Christ was the fulfillment of every bloody sacrifice the Old Testament. Every lamb slain upon Israel's altars was a picture of Jesus Christ the Lamb of God, Who was to be slain upon Calvary's altar. Jesus is the sacrificial Lamb of God sent to die vicariously for whosoever will come to Him and be saved. The Jews were well familiar with the significance of the lamb as a sacrificial animal. Here the sacrificed and risen Lamb of God is seen standing victoriously on Mount Sion.

The Standing On The Mount

... stood on the mount Sion, (Revelation 14:1b) Mount Sion is a place of worship that is especially connected to the Jew and Jerusalem. Remember that this is a prophetic vision. So, let us also keep in mind that this is an earthly scene. We know that there is also a heavenly Jerusalem referred to by Paul in the book of Hebrews.

> **But ye are come unto mount Sion, and unto the city of the living God, the heavenly Jerusalem, and to an innumerable company of angels. (Hebrews 12:22)**

There is no doubt that there is both a heavenly place and an earthly place called by the same name. However, when we consider the context, we learn that this passage here refers to the earthly Mt. Zion in Jerusalem.

The Size Of The Multitude

... and with him an hundred forty and four thousand, having his Father's name written in their foreheads. (Revelation 14:1c) This is the second time in the book of Revelation that we've come across the 144,000. Back in chapter

7, we were first introduced to them and saw that they were given the seal of God in their foreheads. Now this is a tremendous sight! Here stands the Lamb of God on Mount Zion along with those who belong to Him. What John saw in this scene is a vision of the triumphant Lamb of God and the 144,000 gathered in Jerusalem at the end of the Great Tribulation.

> **Yet have I set my king upon my holy hill of Zion. I will declare the decree: the LORD hath said unto me, Thou art my Son; this day have I begotten thee. Ask of me, and I shall give thee the heathen for thine inheritance, and the uttermost parts of the earth for thy possession. Thou shalt break them with a rod of iron; thou shalt dash them in pieces like a potter's vessel. (Psalm 2:6-9)**
>
> **Then the moon shall be confounded, and the sun ashamed, when the LORD of hosts shall reign in mount Zion, and in Jerusalem, and before his ancients gloriously. (Isaiah 24:23)**
>
> **And I will pour upon the house of David, and upon the inhabitants of Jerusalem, the spirit of grace and of supplications: and they shall look upon me whom they have pierced, and they shall mourn for him, as one mourneth for his only son, and shall be in bitterness for him, as one that is in bitterness for his firstborn. (Zechariah 12:10)**

What a grand and glorious day this will be for Israel when she at last recognizes and receives her Messiah. This scene will literally take place at the end of the Tribulation Period and just preceding the beginning of Christ's Millennial reign. This will be a glorious day for the nation of Israel.

THEIR PERSUASION

And I heard a voice from heaven, as the voice of many waters, and as the voice of a great thunder... (Revelation 14:2a) Notice how the victory of these faithful followers have an impact and influence in Heaven. A voice as many waters is heard from Heaven. This voice has been heard several times in the book of Revelation (4:5; 6:1; 8:5; 11:19). This particular voice belongs to none other than Almighty God.

> **The LORD on high is mightier than the noise of many waters, yea, than the mighty waves of the sea. (Psalm 93:4)**

When Christ returns from Heaven, He will take His seat on the throne of David atop Jerusalem's Mount Zion and rule from there with a rod of iron for a thousand years.

... and I heard the voice of harpers harping with their harps. (Revelation 14:2b) When the victory of the Lamb and His faithful remnant is announced in Heaven and rejoicing breaks out. The heavenly choir is accompanied by harps. These are symbols of joy and gladness. This joy is associated with Christ's redemption. The **voice of harpers** is the voice of the saints. They are those who have been redeemed by the blood of the Lamb. Heaven will be a place of music and merriment as the blood bough redeemed of the Lord sing to His glory.

THEIR PRAISE

And they sung as it were a new song before the throne, and before the four beasts, and the elders... (Revelation 14:3a) Heaven will be full of praise and worship. These 144,000 will have a special song of victory to sing—it is a new song. At this time the tribulation period will have ended, and the millennial reign of Christ established. These soldiers of Christ have labored extensively for seven years. At last, they stand at the threshold of eternity. They shall live forevermore in the presence of our great God and Saviour, the Lord Jesus Christ. When they arrive victorious and triumphant, they will sing a **new song.** It is a wonderful thing that God has a new song for His children.

> **Sing unto him a new song ... (Psalm 33:3)**
>
> **And he hath put a new song in my mouth ... (Psalm 40:3)**
>
> **O sing unto the LORD a new song ... (Psalms 96:1, Psalm 98:1)**

> I will sing a new song unto thee, O God ... (Psalm 144:9)
>
> Praise ye the LORD. Sing unto the LORD a new song ... (Psalm 149:1)

This will be a time when they will experience the truth that the psalmist spoke of.

> For his anger endureth but a moment; in his favour is life: weeping may endure for a night, but joy cometh in the morning. (Psalm 30:5)

Praise God! There is a glad morning is coming! There is coming a day when our wonderful Saviour will wipe away every tear from our eyes and the heartaches and hurts of this life will be remembered no more. What a time of praising God it will be when the redeemed stands in His presence. The Bible has a great deal to say about praising God.

> The LORD is my strength and my shield; my heart trusted in him, and I am helped: therefore my heart greatly rejoiceth; and with my song will I praise him. (Psalm 28:7)

God's people ought to be a shouting and singing people. If anyone has anything to sing and shout about, it is God's blood bought people. Oh! How we ought to praise His Holy Name. Think about the worship and praise of Heaven's people! We ought to get a head start will we are here.

THEIR PRIVILEGE

And no man could learn that song but the hundred and forty and four thousand, which were redeemed from the earth. (Revelation 14:3b) Of all of God's redeemed people only the 144,000 could learn and sing this song. This is a song particular to the 144,000—only they will be able to sing it. No one else can sing this song because no one else has experienced what they have. Not one of the 144,000 were harmed or lost—they came through the Tribulation Period unscathed. They have been faithful in their witness and testimony for Christ during the darkest hours to ever fall on this earth. Though many had been saved during the tribulation they did not endure the entire seven years. No one else had experienced what these faithful 144,000 witnesses had and only they could praise God for it. What a lesson for us today. We are indeed a blessed people we are! We serve a good God. We ought to occupy ourselves with praising Him.

> **Bless the LORD, O my soul, and forget not all his benefits. (Psalm 103:2)**

The Psalmist asked ...

> **What shall I render unto the LORD for all his benefits toward me? (Psalm 116:12)**
>
> **I will bless the LORD at all times: his praise shall continually be in my mouth. (Psalm 34:1)**
>
> **By him therefore let us offer the sacrifice of praise to God continually, that is, the fruit of our lips giving thanks to his name. (Hebrews 13:15)**
>
> **Praise him for his mighty acts: praise him according to his excellent greatness. (Psalm 150:2)**

God has done so much for His people. How about our praise? There are things that God has done for us personally. His precious and protective hand has been upon us. Are we faithful to praise Him for His mighty works?

THEIR PURITY

These are they which were not defiled with women; for they are virgins. These are they which follow the Lamb whithersoever he goeth. These were redeemed from among men, being the firstfruits unto God and to the Lamb. And in their mouth was found no guile: for they are without fault before the throne of God. (Revelation 14:4a-5) These 144,000 Jews will be virgins; they will never marry. Many commentators have gone to great lengths to attempt to show that this text means that they were spiritual virgins, and that this passage symbolizes their purity in Christ. However, the text is clear that these men were virgins in the sense that they were not defiled with women. To remain single is God's plan for their life. God has a purpose for His requirements. Paul spoke of celibacy as being a gift from God.

> Now concerning the things whereof ye wrote unto me: It is good for a man not to touch a woman ... For I would that all men were even as I myself. But every man hath his proper gift of God, one after this manner, and another after that. I say therefore to the unmarried and widows, It is good for them if they abide even as I. But if they cannot contain, let them marry: for it is better to marry than to burn. (1 Corinthians 7:1, 7-9)

Paul taught that both marriage and celibacy is good. While celibacy is good because it allows a man to focus his whole attention on the work of God, it can also be dangerous if God has not given the gift of being celibate. We must remember that it was God who established marriage. He did so because man needed a wife.

> And the LORD God said, It is not good that the man should be alone; I will make him an help meet for him. (Genesis 2:18)

God set marriage up for man, and only God can give man the gift and grace to be celibate. The Roman Catholic Church has forced celibacy on her priests and the result has been disastrous. Notice Paul's warning, **But if they cannot contain, let them marry: for it is better to marry than to burn.** If one does not have the gift of celibacy, it is better for him to marry rather than to burn inwardly with lust. The tribulation will be an awful time of destruction, disease, and danger. Just think of trying to care for and raise a family in such times. It would be nearly impossible for these men of God to be faithful in both serving God and caring for their families. Therefore, these 144,000 were given the special gift of celibacy so that all their time and energy could go into serving God.

THEIR PATH

These are they which follow the Lamb whithersoever he goeth. (Revelation 14:4b) If we follow the Lamb we will end up in the right place. These men are faithful followers of Christ—

they are committed. Nothing will stop them from serving and they will refuse no path that Christ sets them on. Jesus said:

> **My sheep hear my voice, and I know them, and they follow me. (John 10:27)**

The 144,000 heard their Saviour and faithfully followed. We must realize that this is the kind of loyalty which Christ desires and demands of His followers, even today.

ANGELIC MESSENGERS
Revelation 14:6-13

The gospel message is dear to the heart of God. Even during the fierce judgment of the Tribulation Period, the gospel is still a high priority as God deals with the lost world. One of God's great desires is that sinners come to Christ. So, much so that He gave His only begotten Son as a sacrifice for man's sin.

THE DECLARATION OF THE GOSPEL

In this vision, an angel was sent for the purpose of declaring the everlasting gospel to the world. Angels will play a major role in the end-time events (Matthew 24:31, 25:31; 2 Thessalonians 1:7; Revelation, 8:6; 11:15; 16:1). In this passage we see three truths concerning the angel's message.

An Everlasting Message

And I saw another angel fly in the midst of heaven, having the everlasting gospel to preach unto them that dwell on the earth, and to every nation, and kindred, and tongue, and people, (Revelation 14:6) This everlasting gospel is to be preached to the people of **every nation, and kindred, and tongue** at the end of the Great Tribulation Period, immediately preceding the judgment of all nations when the sheep will be divided from the goats (Matthew25:31-46). The word **gospel** means *"good news."* It is indeed good news that people in any dispensation or situation can be forgiven and saved through faith. Notice it is described as the **everlasting** gospel. John Walvoord said:

> *It is everlasting in the sense that it is ageless, not for any specific period.*

Here the everlasting gospel also includes the good news that God is ready to conclude His judgments on the government of the antichrist and the satanic one world church. Notice this gospel message is directed to them that dwell on the earth. This phrase refers to the lost (Revelation 3:10; 6:10; 8:13; 11:10; 13:8, 12, 14; 17:2, 8).

An Essential Message

Saying with a loud voice, Fear God, (Revelation 14:7a) Included in this gospel message, is the call to repent and turn to Christ for salvation. For those who have not taken the mark of the beast there is hope. **Fear God, and give glory to him** is the cry of this Angel. Their hope begins with the fear of God. The fear of God is missing in today's world. This world lives from day to day, as if there is no God to answer to. In these last days, the fact that this world does not fear God is clearly seen in their actions. Our news is filled with school shootings, murders, rapes, robberies, and all sorts of wickedness. With over 4,000 babies murdered every day in their mother's wombs, it is clear that there is no respect for life. Our televisions and movie screens are filled with violence, death, and sex. Many programs on television openly glorify and promote the sodomite lifestyle. The air waves are filled with raw blasphemy. We have children killing children, adults killing unborn children, and our homes flooded with violence and wickedness. We are living amidst what the Bible calls a **perverse and crooked generation.**

If it is this bad now, how much worse it will be during the tribulation, when all restraints are removed? During the Tribulation Period, men will live as if there is no God to answer to. Like the ungodly crowd Paul spoke of:

> **There is no fear of God before their eyes. (Romans 3:18)**

The Bible declares that:

> **The fear of the LORD is the beginning of knowledge: but fools despise wisdom and instruction. (Proverbs 1:7)**

Saved people fear God as they ought and therefore, they live to please Him. However, fools live without considering the fact that they must answer to the Holy God of Heaven for their ways. They live on in sin not considering what their end will be. Therefore, they live wicked and sinful lives, enjoying the...

... pleasures of sin for a season. (Hebrews 11:25)

What precious mercy and grace we see here as our Great God once again issues the call for people to repent and glorify Him. God wants people to be saved. He continues to be merciful to the very last minute.

An Exalting Message

... and give glory to him; for the hour of his judgment is come: and worship him that made heaven, and earth, and the sea, and the fountains of waters. (Revelation 14:7b) Here our attention is directed to the God of creation. He is the God that **made heaven, and earth, and the sea, and the fountains of waters.** This pronouncement emphasizes the omnipotence and omniscience that God exhibited in the creation. He is the Almighty!

THE DOWNFALL OF BABYLON

And there followed another angel, saying, Babylon is fallen, is fallen, that great city, because she made all nations drink of the wine of the wrath of her fornication. (Revelation 14:8) The next Angel clearly announces the destruction of Babylon—the center of the antichrist's empire. Babylon will be the capital of the antichrist's political and religious empire. The city of Babylon is mentioned here because it is the capital. However, God's judgment will include the entire empire as we will see in chapters 17 and 18.

THE DOOM OF THE DEFECTORS

And the third angel followed them, (Revelation 14:9a) A third angel announces the severe judgment of those who follow the antichrist. These are people who choose their wicked over God's way. Notice three things here.

The Solemn Declaration

... saying with a loud voice, If any man worship the beast and his image, and receive his mark in his forehead, or in his hand, (Revelation 14:9b) God's judgment awaits anyone who worships the image of the anti-christ or who receives the mark of the beast. Millions worldwide will follow the antichrist. We learned earlier concerning the false prophet that ...

> **... he causeth all, both small and great, rich and poor, free and bond, to receive a mark in their right hand, or in their foreheads: (Revelation 13:16)**

The false prophet will exalt the antichrist deceiving many and motivating them to worship the beast. Those who receive the mark of the beast acknowledge that they accept the anti-Christ's claim to be god and recognize him as such.

The Sure Damnation

The same shall drink of the wine of the wrath of God, which is poured out without mixture into the cup of his indignation; and he shall be tormented with fire and brimstone in the presence of the holy angels, and in the presence of the Lamb: (Revelation 14:10) These are startling and sure words. Those who take the mark of the beast will lose all hope of redemption and will suffer the torments and horrors of the lake of fire throughout all eternity. What a contrast we have here between God's people and the antichrist's followers.

> **And the smoke of their torment ascendeth up forever and ever, and they have no rest day nor night, who worship the beast and his image.**

While the redeemed of God will live in a land of fadeless eternal day, the wicked will suffer in Hell both day and night forever. What an awful place Hell is. We read of its horrors and yet we cannot fully comprehend it.

> **And it came to pass, that the beggar died, and was carried by the angels into Abraham's bosom:**

the rich man also died, and was buried; And in hell he lift up his eyes, being in torments, and seeth Abraham afar off, and Lazarus in his bosom. (Luke16:22–23)

This is one of the saddest passages in all the Bible. It is sad because it is the account of a man losing his soul. The tragic results are the same for everyone who dies without Christ. The Bible says, **And in hell he lift up his eyes, being in torments**. One of the most difficult things in the world is to get folks to believe that God means what He says. The unsaved attempt to explain Hell away, but my friend that does not change what God has said. Folks laugh and joke about Hell, but that does not change things. Many times, I've heard the old saying, *"I don't mind going to Hell, I have plenty of friends there."* You'll mind it once you get there. I have news for you! The party in Hell has been canceled due to fire. All your joking and laughing will be over!

The Set Duration

And the smoke of their torment ascendeth up for ever and ever: and they have no rest day nor night, who worship the beast and his image, and whosoever receiveth the mark of his name. (Revelation 14:11) Notice the words, **forever and ever**. The lake of fire is an eternal place. A never-ending place where there is no such thing as a second chance. People who die lost and go to Hell will be there for eternity. The saddest thing about a man losing his soul is that it is lost for forever! Hell is a place where the lost go for eternity. When we think of being lost and going to this awful place of torment, for eternity, it is more than the human mind can comprehend. What is your eternal destiny?

THE DEATH OF THE SAINTS

Here is the patience of the saints: here are they that keep the commandments of God, and the faith of Jesus. And I heard a voice from heaven saying unto me, Write, Blessed are the dead which die in the Lord from henceforth: Yea, saith the Spirit, that they may rest from their labours; and their works do follow them. (Revelation 14:12-13) When the heat is turned up, the persecution of God's people will intensify at the hand of the antichrist and false prophet. God announces this message of hope and Heaven for the martyred saints of the tribulation. So cold and cruel is the antichrist's pursuit of the saints that God especially reminds them of the reward awaiting all who for His sake suffer unto death. God has the last word. Tribulation saints will be martyred for their faith and allegiance to Christ and Satan will laugh as if he has won. However, God says **Blessed are the dead which die in the Lord.** To die in the Lord is no tragedy.

WHEN THE WICKED REAP THE WRATH OF GOD
Revelation 14:14-20

Here we have two more angels who announce judgments that will come at the end of the Tribulation Period. These prophecies speak of the terrible and dreaded battle known as Armageddon. This battle will take place in the valley of Megiddo. The metaphor used to describe the awful events of this battle are taken from the treading of ripe grapes in the winepress.

THE REAPER

And I looked, and behold a white cloud, and upon the cloud one sat like unto the Son of man, having on his head a golden crown, and in his hand a sharp sickle. (Revelation 14:14) The first thing we see here is a man sitting upon a cloud. He is likened unto the **Son of man.** Of course, the Lord Jesus is the **Son of man** who will come in judgment. From the description given we can see that this is Jesus Christ Who is returning as Lord of lords and King of kings. So, this is a reference to the Second Coming of Christ (Revelation 19:11-16) Let's take note of several characteristics of our Lord here in this verse.

His Cloud

And I looked, and behold a white cloud... (Revelation 14:14a) You will remember our earlier study of how the cloud speaks of Divine presence. We are told of God that:

> **He maketh the clouds His chariot. (Psalm 104:3)**

The Lord led Israel by day in:

> **... a pillar of a cloud. (Exodus 13:21)**

When Israel murmured:

> **... the glory of the LORD appeared in the cloud. (Exodus 16:10)**

At Sinai He descended in:
> ... a thick cloud. (Exodus 19:9,16)

When the tables of stone were renewed to replace the broken ones:
> **The LORD descended in the cloud. (Exodus 34:4-5)**

When the tabernacle was completed:
> **...a cloud covered the tent of the congregation, and the glory of the LORD filled the tabernacle. (Exodus 40:34)**

This cloud was called the:
> ... cloud of the LORD. (Exodus 40:38)

God had said:
> **I will appear in the cloud upon the mercy seat. (Leviticus 16:2)**

On the Mount Of Transfiguration:
> **A bright cloud overshadowed them: (Matthew 17:5)**

When Christ ascended into Heaven:
> ... a cloud received Him. (Acts 1:9)

Of His second coming He said:
> **They shall see the Son of Man coming in a cloud with power and great glory. (Luke 21:27)**

Referring to this time when Christ would return in His Glory the Bible says:
> **Behold, He cometh with clouds. (Revelation 1:7)**

This passage here in Revelation is a direct fulfillment of Daniel's prophecy of the Ancient of Days coming to establish His kingdom.

> **I saw in the night visions, and, behold, one like the Son of man came with the clouds of heaven, and came to the Ancient of days, and they brought him near before him. And there was given him**

> dominion, and glory, and a kingdom, that all people, nations, and languages, should serve him: his dominion is an everlasting dominion, which shall not pass away, and his kingdom that which shall not be destroyed. (Daniel 7:13-14)

This One sitting on this cloud is the King of kings and Lord of lords—the Lord Jesus Christ in His glory.

His Character

...and upon the cloud one sat like unto the Son of man... (Revelation 14:14b) This is a title that Christ used often of Himself (Matthew 8:20; 9:6; 24:27,30; Mark 2:10, 28; 8:31; 9:9; Luke 6:22; 7:34; 9:22;12:8; John 5:27; 6:27,62; 8:28). This is the Lord Jesus returning in glory. At this time the victorious Christ will take His throne and rule with a rod of iron.

His Crown

... having on his head a golden crown. (Revelation 14:14c) As the God's anointed Jesus He wears a golden crown. He is crowned and coming as King. The **golden crown** symbolizes Christ's royalty and right to reign over the nations. The word for **crown** is *"stephanos."* Another common work for crown is *"diadem."* The *"diadem"* is the crown of the king. The *"stephanos"* is the victor's crown. It is the crown of the conqueror. Here we see Jesus coming back to earth to conquer, and to be victor. This is the Sovereign Christ coming to conquer the wicked and take His rightful place as Ruler. He will rule with a rod of iron.

> **Thou shalt break them with a rod of iron; thou shalt dash them in pieces like a potter's vessel. (Psalm 2:9)**

This event was described by Zechariah the prophet.

> **And his feet shall stand in that day upon the mount of Olives, which is before Jerusalem on the east, and the mount of Olives shall cleave in the midst thereof toward the east and toward the west, and there shall be a very great valley; and half of the mountain shall remove toward the north, and half of it toward the south. (Zechariah 14:4)**

This will be a devastating time for this world, but a glorious one for Christ and His people. His cause, He is coming for a reason **and in his hand a sharp sickle.** The harvest is in view here as our Saviour stands with His sickle. Praise God for these days of grace. However, the day is coming when the wicked of this world will pass the deadline and Christ will come in judgment.

THE REAPING

Here we come to the time of reaping. It is time to thrust in the sickle and wipe all wickedness from the earth. The angels of God will be used in this reaping.

The Announcement Of Retribution

And another angel came out of the temple ... (Revelation 14:15a) This is the fourth angel mentioned in this chapter (vs. 6, 8, 9), appears on the scene. The first three angels announced the judgment while this fourth angel delivers the command to execute God's wrath.

... crying with a loud voice to him that sat on the cloud, Thrust in thy sickle, and reap: for the time is come for thee to reap; for the harvest of the earth is ripe. (Revelation 14:15b) This prophecy foresees a ripe harvest. The phrase **the time is come** indicates that God has a specific hour appointed in which He will execute His wrath. This will be a time when sinful man's iniquity has reached its peak. It is time for the Lord to deal with the crop of wickedness.

> **Be not deceived; God is not mocked: for whatsoever a man soweth, that shall he also reap. For he that soweth to his flesh shall of the flesh reap corruption; but he that soweth to the Spirit shall of the Spirit reap life everlasting. (Galatians 6:7-8)**

It is Jesus Who begins the reaping of the harvest as foretold in Scripture. John the Baptist spoke of this day when he identified Christ as the One:

> **Whose fan is in his hand, and he will thoroughly purge his floor, and gather his wheat into the garner; but he will burn up the chaff with unquenchable fire. (Matthew 3:12)**

In the gospel of Mark, Jesus Himself said:

> **So is the kingdom of God, as if a man should cast seed into the ground; And should sleep, and rise night and day, and the seed should spring and grow up, he knoweth not how. For the earth bringeth forth fruit of herself; first the blade, then the ear, after that the full corn in the ear. But when the fruit is brought forth, immediately he putteth in the sickle, because the harvest is come. (Mark 4:26-29)**

The phrase, **the harvest of the earth,** speaks of the inhabitants of the earth, those who have rejected the Lord Jesus Christ and followed the anti-Christ. The prophet Joel spoke of this harvest.

> **Assemble yourselves, and come, all ye heathen, and gather yourselves together round about: thither cause thy mighty ones to come down, O LORD. Let the heathen be wakened, and come up to the valley of Jehoshaphat: for there will I sit to judge all the heathen round about. Put ye in the sickle, for the harvest is ripe: come, get you down; for the press is full, the fats overflow; for their wickedness is great. Multitudes, multitudes in the valley of decision: for the day of the LORD is near in the valley of decision. The sun and the moon shall be darkened, and the stars shall withdraw their shining. The LORD also shall roar out of Zion, and utter his voice from Jerusalem; and the heavens and the earth shall shake: but the LORD will be the hope of his people, and the strength of the children of Israel. (Joel 3:11–16)**

The lost world will reap the fruit of its ways. When this time of judgment comes no one will be left out. Everyone will answer to God. All the wicked of the earth will be harvested and cast into the lake of fire. At this time the victorious Christ will take His throne and rule with a rod of iron.

The Action Of Reaping

And he that sat on the cloud thrust in his sickle on the earth; and the earth was reaped. (Revelation 14:16) The sickle is a tool used to reap the harvest of grain. Jesus is coming as the victor, to reap the harvest of earth (Joel 3:12, 13; Matthew 9:38; John 4:35-38). The reaper sits on a **cloud** which takes us back to the book of Daniel.

> **I saw in the night visions, and, behold, one like the Son of man came with the clouds of heaven, and came to the Ancient of days, and they brought him near before him. And there was given him dominion, and glory, and a kingdom, that all people, nations, and languages, should serve him: his dominion is an everlasting dominion, which shall not pass away, and his kingdom that which shall not be destroyed. (Daniel 7:13–14)**

Matthew also spoke of the clouds in association to Christ's second coming.

> **And then shall appear the sign of the Son of man in heaven: and then shall all the tribes of the earth mourn, and they shall see the Son of man coming in the clouds of heaven with power and great glory. (Matthew 24:30)**

The judgment will be carried out by Christ Himself. This will occur when He returns to the earth in power and glory and defeats the anti-Christ and his forces (Revelation 19:11-15). We notice that when Christ comes His judgment will be swift and immediate. He is coming in wrath to reap the harvest of the earth.

And another angel came out of the temple which is in heaven, he also having a sharp sickle. (Revelation 14:17) We continue to see the important role of the angels in God's judgment. The reapers are the angels (Matthew 13:39), with Jesus Christ as their leader. Throughout Scripture angels have played a prominent role in administering God's wrath. Here is **another angel** that is depicted as a reaper **having a sharp sickle**. The prophet Joel said:

> **Put ye in the sickle, for the harvest is ripe: come, get you down; for the press is full, the fats overflow; for their wickedness is great. Multitudes, multitudes in the valley of decision: for the day of the LORD is near in the valley of decision. (Joel 3:13-14)**

The imagery here that that of cutting down and gathering the harvest. Again, this judgment will take place at the Second Coming of Christ. With the Word from His mouth, He will ...

> **.... smite the nations: (Revelation 19:15)**

It is referred to as ...

> **... the battle of that great day of God Almighty. (Revelation 16:14)**

This will be Armageddon. The Word of God confirms that the angels will take part the wrath of the Lamb at His coming in glory.

> **The enemy that sowed them is the devil; the harvest is the end of the world; and the reapers are the angels. (Matthew 13:39)**

> **And to you who are troubled rest with us, when the Lord Jesus shall be revealed from heaven with his mighty angels, (2 Thessalonians 1:7)**

When the time comes, God will pour out His full vengeance on the ungodly. God's mighty angels will play a major part in the punishment and judgment of the wicked at the time of Armageddon.

And another angel came out from the altar, which had power over fire; and cried with a loud cry to him that had the sharp sickle, saying, Thrust in thy sharp sickle, and gather the clusters of the vine of the earth; for her grapes are fully ripe. (Revelation 14:18) Now the seventh and final angel comes from the altar. The harvest continues as the angel is given instructions to thrust his sickle in and gather the clusters.

This is not a repeat of the previous verses. This is yet another judgment. This is the judgment of the **vines** and **clusters**. In God's Word we often see the vine used a figure for Israel (Isaiah 5, Psalm 80). This is the judgment of wayward Israel. The phrase fully ripe depicts a vineyard where the vines are full of huge clusters of grapes that are so ripe, they are on the verge of rotting. At this point, sin's harvest is **fully ripe**, and it is time to reap. When Christ returns to earth in power and glory, the inhabitants of the earth will be fully ripe for the judgment He will deliver.

And the angel thrust in his sickle into the earth, and gathered the vine of the earth, and cast it into the great winepress of the wrath of God. (Revelation 14:19) We know that the holy angels will have an active part in the end time judgments.

> **And he shall send his angels with a great sound of a trumpet, and they shall gather together his elect from the four winds, from one end of heaven to the other. (Matthew 24:31)**

The angel is told to **thrust in thy sharp sickle, and gather the clusters of the vine of the earth; for her grapes are fully ripe.** This will be the fulfillment of Joel's prophecy that we mentioned earlier.

> **Let the heathen be wakened, and come up to the valley of Jehoshaphat: for there will I sit to judge all the heathen round about. Put ye in the sickle, for the harvest is ripe: come, get you down; for the press is full, the vats overflow; for their wickedness is great. (Joel 3:12-13)**

The wicked of the world are here symbolized as clusters of grapes. The depiction is that wickedness has reached its peak and God is not going to allow evil to go any further. The sharp sickle of Divine judgment will strike, and the vine of the earth cut down and cast into the great **winepress of the wrath of God**. One of the saddest things about this is that God will withdraw all mercy.

> When the boughs thereof are withered, they shall be broken off: the women come, and set them on fire: for it is a people of no understanding: therefore he that made them will not have mercy on them, and he that formed them will shew them no favour. (Isaiah 27:11)

Armageddon is God's winepress of wrath. This will be a sad day when the Almighty's mercy is withdrawn, and His fierce judgment executed upon the ungodly.

THE REALITY

> And the winepress was trodden without the city, and blood came out of the winepress, even unto the horse bridles, by the space of a thousand and six hundred furlongs. (Revelation 14:20)

The terminology of the winepress here is very clear. In Bible days, the grapes were harvested and dumped into the wine press. Then the grapes were stomped until all the juice ran out and was collected in the vats. The stain from the juice and the staining of one's feet and garments serve as a picture of divine judgment.

> Who is this that cometh from Edom, with dyed garments from Bozrah? this that is glorious in his apparel, travelling in the greatness of his strength? I that speak in righteousness, mighty to save. Wherefore art thou red in thine apparel, and thy garments like him that treadeth in the winefat? I have trodden the winepress alone; and of the people there was none with me: for I will tread them in mine anger, and trample them in my fury; and their blood shall be sprinkled upon my garments, and I will stain all my raiment. For the day of vengeance is in mine heart, and the year of my redeemed is come. (Isaiah 63:1-4)

The prophecy of Christ's second coming pictures Him as ...

> ... clothed with a vesture dipped in blood. (Revelation 19:13)

Under the judgment of God, blood will flow like juice from a winepress. A river of blood up to the horse's bridle and the length of 1,600 furlongs will flow through the streets of Palestine. Think about that! A river of blood 4 to 4 ½ feet deep and almost 200 miles long will run from the veins of the enemies of God. In chapter 19 this judgment will end with ...

> **... the supper of the great God. (Revelation 19:17)**

At the end of the Tribulation Period God will call the fowls of the air together to feed on the carnage. The world has never seen such a battle as will take place at Christ's coming. This is a prophecy of the complete annihilation of the antichrist's armies. The slaughter and carnage of this battle will cover the Megiddo Valley. This describes the intense wrath of the Almighty.

PREPARING FOR THE VIAL JUDGMENTS
Revelation 15:1-8

In chapter fifteen we come to the introduction to the seven vial judgments of chapter sixteen, and which finalize the wrath of God. Chronologically, the seven vial judgments will be poured out during the last half of the Tribulation Period. As we saw earlier, this is the time known as the *Great Tribulation.* Thus, these vial judgments will bring us to the end of the Great Tribulation. The Lord's wrath continues building to a majestic climax upon the lost world.

THE SIGN IN HEAVEN

Chapter fifteen is short as far as verses go, but as we shall see, it does not come up short on content. In this chapter we will see the seven angels who have the seven last plagues to be poured out upon the earth. These angels have the seven vials of the wrath of Almighty God.

The Awe Of The Sign

And I saw another sign in heaven, great and marvellous, (Revelation 15:1a) Here we see the scene change from earth to heaven. John described this **sign** as **great and marvellous**. The word **great** denotes *"size, magnitude and intensity."* The word **marvellous** comes from *"thaumastos"* and describes a spectacle that is wonderful and amazing. This is a stunning and awe-inspiring sign.

The Angels And The Plagues

... seven angels having the seven last plagues; (Revelation 15:1b) The Word of God states that these are **the seven last plagues.** The word **last** comes from *"eschatos"* and is the word from which eschatology is derived. Eschatology is the study of *"last things."* These are the last of the Tribulation judgments that will bring this period to an end. In other words when the vials of wrath are poured out, God's judgment will come to a climax.

The Acknowledgement Of His Wrath

... for in them is filled up the wrath of God. (Revelation 15:1c) Also, in these seven last plagues **is filled up the wrath of God.** This is a vision of judgment and Divine wrath. Let's keep in mind that this is a decisive and an absolute reaction of perfect holiness to all sin. When these judgments are finished, the Lord Jesus Christ will return in Glory to establish His Millennial reign in Jerusalem. God's greatest fury will be released up against the Antichrist, his cohorts, and his religious system. The word **wrath** comes from *"thumos"* speaks of fierceness indignation. It is a very strong word, describing rage, or an intense outburst of anger. This will be a time when God's anger will be expressed against all unforgiven sinners.

THE SEA OF GLASS

And I saw as it were a sea of glass mingled with fire: and them that had gotten the victory over the beast, and over his image, and over his mark, and over the number of his name, stand on the sea of glass, having the harps of God. (Revelation 15:2) This is the same sea we saw back in chapter four where we found it to be typical of the laver where the priest would wash before entering God's presence. Notice that his is not a sea of water, but a **sea of glass.** The **glass** speaks of the believer's fixed state of holiness in Heaven. There will be no sin there and no need for further cleansing.

This time we see it **mingled with fire**. The fire here probably speaks of the trials of fire endured by the tribulation saints. Notice that those standing on the sea of glass have won the **victory over the b**east. Praise God! There is victory in Jesus! The faithful martyrs have refused to worship the beast and take his mark. The price they paid was high. They sealed their loyalty to Christ with their life's blood. They die as martyrs for Christ. They lose their lives on earth, but they are victorious in the presence of God. The missionary martyr, Jim Elliot, penned the following words in his diary just a few days before he was murdered by the very people he was trying to reach for Christ. *"He is no fool who gives what he cannot keep to gain that which he cannot lose."* Elliot had the right perspective on the value of eternal things. Serving God can be hard at times, but it pays great dividends.

THE SONGS OF WORSHIP

The song of Moses and the song of the Lamb speak of deliverance, victory, and salvation. Moses sang about God leading Israel out of physical captivity and into the Promise Land. The song of the Lamb speaks of Christ leading a lost world out of spiritual bondage and into eternal life.

The Songs Of Redemption

And they sing the song of Moses the servant of God, (Revelation 15:3a) Well, once again we see that these tribulation events are clearly Jewish in nature. The Church is not seen here, but rather God is dealing with the Jews. This period is known as the ...

... time of Jacob's trouble. (Jeremiah 30:7),

We are told that these faithful servants sing t**he song of Moses**. The song of Moses is a song of victory and deliverance and is found in Exodus 15. The Song of Moses takes us back to Israel's exodus from Egypt. The nation had been delivered from Pharaoh by the blood of the lamb and God destroyed the Egyptian army in the Red Sea. In worship and thankfulness to God, His people stood by the sea and sang **the song of Moses** (Exodus 15). This is a song of praise concerning the mighty power and justice of God. This is a song that reminds us of God's power, faithfulness, and deliverance. Just as the Children of Israel escaped from the hands of Pharaoh and his armies, so will these faithful martyrs of the tribulation period escape the antichrist.

... and the song of the Lamb, (Revelation 15:3b) The song of the Lamb celebrates the marvelous redemption from sin by the sacrifice of Jesus Christ—the Lamb of God. Our redemption was purchased by the shed blood of the Lamb on Calvary. This is a song of eternal redemption. Throughout eternity the Lord Jesus will be praised and worshiped.

The Song Of Reverence

... saying, Great and marvellous are thy works, Lord God Almighty; just and true are thy ways, thou King of saints. Who shall not fear thee, O Lord, and glorify thy name? for thou only art holy: for all nations shall come and worship before thee; for thy judgments are made manifest. (Revelation 15:3c-4) As the Singers sing about redemption through the blood of the Lamb, they also proclaim the holiness of God, His works, justice, and name. They sing that all nations shall come and worship before Jesus after the final judgments are poured out. They remind us that the **Lord God Almighty** is to be feared, honored, and obeyed.

THE SANCTUARY OPENED

And after that I looked, and, behold, the temple of the tabernacle of the testimony in heaven was opened. (Revelation 15:5) As we have previously studied, we know that the Tabernacle which Moses built, with its altar and other articles of furniture, was made after the pattern of the true Tabernacle in the Heavenlies. In the earthly tabernacle there was the outer court, the holy place, and the holy of holies. The Ark of the Covenant, containing the two tables of stone on which were written the ten commandments was in the holy of holies. It was there in the holy of holies that God appeared in His Shekinah glory over the mercy seat. Our text says that, **the temple of the tabernacle of the testimony in heaven was opened.** Here John sees the holy place open up. Lehman Strauss says:

> *"The 'temple of the tabernacle' is the holy of holies where the ark of the testimony was kept. The ark speaks of the faithfulness of God in keeping His covenants. Under the Law of Moses, the holiest of all was concealed from the eyes of the people. Mystery shrouded that sacred area. But here the mystery of God is finished. (see 10:7) The way into the holiest is*

now open to all the redeemed, including the tribulation saints. (see 11:19) This is God's dwelling place, where He is approached and worshiped, and from which issues His just judgments."

This fact that the temple is opened indicates that the plans and purposes of God will no longer be kept secret but will be made known to all.

THE SEVEN VIALS

Now we come to the last seven judgements. These are the vial judgments. The have to do with the seven last plagues that will come on all those who reject God's offer of salvation and who worship the antichrist.

The Appearing Of The Angels

And the seven angels came out of the temple, having the seven plagues, clothed in pure and white linen, and having their breasts girded with golden girdles. (Revelation 15:6) John saw the heavenly temple open and seven angels exit carrying **seven plagues**. Notice that the seven angles and the vials of judgment come from the temple, or the very presence of God. The angels' clothing, being **in pure and white linen** speaks of purity and holiness. Having **their breasts girded with golden girdles** reminds us of the priestly garments worn during service in the tabernacle. Here we see the angels come out from the presence of God and acting on His behalf, to execute final judgment and justice on the world.

The Action Of The Beast

And one of the four beasts gave unto the seven angels seven golden vials full of the wrath of God, who liveth for ever and ever. (Revelation 15:7) Notice carefully the inspired words of this text. These angels are given seven vials, **full of the wrath of God.** We are told that these vials are **full of the wrath of God.** The longsuffering patience of a gracious and forgiving God has come to an end—the world in all of her wickedness has passed the deadline! Today God is:

> **... longsuffering to us-ward, not willing that any should perish. (2 Peter 3:9)**

However, the cup of His wrath is filling fast and someday will overflow. When it does, the judgments of God will be dreadful to those who will have to drink of the cup of His wrath.

> **For in the hand of the lord there is a cup, and the wine is red; it is full of mixture; and he poureth out of the same: but the dregs thereof, all the wicked of the earth shall wring them out, and drink them. (Psalm 75:8)**

Earlier we learned that His wrath would be poured out without mixture.

> **The same shall drink of the wine of the wrath of God, which is poured out without mixture into the cup of his indignation; and he shall be tormented with fire and brimstone in the presence of the holy angels, and in the presence of the Lamb. (Revelation 14:10)**

The term **without mixture** means that it will be pure judgment and wrath with no mixture of mercy. Here in chapter 15:8 we are told that the vials are **full of the wrath of God.** The vials being full of wrath means that there is no room for mercy. What dreadful days await the wicked! Paul warns ...

> **Behold therefore the goodness and severity of God: (Romans 11:22)**

The Psalmist declared ...

> **... God is angry with the wicked every day. (Psalm 7:11b)**

. The Word of God declares that God is longsuffering and patient. He is good. He is merciful and He is kind; but He is also a God of justice and judgment.

THE SMOKE IN THE TEMPLE

And the temple was filled with smoke from the glory of God, and from his power; and no man was able to enter into the temple, till the seven plagues of the seven angels were

fulfilled. (Revelation 15:8) The glory of God being symbolized by smoke is a familiar one in relation to the **glory of God**, especially in the Old Testament. After the Israelites completed the building of the tabernacle and placed the Ark of the Covenant within the Holy of Holies, the glory of the Lord filled that place.

> **Then a cloud covered the tent of the congregation, and the glory of the LORD filled the tabernacle. And Moses was not able to enter into the tent of the congregation, because the cloud abode thereon, and the glory of the LORD filled the tabernacle. (Exodus 40:34-35)**

Also see the dedication service of the Temple when God came in all His glory and filled the place (2 Chronicles 7:1-4). Isaiah also testified of the same truth:

> **In the year that king Uzziah died I saw also the Lord sitting upon a throne, high and lifted up, and his train filled the temple. Above it stood the seraphims: each one had six wings; with twain he covered his face, and with twain he covered his feet, and with twain he did fly. And one cried unto another, and said, Holy, holy, holy, is the LORD of hosts: the whole earth is full of his glory. And the posts of the door moved at the voice of him that cried, and the house was filled with smoke. (Isaiah 6:1-4)**

This smoke, likewise, is evidence of God's presence and glory. You will remember back in Exodus when ...

> **... a cloud covered the tent of the congregation, and the glory of the LORD filled the tabernacle. And Moses was not able to enter into the tent of the congregation, because the cloud abode thereon, and the glory of the LORD filled the tabernacle. (Exodus 40:34–35)**

The same thing happens here. We are told that ...

> **... no man was able to enter into the temple, till the seven plagues of the seven angels were fulfilled. (Revelation 15:8)**

Robert Mounce in his commentary on the book of Revelation summarizes this chapter as follows:

> "Until the seven plagues are finished, no one is able to enter the temple. Once the time of final judgment has come, none can stay the hand of God. The time for intercession is past. God in His unapproachable majesty and power has declared that the end has come. No longer does He stand knocking: He enters to act in sovereign judgment."

No one can enter the temple until the angels complete their work. Everything comes to a standstill in Heaven until the angels complete their work and the seven vial judgments are poured out.

THE SEVEN VIAL JUDGMENTS
Revelation 16:1-21

And I heard a great voice out of the temple saying to the seven angels, Go your ways, and pour out the vials of the wrath of God upon the earth. (Revelation 16:1) This chapter begins the outpouring of the vials of God's final wrath. This is the final set of seven judgments to be poured out upon the earth. The **great voice out of the temple** is the voice of God—the Almighty. The seven angels holding the vials are now commanded by God to **pour out the vials of the wrath of God upon the earth.** The **seven angels** can only execute these final judgments with God's permission. When the sealed book was opened by the Lamb of God, the seventh seal produced seven trumpet judgments (Revelation 8:1-2). Likewise, when the seventh trumpet was blown it started the seven plagues contained in the seven vials of God's wrath (Revelation 11:15-15:1). These vial judgments will conclude the wrath of the Almighty upon the world. The first four vial judgments follow the same order as the first four trumpet judgments—falling upon the earth, the sea, the waters, and the sun. Speaking of the terror and affliction of those days Jesus said ...

> **And except those days should be shortened, there should no flesh be saved: but for the elect's sake those days shall be shortened. (Matthew 24:22)**

During the former judgments God had mercifully restricted His wrath to a third of these areas. However, the Angry God of Heaven now strikes with full force. Thus, at His command, the seven angels begin to pour out God's wrath in rapid succession on a Christ rejecting world.

THE FIRST VIAL

And the first went, and poured out his vial upon the earth; and there fell a noisome and grievous sore upon the men which had the mark of the beast, and upon them which worshipped his image. (Revelation 16:2) The first vial is poured out on the earth and punishes the followers of the beast. It targets those who have the **mark of the beast** on them. With the first plague was men received nasty and dreadful sores. These dreadful boils are similar to those that God poured out on Egypt (Exodus 9:9-11).

Those who have received **the mark of the beast** will reap a harvest of their own sowing. Their payday has come. As their sinful life comes to an end, they are grievously afflicted with ulcer like boils and sores. These awful sores are described as:

Noisome—Webster defines **noisome** as *"Noxious to health; hurtful; mischievous; unwholesome; insalubrious; destructive ... injurious ... Offensive to the smell or other senses; disgusting; fetid."* Now that does not sound so good does it?

Grievous—The word **grievous** means *"to grieve or to have grief."* Webster defines it as *"heavy; oppressive; burdensome ... Afflictive; painful; hard to be borne."* Henry Morris describes these sores as:

> ... a hideous and painful infection on the bodies of men and women everywhere. This infection manifests itself as a loathsome ulcer of some kind, eating into the skin, seemingly malignant and unresponsive to medical treatment.

This first vial will result in a poisonous, putrefying, and painful effect on people's physical bodies. It is for certain that those living during this time will suffer intense, excruciating pain. The prophet Zechariah tells us that those who have worshipped the beast will literally rot away under God's judgment.

> **And this shall be the plague wherewith the LORD will smite all the people that have fought against Jerusalem; Their flesh shall consume away while they stand upon their feet, and their eyes shall consume away in their holes, and their tongue shall consume away in their mouth. (Zechariah 14:12)**

These sores will be incurable. No doctor will be able to help. No medicine will heal them. There will be no help or hope for those who worship the beast. This judgment is similar to the judgment of boils that God poured out upon the Egyptians when they refused to let Israel leave Egypt and go to the Promise Land (Exodus 9:8-11). Also, the disease that God sent upon the who refused to follow the Lord and followed after false gods and idols (Deuteronomy 28:27-35) However, this judgment is much worse and far more devastating. These dreadful sores will be extremely and excruciatingly painful. In addition to the pain, the smell will be almost unbearable.

THE SECOND VIAL

And the second angel poured out his vial upon the sea; and it became as the blood of a dead man: and every living soul died in the sea. (Revelation 16:3) Under the second trumpet judgment. (Revelation 8:8-9), one third of the sea became as blood, but here God's judgment falls in its entirety and the whole sea is affected. This is not to be explained away by claiming it to be symbolic. This is the actual and literal judgment of Almighty God. Not one creature in the sea will survive. Notice carefully the wording of the text. It did not simply say that the sea became as blood. No! But that it **became as the blood of a dead man.** This was not fresh and living blood—it was dead blood. This blood is rotting, foul, and putrid with its nasty odor spreading world-wide. What a horrible condition. Nature lovers are going to have a real problem here. Henry Morris wrote:

> *"Exactly what chemical reactions take place to produce this lethal transformation of the waters of earth's vast oceans we do not know, though chemists could offer speculative suggestions. We can be sure, however, that the angel of the waters knows far more about water chemistry than any modern organic chemist and is well able to initiate and maintain such reactions until, indeed, all the earth's great and wide seas are filled with a deadly solution having the appearance and chemical components of the noxious blood of a human corpse. In this toxic ocean nothing can survive, and soon all the billions of fishes and*

> marine mammals and marine reptiles and the innumerable varieties of marine invertebrates will perish, thus still further poisoning the oceans and contaminating the sea shores of the world. The oceans will have effectively completed their age long function in earth's physical economy, and will die. As God had created every living soul in the waters. (Genesis 1:21), so now every living soul died in the sea."

Just think for a moment about the effects of this judgment. Every creature in the sea will die and the surface of the sea and the shores will be covered with dead and decaying bodies. The nauseating stench of rotten blood and flesh will be incomparable to anything that has ever happened in the history of man. The ships become so bogged down that they will be immovable and all on board will die, further adding to the catastrophe.

THE THIRD VIAL

As we come to the Third Vail, we find that things just keep getting worse for the unsaved world. The wrath keeps coming and it intensifies as it comes.

The Pouring

And the third angel poured out his vial upon the rivers and fountains of waters; and they became blood. (Revelation 16:4) Having destroyed the seas, God now focuses His judgment upon the fresh waters of the earth. Again, it is imperative that we understand these to be literal judgments. In Exodus chapter 7, we find that God literally turned the water to blood in dealing with Pharaoh. There is no reason to suppose that this passage is symbolic. These are literal judgment that will fall upon sinful man during the Great Tribulation. All the fresh waters, wells, streams, and springs are now targeted. All the world's life-sustaining water will be turned into blood. What an awful judgment that men will be made to drink bloody water.

The Praise

And I heard the angel of the waters say, Thou art righteous, O Lord, which art, and wast, and shalt be, because

thou hast judged thus. (Revelation 16:5) The angel of the waters was in absolute agreement with God's divine wrath. This angel states that God had judged righteously in turning the rivers and fountains of water to blood.

> **... Shall not the Judge of all the earth do right? (Genesis 18:25)**

Thou art righteous, O Lord... The Holy God of Heaven is Righteous God. It is clear that the holy God judges and pours out wrath in perfect righteousness.

The Payment

For they have shed the blood of saints and prophets, and thou hast given them blood to drink; for they are worthy. (Revelation 16:6) Notice here the reason for this particular judgment. **For they have shed the blood of saints and prophets.** Mark it down my friend God is just, and evil men will get what is coming to them.

> **Be not deceived; God is not mocked: for whatsoever a man soweth, that shall he also reap. (Galatians 6:7)**

Hateful and wicked men who have shed the blood of saints will now have to drink these bloody waters. Notice that the text says, **for they are worthy.** In other words, they have earned the judgment and wrath of Almighty God.

> **For we know him that hath said, Vengeance belongeth unto me, I will recompense, saith the Lord. And again, The Lord shall judge his people. It is a fearful thing to fall into the hands of the living God. (Hebrews 10:30-31)**

God will hand out just what man has earned—nothing more, nothing less. There will no *"this isn't fair"* defense. The perfect and holy justice of God will see to it that everyone gets his fair judgment.

The Purity

And I heard another out of the altar say, Even so, Lord God Almighty, true and righteous are thy judgments. (Revelation 16:7) Again, God judgment is defended by a voice from the altar. The voice is basically saying, *"They got what was coming to them."* This is an answer to the prayers of the saints under the altar (chapter 6).

THE FOURTH VIAL

And the fourth angel poured out his vial upon the sun; and power was given unto him to scorch men with fire. And men were scorched with great heat, and blasphemed the name of God, which hath power over these plagues: and they repented not to give him glory. (Revelation 16:8-9) What a blessing the sun is to mankind as it gives forth its heat and light for his benefit. Here, however, the sun will be turned into a means of torment. According to our text it is still possible for men to repent; but instead, hardened in their heart from the very depth of their depravity they lash out and blaspheme the very God Who in mercy would save if they would simply call upon Him.

THE FIFTH VIAL

And the fifth angel poured out his vial upon the seat of the beast; and his kingdom was full of darkness; and they gnawed their tongues for pain, And blasphemed the God of heaven because of their pains and their sores, and repented not of their deeds. (Revelation 16:10-11) When the fourth angel sounded his trumpet, a third of the sun was affected causing darkness (8: 12); now as a result of the fourth vial of God's wrath being poured out, the entire sun is affected. What a dreadful time this will be. An awful darkness now covers the earth. The sun which was so intensely hot that man was scorched by its heat is now turned off and an awful darkness engulfs the land. This is the fulfillment of the prophecy of Joel.

> **Blow ye the trumpet in Zion, and sound an alarm in my holy mountain: let all the inhabitants of the land tremble: for the day of the lord cometh, for it is nigh at hand; a day of darkness and of gloominess, a day of clouds and of thick darkness, as the morning spread upon the mountains: a great people and a strong; there hath not been ever the like, neither**

shall be any more after it, even to the years of many generations. (Joel 2:1-2)

The conditions upon earth go from blinding and scorching heat to absolute darkness. So, devastating are these judgments that **they gnawed their tongues for pain.** They had previously used their tongues to blaspheme God will now cry out in agony as they chew their tongue off.

THE SIXTH VIAL

As God's wrath continues, His judgment increases in intensity as the events rush toward Armageddon.

The Daring Commencement

And the sixth angel poured out his vial upon the great river Euphrates; and the water thereof was dried up, that the way of the kings of the east might be prepared. (Revelation 16:12) The final judgement commences when the sixth vial is poured out and the great river Euphrates is dried up, **that the way of the kings of the east might be prepared.** The river Euphrates is one of the mightiest rivers in the world and holds a prominent place in Scripture. This great river will be dried up for the specific purpose of letting the armies of the east cross and enter **a place called in the Hebrew tongue Armageddon.** Isaiah spoke of the day when the Lord would ...

> **... with his mighty wind shall he shake his hand over the river, and shall smite it in the seven streams, and make men go over dryshod. (Isaiah 11:15)**

The foolish kings of the east will come across the dried-up Euphrates to participate in the battle of Armageddon. Little do they know that they are headed to their own destruction.

The Demonic Coalition

And I saw three unclean spirits like frogs come out of the mouth of the dragon, and out of the mouth of the beast, and out of the mouth of the false prophet. (Revelation 16:13) John looked and saw three unclean spirits come forth. One came forth from the mouth of the dragon—the Devil. One came forth from the beast—antichrist. The third one came forth from the false prophet. The text is clear that these are miracle-working demons. Their purpose is to gather the kings of the earth for the great battle of Armageddon.

> **Behold, the day of the LORD cometh, and thy spoil shall be divided in the midst of thee. For I will gather all nations against Jerusalem to battle; and the city shall be taken, and the houses rifled, and the women ravished; and half of the city shall go forth into captivity, and the residue of the people shall not be cut off from the city. Then shall the LORD go forth, and fight against those nations, as when he fought in the day of battle. (Zechariah 14:1-3)**

The three unclean spirits that come out of the mouth of the Satanic trinity have a purpose. They go forth to gather the kings of the earth for the Battle of Armageddon.

The Deceitful Counterfeits

For they are the spirits of devils, working miracles, which go forth unto the kings of the earth and of the whole world, to gather them to the battle of that great day of God Almighty. (Revelation 16:14) These demonic beings go forth from Satan to unite the armies of the world to fight against the Lord. The proud kings of the earth will be deceived by the miracle-working demons and the combined military strength of the nations will gather in the valley of Megiddo against Jesus Christ. The armies will come from all parts of the earth and join forces against Christ. The name **Armageddon** means *"mountain of slaughter"* and that is exactly what it will be. When our Lord is finished with the ungodly armies of this world, He will call the buzzards together to clean up the carnage.

The Divine Counsel

Behold, I come as a thief. Blessed is he that watcheth, and keepeth his garments, lest he walk naked, and they see his shame. (Revelation 16:15) The Church age saints have already been raptured and are in Heaven at this point. Thus, this warning is to Tribulation saints. The Lord Jesus warns these believers that He is coming **as a thief**. As we saw earlier, a thief comes when he is not expected, but when he is not expected. He comes suddenly and without warning. Jesus is warning the Tribulation saints to watch, stay pure and be ready for His coming.

The Deadly Campaign

And he gathered them together into a place called in the Hebrew tongue Armageddon. (Revelation 16:16) As the armies make their way across the Euphrates, they gather into a place **called in the Hebrew tongue Armageddon**. Armageddon means *"Mount of Megiddo "*and is located in the plain of Jezreel in northern Israel. Megiddo will be the staging area for the armies of the Beast as they make war against God. Jezreel runs through the middle of the Holy Land and stretches from the Mediterranean Sea to the Sea of Galilee. It is roughly two hundred miles long and fifteen miles wide. This massive valley is where the Battle of Armageddon is going to be fought. This will not be a single battle but a series of battles that will finally culminate in the battle at Armageddon when the Lord returns.

THE SEVENTH VIAL

We come now to the last of the seven vial judgments. This will be the most catastrophic and most terrible judgment of the Tribulation Period.

The Satanic Domain

And the seventh angel poured out his vial into the air; (Revelation 16:17a) The last of the seven vials was poured out **into the air.** This is the realm where Satan is permitted to reign. Satan is **the prince of the power of the air, (Ephesians 2:2)** The seventh vial will be a Divine attack against the evil realm of Satan. The seven years Tribulation Period is now coming to an end and God is finishing up His wrath upon Satan, his evil trinity along with the wicked of this world.

The Sovereign Declaration

... and there came a great voice out of the temple of heaven, from the throne, saying, It is done. (Revelation 16:17b) When the last vial is poured out a voice was heard coming out of the temple from the throne, saying, It is done. Notice that the **great voice** which John heard was **out of the temple of heaven, from the throne.** This is the voice of God. The Almighty declares **It is done.** What is done? God's wrath is finally poured out and its completion realized. Oliver B. Greene, in his commentary on the book of Revelation wrote:

> *From the seat of the Judge of all, we have the announcement that it is done. This is the climax! When Jesus paid the supreme price for the redemption of sinners, just before He died, He cried "IT IS FINISHED!" On the cross He finished redemption for the soul. Nothing more can be added. Redemption of the soul is complete in Jesus. And now, the judgment of the earth is done. It, too, is finished! Jesus Christ is about to rid the earth of the dragon, the Beast, and the false prophet. The contents of the little seven-sealed book are completed. Every minute detail has been carried out and the whole creation at last will stop "groaning and travailing in pain" (Romans 8:22). IT IS DONE! HALLELUJAH!*

It is done. At this point the Tribulation Period has run its awful course. Hence, as we come to the last vial poured out by the seventh angel here in our text, we are rapidly coming to the end of the seven-year Tribulation Period.

The Seismic Destruction

And there were voices, and thunders, and lightnings; and there was a great earthquake, such as was not since men were upon the earth, so mighty an earthquake, and so great. (Revelation 16:18) The pouring out of the seventh vial will result in the most catastrophic and most terrible judgment of the Tribulation Period. Never in the history of the has there been such calamity, confusion, chaos, confusion, conflict, agitation, upheaval and such cataclysmic events upon this earth as will be when the seventh vial is poured out! There will be a **great earthquake.** This will be the most devastating earthquake the world has known. Notice the phrase **such as was not since men were upon the earth.** This will be the most devasting and destructive earthquake in all of human history.

The Separating Division

And the great city was divided into three parts, and the cities of the nations fell: (Revelation 16:19a) The awful judgments connected to the seventh plague included **the great city**. There is some disagreement among Bible teachers as to the identification of the great city. Some believe it is Jerusalem (11:8) while others believe it is Babylon (17&18). The great city seems to be a reference to Jerusalem for several reasons. Israel is the center of prophecy. Remember that the Tribulation Period is a time of **Jacob's trouble. (Jeremiah 30:7)** Jacob is a reference to Israel. Jerusalem will be the focal point of the Tribulation. The Battle of Armageddon is going to be fought only a few miles in the Valley of Megiddo. Notice that this great city is divided into three parts. Zechariah spoke of this event.

> **And his feet shall stand in that day upon the mount of Olives, which is before Jerusalem on the east, and the mount of Olives shall cleave in the midst thereof toward the east and toward the west, and there shall be a very great valley; and half of the mountain shall remove toward the north, and half of it toward the south. (Zechariah 14:4)**
>
> **And it shall come to pass, that in all the land, saith the LORD, two parts therein shall be cut off and die; but the third shall be left therein. And I will bring the third part through the fire, and will refine them as silver is refined, and will try them as gold is tried: they shall call on my name, and I will hear them: I will say, It is my people: and they shall say, The LORD is my God. (Zechariah 13:8-9).**

A colossal earthquake will shake the entire area and split Jerusalem into **three parts**. This earthquake will be so powerful that the Mount of Olives will break in half, with one half moving toward the east and the other toward the west. This will set in motion a series of geophysical changes that culminate when

Christ returns to earth with His saints at the end of the Tribulation Period.

... and great Babylon came in remembrance before God, to give unto her the cup of the wine of the fierceness of his wrath. (Revelation 16:19b) God's greatest and most fierce judgment is reserved for Babylon, which will receive **the cup of the wine of the fierceness of his wrath.** In the next chapter we will see the effects of this judgment as Babylon falls. Everything plummets into utter ruin.

The Sudden Disappearance

And every island fled away, and the mountains were not found. (Revelation 16:20) So great will be the magnitude of this earthquake and its effect upon the earth, that the islands of the sea and the mountains will vanish away.

The Storms Devastation

And there fell upon men a great hail out of heaven, every stone about the weight of a talent: and men blasphemed God because of the plague of the hail; for the plague thereof was exceeding great. (Revelation 16:21) There will be a great storm with hailstones falling that will weigh from 100 to 115 pounds. Just imagine the destruction that is yet to come. With one stroke of His mighty hand, God will destroy cities and civilizations which proud men labored tirelessly to build. Instead of repenting, **men blasphemed God.** This reveals the utter depravity and hardness of man's heart. Instead of recognizing the power and glory of our Lord, men blaspheme His holy Name.

THE JUDGMENT OF RELIGIOUS BABYLON
Revelation 17:1-18

In the Revelation, there are two main women mentioned. One is pure and the other is a harlot. One is righteous and the other is full of abominations. One is of God and the other is of Satan. Both are splendidly dressed; one with heavenly garments and the other with worldly religious garments. In this chapter we see the one world church in its last days—this is religious Babylon. In chapter 18 we will see political Babylon judged. Chapters 17 and 18 refer to the revived Roman Empire. We have already studied this in chapter 13. The head that was wounded, as it were dead, refers to the political death of the Roman empire. However, Satan will miraculously resurrect this kingdom during the Tribulation thereby deceiving and capturing the hearts of untold thousands. Rome fell in A. D. 476. Since that time, it has been an insignificant power. But it will rise again after the Rapture of the Church. A ten-nation confederacy from Europe will form the Revived Roman Empire. While everything about this harlot parallels with Rome we must be careful to understand that she is not alone but is united with all of apostate Christendom. This chapter describes the **mystery of iniquity** in its final day. The Apostle Paul said in his day:

> **For the mystery of iniquity doth already work... (2 Thessalonians 2:7a)**

Paul spoke those words two thousand years ago. He saw the apostasy and assault of unbelieving wickedness back then. Paul went on in the second part of the same verse to say:

> **... only he who now letteth will let, until he be taken out of the way. (2 Thessalonians 2:7b)**

He is referring to the Holy Spirit Who holds back and hinders the progress of wickedness through the Christian. The Christian is the salt and light of the world. As long as we are on earth apostasy and wickedness cannot reach its peak. However, Paul says that He, (the Holy Spirit), will be **taken out of the way.** When the Rapture of the Church occurs and Christians are removed, apostasy will flood the world. The ecumenical apostate church will not leave in the Rapture for it is made up of unbelievers. These false believers will unite with Rome Catholicism along with all other religions and the one world church will be formed under the leadership of the antichrist. Even today we see a breaking down of the walls of separation. Many religions are uniting. The groundwork is being laid now for the forming of the ecumenical, apostate one world church.

HER CHARACTER

And there came one of the seven angels which had the seven vials, and talked with me, saying unto me, Come hither; I will show unto thee the judgment of the great whore ... (Revelation 17:1a) The Holy Spirit does not mince words when He labels this woman as a **great whore.** The word **whore** comes from *"porneia"* and speaks of *"fornication, adultery, or prostitution."* It speaks of immoral and illicit behavior. In our text it has to do with Babylon's wretched religious idolatry. The angel portrays her with the startling imagery of a drunken harlot who seduces, spoils and slaughters. In the Bible, a whore is immoral and sexually promiscuous. The great whore is loose and immoral with the truth of God's. The whore offers sexual gratification outside of marriage. Babylon's whorish religion offers religious satisfaction apart from the principles of God's Word. Hence this Babylonian religious system of the great whore (the one world church) will be judged by God.

... that sitteth upon many waters. (Revelation 17:1b) She is described as setting upon many waters. A bit later the **many waters** are explained.

> **... The waters which thou sawest, where the whore sitteth, are peoples, and multitudes, and nations, and tongues. (Revelation 17:15)**

Many will be the people who align themselves with the one world church. Religious Babylon will gain worldwide influence by permeating society. Babylon will be the head of the apostate religious and political system of the Tribulation Period.

HER COMPROMISE

With whom the kings of the earth have committed fornication, and the inhabitants of the earth have been made drunk with the wine of her fornication. (Revelation 17:2) We have already seen this woman labeled a whore. Throughout the Bible, God has used harlotry as the symbol for idolatry and apostasy. When God's people abandon His Word and worship and give their hearts to idols or anything else that takes the place of God in their life, He calls it whoredom, adultery, or fornication. Jeremiah said:

> **... thou hast played the harlot with many lovers; yet return again to me, saith the LORD. (Jeremiah 3:1)**
>
> **The LORD said also unto me in the days of Josiah the king, Hast thou seen that which backsliding Israel hath done? she is gone up upon every high mountain and under every green tree, and there hath played the harlot. And I said after she had done all these things, Turn thou unto me. But she returned not. And her treacherous sister Judah saw it. And I saw, when for all the causes whereby backsliding Israel committed adultery I had put her away, and given her a bill of divorce; yet her treacherous sister Judah feared not, but went and played the harlot also. And it came to pass through the lightness of her whoredom, that she defiled the land, and committed adultery with stones and with stocks. (Jeremiah 3:6-9)**

We see the same terminology throughout Scripture. Isaiah, speaking of Jerusalem said:

> **How is the faithful city become an harlot! (Isaiah 1:21)**

Ezekiel spoke the same:

> **Thou hast played the whore also with the Assyrians, because thou wast unsatiable; yea, thou hast played the harlot with them, and yet couldest not be satisfied. Thou hast moreover multiplied thy fornication in the land of Canaan unto Chaldea; and yet thou wast not satisfied herewith. (Ezekiel 16:28-29)**

Strong words! Yes! But remember, this God speaking. God takes it seriously when people leave Him for another love, whether it be religion, work, sports, riches, or anything else. Here in Revelation 17, we see that this ecumenical church has:

> **... committed fornication and that the inhabitants of the earth have been made drunk with the wine of her fornication.**

The ecumenical church's condition is one of compromise and corruption. She has abandoned the One True God, Who was to be her true love. She has chosen to forsake Him and join in union with the wicked. She has married the world and its false religion. Such is the sad state of many churches in our day. My friend, you cannot live in two realms. God requires our faithfulness to Him. We are to separate from the world and unto God.

> **Love not the world, neither the things that are in the world. If any man love the world, the love of the Father is not in him. (1 John 2:15)**

Jesus warned:

> **No servant can serve two masters: for either he will hate the one, and love the other; or else he will hold to the one, and despise the other. Ye cannot serve God and mammon. (Luke 16:13)**

God requires that we serve Him with the whole heart. God will not share your love and loyalty with another lover. When believers have a love affair with the world, God sees it as adultery.

> **Ye adulterers and adulteresses, know ye not that the friendship of the world is enmity with God? whosoever therefore will be a friend of the world is the enemy of God. (James 4:4)**

God not only deserves but demands our loyalty. This one world church is a compromising church—unfaithful and disloyal to the God of Heaven. Her god is the power, pomp, prestige, and possessions of the world. The combination of drunkenness and fornication speaks of the moral depravity and filth with which she has lured men from the love of God into her own arms.

HER CORRUPTION

So he carried me away in the spirit into the wilderness: and I saw a woman sit upon a scarlet coloured beast, full of names of blasphemy, having seven heads and ten horns. (Revelation 17:3) The idea of a beast reminds us of something that is vicious and violent. This color is red—a color that is generally associated with blood. This beast has been responsible for shedding the blood of millions of Christians throughout the years of her existence. Without a doubt, the beast upon which the woman sits is the same beast that we studied in Revelation 13:1. That beast is the antichrist who derives his power and authority from Satan. This woman represents a system of false religion This is Satan's one world ecumenical church that is seated upon the antichrist. This is the evil religious system that we see taking shape in our day. We are seeing an unprecedented union of religion with the world. Modern religion and churchianity is a thoroughly corrupt, rebellious, and powerful movement that will culminate during the final days of the Tribulation Period.

HER CLOTHING

And the woman was arrayed in purple and scarlet colour, and decked with gold and precious stones and pearls, (Revelation 17:4a) This is a clear description of this woman and her seductiveness. Her clothing and jewelry, her golden cup, as well as the **gold and precious stones and pearls** speak of her great wealth. Depraved men love riches, glamour, and beauty.

For the love of money is the root of all evil: which while some coveted after, they have erred

from the faith, and pierced themselves through with many sorrows. (1 Timothy 6:10)

This harlot will woe multiple thousands into her bed. The one world church is described as a beautiful temptress who will seduce and lure untold hundreds of thousands into her deadly bed.

... having a golden cup in her hand full of abominations and filthiness of her fornication. (Revelation 17:4b) The contents of her cup are described as **full of abominations and filthiness.** The great whore has committed spiritual **fornication** by leading people away from the true worship of God. Thousands upon thousands have been seduced by her. They have been drawn away from the True and Almighty God of Heaven and are drinking from her cup of wickedness.

HER CAPTION

And upon her forehead was a name written, MYSTERY, BABYLON THE GREAT, THE MOTHER OF HARLOTS AND ABOMINATIONS OF THE EARTH. (Revelation 17:5) The Holy Spirit now goes further in His description of this woman. He identifies her not only as a harlot, but as the **MOTHER OF HARLOTS AND ABOMINATIONS OF THE EARTH.** The false religious system with the ecumenical one world church will come to a climax during the Great Tribulation. Satan is a great counterfeiter. He will produce his own church, headed up by the false prophet and by this Babylonian harlot. She is not simply a harlot but the **MOTHER OF HARLOTS.** Her wicked and illicit relationship with the world has produced offspring. Their fruit is the **ABOMINATIONS OF THE EARTH.** Notice that this name was written upon her forehead. Up until this time she has been able to hide her true character. However, God will reveal her for what she really is and for all the world to see.

HER CRUELTY

And I saw the woman drunken with the blood of the saints, and with the blood of the martyrs of Jesus: and when I saw her, I wondered with great admiration. (Revelation

17:6) What a sobering passage of Scripture! Again, God uses graphic words here. This harlot is described as **drunken with the blood of the saints and the martyrs of Jesus.** Here, she is seen as the persecutor of true Christians. Over the years, Rome has been guilty of the shedding of the blood of more Christians than any other outfit that can be found. History proves this to be the case. It is a well-established and documented fact that down through the years, apostate religion has always persecuted true Christianity. Read Foxes book of martyrs. It is filled with the historical accounts of men and women who were persecuted, tortured, and murdered by religious zealots who knew nothing of true Christianity. The Church of Rome stood at the forefront when it came to the persecution of God's people. The facts of their atrocities would fill volumes, but it is doubtful that one would have the stomach to read them. During the years of the Inquisition, one million Christians were put to death. Their crime was one of believing in salvation by grace plus nothing, as the Word of God teaches.

Throughout history, untold numbers have been crucified and burned at the stake, while others were covered with animal skins and ripped to death by wild dogs. Many were covered in tar and set on fire as human torches. Some were boiled in oil and burned at the stake while others endured the torture chambers of Rome before dying. When millions of Christians throughout France were murdered for their faith in Christ, Rome called special services of thanksgiving. Sir Robert Anderson estimates that she is guilty of the death of fifty million Christians. Millions have died down through the years, as a result of standing for the gospel of our Lord Jesus Christ and Rome stands guilty for most of it. In Revelation 17, God calls her into account.

HER CARRIER

And the angel said unto me, Wherefore didst thou marvel? I will tell thee the mystery of the woman, and of the beast that carrieth her, which hath the seven heads and ten horns. The beast that thou sawest was, and is not; and shall ascend out of the bottomless pit, and go into perdition: and

they that dwell on the earth shall wonder, whose names were not written in the book of life from the foundation of the world, when they behold the beast that was, and is not, and yet is. (Revelation 17:7-8)** In verse 3 John said, **I saw a woman sit upon a scarlet coloured beast.** Again, this beast is the antichrist. Here in verse seven, we are told that the beast **carrieth her.** The analogy of the beast carrying this woman refers to the fact that he is her support. This one world church is once again seen as the movement of the antichrist.

HER CITY

And here is the mind which hath wisdom. The seven heads are seven mountains, on which the woman sitteth. And there are seven kings: five are fallen, and one is, and the other is not yet come; and when he cometh, he must continue a short space. And the beast that was, and is not, even he is the eighth, and is of the seven, and goeth into perdition. (Revelation 17:9-11) The only city in history that fits this description is Rome. Again, Rome is not alone in her one world religion and ecumenical church. While it involves all apostate religions, Rome is the headquarters of it. There are seven kings or kingdoms. We notice three divisions here. *First*, of these seven kingdoms, five are fallen. They have passed away and are no longer world powers. These are Egypt, Assyria, Babylonia, Persia, and Greece. *Secondly*, of another kingdom we are told that **one is**. That present tense is referring to the time period in which John was writing. During John's Day, Rome was the world power and so it fits the description of the one that is. Third, there is a kingdom mentioned that is not yet come. It is yet future. This refers to the ten-nation confederacy represented by the ten horns on the beast that we saw in Revelation 13:1.

HER CLAN

And the ten horns which thou sawest are ten kings, which have received no kingdom as yet; but receive power as kings one hour with the beast. These have one mind, and shall give their power and strength unto the beast. (Revelation

17:12-13) The ten horns are kings who will rule with the antichrist. The ten kings are of one mind—they are united in power and purpose. This ten-nation confederacy will delegate all their power and authority to the beast.

And he saith unto me, The waters which thou sawest, where the whore sitteth, are peoples, and multitudes, and nations, and tongues. (Revelation 17:15) Imagine the awesome power and great prestige that the beast will have when he has deceived and stolen the hearts of the nations. Our text says that he will be supported by **multitudes and nations and languages.** The idea is that practically everyone will join the one world church. It will ecumenical and worldwide. Thus, the groundwork for the church of the Tribulation Period is being laid, even in our day. The church of our time is quickly becoming more cultural than Christian. Most Churches are more interested in pleasing people than in pleasing God.

HER COLLAPSE

These shall make war with the Lamb, and the Lamb shall overcome them: for he is Lord of lords, and King of kings: and they that are with him are called, and chosen, and faithful. (Revelation 17:14) This is mind biologging! This ten-nation confederacy under the leadership of the conceited antichrist will make war with Christ. This will be at the battle of Armageddon, which takes place when our Lord returns in glory. God guarantees that **the Lamb shall overcome them.** All the armies of the world, including their leader, the antichrist, will meet their end when Jesus Christ returns at the end of the Tribulation Period.

> **And then shall that Wicked be revealed, whom the Lord shall consume with the spirit of his mouth, and shall destroy with the brightness of his coming. (2 Thessalonians 2:8)**

Isaiah prophesied:

> **But with righteousness shall he judge the poor, and reprove with equity for the meek of the earth: and he shall smite the earth with the rod of his**

mouth, and with the breath of his lips shall he slay the wicked. (Isaiah 11:4)

The Psalmist spoke of the day when ...

The kings of the earth set themselves, and the rulers take counsel together, against the LORD, and against his anointed ... (Psalm 2:2)

When the mystery of iniquity runs its course and when the time of the end comes, we find the antichrist is so arrogant and conceited that he will gather the kings of the earth and lead a military campaign against Christ and His saints, but to no avail.

HER CALAMITY

And the ten horns which thou sawest upon the beast, these shall hate the whore, and shall make her desolate and naked, and shall eat her flesh, and burn her with fire. (Revelation 17:16) Now there is division in the camp. This great city for some time has been the center of ecumenical worship, but it is about to end. Here we see a great change of heart and alliance between the beast and great city. In verse seven, the beast is seen carrying the whore, but now the kings who form the ten-nation confederacy along with the beast, hate her and proceed to destroy and devour her.

For God hath put in their hearts to fulfil his will, and to agree, and give their kingdom unto the beast, until the words of God shall be fulfilled. And the woman which thou sawest is that great city, which reigneth over the kings of the earth. (Revelation 17:17-18) Religious Babylon, (the one world ecumenical church), will be utterly destroyed by the antichrist and his confederacy. It is God in His omnipotent and Sovereign power Who is ultimately the One Who brings about her fall. God is in control of the nations. During the Tribulation He moves upon the hearts of the ten kings to give their power to the antichrist and then, for all of them to turn against the harlot.

GOD'S JUDGMENT OF POLITICAL BABYLON
Revelation 18:1-24

The previous chapter closed with the destruction of religious Babylon—the headquarters of the ecumenical one world Church. In Chapter 18, God overthrows the antichrist and his commercial center. Babylon is a key city in Bible prophecy. She is the second most mentioned city in the Word of God; only Jerusalem is mentioned more times than her. This chapter describes the fall of political and commercial Babylon. This city will be a massive empire and will be the center-point of world commerce and trade during the tribulation. All the riches and wealth of the world will be tied to this city. There will be a great and devastating financial collapse when this takes place. Keep in mind that the name Babylon means *"confusion,"* and this will be a time of confusion and chaos.

THE DESCRIPTION OF BABYLON

Political Babylon will be a great world empire. It will be the financial center of the tribulation period. She will be the glory of the antichrist and his kingdom. Tragically, men love and worship their empires, their possessions, and their power. They focus on the temporal and neglect the eternal. We are warned:

> **But seek ye first the kingdom of God, and his righteousness; and all these things shall be added unto you. (Matthew 6:33)**

Man has always had a problem with putting first things first. We notice that political Babylon is the habitation of devils and wicked spirits. This will be the most vile and wicked place on earth. The description of this evil place is laid out s in detail.

The Angel

And after these things I saw another angel come down from heaven, having great power; (Revelation 18:1a) When this angel appears from Heaven with great power, He shed light on the earth **with his glory.** There is good cause to believe that the Angel with **great power** that John saw was none other than Jesus Christ. The word **power** in this verse comes from *"exousia"* and carries the idea of *"authority."* The great power possessed by this Angel reminds us of that given to Christ by the Father.

> **... hath given him authority to execute judgment also, because he is the Son of man. (John 5:27)**

The Bible also says:

> **And Jesus came and spake unto them, saying, All power is given unto me in heaven and in earth. (Matthew 28:18)**

... the earth was lightened with his glory. (Revelation 18:1b) This certainly does not refer to an ordinary Angel. It is, however, a description of the appearance of the Lord Jesus Christ.

> **Holy, holy, holy, is the LORD of hosts: the whole earth is full of his glory. (Isaiah 6:3)**

This Angels appearance lightens the entire world. It seems reasonable to concludes that only a Divine Being could cause the earth to be lightened with glory. Remember that when the fifth vial was poured out the world was thrust into deep darkness.

> **And the fifth angel poured out his vial upon the seat of the beast; and his kingdom was full of darkness; and they gnawed their tongues for pain, (Revelation 16:10)**

Now in the pitch dark there is suddenly the blinding and brilliant appearance of the Lord Jesus Christ in glory. The antichrist, his dominion, and his power are going to be brought to complete destruction. He will learn that there is pleasure in sin only for a season. It is Jesus Christ, the King of king and Lord of Lords, Who will bring antichrist to his end.

The Announcement

And he cried mightily with a strong voice, saying, Babylon the great is fallen, is fallen, and is become the habitation of

devils, and the hold of every foul spirit, and a cage of every unclean and hateful bird. (Revelation 18:2)** The Angel's announcement goes forth with great power. **Babylon the great is fallen.** There is a similar verse back in Isaiah.

> **And, behold, here cometh a chariot of men, with a couple of horsemen. And he answered and said, Babylon is fallen, is fallen; and all the graven images of her gods he hath broken unto the ground. (Isaiah 21:9)**

Notice that twice the Angel says that Babylon is fallen. It speaks of the two-fold destruction of the city. One fall refers to the system of false worship—the ecumenical church of chapter 17. The other fall refers to the literal city—commercial and political Babylon. So horrible and gruesome is the desolation of the city that it will become **the habitation of devils, and the hold of every foul spirit, and a cage of every unclean and hateful bird.**

The Apostasy

For all nations have drunk of the wine of the wrath of her fornication, and the kings of the earth have committed fornication with her, and the merchants of the earth are waxed rich through the abundance of her delicacies. (Revelation 18:3) As we saw in the last chapter, the word **fornication** is used as a symbol of idolatry and apostasy. When God's people abandon Him and follow after false gods, He calls it whoredom, adultery, or fornication. The Word of God stresses many time the evil, as well as the punishment of such sin.

> **Thou hast played the whore also with the Assyrians, because thou wast unsatiable; yea, thou hast played the harlot with them, and yet couldest not be satisfied. Thou hast moreover multiplied thy fornication in the land of Canaan unto Chaldea; and yet thou wast not satisfied herewith. (Ezekiel 16:28–29)**

> **How is the faithful city become an harlot! it was full of judgment; righteousness lodged in it; but now murderers. (Isaiah 1:21)**

> **Ye adulterers and adulteresses, know ye not that the friendship of the world is enmity with God? whosoever therefore will be a friend of the world is the enemy of God. (James 4:4)**

It is a serious matter to abandon the true God and go after other gods. Thus, the Almighty announces His charges against Babylon, the great mother of harlots. Babylon is not only the capital of the world, but she has become the capital of wickedness and idolatry as well. At this point the religious world will be steeped in debauchery. Oliver B. Greene calls Babylon:

> ... *a cesspool of corruption and abomination in the sight of a holy God.*

She has led the nations and their rulers into an adulterous relationship with the world. This sinful world is becoming bolder in its practice of sin. Their wickedness is flaunted and rampant during these days. As we hasten toward the end, the wicked condition will become even worse. However, sin will reach its climax during the Tribulation Period.

THE DEGRADATION OF BABYLON

Here the call is issued for believers in the tribulation to separate themselves from Babylon. God's people have no part in this world or its ungodly system. God has a faithful remnant, even in Babylon.

The Call To Separate

And I heard another voice from heaven, saying, Come out of her, my people, that ye be not partakers of her sins, and that ye receive not of her plagues. (Revelation 18:4) Before God strikes in judgment, He calls His people out. He called Enoch out before He destroyed the world. He called Lot out before He destroyed Sodom. He will call the Church out before His judgment begins and here we see Him calling the faithful Jews out of Babylon before it is destroyed.

The Consequences Of Sin

For her sins have reached unto heaven, and God hath remembered her iniquities. Reward her even as she

rewarded you, and double unto her double according to her works: in the cup which she hath filled fill to her double. (Revelation 18:5-6)** God's longsuffering patience has come to an end. Babylon's sin has reached unto Heaven and God is angry. May this be a warning to us today—God sees our sin.

> **For the ways of man are before the eyes of the LORD, and he pondereth all his goings. (Proverbs 5:21)**

Nothing eludes the all-seeing eyes of Almighty God. John said that the eyes of God are as a **flame of fire. (Revelation 1:14)** There is no place where man can get away from God. He is everywhere and knows everything. It is impossible to sin without Him knowing it.

> **The eyes of the LORD are in every place, beholding the evil and the good. (Proverbs 15:3)**

Even sin in the heart is seen by God.

> **For the LORD seeth not as man seeth; for man looketh on the outward appearance, but the LORD looketh on the heart. (1 Samuel 16:7b)**

His eyes will search in judgment. They pierce, they penetrate, they commend or condemn. There is absolutely no person or thing that will escape the examination of His eyes of fire. Everything will be laid open and exposed before His eyes. God is aware of sin and, mark it down, it is impossible to sin and get away with it.

The Complacency Of Her Situation

How much she hath glorified herself, and lived deliciously, so much torment and sorrow give her: for she saith in her heart, I sit a queen, and am no widow, and shall see no sorrow. (Revelation 18:7) What pride she now exhibits! She is pride personified. She is up to her eyes in sin and boasting. She glorifies herself and brags that she shall see no sorrow. Babylon thinks that she is invincible. She believes that nothing or no one can conquer her. She is drunk on pride and self-deceit.

> **Pride goeth before destruction, and a haughty spirit before a fall. (Proverbs 16:18)**

We are warned in the Word of God that:

> ... **a man's pride shall bring him low** ... **(Proverbs 29:23)**

Babylon is about to learn this lesson the hard way. She has stubbornly hardened herself against the call and correction of God for seven years of tribulation and God will now move to correct the situation. Babylon has stubbornly set her will and glory above God's and now she will meet with destruction, without remedy. Never again will she rear her ugly head in pride against the Holy and Almighty God of Heaven.

THE DESTRUCTION OF BABYLON

Therefore shall her plagues come in one day, death, and mourning, and famine; and she shall be utterly burned with fire: for strong is the Lord God who judgeth her. (Revelation 18:8) Jeremiah, the weeping prophet lived through Babylon's conquest of Jerusalem. However, God allowed the broken-hearted Prophet to write of this final day when God would judge Babylon.

> **As God overthrew Sodom and Gomorrah and the neighbour cities thereof, saith the LORD; so shall no man abide there, neither shall any son of man dwell therein. (Jeremiah 50:40)**
>
> **Babylon hath been a golden cup in the LORD'S hand, that made all the earth drunken: the nations have drunken of her wine; therefore the nations are mad. Babylon is suddenly fallen and destroyed: howl for her; take balm for her pain, if so be she may be healed. We would have healed Babylon, but she is not healed: forsake her, and let us go every one into his own country: for her judgment reacheth unto heaven, and is lifted up even to the skies. The LORD hath brought forth our righteousness: come, and let us declare in Zion the work of the LORD our God. (Jeremiah 51:7-10)**

In a single display, the wrath of God will demolish the so-called great city of Babylon. God's wrath is a serious matter.

> Thou shalt make them as a fiery oven in the time of thine anger: the LORD shall swallow them up in his wrath, and the fire shall devour them. (Psalm 21:9)

Verse 10 sheds further light on this, **for in one hour is thy judgment come** meaning that God's judgment will be immediate and instantaneous. Speak of sudden and final destruction!

THE DIRGE OF BABYLON

Talk about the market crashing! This will be devastating. The destruction of the world's political and commercial headquarters will be disastrous for those associated with it. Babylon is dead—now it is time for the funeral! The mourners are abundant. Notice the list of mourners who show up at this funeral.

The Monarchs Degrade

> And the kings of the earth, who have committed fornication and lived deliciously with her, shall bewail her, and lament for her, when they shall see the smoke of her burning, Standing afar off for the fear of her torment, saying, Alas, alas, that great city Babylon, that mighty city! for in one hour is thy judgment come. (Revelation 18:9-10)

The kings of the earth have **committed fornication** with Babylon—they have a close union with her, and they have become dependent upon her. Notice that they have **lived deliciously with her.** They have enjoyed the best of her luxuries. These are the political rulers of the world. They have stood for that which was politically correct instead of what was Scripturally correct. Now their political and economic kingdoms crumble, but God and His people live on. They can do nothing but stand by and watch as their bank accounts, their stocks, and all that they are worth, goes up in smoke.

The Merchant's Despair

> And the merchants of the earth shall weep and mourn over her; for no man buyeth their merchandise any more: (Revelation 18:11)

The Babylon of the Tribulation Period will be the commercial trade center of the entire world. However, when God's judgment reached its climax, the bottom will fall out for Babylon. The merchants will be overwhelmed with grief. Their god is money and Babylon's destruction means that they are out of business. All at once the wheels of commerce stand still. Like the kings of the earth, their mourning isn't over their wickedness, or even for the city, but rather, because the financial market has collapsed. They are shocked beyond measure that no one **buyeth their merchandise any more.** With one stroke of God's mighty hand, the world center of commerce will come to its end.

The Merchandise Destroyed

The merchandise of gold, and silver, and precious stones, and of pearls, and fine linen, and purple, and silk, and scarlet, and all thyine wood, and all manner vessels of ivory, and all manner vessels of most precious wood, and of brass, and iron, and marble, And cinnamon, and odours, and ointments, and frankincense, and wine, and oil, and fine flour, and wheat, and beasts, and sheep, and horses, and chariots, and slaves, and souls of men. (Revelation 18:12-13) Babylon has her hands in many businesses throughout all the world, but once judgment falls, she will come to nothing. This is the way is for those give their life to the god of riches. The Lord Jesus warned us about giving our heart world treasures.

> **Lay not up for yourselves treasures upon earth, where moth and rust doth corrupt, and where thieves break through and steal: But lay up for yourselves treasures in heaven, where neither moth nor rust doth corrupt, and where thieves do not break through nor steal: For where your treasure is, there will your heart be also. (Matthew 6:19-21)**

Notice also that this false religious also merchandises in the **souls of men**. Untold millions have been the souls claimed by her down through the centuries. But now her end has come. No one else will ever be misled and taken to Hell by her.

And the fruits that thy soul lusted after are departed from thee, and all things which were dainty and goodly are

departed from thee, and thou shalt find them no more at all. The merchants of these things, which were made rich by her, shall stand afar off for the fear of her torment, weeping and wailing, (Revelation 18:14-15)** Everything the merchants **lusted after** is gone and they **shalt find them no more at all.** There will be no more luxuries and dainties to lust after. All the merchants of Babylon could do was at this point was to stand back **weeping and wailing** and watch her valuable merchandise go up in smoke. The merchants of the world made rich, through commerce with this religious system can do nothing but mourn.

And saying, Alas, alas, that great city, that was clothed in fine linen, and purple, and scarlet, and decked with gold, and precious stones, and pearls! (Revelation 18:16) The word **alas** speaks of misery and woe. It is a statement of extreme grief and anguish. The merchants will respond the same way as the kings of the earth. They plummet into total anguish and sorrow.

The Mariner's Despair

The sea captains and sailors who make their living by moving merchandise across the sea will mourn as if they are at a funeral. In one hour, everything they have will come to nothing. They have grown rich and prospered by trafficking her merchandise, but now it is over, and the worst is yet to come.

The Riches They Lost. **For in one hour so great riches is come to nought. And every shipmaster, and all the company in ships, and sailors, and as many as trade by sea, stood afar off, And cried when they saw the smoke of her burning, saying, What city is like unto this great city! (Revelation 18:17-18)** Note that phrase **so great riches is come to nought**. The bottom fell out and their business, bank accounts and avenues of trade came to nothing. Notice that they **stood afar off** from Babylon as the wrath of God fell.

The Reason They Lamented. **And they cast dust on their heads, and cried, weeping and wailing, saying, Alas, alas, that great city, wherein were made rich all that had ships in the sea by reason of her costliness! for in one hour is she made desolate. (Revelation 18:19)** The phrase **cast dust on**

their heads expresses severe grieving and deep mourning at the hopelessness of a situation. The **weeping and wailing** denotes the wrenching anguish and deep despondency over their situation. **Alas, alas** describes the extreme grief of their souls. The merchants and mariners of the world will be **made rich** by way of their partnership with Babylon. Now they are seen standing back weeping and wailing at her destruction and ruin.

THE DESOLATION OF BABYLON

Now we come to the final words concerning political Babylon. There is a heavenly call for God's people to rejoice at her demise. It appears that God will repay Babylon with the same infliction she poured out in the martyrdom of His saints. At the hand of the Almighty, she will reap what she has sown.

The Cause To Be Delighted

Rejoice over her, thou heaven, and ye holy apostles and prophets; for God hath avenged you on her. (Revelation 18:20) This describes a great praise meeting that takes place in Heaven when Babylon is annihilated. Over the years, false religion has relentlessly persecuted the followers of the true God. They have often hunted and pursued them, by taking their possessions and even taking their lives. But God gets the last word. He will avenge His people. The destruction of religious Babylon will be divine vengeance.

As the lost world weeps over the destruction of Babylon, all heaven breaks forth in song and praise to God. The kings of the earth along with merchants and mariners weep and mourn at her demise, but Heaven rejoices. While the sinners weep, the saints rejoice. While the whole world is filled with lamenting and grief, the inhabitants of Heaven break out in rejoicing and song. The reason for the rejoicing is because **God hath avenged** their blood. This is the awful payday for those who participated in the death of the Tribulation saints.

The Casting Into The Deep

And a mighty angel took up a stone like a great millstone, and cast it into the sea, saying, Thus with violence shall that

great city Babylon be thrown down, and shall be found no more at all. (Revelation 18:21) Why rejoice? Because God has brought an end to evil. Through all the ages, God's preachers and people have preached and stood against the evils of this world. As God's messengers, we have always been in the minority. The world, and in many cases, even the Church, has rejected our cry. God's people are ridiculed, scorned, mocked, and hated in this world. What we stand for goes against the grain of society, and they hate us for it. But the day will come when all that they have accomplished and trusted will be reduced to ashes. God will settle the score! Never again will anyone raise a hand against God or His people. On this we have God's assurance.

The Completeness Of Her Destruction

The destruction of Babylon will be complete and final—she will be forever gone. The phrase **no more** speaks of the extent and finality of God's judgment upon her. She becomes silent before God and man. Her influence and power have come to nothing. The list given tells us that all activity will cease.

There will be _No More Music_. **And the voice of harpers, and musicians, and of pipers, and trumpeters, shall be heard no more at all in thee; (Revelation 18:22a)** Imagine a place where there is no music. Babylon famous for her musicians, has become a silent city. The sound of music will not be again. The entertainment industry will not make rake in its millions anymore. This great city once full of sound and activity has become soundless. The silence is the result of God's overwhelming judgment.

There will be _No More Manufacturing_. **.... and no craftsman, of whatsoever craft he be, shall be found any more in thee; and the sound of a millstone shall be heard no more at all in thee; (Revelation 18:22b)** The manufacturing industry likewise will come to a standstill. The carpenter and craftsmen will no longer be found in her for she is forever destroyed. No longer will the grinding of a millstone be heard. The products and luxuries that once comforted the wicked will be produced no more. The sounds of her massive industry will be silenced.

There will be *No More Marriages*. **And the light of a candle shall shine no more at all in thee; and the voice of the bridegroom and of the bride shall be heard no more at all in thee: (Revelation 18:23a)** The magnificent glow that once lit the city will be **no more**. The flashing and glistening of the lights will go out and cease to shine. The **voice of the bridegroom and of the bride shall be heard no more at all**. Marriage and the festivities associated with them no longer happen inside the city.

There will be *No More Misleading*. **... for thy merchants were the great men of the earth; for by thy sorceries were all nations deceived. (Revelation 18:23c)** The word **sorcery** comes from "*pharmakeia*" and is the word from which we get the English "*pharmacy.*" Today millions of people are duped by doctors who describe medicines that deaden the mind make people susceptible to deception.

There will be *No More Martyrs*. **And in her was found the blood of prophets, and of saints, and of all that were slain upon the earth. (Revelation 18:24)** What an inditement! Here Babylon stands naked before God and man. All of her worldly beauty is wiped away. Pleasure and commerce have come to nothing. Her pride has brought her low. Here we see the city of Babylon as God sees her—naked and guilty of the blood of His saints.

HEAVEN'S ALLELUIA CHORUS
Revelation 19:1-6

As we come to this chapter, there is a change in John vision. We move from the earthly to a heavenly scene. As we began, we enter a great praise service that is taking place in Heaven. The reason for these praises is that the great whore has been judged and wiped from the face of the earth. This is Heaven's wonderful song of victory for God's vengeance on Babylon. At this point, both political and religious Babylon will have been destroyed. This will bring the Great Tribulation Period to an end. Now we hear four Alleluias ring out in Heaven choir. Each of these four hallelujahs reveal something great about the Lord Jesus.

ALLELUIA OF REDEMPTION

God has provided a wonderful redemption for lost man. Whosoever will may come to Christ. In Heaven there will be a lot of praise offered to God for His grace and salvation. As we come to the first **Alleluia** the subject of salvation comes to mind.

The Start Of Their Praise

And after these things ... (Revelation 19:1a) The phrase **after these things** signals that there is a change from the events of the destruction of Babylon in chapters 17 and 18 which will bring the seven-year tribulation to an end. What a day that will be when we can sing in His presence. The glory, honor and power of the Lord is so majestic and mighty that the entire population of Heaven cries out, Alleluia!

The Sound Of Their Praise

... great voice of much people. (Revelation 19:1b) The sound heard in Heaven came the great of a multitude. I sometimes hear fold talk as if only they and maybe a few others will actually go Heaven. They are wrong! Heaven is a place of **much people** shouting praise to God. It is sad that in our day of dead religion and defeated churches that believers are silent. Oliver B. Greene said ...

> *God has never had the praise and honor due Him, but at this point and throughout eternity to follow He will be praised by the heavenly host, and His enemies will be in the lake of fire.*

In Heaven everyone will praise God. Wouldn't it be wonderful if God's people would start practicing now? May the sound of praising God be heard from His people.

The Sovereign Of Their Praise

... saying, Alleluia ... unto the Lord our God. (Revelation 19:1c, 1e) This praise is unto the **Lord our God**. He gets all of the glory. The great voice of **much people** was saying, **Alleluia**. Great rejoicing breaks out in Heaven. The word **Alleluia** is a transliteration of the word Hallelujah. Hallelujah is a combination of three words: *"halel"* meaning *"praise,"* *"u"* meaning *"ye,"* and *"yah"* meaning *"the Lord."* The phrase is literally translated many times in the Word of God as *"Praise ye the Lord."* This word occurs twenty-four times in the Old Testament, but only four times in the New Testament—all four times right here in Revelation 19. It is a triumphant cry of victory in which praise is given to God by His people. **Alleluia** is a word that belongs exclusively to God's people. Only those who have experienced salvation can praise God for it. Others can repeat the words, but unless they have experienced salvation—the phrase is simply empty.

The Subjects Of Their Praise

... Salvation, (Revelation 19:1h) The first **Alleluia** has to do with salvation! We have a habit of talking about *"our"* salvation and certainly it is ours in the sense that we are saved. However, salvation actually belongs to God.

> **Salvation belongeth unto the LORD: thy blessing is upon thy people. Selah. (Psalm 3:8)**

Salvation is a wonderful provision of God. His people need to be about the business of praising Him for His salvation.

The Marriage Of The Lamb

Let the redeemed of the LORD say so... (Psalm 107:2) There should be a lot more praising God for the salvation He has provided to fallen man. We have been saved by His grave, redeemed by the blood of Jesus Christ. That is something to shout about! God *Planned It*, *Provided It*, *Propagated It*, *Purchased It*, and He is now *Protecting It*. Hallelujah!

... and glory, (Revelation 19:1e) The world is enamored with the luster of material wealth. But the glory of God is His beauty and brightness which demonstrates His purity and holiness. Glory is the manifestation of God's character and nature. Here Heaven is seen praising God for the Glory that He alone possesses. This is the same glory that will be light of the Heavenly city where the saints of God will dwell for eternity (Revelation 21:23).

... and honour, (Revelation 19:1f) He word **honour** comes from *"time"* and carries the idea of *"respect, reverence, esteem."* Men love to be honored. They love titles, positions, and degrees. While there are some truly honorable men in this world, let us understand that true honor belongs to God and His Son.

... and power, (Revelation 19:1g) The word **power** comes from *"dynamis"* and denotes strength or ability. Our God is the all-powerful One. The title **Almighty** is used fifty-seven times in the Bible describing God. It speaks of His omnipotence. God possesses all power within Himself.

ALLELUIA OF RETRIBUTION

The second **Alleluia** has to do with God's righteous judgment Babylon's wickedness will meet with God's judgment. As we have already learned, the enemies of God will get exactly what they deserve.

The Righteousness Sovereign

For true and righteous are his judgments: (Revelation 19:2a) The words **true and righteous** are also character traits of God. God is perfect and always consistent in His character. His judgments are always righteous! His judgment is never too lenient or too hard. God is never unfair. His perfect righteous justice treats everyone equitably.

> **TZADDI. Righteous art thou, O LORD, and upright are thy judgments. (Psalm 119:137)**

Every judgment of God is perfectly consistent with His righteous character. Everyone will get from the hand of God exactly what they deserve when His judgment falls. God will justly exercise wrath according to Babylon's wickedness.

The Religious System

... for he hath judged the great whore, (Revelation 19:2b) It is clear that God's judgment upon the antichrist and his wicked world system will be just. Heaven is praising God because He **hath judged the great whore.** Many in our day do not like the idea of God's judgment. However, the Word of God teaches us that His holiness and justice requires the judgment of sin.

.... did corrupt the earth with her fornication. (Revelation 19:2c) The word **corrupt** comes from the Greek *"phtheirō"* and means *"to defile, to spoil."* The word **fornication** speaks of harlotry and adultery.

> **Babylon is fallen, is fallen, that great city, because she made all nations drink of the wine of the wrath of her fornication. (Revelation 14:8)**

> **With whom the kings of the earth have committed fornication, and the inhabitants of the earth have been made drunk with the wine of her fornication. (Revelation 17:2)**

Babylon will be a great fornicator. She will seduce millions luring them into her embrace only to take them to Hell with her.

... and hath avenged the blood of his servants at her hand. (Revelation 19:2d) The word **avenged** comes from *"ekdikeō"* and means to *"to vindicate, retaliate, punish."* The great whore will not escape God's vengeance for the blood she spilled. The last verse of chapter 18 reminds us that ...

> **... in her was found the blood of prophets, and of saints, and of all that were slain upon the earth. (Revelation 18:24)**

The day is coming when God will avenge every dead prophet, every dead preacher, every dead saint, and all those that were slain upon the earth by religious Babylon.

The Repeated Shout

And again they said, Alleluia. (Revelation 19:3a) Again, triumphant cry of victory is heard in Heaven. The multitude again breaks out in praise to God. The praise here is for His victory over those who corrupted the earth with wickedness and who persecuted the saints.

The Rising Smoke

... And her smoke rose up for ever and ever. (Revelation 19:3b) The rise of the smoke assures the inhabitants of Heaven that Babylon's wickedness has been dealt with completely and forever. Solomon said:

> **I know that, whatsoever God doeth, it shall be for ever: nothing can be put to it, nor any thing taken from it: and God doeth it, that men should fear before him. (Ecclesiastes 3:14)**

When God finishes with this wicked world system, it is finished forever—never to rise again.

ALLELUIA OF REVERENCE

With this third **Alleluia** we see that God is to get the glory for the judgment and destruction of the one world church.

The Affirmation Reiterated

And the four and twenty elders and the four beasts fell down and worshipped God that sat on the throne, saying, Amen; Alleluia. (Revelation 19:4) Now we come to another group who is praising God. This chorus is made up of the four and twenty elders and the four beasts. We were first introduced to these elders back in chapter four when we were first allowed to see inside Heaven's Throne Room.

> **And round about the throne were four and twenty seats: and upon the seats I saw four and twenty elders sitting, clothed in white raiment; and**

they had on their heads crowns of gold. (Revelation 4:4)

You will remember that in the Old Testament David divided the Priesthood into twenty-four orders or courses and these twenty-four orders represented all of God's people (1 Chronicles 24 and 25). We see that same idea here as the twenty-four elders represent the redeemed saints of the Church age, in the same way that the twenty-four elders of the Old Testament represented the complete body of priests. Bear in mind that the first time we saw these raptured Church age saints was at the close of the Church age just as the tribulation was beginning. We saw them sharing in God's throne, clothed in the white garments, with crowns of gold, and enthroned in glory with the Lord and Saviour. Here, in chapter 19, we see them seven years later—still praising God and the praise will ring out for all eternity. We call this the Alleluia of reality because only then, when we are in His presence, and in our glorified state, will we have a real grasp on His Majesty and Might.

Beloved, now are we the sons of God, and it doth not yet appear what we shall be: but we know that, when he shall appear, we shall be like him; for we shall see him as he is. (1 John 3:2)

What precious words! **We shall be like him; for we shall see him as he is.** God's desire for every believer will be realized at last. This verse speaks of the glorification of the Christian.

For whom he did foreknow, he also did predestinate to be conformed to the image of his Son, that he might be the firstborn among many brethren. (Romans 8:29)

When we are in His presence, our glorification will be a reality and we will be conformed to the image of Christ. Alleluia! We shall see Him as He is.

The Action Required

And a voice came out of the throne, saying, Praise our God, all ye his servants, and ye that fear him, both small and great. (Revelation 19:5) Now a **voice came out of the throne**

requiring that all **Praise our God.** All who are His **servants** and **fear** Him are encouraged small **and great**, to join in and sing praises to God.

ALLELUIA OF REIGN

The great multitude in Heaven responds with singing and shouting at the truth of God's reign. No longer does Babylon have any control, the sovereign God sits on the throne, and He reigns.

The Singer's Response

And I heard as it were the voice of a great multitude, and as the voice of many waters, and as the voice of mighty thunderings, saying, Alleluia: (Revelation 19:6a) Just imagine what this singing must sound like! The combined voices of Heaven resonate so loud that the roar is likened to **the voice of a great multitude, and as the voice of many waters, and as the voice of mighty thunderings.** The metaphor of **many waters** refers to a continuous roar, such as that of a massive waterfall. The sound of **mighty thunderings** speaks to the mighty rumble and power of this heavenly choir. What an awesome climax to the four-fold Alleluia chorus!

The Sovereign Reign

... for the Lord God omnipotent reigneth. (Revelation 19:6b) The redeemed of God in the closing stanza burst out with, **Alleluia: for the Lord God omnipotent reigneth.** God is going to reign forever in sovereign power upon the earth. All wickedness will be forever dealt with. To see this day should be the longing of our heart. Again, we are reminded of that wonderful day when we have entered into our glorified state.

> **Because the creature itself also shall be delivered from the bondage of corruption into the glorious liberty of the children of God. For we know that the whole creation groaneth and travaileth in pain together until now. And not only they, but ourselves also, which have the firstfruits of the Spirit, even we ourselves groan within ourselves, waiting for the adoption, to wit, the redemption of our body. (Romans 8:21-23)**

Like a woman in labor this world is in a time of pain and suffering, but praise God, labor doesn't last forever—there comes a delivery and one day God is going to step out of the Heavens to deliver this sin cursed world. The prayer of God's people, **Thy kingdom come,** will no longer be a prayer, but a reality. Our song will be **Alleluia: for the Lord God omnipotent reigneth.** What a shouting time we will have in Heaven. Folks who don't believe in praising God will have to make some adjustments when they get to glory. Dr. Harold B. Sightler said:

> *You know, sometimes I get rather amused at people in this life when somebody becomes excited about the Lord or somebody dares to shout the praises of the Lord. Folk will say, that is not being reverent, and I think that we need to be quiet. Let us enter into the house of God in silence, and I do not think that you ought to make much noise and commotion and become so emotional about salvation. Well, my friend, have you ever thought that when you go to heaven, heaven is not going to be a quiet place. The quietest world you will ever live in is this one, and when you get to heaven, you are going to hear many people saying, Hallelujah, to the top of their voices. And not only will you hear many people saying, Hallelujah, but you are going to be one of them yourself. You might have never shouted in this world. You may live a lifetime and never praise God outwardly in this world, but there is one thing for sure. When you go to heaven and see the salvation, and the glory, and the honour, and the power of the Lord our God, you are going to [shout] like all the others ...*

What a blessing as we read this passage and realize that those of us who are upon earth now and are redeemed through faith in the Lord Jesus Christ, whose sins are blotted out and paid for by the precious blood of Christ, will be part of that great multitude and will join in the singing and worshipping of God.

THE MARRIAGE OF THE LAMB
Revelation 19:7-10

In this section there is great rejoicing because the wedding of the Lamb has come. No longer is the emphasis on the Harlot Babylon, but upon the Holy Bride. The guests have been called, and we learn from the Gospel of Luke that the Marriage Supper will take place on earth following the marriage (Luke 22:16-30). What a day that will be when my Saviour I shall see! We notice several truths concerning this great wedding.

THE GROOM

Let us be glad and rejoice, and give honour to him: for the marriage of the Lamb is come... (Revelation 19:7a) From the start this event is called **the marriage of the lamb.** As to who the Groom is, there is no doubt. He is the Lamb of God, the Lord Jesus Christ. Speaking of Jesus and the glorified Church Paul said:

> **That he might present it to himself a glorious church, not having spot, or wrinkle, or any such thing; but that it should be holy and without blemish. (Ephesians 5:27)**

As a Pastor I have performed many weddings and have attended many others. There is one thing that always stands out at a wedding, and that is the bride—she is always the center of attention. When the music begins, all heads turn and every eye in the place is fixed upon her, as she comes down the aisle. At the reception, the main subject is how beautiful the bride is.

However, things will be different at the **Marriage of the Lamb.** The bride will not be the center of attention there—it will be the bridegroom Who gets all the attention. All of Heaven will be present to give honor to Him.

THE GLORIFIED

Now we come to the bride. The text states, **and his wife hath made herself ready. (Revelation 19:7b)** Who is the wife? There are different ideas, but the issue is cleared up when we study and rightly divide the Word of truth. Throughout the Bible we see such terms as **bride, virgin, husband, marriage,** and **espoused** used in connection with Christ and the Church.

> For this cause shall a man leave his father and mother, and shall be joined unto his wife, and they two shall be one flesh. This is a great mystery: but I speak concerning Christ and the church. (Ephesians 5:31-32)
>
> For I am jealous over you with godly jealousy: for I have espoused you to one husband, that I may present you as a chaste virgin to Christ. (2 Corinthians 11:2)

It is evident from these passages that this marriage is referring to the marriage of Jesus Christ to the glorified Church. That being said, we want to pay close attention to the statement **his wife hath made herself ready.** The word **made** comers from *"hetoimazō"* and means *"to prepare or to provide."* It is clear that those who make up the bride have done something to prepare. Not just anyone can be part of the bride of Christ. Everyone who is saved will spend eternity in Heaven, but not everyone will enjoy the high and honored position of being part of the bride. One becomes a child of God by faith in the Lord Jesus Christ. At that point he or she is cleansed by the blood of Christ and becomes and eternal child of God. But the fact that the bride has **made herself ready** signifies that the believer must do something to be part of the Bride of Christ. A believer, before he can reign with Christ, must make himself ready by serving Christ. He must surrender himself to the Holy Spirit and separate himself from the world and its wickedness. He must identify with the Saviour. In the next verse we will come to **the righteousness of saints.**

THE GARMENTS

And to her was granted that she should be arrayed in fine linen, clean and white: for the fine linen is the righteousness of saints. (Revelation 19:8) First of all, we me point out that there is a great contrast between the attire of the bride and the attire

The Marriage Of The Lamb

of the great whore back in chapter 17. The great whore was clothed in purple and scarlet and decked with gold, and precious stones, and pearl. But in contrast the bride of the Lamb is arrayed in fine linen, clean and white.

Do not misunderstand this verse. The righteousness referred to here is not the imputed righteousness whereby we get to Heaven. No! This **righteousness of saints** has to do with our works while we were saved. One thing is for certain! We are not going to get to Heaven and share and share alike. Just as there are different degrees of punishment in Hell there are different degrees of reward in Heaven.

According to the Word of God, one of the great future events will be the Judgment Seat of Christ.

> **For we must all appear before the judgment seat of Christ; that every one may receive the things done in his body, according to that he hath done, whether it be good or bad. (2 Corinthians 5:10)**

The Judgment Seat takes place sometime between the Rapture, (Revelation 4:1), when Christ comes for His Church, and the Revelation, (Revelation 19:11), when He comes back to earth with His Church. The Judgment Seat is that event when Jesus Christ will judge the saints, to determine their eternal rewards for their faithfulness. Those who have been faithful will be rewarded and those who have not been faithful will receiver no reward. It is after the Judgment Seat judgment, and just before Christ's glorious return to earth, that we have the Marriage of the Lamb.

A lot of Christians seem to have an *"I'm saved and going to Heaven, what else matters"* attitude about the Judgment Seat of Christ. These foolishly believe that Heaven will be the same for everyone. But my friend this will be a serious and solemn time when we will give account to God. We need to be careful that we do not develop a passive and carefree attitude about the Judgment Seat. To stand before Christ will be a serious matter. This will be a time when every believer will be examined and judged by the Saviour.

Every man's work shall be made manifest: for the day shall declare it, because it shall be revealed by fire; and the fire shall try every man's work of what sort it is. If any man's work abide which he hath built thereupon, he shall receive a reward. (1 Corinthians 3:13-14)

Knowing that our Ministries, Methods, and even Motives are going to be examined by the omniscient Christ, ought to significantly change the way we live and serve the Lord. The Judgment Seat of Christ will be a time of _Reality_, a time of _Revealing_, a time of _Rewarding_, and a time of _Remorse_. Robert Ketcham wrote:

> _"What our eyes looked on, what our ears listened to, what our hearts loved, what our minds believed, what our lips said, what our hands did, where our feet walked, our secrets, our motives, and our decisions all come out under the fire of His holy eye. We will tell Him all, not only what we did but why we did it! In the light of that record we will receive 'good' or 'bad.'"_

Again, let me point out that this judgment has nothing to do with our Standing. Every Christian is saved for eternity and will spend that eternity in Heaven. However, we must face the fact that we are going to be judged for our faithfulness in Service and we will receive a garment that corresponds with our faithfulness. At the Marriage of the Lamb, each Christian will be wearing a garment of their own making. What you will have to wear for all eternity will reflect your walk for Christ on this earth.

There are many carnal and self-centered Christians who live worldly and selfish lives. The live to serve and satisfy themselves. When they pass through the fire of the judgment seat, all of their works will be burned. Yes, that is right! Some works will be burned.

If any man's work abide which he hath built thereupon, he shall receive a reward. If any man's work shall be burned, he shall suffer loss: but he

> himself shall be saved; yet so as by fire. (1 Corinthians 3:14-15)

Anything that does not bring glory and honor to Christ will burn. For many, the judgment seat will be a time of remorse when they realize that all their work amounted to nothing, so far as bringing glory to Christ is concerned. Let us be careful that what we do, we do to the glory of God. God will not share His glory with anyone. God has already determined:

> ... that no flesh should glory in his presence. (1 Corinthians 1:29)

The boastful and proud Christian that serves to be seen of men already has his reward.

> And when thou prayest, thou shalt not be as the hypocrites are: for they love to pray standing in the synagogues and in the corners of the streets, that they may be seen of men. Verily I say unto you, They have their reward. (Matthew 6:5)

Sadly, many will receive nothing at the judgment. Others will lose their rewards. What a tragic thing to earn reward and then lose them because of unfaithfulness. John warns us:

> Look to yourselves, that we lose not those things which we have wrought, but that we receive a full reward. (2 John 8)

The works of those who served to be seen of men will be burned at the Judgment Seat. Those who have performed their service in the energy of the flesh will suffer great loss. Only those who have served to bring glory to God will be rewarded.

THE GUESTS

And he saith unto me, Write, Blessed are they which are called unto the marriage supper of the Lamb. And he saith unto me, These are the true sayings of God. (Revelation 19:9) Here is another passage where there seems to be much confusion. Many have gotten the notion that the **called** of this verse is the Church. This is not the case! Notice that the guests are called to **the marriage supper of the Lamb.** This is not referring to the marriage ceremony, but to the marriage supper. The Church is the bride—the bride does not need to be called to the reception. Who is usually invited to the reception? The friends and the family of the groom and bride are called. Those called to the supper here are the Old Testament saints and probably the tribulation saints. This truth is clearly taught in the Word of God.

> **Ye yourselves bear me witness, that I said, I am not the Christ, but that I am sent before him. He that hath the bride is the bridegroom: but the friend of the bridegroom, which standeth and heareth him, rejoiceth greatly because of the bridegroom's voice: this my joy therefore is fulfilled. (John 3:28-29)**

John the Baptist was an Old Testament prophet and identified himself as a friend of the bridegroom. Only New Testament Christians will make up the Church—no other saints will have part in that glorious privilege. However, all of God's people will be present. This will be a blessed and glorious event when all the redeemed of all the ages will gather at this event.

> **And I fell at his feet to worship him. And he said unto me, See thou do it not: I am thy fellowservant, and of thy brethren that have the testimony of Jesus: worship God: for the testimony of Jesus is the spirit of prophecy. (Revelation 19:10)**

So overwhelming and glorious was this wonderful message that John fell down to worship the messenger. The angel quickly corrected John and the glory was directed to Jesus Christ.

THE CONQUERING KING RETURNS
Revelation 19:11-16

At we come to this section, John sees the door of Heaven open for the second time. If you recall, the first time the door of Heaven opened was in Revelation 4:1 when the Rapture took place. Now the door opens again for the Lord Jesus and His bride to return to earth. This event of Christ's Second Coming is without a doubt the high point of the book of Revelation. Back in the beginning of this book, the Apostle prophesied Christ's return.

> **Behold, he cometh with clouds; and every eye shall see him, and they also which pierced him: and all kindreds of the earth shall wail because of him. Even so, Amen. (Revelation 1:7)**

The Second Coming of Christ is one of the most prophesied and promised events in all of the Word of God (Deuteronomy 30:3; Psalm 2:6-9; Isaiah 40:10; Ezekiel 21:27; Daniel 7:13-14; Joel 3:1-2, 12-14; Zechariah 12:3-9, 14:3-4; Malachi 3:1-2). Many times, the Lord Jesus Christ Himself spoke of the Rapture and His Second Coming in glory and judgment (John 14:1-6; Matthew 24:27, 30, 37-44; 25:31; 26:64). This is the fulfillment. There are several thoughts to consider here.

HIS ARRIVAL

And I saw heaven opened, and behold a white horse; and he that sat upon him was called Faithful and True, and in righteousness he doth judge and make war. (Revelation 19:11) Of course the rider of this white steed is none other than our Lord Jesus Christ. The text clearly identifies Him as the **Word of God. (13)** and the **KING OF KINGS, AND LORD OF LORDS. (16)** Here we see Christ in His glory returning to earth with His bride. The first time He came He was crucified. This time He comes to conquer. The first time He came, He received a crown of thorns. This time, He comes wearing many crowns. No longer is He the meek and lowly Saviour riding into Jerusalem on a colt. Instead, He arrives in all His splendor, riding out of Heaven on a white steed, as a Mighty Conqueror going to war. This will be a most glorious scene! Bear in mind that the whole world will be in total darkness because of the fifth vial judgment.

> **And the fifth angel poured out his vial upon the seat of the beast; and his kingdom was full of darkness; and they gnawed their tongues for pain. (Revelation 16:10)**

The prophet Joel also spoke of this time as:

> **A day of darkness and of gloominess, a day of clouds and of thick darkness... (Joel 2:2)**

Imagine the scene! The earth has been engulfed in thick darkness for perhaps months as the fierce judgment of God fell. All at once there is a glow shining in the Heavens, as our Lord appears in the light of His glory. But the hope fades when the wicked of this world realize that they have passed the deadline. He is not coming back to save:

> **So Christ was once offered to bear the sins of many; and unto them that look for him shall he appear the second time without sin unto salvation. (Hebrews 9:28)**

His second coming will be to judge the world and set up His Kingdom on earth. The imagery of riding in on a **white horse** is in keeping with the custom of ancient times, when the victorious Roman General would return from war riding on a white horse with His faithful army following behind him.

HIS ATTRIBUTES

His eyes were as a flame of fire, and on his head were many crowns; and he had a name written, that no man knew, but he himself. (Revelation 19:12) When our Lord returns, He is coming in judgment and righteousness.

> **And Enoch also, the seventh from Adam, prophesied of these, saying, Behold, the Lord cometh with ten thousands of his saints, To execute judgment upon all, and to convince all that**

are ungodly among them of all their ungodly deeds which they have ungodly committed, and of all their hard speeches which ungodly sinners have spoken against him. (Jude 1:14-15)

As we consider our Lord's attributes in this passage, they help us to grasp some important truths about His Second Coming.

He is **Faithful and True. (Revelation 19:11a)** Jesus is identified from the start as **Faithful and True.** This name attests to the fact that He is absolutely reliable and trustworthy. This is in stark contrast to the impersonator who came as a rider on a white horse in Revelation 6:2. That rider was the antichrist. He was the exact opposite in his character than that of the Lord Jesus. He came as an impostor and an impersonator, showing himself to the people of the world as their deliverer, when in fact, he led them into Satan's clutches and eventually into Hell.

His eyes were as a flame of fire. (Revelation 19:12) The eyes of fire represent the Lord's penetrating gaze that can search the hearts and minds of man.

> **For the LORD seeth not as man seeth; for man looketh on the outward appearance, but the LORD looketh on the heart. (1 Samuel 16:7b)**

His eyes will search in judgment. There is absolutely no person or thing that will escape the examination of His eyes.

> **The eyes of the LORD are in every place, beholding the evil and the good. (Proverbs 15:3)**

Everything will be laid open and exposed before His eyes. Therefore, the eyes as flames of fire speak of His complete and righteous judgment upon sin.

On his head were many crowns. (Revelation 19:12) The crowns speak of His absolute rule and Sovereignty. You will notice that He wears **many crowns.** This too is very descriptive imagery. Collecting the crown of a defeated king was the tradition in Bible times. When David defeated the Ammonite:

> **... he took their king's crown from off his head, the weight whereof was a talent of gold with the precious stones: and it was set on David's head.**

> **And he brought forth the spoil of the city in great abundance. (2 Samuel 12:30)**

The fact that Jesus is wearing many crowns signifies that He has defeated the kings of the world and taken their crowns. At last ...

> **The kingdoms of this world are become the kingdoms of our Lord, and of his Christ; and he shall reign for ever and ever. (Revelation 11:15)**

He had a name written, that no man knew, but he himself. (Revelation 19:12) Though many have, I see no need or warrant for speculating as to the meaning of this name. No man knows what this name is—only Jesus Himself knows. Notice that John saw the name and could not comprehend it. When the text is so clear about the secrecy of this name, we should heed the word of God and simply keep silent about it until that day when, perhaps, Christ will reveal that name to us.

And his name is called The Word of God. (Revelation 19:13) Notice that **Word** is capitalized. This is a proper name that belongs exclusively to the Lord Jesus Christ.

> **In the beginning was the Word, and the Word was with God, and the Word was God. The same was in the beginning with God ...And the Word was made flesh, and dwelt among us, (and we beheld his glory, the glory as of the only begotten of the Father,) full of grace and truth. (John 1:1-2, 14)**

... name written, KING OF KINGS, AND LORD OF LORDS. (Revelation 19:16) The title stresses Christ's authority and rule over all other kings and rulers. He is the supreme and sovereign King. In his commentary on Revelation, David Levy said:

> *This title is a summation of His rightful claim to reign and rule over all of creation in absolute sovereignty.*

Paul used this title in describing Jesus as ...

> **... the blessed and only Potentate, the King of kings, and Lord of lords; (1 Timothy 6:15)**

You will remember how that, at Jesus' first coming, the ungodly crowd mocked Him.

> **And when they had platted a crown of thorns, they put it upon his head, and a reed in his right hand: and they bowed the knee before him, and mocked him, saying, Hail, King of the Jews! (Matthew 27:29)**

While He hung on the cross, dying for the sins of mankind, the mocking continued:

> **And set up over his head his accusation written, THIS IS JESUS THE KING OF THE JEWS. (Matthew 27:37)**

Now He has the final word, and He comes wearing His title! He is not merely a King—He is the **KING OF KINGS, AND LORD OF LORDS.** When Jesus returns all other rulers will be conquered and Christ alone will reign supreme as King and Lord of all the earth.

HIS APPAREL

And he was clothed with a vesture dipped in blood: (Revelation 19:13a) The blood on Christ's clothing is not His Blood, but the blood of His enemies. In verse 15, we are told that Jesus will execute judgment with the ...

> **.... fierceness and wrath of Almighty God. (Revelation 19:15)**

At His Second Coming Jesus will defeat every enemy once and for all.

> **Who is this that cometh from Edom, with dyed garments from Bozrah? this that is glorious in his apparel, travelling in the greatness of his strength? I that speak in righteousness, mighty to save. Wherefore art thou red in thine apparel, and thy garments like him that treadeth in the winefat? I have trodden the winepress alone; and of the people there was none with me: for I will tread them in mine anger, and trample them in my fury; and their blood shall be sprinkled upon my**

garments, and I will stain all my raiment. For the day of vengeance is in mine heart, and the year of my redeemed is come. (Isaiah 63:1-4)

The imagery of the winepress and the stained garments is drawn from the ancient custom of stomping grapes to mash the juice out. In doing so the clothing would become stained with the juice of the grapes. As the grapes in the winefat were crushed until every ounce of juice was extracted, so Christ will spill the blood of His enemies. The stain from the juice and the staining of one's feet and garments serve as a picture of Divine judgment.

.... and his name is called The Word of God. (Revelation 19:13b) The Word of God speaks of absolute authority. This is Christ coming in power and authority to execute judgment. Oliver B. Greene stated:

> *Christ, the Word of God, is the absolute and final expression of God in righteous judgment about to take place just before the beginning of the Millennium ...*

Make no mistake about it. Those who have foolishly rejected the Word of God will answer directly to Christ at His coming.

HIS ARMY

And the armies which were in heaven followed him upon white horses, clothed in fine linen, white and clean. (Revelation 19:14) The armies of the Lord include all the redeemed of the Church age. (v:8), the Old Testament believers. (Jude 1:14-15; Daniel 12:1-2), the tribulation saints. (7:13-14; 20:4), and the holy angels. (Matthew 25:31).

> **And Enoch also, the seventh from Adam, prophesied of these, saying, Behold, the Lord cometh with ten thousands of his saints, To execute judgment upon all, and to convince all that are ungodly among them of all their ungodly deeds which they have ungodly committed, and of all their hard speeches which ungodly sinners have spoken against him. (Jude 1:14-15)**

This will be the greatest army to ever ride into battle. It will be the greatest victory ever won.

> **The LORD shall go forth as a mighty man, he shall stir up jealousy like a man of war: he shall cry, yea, roar; he shall prevail against his enemies. (Isaiah 42:13)**

This victory has nothing to do with the army, it has everything to do with the Leader. Jesus is the Mighty Warrior. He is the mighty Conqueror.

HIS AUTHORITY

Again, we are reminded of Christ's absolute authority. When Jesus returns, He will speak and rule with supreme sovereignty.

The Sword And The Word

And out of his mouth goeth a sharp sword, ... (Revelation 19:15a) We are told that **out of his mouth goeth a sharp sword**... Of course, this is not a literal sword, but a symbol speaking of the Word of God. The Word of God is called a sword many times in the Bible.

> **For the word of God is quick, and powerful, and sharper than any twoedged sword, piercing even to the dividing asunder of soul and spirit, and of the joints and marrow, and is a discerner of the thoughts and intents of the heart. (Hebrews 4:12)**

It is referred to as the **sword of the Spirit. (Ephesians 6:17)** With the very words of His mouth the Lord Jesus Christ will conquer His enemies. He will simply speak the words and it will be done. His Word is irrefutable, irresistible, and inclusive. We get a hint of the power of His spoken word back in Gethsemane, Judas and his mob came to arrest Jesus. The Bible says:

> **As soon then as he had said unto them, I am he, they went backward, and fell to the ground. (John 18:5)**

If this is the result of Him simply identifying Himself, how much more will be the force when He speaks in wrath? The

Word of God is likened to a twoedged sword. Christ will return with the Sword of His Word, speaking and delivering judgment.

His Smiting Of The Wicked

He will **smite the nations: and he shall rule them with a rod of iron. (Revelation 19:15b)** This is a reference to His millennial reign.

> **Thou shalt break them with a rod of iron; thou shalt dash them in pieces like a potter's vessel. (Psalm 2:9)**

Our Lord will rule the nations with unyielding authority from His throne in Jerusalem. The rod reminds us of the Shepherd's rod, which serves to conform, correct and comfort. Jesus Christ is the **Good shepherd. (John 10:11)**, the **Great Shepherd. (Hebrews 13:20)**, and the **Chief Shepherd. (1 Peter 5:4)** who will rule the nations.

HIS ANGER

And he treadeth the winepress of the fierceness and wrath of Almighty God. (Revelation 19:15b) Jesus is coming and boy, is He mad! He will come as One Who **treadeth the winepress of the fierceness and wrath of Almighty God.** This illustration of the winepress was used earlier, speaking of Christ's coming and the war of Armageddon.

> **And the winepress was trodden without the city, and there came out blood from the winepress, even unto the bridles of the horses, as far as a thousand and six hundred furlongs. (Revelation 14:20)**

We have already seen Christ **clothed with a vesture dipped in blood. (Revelation 19:13)** Under the judgment of God the blood of His enemies will flow like juice from a winepress. A river of blood, up to the horse's bridles, and the length of 1,600 furlongs, will flow through the streets of Palestine. A river of blood 4 to 4 ½ feet deep and almost 200 miles long will run from the veins of the enemies of God.

THE BATTLE OF ARMAGEDDON
Revelation 19:17-21

And he gathered them together into a place called in the Hebrew tongue Armageddon. (Revelation 16:16) This will be the war of all wars—the war that will end civilization as we know it. This will be the fiercest event to ever fall upon this earth. This is the same war previously mentioned by John as the:

> ... great day of God Almighty. (Revelation 16:14)

This is identified as the war of Armageddon. This will be the fulfillment of the prophecy of Jesus in His Olivet discourse (Matthew 24:27-31). The word itself speaks to the nature of this war. **Armageddon** means *"Mount of Slaughter"* and as we shall see, that is exactly what it will be when our Lord Jesus Christ unleashes the full force of His fury on Satan, and this wicked world. Let's look at several aspects of this war.

A GREAT MEAL

And I saw an angel standing in the sun; and he cried with a loud voice, saying to all the fowls that fly in the midst of heaven, Come and gather yourselves together unto the supper of the great God. (Revelation 19:17) Immediately following the battle of Armageddon, the birds are invited to come for a great feast. The supper of the great God describes the slaughter of the armies of the world when they gather against Christ. This parallels Christ's teaching on the Tribulation Period.

> For as the lightning cometh out of the east, and shineth even unto the west; so shall also the coming of the Son of man be. For wheresoever the carcase is, there will the eagles be gathered together. (Matthew 24:27-28)

It is interesting to note that hundreds of thousands of birds of prey migrate each year between their nesting places in Africa to the south, and Europe and Asia to the north. They cross the only land bridge that connects these continents—that is Palestine. Our Sovereign God already has the birds ready. Everything is set up and awaiting His command when He summons the vultures to gather. The prophet Zephaniah said:

> **Hold thy peace at the presence of the Lord GOD: for the day of the LORD is at hand: for the LORD hath prepared a sacrifice, he hath bid his guests. (Zephaniah 1:7)**

This is the second supper mentioned in this chapter—the first being the marriage supper of the Lamb. What a contrast between these two suppers. The marriage supper is a time for rejoicing while the supper of the great God is a time of retribution. The participants at the marriage supper go on into a glorious eternity with Christ. The participants of the supper of the great God will be cast into the lake of fire for all eternity. Those who attend the Marriage Supper will eat and feast. All those that attend the **supper of the great God** will be eaten.

A GROTESQUE MENU

That ye may eat the flesh of kings, and the flesh of captains, and the flesh of mighty men, and the flesh of horses, and of them that sit on them, and the flesh of all men, both free and bond, both small and great. (Revelation 19:18) An angel appears and calls the buzzards to a great feast. This is called the **supper of the great God.** The menu is made up of **kings, and the flesh of captains, and the flesh of mighty men, and the flesh of horses, and of them that sit on them, and the flesh of all men, both free and bond, both small and great.** Joseph Seiss wrote:

> *"This tells an awful story. It tells of the greatest of men made food for the vultures;—of kings and leaders, strong and confident, devoured on the field, with no one to bury them;—of those who thought to conquer Heaven's anointed King rendered helpless even against the timid birds;—of vaunting gods of nature turned into its cast off and most dishonored*

dregs. And what is thus foreintimated soon becomes reality. The Great Conqueror bows the heavens and comes down. He rides upon the cherub horse, and flies upon the wings of the wind. Smoke goes up from his nostrils, and devouring fire out of his mouth. He moves amid storms and darkness, from which the lightnings hurl their bolts, and hailstones mingle with the fire. He roars out of Zion, and utters his voice from Jerusalem, till the heavens and the earth shake. He dashes forth in the fury of his incensed greatness amid clouds, and fire, and pillars of smoke. The sun frowns. The day is neither light nor dark. The mountains melt and cleave asunder at his presence. The hills bound from their seats and skip like lambs. The waters are dislodged from their channels, The sea rolls back with howling trepidation. The sky is rent and folds upon itself like a collapsed tent. It is the day for executing an armed world, —world in covenant with Hell to overthrow the authority and throne of God, —and everything in terrified Nature joins to signalize the deserved vengeance."

The proud armies of the world imagine themselves to be invincible. However, they will become buzzard food under the mighty word of God.

A man's pride shall bring him low. (Proverbs 29:23)

What a sad end to human life. There will not even be a funeral for them. No honor will be given to them. There will be no pomp and no ceremony—there will be no burial. They are simply devoured by the buzzards.

A GATHERING MILITARY

And I saw the beast, and the kings of the earth, and their armies, gathered together... (Revelation 19:19a) One can hardly imagine this being seen, as all the military might of the world is gathered together, and not only the armies, but the antichrist and the political leaders of the earth. These military powers will gather in the land of Palestine from Megiddo in the north to Bozrah in the south. The theater of battle will span 200 miles from north to south, and 100 miles from east to west.

> **Behold, the day of the LORD cometh, and thy spoil shall be divided in the midst of thee. For I will gather all nations against Jerusalem to battle; and the city shall be taken, and the houses rifled, and the women ravished; and half of the city shall go forth into captivity, and the residue of the people shall not be cut off from the city. Then shall the LORD go forth, and fight against those nations, as when he fought in the day of battle. And his feet shall stand in that day upon the mount of Olives, which is before Jerusalem on the east, and the mount of Olives shall cleave in the midst thereof toward the east and toward the west, and there shall be a very great valley; and half of the mountain shall remove toward the north, and half of it toward the south. (Zechariah 14:1-4)**

The Jews have always been a hated and despised people, and the armies of the world will gather for the purpose of once and for all exterminating the Jewish people. However, these powerful armies though backed by the power of Satan, are no match for Christ. You will remember that the Lord Jesus Christ ascended into heaven from the mount of Olives, the promise was:

> **This same Jesus, which is taken up from you into heaven, shall so come in like manner as ye have seen him go into heaven. (Acts 1:11)**

We learn from Zechariah that when Jesus returns and stands on the Mount of Olives, He will split the mountain in two from east to west, forming a valley through which the Jewish people can escape. Joel described this awful day.

> **Proclaim ye this among the Gentiles; Prepare war, wake up the mighty men, let all the men of war draw near; let them come up: Beat your plowshares into swords, and your pruninghooks into spears: let the weak say, I am strong. Assemble yourselves, and come, all ye heathen, and gather yourselves together round about: thither cause thy mighty ones to come**

down, O LORD. Let the heathen be wakened, and come up to the valley of Jehoshaphat: for there will I sit to judge all the heathen round about. Put ye in the sickle, for the harvest is ripe: come, get you down; for the press is full, the vats overflow; for their wickedness is great. Multitudes, multitudes in the valley of decision: for the day of the LORD is near in the valley of decision. The sun and the moon shall be darkened, and the stars shall withdraw their shining. The LORD also shall roar out of Zion, and utter his voice from Jerusalem; and the heavens and the earth shall shake: but the LORD will be the hope of his people, and the strength of the children of Israel. (Joel 3:9-16)**

What a clear description Joel gives of this terrible scene. Army upon army gathering from every nation under Heaven. They will be equipped with their modern weapons and rely on the latest technology and tactics of warfare. Yet, they don't stand a chance against the King of kings and Lord of lords. He will speak with all authority and His enemies will be defeated.

A GRAVE MISTAKE

The purpose of their gathering was **to make war against him that sat on the horse, and against his army. (Revelation 19:19b)** He that sat on the horse is the Lord Jesus Christ, the King of kings and Lord of lords. His army is made up of the redeemed, the born again, blood washed believers, clothed in fine linen, clean and white, who return with Him at the end of the seven years of the Tribulation Period. When He returns the wicked men of the earth will be gathered **to make war against him that sat on the horse, and against his army.** It is hard to even imagine such pride! Pride is man's biggest problem. To gather an army for the purpose of fighting against the Glorious Son of God shows to what depth the depraved heart of man can plummet. As it was back in Genesis, so it is today. God said of man ...

> **... every imagination of the thoughts of his heart was only evil continually. (Genesis 6:5)**

How will God answer them? He will laugh at them. The Psalmist spoke of this day.

> **Why do the heathen rage, and the people imagine a vain thing? The kings of the earth set themselves, and the rulers take counsel together, against the LORD, and against his anointed, saying, Let us break their bands asunder, and cast away their cords from us. He that sitteth in the heavens shall laugh: the Lord shall have them in derision. (Psalm 2:1-4)**

In his commentary on the Book of Revelation, Donald Grey Barnhouse said:

> *The battle of Armageddon is the laughter of God against the climax of man's arrogance. The carnal mind is enmity against God. That carnal enmity crucified Christ. That carnal enmity will dare take up arms against the visible power of God ... the pride of man is so blind, when pushed by the Satanic powers, that he will dare to lift up his hand against God. The Lord shall have them in derision.*

Wicked man will convene and conspire to come against the Holy God of Heaven. Their efforts will prove futile. God will **laugh** at them from Heaven.

> **He that sitteth in the heavens shall laugh: the Lord shall have them in derision. (Psalm 2:4)**

The word **derision** carries the idea of *"laughing at in contempt and being a laughing-stock."* They have dared to attack the Son of God and now they will not only receive His fury, but His scorn as well. The same awaits those to mock and laugh at and reject His counsel (Psalm 1). God has the final Word!

A GRAND MOVE

And the beast was taken, and with him the false prophet that wrought miracles before him, with which he deceived them that had received the mark of the beast, and them that worshipped his image. These both were cast alive into a lake of fire burning with brimstone. (Revelation 19:20) The beast and the false prophet have had their day, but now it is over—it's payday. You will remember the cry and worship of the people when the beast appeared.

> **And they worshipped the dragon which gave power unto the beast: and they worshipped the beast, saying, Who is like unto the beast? who is able to make war with him? (Revelation 13:4)**

... **who is able to make war with him?** That question is answered in the presence of all the great military powers of the world. The answer is clear! Jesus Christ, the King of kings and Lord of lords will take hold of the beast and the false prophet and cast them into the lake of fire where they will spend eternity. The once proud and powerful enemies are taken from the battlefield as powerless prisoners. These, who boasted of their power and stole the hearts of men away from God, are now powerless to help themselves. They are defeated! Even today Hell is waiting to receive these two.

A GRIM MASSACRE

And the remnant were slain with the sword of him that sat upon the horse, which sword proceeded out of his mouth: and all the fowls were filled with their flesh. (Revelation 19:21) In chapter 19, this judgment will end with the supper of the great God. (Revelation 19:17) in which God will call the fowls of the air together to feed on the carnage of the wicked. The world has never seen such a battle as will take place at Christ's coming. Millions will be slaughtered! This will be the banquet of the buzzards and blood. Jesus spoke of this grim massacre.

> **For wheresoever the carcass is, there will the eagles be gathered together. (Matthew 24:28)**
>
> **And he said unto them, Wheresoever the body is, thither will the eagles be gathered together. (Luke 17:37)**

Eagles, buzzards, ravens, crows, hawks, and all birds of prey will be directed by God to have their fill and gorge themselves on the carcasses of the slain. The awful pride of man has led to his destruction! These men were the great military leaders of the world, yet Christ brought them to nothing in one battle.

A GLORIOUS MOMENT

With His enemies defeated, Jesus Christ the Victor, will set up His Kingdom and rule from Jerusalem for a thousand years. This will be the fulfillment of Zechariah's prophecy.

> **Behold, the day of the LORD cometh, and thy spoil shall be divided in the midst of thee. For I will gather all nations against Jerusalem to battle; and the city shall be taken, and the houses rifled, and the women ravished; and half of the city shall go forth into captivity, and the residue of the people shall not be cut off from the city. Then shall the LORD go forth, and fight against those nations, as when he fought in the day of battle. And his feet shall stand in that day upon the mount of Olives, which is before Jerusalem on the east, and the mount of Olives shall cleave in the midst thereof toward the east and toward the west, and there shall be a very great valley; and half of the mountain shall remove toward the north, and half of it toward the south. (Zechariah 14:1–4)**

It was from the Mount of Olives that the Lord Jesus ascended into Heaven and a great promise was given.

> **This same Jesus, which is taken up from you into heaven, shall so come in like manner as ye have seen him go into heaven. (Acts 1:11)**

When Jesus comes back, He will descend upon the Mount of Olives, overlooking the city of Jerusalem. So great will be the power of His return that the mountain will split in two from east to west. What a glorious sight it will be as Jesus Christ returns to this earth to establish His earthly kingdom.

THE MILLENNIAL REIGN
Revelation 20:1-10

As we come to this chapter the Tribulation Period has come to an end. The time of Jacob's Trouble is over. Thus, we now come to the setting up of Christ's long-awaited Kingdom on earth. This will take place at the end of the tribulation when Israel turns to Christ and a nation will be ...

... born at once. (Isaiah 66:8)

The Millennial Kingdom is a major theme of Bible prophecy. The Jews, in unbelief, missed the Kingdom when Christ came the first time.

He came unto his own, and his own received him not. (John 1:11)

Because of Israel's rejection of their Messiah at His first coming, God temporally set them aside and is today grafting in the wild branch (Romans 11). He is in the process of calling out the bride. Once our Lord raptures His people, He will once again take up the business of dealing with Israel and the Kingdom.

The Tribulation Period began back in chapter six of the book of Revelation and runs through and into chapter number nineteen of the book. Chapter twenty concerns the establishing of Christ's earthly kingdom. The Word of God abounds with references that speak of a literal Kingdom of God upon this earth (Deuteronomy 30:1-5; 2 Samuel 7:12-16; Psalm 2:6-12; Isaiah 2:2-4; 11:1-10; 12:1-6; 24:23; 32:15-20; 35:1-2; 60:10-18; 65:20-22; Jeremiah 3:14-18; 23:5-6; 30:3; 31:35-40; 33:14-18; Ezekiel 34:23-24; 36:16-38; 37:15-28; Daniel 2:44-45; Hosea 3:4-5; Joel 3:18-21; Amos 9:11-15; Micah 4:1-8; Zephaniah 3:14-20; Zechariah 14:9-11).

The word *millennium* comes from two Latin words, *"mille"* meaning *"thousand,"* and *"annus"* meaning *"year."* These two words together literally mean *"a thousand years."* The phrase thousand years is used six times in this chapter. This without a doubt establishes the length of the earthly kingdom and is therefore called the Millennium or the Millennial Kingdom. This will be a literal one-thousand-year reign of Christ upon this earth. I emphasis literal kingdom because we have so many reformed theologians running around trying to symbolize the Bible and teaching and amillennial position. The *"a"* in the Greek means no or none. They believe in a no millennial theology. But we need to follow Scripture and ...

> ... **let God be true, but every man a liar; (Romans 3:4)**

The Lord Jesus as the King of kings will sit upon the Throne of David in Jerusalem and rule with a rod of iron.

THE RESTRAINT OF SATAN

The Millennium begins with the restraining of Satan. In order to implement the kind of conditions which the Bible reveals concerning the Millennium, the Devil will have to be restrained. There will never be peace on earth with Satan loose.

The Authoritative Power

And I saw an angel come down from heaven, having the key of the bottomless pit and a great chain in his hand. (Revelation 20:1) The next thing John sees is an angel come down out of Heaven. We do not have to guess at and wonder who this angel is. He holds **key of the bottomless pit.** This Angel is Christ Himself. We read earlier that Jesus has ...

> ... **the keys of hell and of death. (Revelation 1:18)**

This bottomless pit is the abode of the wicked dead and the prison house of the demons. Christ is the keeper of the keys to this awful place.

The Adversary Prevented

And he laid hold on the dragon, that old serpent, which is the Devil, and Satan, (Revelation 20:2a) The old adversary, Satan, will be prevented from spreading his evil and corruption during the Millennium. The great archenemy of God and man has done his best to thwart the plans and purposes of God. He has

The Millennial Reign

poured his wrath and hatred out upon the people of God down through the ages. He has been the moving power and mastermind behind the spilling of the blood of the martyrs. He has sought to dethrone God and establish his own kingdom in the earth (Isaiah 14:12-15). We notice he is called by four names. His names reveal who and what he is.

He is the **dragon**. The word dragon is used of Satan only in the book of Revelation. (Revelation 12:3-4, 7,9, 13, 16-17; 13:2, 4,11; 16:13; 20:2) It speaks of him as an administrator—the power behind the antichrist and the evil world system. Keep in mind that though he is powerful, he is not all-powerful. The Bible clearly identifies him as the ...

... god of this world. (2 Corinthians 4:4)

He is called the **old serpent.** This name takes us back to the Garden where he slithered into the presence of God's creation and deceptively brought about the fall of man.

He is called the **devil.** The name devil literally means slanderer and liar, demonstrating how he falsely accuses and opposes the children of God. This has been one of the leading characteristics of the devil down through the ages. Jesus refers to him not only as a liar, but the father of lies (John 8:44).

He is called **Satan.** This name identifies him as our adversary. The name Satan is used over fifty times in the Bible demonstrating how he opposes the child of God (1 Peter 5:8).

The Awful Prison

... and bound him a thousand years, And cast him into the bottomless pit, and shut him up, and set a seal upon him, that he should deceive the nations no more, (Revelation 20:2b-3a) Satan is taken hold of by an angel and thrown into the bottomless pit. Remember that in chapter nine the bottomless pit was opened, and demons let out. The bottomless pit is the place of torment where the fallen angels are held. This is Hell's prison house. It is the place where the angels who followed Satan in his rebellion against God are chained in darkness. (Jude 1:6, 2 Peter 2:4) Demons hate the pit, but they will all eventually end up there. In Luke 8:31, the demons asked Jesus not to send them to the pit. This lines up with their request that He not torment them, in Luke 8:28. The bottomless pit is just a holding place for Satan. Christ at this time does not cast the devil to his final doom because He has a further purpose to accomplish in relation to the nations. The duration of the devil's imprisonment is one thousand years—he will be bound for the entire Millennium Kingdom of Christ. Without his influence, the world would be perfect and sinless.

The Astonishing Purpose

... till the thousand years should be fulfilled: and after that he must be loosed a little season. (Revelation 20:3b) God will allow the Devil to be released for a **little season** at the end of the Millennium. So, why would God let Satan out of prison? We know that for a thousand-years Satan's evil influence on the world will cease as he is incarcerated in the bottomless pit. For 1,000 years Satan's will not be allowed to tempt and influence man. Earth will be rid of his influence and temptation, and thus man's fallen nature will not be tempted. During the Millennium people will live in a perfect environment. There will be perfect health, a perfect government, perfect climate, and wild animals will be tame. There will be perfect justice and peace. So then, at the end of the Millennium there will be millions on earth who have never been tempted by Satan. However, the Just God cannot simply give these people eternal life. They must be tested and make a choice as to whether not they will trust Christ for their salvation. Our God is just and no respecter of persons. As the Millennium comes to an end and Satan is loosed and the people will face temptation. We will study this a bit more when we come to verse seven of this chapter.

THE REIGN OF THE SAINTS

The overcomers who were faithful in their earthly life are seen sitting upon their thrones and ruling Him.

Their Seat

And I saw thrones, and they sat upon them, (Revelation 20:4a) Here we have a description of God's overcoming saints

The Millennial Reign

ruling with Christ during the Millennium. It will be a marvelous time when the child of God reigns with Him in glory.

Their Sanction

... and judgment was given unto them: (Revelation 20:4b) These believers who sit on these thrones here are sanctioned by God with His authority to conduct His business. This is not a small thing! These enthroned believers will administer judgment in Christ's reign over the nations. The Lord spoke about this event at other times.

> **Then answered Peter and said unto him, Behold, we have forsaken all, and followed thee; what shall we have therefore? And Jesus said unto them, Verily I say unto you, That ye which have followed me, in the regeneration when the Son of man shall sit in the throne of his glory, ye also shall sit upon twelve thrones, judging the twelve tribes of Israel. (Matthew 19:27-28)**

> **To him that overcometh will I grant to sit with me in my throne, even as I also overcame, and am set down with my Father in his throne. (Revelation 3:21)**

During the thousand-year reign of the Lord Jesus Christ, the Old Testament saints, the Church, along with the Tribulation saints will work with Christ in His earthly kingdom. This is a promise to the overcomer.

Their Statement

... and I saw the souls of them that were beheaded for the witness of Jesus, and for the word of God, and which had not worshipped the beast, neither his image, neither had received his mark upon their foreheads, or in their hands; (Revelation 20:4c) These are the faithful martyrs who were beheaded for their testimony during the Tribulation Period. They refused to worship the beast or his image. Furthermore, they would not take the mark of the beast. Now we see them resurrected to join the New Testament saints who were resurrected and raptured at the beginning of the Tribulation

Period. These faithful saints are rewarded and will reign with Christ during the Millennium.

> **He that over cometh, I will give to him to sit down with me in my throne, as I also overcame, and sat down with my Father in his throne. (Revelation 3:21)**

Notice that the Lord specifically mentions His martyred saints. Satan had viciously brought about their death. However, they now rule with Christ on His throne, while Satan is incarcerated in the bottomless pit. God's people always come out on top.

Their Success

... and they lived and reigned with Christ a thousand years. (Revelation 20:4d) Now, the promised Messiah is on the throne, and the government is upon His shoulder as prophesied before His birth (Isaiah 9:6-7). The children of God who have overcome and succeeded in the Christian life will be given greater responsibilities in Christ's Kingdom. Jesus along with the faithful saints of the ages are sitting upon their thrones and His kingdom is established on earth.

... This is the first resurrection. (Revelation 20:4e) The **first resurrection** includes the resurrection of the saints at the Rapture and the resurrection of the tribulation saints at the close of the tribulation. Jesus said ...

> **... they that have done good, unto the resurrection of life; and they that have done evil, unto the resurrection of damnation. (John 5:29)**

This verse does not suggest the idea of a general resurrection as some suppose. Rather it speaks of two separate resurrections for two different kinds of people. It is the **resurrection life** for God's people, but the **resurrection of damnation** for the lost. Those who reject Christ will be damned for eternity.

But the rest of the dead lived not again until the thousand years were finished. This is the first resurrection. (Revelation 20:5) It is only those who are saved, and overcomers that will have part in the first resurrection. The unsaved, the wicked dead, live not again until after the Millennial Reign of Christ. The resurrection of the wicked is not a resurrection unto life that Jesus spoke of, but unto eternal damnation.

Their Sanctification

Blessed and holy is he that hath part in the first resurrection: on such the second death hath no power, (Revelation 20:6a) Here it is reiterated that only **holy** people (saved) will have part in the **first resurrection**. These are people who have trusted Christ and are saved. Further, these are people of whom **the second death hath no power.** Only these people will be resurrected in the first resurrection.

Their Service

... but they shall be priests of God and of Christ, and shall reign with him a thousand years. (Revelation 20:6b) The overcomers who take part in the first resurrection The Rapture will rule with Christ.

> **And he that overcometh, and keepeth my works unto the end, to him will I give power over the nations: (Revelation 2:26)**

John Walvoord says that the phrase **priests of God and of Christ,** is ...

> ... a designation of a privileged rank similar to that which the church enjoys in this present age under Christ our High Priest.

Back in the Old Testament the priests were given the important task of teaching God's people and leading them in the worship of the Lord. Likewise, during the Millennium, the overcomers of the first resurrection will teach the nations about the ways of God.

THE RELEASE OF SATAN

And when the thousand years are expired, Satan shall be loosed out of his prison. (Revelation 20:7) Again, we are reminded that after the thousand-year reign of Christ, Satan will be let out of Hell's prison house. We should take aa few moments to look at this again. This is Satan's last stand! We must be careful not to doubt the wisdom of God here. The fact that Satan is loosed is part of the eternal plan and purpose of God. In fact, the inspired writer says of Satan that ...

> ... he **MUST** be loosed, a little season. (Revelation 20:3)

Notice the **must**. Satan must be loosed—there is no way around it. Satan is released from the bottomless pit and after a thousand-year imprisonment he is unchanged. He is still the archenemy of God and the deceiver of mankind. He still has the same wicked heart and motives that he always had. It is not incarceration that changes a wicked heart, but regeneration.

There will be millions of people born during the Millennium who have not made a decision to trust Christ as their Saviour. Satan has been bound. Therefore, there has been no temptation. It has been a perfect environment as Christ ruled with a rod of iron. During this time there will be no murder, no stealing, no adultery, no drunkenness—there will be no sin. However, we must understand that the kingdom has not been perfect because of man's goodness, but because of Christ's righteous rule, and the fact that the Devil has been bound and unable to tempt the depraved heart of man. Remember the words of Jesus:

> **That which is born of the flesh is flesh; and that which is born of the Spirit is spirit. (John 3:6)**

All those who have been born during the Millennial reign of Christ were born in the flesh, but not in the Spirit.

> **Because the carnal mind is enmity against God: for it is not subject to the law of God, neither indeed can be. (Romans 8:7)**

When Satan is loosed, man will once again prove his depravity. Not only will Satan be loosed, but the gospel will go forth once again as well.

> **Look unto me, and be ye saved, all the ends of the earth: for I am God, and there is none else. (Isaiah 45:22)**

The Millennial Reign

People will have to make a choice. Unfortunately, when Satan comes to them offering an alternative to Christ, many people who have not been saved will follow him to death. However, God is no respecter of persons (Acts 10:34) and must give them the opportunity to choose the Lord or continue on unsaved.

For there is no respect of persons with God. (Romans 2:11)

The fact that Satan is released at the end of the Millennium shows the fairness of God concerning the matter of salvation. God could not let them into Heaven without being saved and He could not deny them entrance without giving them the opportunity to trust Christ. He is indeed a good and merciful God.

THE REBELLION OF SOCIETY

Isn't it amazing that after a thousand-year utopia on the earth that man would be deceived into following a diabolical plan to attempt to overthrow Almighty God? Yet this will be the case.

The Deception Of The Adversary

And shall go out to deceive the nations which are in the four quarters of the earth, Gog and Magog, to gather them together to battle: the number of whom is as the sand of the sea. (Revelation 20:8) The Millennium comes to an end Satan will immediately go out and **deceive the nations**. When Satan comes to them offering an alternative to Christ's rule, multitudes will join with him against Jesus. Having been born and raised in a perfect environment, as soon as they are tempted, they go astray. Psychologists teach that all man really needs is a better world or a better environment and he will do better. This proves their idea to be wrong. Man's problem is not environment—it is depravity (Jeremiah 17:9). Satan goes out and deceives the nations and from the four quarters of the earth, he gathers an army, the number of whom is as the sand of the sea, to attack Jesus and His people. Satan and his army are permitted to enter Palestine and encircle Jerusalem.

It should be noted that the term **Gog and Magog** is not a reference to Ezekiel 38. The prophecies regarding Gog and Magog in Ezekiel 38-39 will take place just before or just after the Tribulation Period begins. The terms Gog and Magog here are symbolic of the enemies of God and His people.

The Desire Of The Aggressors

And they went up on the breadth of the earth, and compassed the camp of the saints about, and the beloved city: (Revelation 20:9a) The phrase **the breadth of the earth** emphasizes the masses of unsaved people who will come out of the Millennium and join up with Satan to fight against Christ. Satan and his armies surround **the camp of the saints** and **the beloved city** Jerusalem. This is Satan's last-ditch effort to overthrow Christ and take His throne.

The Destruction Of The Armies

... and fire came down from God out of heaven, and devoured them. (Revelation 20: 9b) Satan's last great act of rebellion will be quashed by fire from the Almighty. When Jerusalem is completely cut off from all outside help and surrounded by millions of soldiers, God will step in. God deals with rebellion fully and finally as **fire came down from God out of heaven, and devoured them.** Satan and his armies will be wiped from the face of the earth.

THE RECOMPENSE FOR SATAN

And the devil that deceived them was cast into the lake of fire and brimstone, where the beast and the false prophet are, and shall be tormented day and night for ever and ever. (Revelation 20:10) This doom of Satan has been long foretold. (Ezekiel 28:18) For thousands of years he has deceived men and fought against the very God Who created him. Now his day has come, and he is cast into the lake of fire and brimstone and shall be tormented day and night forever and ever. This is the place that was specifically prepared for him. (Matthew 25:41) This will be the end of Satan.

THE GREAT WHITE THRONE JUDGMENT
Revelation 20:11-15

At this point the Millennial Kingdom has come to an end. Satan and his army have been cast into the lake of fire. Now, we come to the Great White Throne Judgment. This is where the unsaved of all ages will be resurrected to stand before Christ in judgment. Everyone who has refused to receive Jesus Christ as Saviour will be judged according to his or her works and thrown into the lake of fire. The people being judged here are **the rest of the dead** that we saw back in verse 5. These died without God and therefore have no hope of Heaven. This is the Great White Throne Judgment. This is the judgment of the unsaved dead. Bear in mind that no saved person will ever be judged at the White Throne Judgment. It is here that the unsaved will stand before God in his filthy rags and suffer the consequences of his wickedness.

A FEARFUL SIGHT

This scene here is overwhelmingly solemn. Here is the Holy, Righteous, and Angry God of Heaven sitting upon His throne in judgment.

The Frightening Reality

And I saw a great white throne, and him that sat on it, (Revelation 20:11a) The word **great** comes from *"megas"* and denotes size. It carries the idea of *"exceeding, great, large, loud, mighty."* It is a great throne of the Great and Almighty God. The word **white** speaks of righteousness, holiness, and purity. All those judged here will receive a righteous verdict.

> **But the LORD shall endure for ever: he hath prepared his throne for judgment. And he shall judge the world in righteousness, he shall minister**

> judgment to the people in uprightness. (Psalm 9:7-8)
>
> **But after thy hardness and impenitent heart treasurest up unto thyself wrath against the day of wrath and revelation of the righteous judgment of God; (Romans 2:5)**

This is the same scene described by Daniel (Daniel 7:9-10). The phrase **him that sat on it** denotes the Lord Jesus. Here the Son of God takes His place as the Supreme Judge of all the earth. Here He judges the unsaved dead.

> **For the Father judgeth no man, but hath committed all judgment unto the Son. (John 5:22)**

All judgment is committed into the hands of Christ, and we see Him seated on a **great white throne** where He will judge the unsaved. This is not the judgment of believers, but of the wicked dead. This will be a fierce time for those who died in unbelief. Many scoffers ask, *"where is the promise of His coming."* They refuse to except what the Bible says about the return of Christ. But one day they will realize that they made the mistake of their lives when they stand before Him in judgment.

The Fleeing Response

... from whose face the earth and the heaven fled away; and there was found no place for them. (Revelation 20:11b) Notice the response to Jesus Christ and His Sovereign Majesty as He sits on His throne. **The earth and the heaven fled away; and there was found no place for them.** Not only did the earth and heaven flee away, but **there was found no place for them.** They simply cease to be—the old heaven and earth are no more. In the next chapter we see a ...

> **... new heaven and a new earth: for the first heaven and the first earth were passed away. (Revelation 21:1)**

Imagine the scene when Christ takes His throne and the heavens and earth flee from his presence. This is not only the judgment of lost man, but of all creation. This world, tainted by sin, will not be allowed to continue into eternity. We will study this in a little more detail in the next chapter.

A FINAL SUMMONS

And I saw the dead, small and great, stand before God ... And the sea gave up the dead which were in it; and death and hell delivered up the dead which were in them: and they were judged every man according to their works. (Revelation 20:12-13) There shall not be one saved person at the White Throne Judgment. Here is a judgment entirely for the wicked dead. Saved people's sins have been paid for and taken away by the blood of Christ. What a serious moment when the millions upon millions of the unrighteous dead are summoned from their graves to answer to God. The Bible declares that it is:

> **...appointed unto men once to die, but after this the judgment. (Hebrews 9:27)**

Everyone must die—death is by divine appointment. The Great White Throne is another Divine appointment that the unsaved have with God.

The **small and great, stand before God** in judgment. No one gets away from his just punishment. There are no escapees. This judgment will include all of the unsaved. In his commentary on Revelation, John Phillips said:

> *The dead, small and great, stand before God. Dead souls are united to dead bodies in a fellowship of horror and despair. Little men and paltry women whose lives were filled with pettiness, selfishness, and nasty little sins will be there. Those whose lives amounted to nothing will be there, whose very sins were drab and dowdy, mean, spiteful, peevish, groveling, vulgar, common, and cheap. The great will be there, men who sinned with a high hand, with dash, and courage and flair. Men like Alexander and Napoleon. Hitler and Stalin will be present, men who went in for wickedness on a grand scale with the world for their stage and who died*

> *unrepentant at last. Now one and all are arraigned and, on their way, to be damned: a horrible fellowship congregated together for the first and last time.*

There are no big shots at this judgment. God is no respecter of persons. It will make no difference whether it is a man or woman. It will make no difference whether they were moral people or immoral. Because they do not know Christ as their Saviour, they will be called before the Supreme Judge of Heaven, and one by one, judged for their sin.

A FACTUAL STATEMENT

And the books were opened: and another book was opened, which is the book of life: and the dead were judged out of those things which were written in the books... (Revelation 20:12) Though some have attempted to teach a general resurrection and judgment. They believe that saints and sinners will be raised at the same time to face judgment. However, the Scriptures are clear that this is not the case. The Great White Throne will be the judgment of the wicked dead, not the saved.

We see that the **books** (plural) were opened: and another **book** (singular) was opened, which is the **book of life.** When a person is born into the world his name is recorded in the Book of Life. When he dies, if he has not received Jesus Christ as Saviour, his name is blotted out of this book, leaving a blank spot where the name once was. At the Great White Throne, therefore, the Book of Life is brought forth as evidence to prove to the unbelievers that their names are not there. It is this book of life that the Psalmist referred to when he said ...

> **Let them be blotted out of the book of the living, and not be written with the righteous. (Psalm 69:28)**

One of the other books mentioned is the Word of God. The very Bible that God gave to man to instruct him, will now be opened to convict and damn him. All sixty-six books will be there to testify of every man's sin.

> **In the day when God shall judge the secrets of men by Jesus Christ according to my gospel. (Romans 2:16)**

Jesus said,

> **He that rejecteth me, and receiveth not my words, hath one that judgeth him: the word that I have spoken, the same shall judge him in the last day. (John 12:48)**

Another book opened will be the record of man's deeds (Daniel 7:10, Isaiah 65:6, Malachi 3:16). Everything we have ever done is recorded in Heaven. There is nothing hidden from God. We have no secret that He doesn't know (Ecclesiastes 12:14). Imagine standing before a Judge Who knows everything about you. He knows every detail of our life. He knows every thought that ever crossed our mind. He knows every word that ever fell from our lips.

> **For God shall bring every work into judgment, with every secret thing, whether it be good, or whether it be evil. (Ecclesiastes 12:14)**

At the judgment, nothing will be forgotten. Nothing will be overlooked. Sinful man will get away with absolutely nothing when he stands before God. What a solemn thought! There is not one thing in our lives that He does not know about. He knows every detail of our lives He knows every thought that ever crossed your mind. He knows every word that ever fell from your lips. He knows your every crime.

A FAIR SUMMATION

And they were judged every man according to their works. (Revelation 20:13b) This judgment is based on works. At the Judgment of Christ, believers will be judged to determine how great a reward they will be given for their service. Here, at the Great White Throne Judgment, sinner's deeds will be examined to determine how great a degree of punishment they will receive. Just like there are degrees of reward in Heaven, there are degrees of punishment in Hell. This principle is clearly taught in the Word of God. (Luke 12:47-48) We often hear the phrase "it's not fair." Well, the Great White Throne Judgment will be fair. Man will get exactly what is coming to him.

A FATAL SENTENCE

And death and hell were cast into the lake of fire. This is the second death. And whosoever was not found written in the book of life was cast into the lake of fire. (Revelation 20:14-15) There will be no pay offs, no plea bargaining, no favoritism! Only righteous judgment and everyone at this judgment will end up in the lake of fire. There will be no appeal! The matter is settled! There will be no atonement—the Blood has been rejected. There will be no more amazing grace. Never again will one ever be handed a gospel tract. No one will ever hear another sermon. This will be the final state of all who reject Christ. They will be hopelessly lost forever!

ALL THINGS NEW
Revelation 21:1-8

This will be a precious time for the children of God. In our day we see folks worried silly about the environment. They occupy themselves with trees, lakes, rivers, animals, and the hole in the ozone. Billions are being spent in search of solutions that will ultimately make no difference. God already has the answer.

And he that sat upon the throne said, Behold, I make all things new. And he said unto me, Write: for these words are true and faithful. (Revelation 21:5)

This sinful world is going to be dealt with. It will be destroyed by fire and God will bring a new world into existence according to His great plan and purpose. God will make **all things new.** This will take place at the close of the Millennial Kingdom.

A NEW CREATION

And I saw a new heaven and a new earth: for the first heaven and the first earth were passed away; and there was no more sea. (Revelation 21:1) Now this is an interesting passage! This event could be called the uncreation. In Genesis we read:

In the beginning God created the heaven and the earth. (Genesis 1:1)

What a glorious sight that must have been when God Almighty stepped forth in all His majesty and might and spoke the world into existence. Now, when the end comes and He sits in judgment we see that same majesty and might, but this time creation disappears into nothingness. Just like creation came out of nothing, it will return to nothing.

For, behold, I create new heavens and a new earth: and the former shall not be remembered, nor come into mind. (Isaiah 65:17)

Not only will earth and heaven be destroyed, but it will also not **be remembered, nor come into mind** again. Peter wrote:

> **Nevertheless we, according to his promise, look for new heavens and a new earth, wherein dwelleth righteousness. (2 Peter 3:13)**

The prophet Isaiah wrote:

> **For as the new heavens and the new earth, which I will make, shall remain before me, saith the LORD, (Isaiah 66:22a)**

Jesus said:

> **Heaven and earth shall pass away. (Matthew 24:35)**

Paul wrote:

> **And, Thou, Lord, in the beginning hast laid the foundation of the earth; and the heavens are the works of thine hands: They shall perish; but thou remainest; and they all shall wax old as doth a garment; And as a vesture shalt thou fold them up, and they shall be changed: but thou art the same, and thy years shall not fail. (Hebrews 1:10-12)**

While our God is a God of love, He is also a God of fire and judgment. and we know from Scripture that He will use fire when He destroys the heavens and earth.

> **But the heavens and the earth, which are now, by the same word are kept in store, reserved unto fire against the day of judgment and perdition of ungodly men. But the day of the Lord will come as a thief in the night; in the which the heavens shall pass away with a great noise, and the elements shall melt with fervent heat, the earth also and the works that are therein shall be burned up. Seeing then that all these things shall be dissolved, what manner of persons ought ye to be in all holy conversation and godliness, Looking for and hasting unto the coming of the day of God, wherein the heavens being on fire shall be dissolved, and the elements shall melt with fervent heat. (2 Peter 3:7, 10-12)**

Peter speaks with confidence that **the day of the Lord will come.** There is no question about it. Judgment is coming not only upon fallen man, but the universe as well. Notice the phrases used. The earth and heaven will pass away, the elements shall melt, and the earth also and the works that are therein shall be burned up. Dr. Henry Morris writes:

> "Now, before the amazed John a vision is unfolded of an even grander scene than any he had ever witnessed before. In fact, the spectacle is so blindingly glorious that the very earth itself disintegrates before it. The fire which had fallen from heaven to consume the multitudes following Gog and Magog seems to be nothing less than the unveiled glory, the pure, white hot energy, of the Creator in all His ineffable brilliance. Now that same cosmic power penetrates the very atomic structure of the earth and its atmosphere, and they are vaporized in a gigantic holocaust that brings this present world to an end."

This world cursed by God and contaminated by sin will not be allowed to continue into eternity. The eternal state will be uncontaminated by sin and will be perfectly pure and righteous, just as it was before the fall.

> **Nevertheless we, according to his promise, look for new heavens and a new earth, wherein dwelleth righteousness. (2 Peter 3:13)**
>
> **While we look not at the things which are seen, but at the things which are not seen: for the things which are seen are temporal; but the things which are not seen are eternal. (2 Corinthians 4:18)**

God will not simply renovate; He will replace the earth with a new one. In light of this we can better understand Paul's words. So, this earth will be restored to its original beauty and in its original glory and forever the earth will be what God originally intended it to be.

A NEW CITY

And I John saw the holy city, new Jerusalem, coming down from God out of heaven, prepared as a bride adorned for her husband. (Revelation 21:2) As John looked, he saw a magnificent city coming down from Heaven. It is described as the holy city, and new Jerusalem. In verse 9, concerning this same city, an Angel said to John:

> **Come hither, I will show thee the bride, the Lamb's wife. And he carried me away in the spirit to a great and high mountain, and showed me that great city, the holy Jerusalem, descending out of heaven from God. (Revelation 21:9-10)**

John was told that he would see the Bride, the Lamb's wife, and God shows John the New Jerusalem. The great city of God will be the capital city of the new heavens and earth. But where was the bride? The answer is simple, she is in the New Jerusalem. The New Jerusalem is the home of the bride throughout all eternity. What a magnificent city it will be! We will study the New Jerusalem in greater detail in our next study.

A NEW COMPANY

> **And I heard a great voice out of heaven saying, Behold, the tabernacle of God is with men, and he will dwell with them, and they shall be his people, and God himself shall be with them, and be their God. (Revelation 21:3)** A great voice announces that the **tabernacle of God is with men, and He will dwell with them.** God will personally be present with His people. Just imagine! Dwelling with God! How God loves His children. The conditions were wonderful in the garden as God would come daily to fellowship with Adam and Eve. When that fellowship was interrupted by sin, God no longer came daily in His glory to the garden. The way God fellowships with man will change in the New Jerusalem. Back in Genesis Adam and Eve enjoyed the presence of God daily as He came and fellowshipped with them in the garden. However, we are told that God will **dwell** with His people in the New Jerusalem. Meditate for a while on this great truth! A new intimacy is going to exist between God and His people because sin will no longer be an issue in our relationship with Him. Earlier John wrote:

> **Beloved, now are we the sons of God, and it doth not yet appear what we shall be: but we**

know that, when he shall appear, we shall be like him; for we shall see him as he is. (1 John 3:2)

Speaking of the future when believers have entered their glorified state, John declares **we shall be like him; for we shall see him as he is.** We will be allowed to see God in His glory. In the Eternal State, we will constantly experience God's presence and glory.

A NEW COMFORT

And God shall wipe away all tears from their eyes; and there shall be no more death, neither sorrow, nor crying, neither shall there be any more pain: for the former things are passed away. (Revelation 21:4) Think about living in the very presence of God who made all things and by Whom all things exist. His presence ensures complete protection from those things which cause us pain, both mentally and physically. Because sin will no longer be an issue, the tears and sorrow will also be forever gone. Tears are a major part of human experience. Even with the sympathy of our friends and even with the comfort of God, we still have sorrow and tears. I thank God that we:

... sorrow not, even as others which have no hope. (1 Thessalonians 4:13)

Praise God that no matter what comes our way we can face it with the hope and confidence that it is only temporal, and that Jesus Christ is coming back for us. No matter the circumstances, we are:

Looking for that blessed hope, and the glorious appearing of the great God and our Saviour Jesus Christ. (Titus 2:13)

However, even with the comfort and encouragement of God and friends, there are still tears. We still feel pain, we still carry burdens, and we still experience sorrow. That is because the reason for our pain and sorrow is still present. Kind words and even the hope of Christ's return cannot fully heal a broken heart. But in the eternal state, in the New Jerusalem, God Himself will dry all tears. He will do it by removing the source of our sorrow. We will be glorified! This is the promise of God to every believer.

> **Beloved, now are we the sons of God, and it doth not yet appear what we shall be: but we know that, when he shall appear, we shall be like him; for we shall see him as he is. (1 John 3:2)**

When that day comes, we will be just like Christ. This is God's plan for his children.

> **For whom he did foreknow, he also did predestinate to be conformed to the image of his Son, that he might be the firstborn among many brethren. (Romans 8:29)**

When that day comes, the source of all sorrow and pain will be removed. The depraved heart will be gone, we will be glorified. What a day that will be!

A NEW CONDITION

And he that sat upon the throne said, Behold, I make all things new. And he said unto me, Write: for these words are true and faithful. And he said unto me, It is done. I am Alpha and Omega, the beginning and the end. I will give unto him that is athirst of the fountain of the water of life freely. (Revelation 21:5-6) Here is a snapshot of eternity. The One who sat on the throne emphasizes that He will **make all things new**. Henry Morris said:

> *Presumably this means not only that everything will be made new, but also that everything will then stay new. The entropy law will be "repealed." Nothing will wear out or decay, and no one will age or atrophy anymore.*

In eternity there will be a permanent state of newness. Sin will never again taint God's creation. We are assured that these words are **true and faithful.** The phrase, **these words are true and faithful**, has been recorded three times in this latter portion of the Revelation (19:11; 21:5; 22:6). Such is the test of genuine prophecy.

... **it is done**. This is the third and final time that our Lord has spoken such words of completion. Upon His finished work on Calvary He said, **it is finished. (John 19:30)** This signified the completion of Redemption. When the seventh vial was poured out, He said it is done. This was the completion of Retribution upon this wicked world. Now in our text, redeemed man is brought into perfect fellowship with God. This is the completion of Restoration. We have nothing to worry about concerning our eternal salvation.

The One on the throne now identifies Himself. **I am Alpha and Omega, the beginning and the end.** This is the Lord Jesus Christ (Revelation 1:8; 22:12,13). The Alpha is the first letter, and the Omega is last letter in the Greek alphabet. From eternity past to eternity future, Jesus encompasses everything. As the One Who is true and faithful, the Alpha and Omega, the beginning and the end, Jesus Christ personally guarantees the believer's eternal standing in Heaven.

A NEW CALM

He that overcometh shall inherit all things; and I will be his God, and he shall be my son. (Revelation 21:7) What a wonderful verse that points to the believer's future. But notice here that another reference is made to the overcomer. The overcomers have suffered extreme persecution for their faith, yet they overcame the circumstances and rose to the top. This is the heritage of God's people. Peter tells us that God's grace is the secret of overcoming faith.

> **But the God of all grace, who hath called us unto his eternal glory by Christ Jesus, after that ye have suffered a while, make you perfect, stablish, strengthen, settle you. (1 Peter 5:10)**

Paul wrote:

> **Nay, in all these things we are more than conquerors through him that loved us. (Romans 8:37)**

Every believer is supposed to be an overcomer. God's people are a victorious people. The child of God does not have to be a victim, he is by God's grace a victor. We are **more than conquerors through him.** There is no excuse for believers not to be overcomers. We have the power of the Holy Spirit to enable us. What we cant do the Holy Spirit can do through us.

A NEW CONFINEMENT

But the fearful, and unbelieving, and the abominable, and murderers, and whoremongers, and sorcerers, and idolaters, and all liars, shall have their part in the lake which burneth with fire and brimstone: which is the second death. (Revelation 21:8) The word **but** calls our attention to the fact that there is a great contrast between the Christians who have an eternally righteous standing with God and those who have no standing with God at all. The Holy City, the New Jerusalem is a place designed by God for His people exclusively. God assures His people that they will inherit all things and then lists eight characteristics of the unsaved describing why they will not enter the heavenly city. God's people are going to have a wonderful and glorious fellowship with God and one another for eternity. This list in our text, however, describes the "Eternal Fellowship Of The Damned."

The Fearful

The Devil uses fear to capture and control man. The word **fearful** comes from *"deilos"* and means *"timid or cowardly."* There are many today who will not be saved and serve Christ for fear of others. Their fear of friends and family hinders them from coming to Christ. They are afraid to take their stand for the Lord Jesus Christ. Paul spoke of such people ...

> **Now the just shall live by faith: but if any man draw back, my soul shall have no pleasure in him. But we are not of them who draw back unto perdition; but of them that believe to the saving of the soul. (Hebrews 10:38–39)**

Jesus said ...

> **... No man, having put his hand to the plough, and looking back, is fit for the kingdom of God. (Luke 9:62)**

John describes those whose cowardice hindered them from taking a stand and speaking out for Christ. As a result of fear, they enjoy no peace or place in Heaven. The pit of Hell will be populated with such people.

The Unbelieving

The **unbelieving** will never enter into the city of God. An unbeliever will never know what it is like to dwell with God. There is no hope of salvation after death.

> **And as it is appointed unto men once to die, but after this the judgment: (Hebrews 9:27)**

The state of the dead is forever fixed. He will be hopelessly lost for eternity.

The Abominable

This word abominable carries the idea of *"detestable or loathsome."* It carries the idea of being polluted, loathsome, abominable. Noah Webster says this word *"is applicable to whatever is odious to the mind or offensive to the senses."* It refers to those polluted and given to unnatural lust. Man is polluted with depravity and the lost will remain in such a condition for eternity.

The Murderer

Murderers will be locked out of Heaven. Man, places little value on human life, unless it is his own. Violence and bloodshed have increased, and murder has actually become big business, with over four thousand babies murdered every day in America. Politicians, doctors and would be mothers care nothing about the unborn. They butcher the unborn in the womb. However, life is sacred to God and all those who are murders will be removed from His presence for all eternity. Untold millions of unforgiven murderers will populate Hell.

The Whoremonger

Whoremongers are those who are sexually immoral. The word **whoremonger** comes from *"pornos"* from which we get the English pornography. It speaks of any kind of illicit sexual sin. Adulterers, rapists, fornicators, prostitutes' pedophiles, and providers of pornography. Many are guilty of these sins. They will be turned away from the Holy City. We live in a day when many are serving the god of sex. They worship at the altar of pleasure. We live in an immoral world and the world loves it; they live for it. But God hates it and banishes such wickedness forever from His home to spend eternity in the lake of fire.

The Sorcerer

Sorcerers will have no place in the city of God. The word for sorcerers is the word from which the English word pharmacy is derived. It is a word that has to do with dealing and dabbling with drugs. It involves dealing with witchcraft, magical arts, potions, and incantations. In this context it would include all forms of sorcery including astrology, palm reading, séances, fortune telling, crystals, and other forms of witchcraft.

The Idolater

Idolaters will be banned from God's city. This world is full of idolatry. We think of idols as statues or false gods, and that is true. However, it goes much further than that. An idol is anything that takes the place of God in someone's life. It could be your work, food, books, education, possessions, television, or fashion. Anything that squeezes God out of your life is an idol. People idolize ball players, Hollywood stars, musicians, and other worldly people.

The Liar

All Liars will be cast into the lake of fire. Their deceitfulness will not be allowed in Heaven. God will cast them into a Christ less, Godless eternity. Only absolute truth will be allowed to exist in Heaven. There will be no liars in Heaven.

Many kinds of people dwell in earthly cities. It is not safe to walk the streets of America at night, and in some cities, it is not safe to be out during the day. This will not be the case in the New Jerusalem. Those who would pervert the city with crime and sin, have long rejected the Saviour and will not be permitted to enter the city of God. The heavenly and holy city of New Jerusalem will be a calm and peaceful place.

THE NEW JERUSALEM
Revelation 21:9-22:5

In this section we find some details about the wonderful city of God. Like Abraham, we long and look for this city not made with hands (Hebrews 11:10). No human architect drew up the plans and blueprints for this magnificent city. No human hand will ever be employed in its construction. The New Jerusalem is the city **whose builder and maker is God.** As Jesus was coming to the end of His earthly ministry, He made a wonderful promise to his disciples:

> **In my Father's house are many mansions: if it were not so, I would have told you. I go to prepare a place for you. And if I go and prepare a place for you, I will come again, and receive you unto myself; that where I am, there ye may be also. (John 14:2-3)**

This holy city has been in the making since Jesus ascended to Heaven after His resurrection. He is preparing it for us as our eternal home with Him. What wonderful promises the children of God have! The Lord Jesus Christ is in Heaven now preparing mansions in the city of God for His people and He is coming again for us that we may be there with Him.

THE DESCENT

John begins by describing the wonderful city of God. In these verses the Lord shows the Apostle and us, just how beautiful Heaven is. After being caught up into Heaven and allowed to it beauty, the Apostle Paul said that ...

> **... he was caught up into paradise, and heard unspeakable words, which it is not lawful for a man to utter. (2 Corinthians 12:4)**

The word unspeakable means that God's gift is *"incapable of being adequately described."* Since there are things in Heaven that are **unspeakable**, this section does not fully describe the

Holy City. Rather, it simply gives us a glimpse of the unspeakable beauty of the place God is preparing for His people.

The Announcement Of The City

And there came unto me one of the seven angels which had the seven vials full of the seven last plagues, and talked with me, saying, Come hither, I will shew thee the bride, the Lamb's wife. (Revelation 21:9) One of the seven angels that had the vials full of the last plagues called John to look up and see the New Jerusalem descending out of Heaven. In the following verses will see the beauty of the bride of Christ. The designation used is of the **Lamb's wife** is drawn from the idea of a wedding. It speaks of beauty and love and everything else that is associated with a pure and godly wedding.

The Arrival Of The City

And he carried me away in the spirit to a great and high mountain, and shewed me that great city, the holy Jerusalem, descending out of heaven from God, (Revelation 21:10) The Apostle John was carried away, that is, he was transported **in the spirit** to a **great and high mountain**, where he receives this vision. It is exciting that what John saw this in the Spirit, we will one day literally see with our own eyes. John sees the holy city **descending out of heaven from God.** Thus, we see that the New Jerusalem is of Divine origin as it descends out of Heaven from God. There is no need to spiritualize and symbolize the New Jerusalem. We can take every detail of this passage literally. This is a real city in which the Lord Jesus Christ dwells with His glorified saints.

The Appearance Of The City

Having the glory of God: and her light was like unto a stone most precious, even like a jasper stone, clear as crystal; (Revelation 21:11) This city is beautiful beyond comparison to anything known by mortal man. Everything about the New Jerusalem speaks of the glory and greatness of God.

The first thing John saw was the **glory of God**. The holy city glows with the glory and radiance of God.

The New Jerusalem

> And the city had no need of the sun, neither of the moon, to shine in it: for the glory of God did lighten it, and the Lamb is the light thereof. (Revelation 21:23)
>
> And there shall be no night there; and they need no candle, neither light of the sun; for the Lord God giveth them light: and they shall reign for ever and ever. (Revelation 22:5)

God's very presence fills this city, and it glows with the gleam of God like a precious jewel, radiating the Shekinah glory of its Divine Architect.

THE DESIGN

What a magnificent city! The design of this city is like no other. It was designed and built by the Divine Architect. This is the city whose builder and maker is God.

The Safety Of The City

> And had a wall great and high, and had twelve gates, and at the gates twelve angels, and names written thereon, which are the names of the twelve tribes of the children of Israel: On the east three gates; on the north three gates; on the south three gates; and on the west three gates. And the wall of the city had twelve foundations, and in them the names of the twelve apostles of the Lamb. (Revelation 21:12-14)

Our attention, first of all, is drawn to the gates and walls. The Apostle John saw an enormous city surrounded by high walls with twelve gates and an angel at each gate. The walls of ancient eastern cities were designed for protection and was the main defense against attack on the city. Tim Lahaye, in his book, *"Revelation Illustrated And Made Plain,"* said:

> "The great wall around this city suggests that it is an exclusive city. It is not built for protection, of course, since no enemies w builder and maker is God ill threaten in the eternal order, but it stands as a visual reminder that all men do not have access to God."

The New Jerusalem will not be threatened by the enemy. The gates are never closed (Revelation 21:25). Since there are no enemies to fear, the walls of this city probably represent strength and security.

There are **twelve gates**, three at each side of the city, east, north, south, and west. Upon these gates are the names of the twelve tribes of Israel reminding us that ...

> ... salvation is of the Jews. (John 4:22)

Notice that the number 12 stands out in this city; it has 12 gates, 12 angels, 12 foundation stones, 12 apostles, 12 pearls, and 12 kinds of fruit. In biblical numerology 12 signifies Governmental Perfection.

The Size of the City

And he that talked with me had a golden reed to measure the city, and the gates thereof, and the wall thereof. And the city lieth foursquare, and the length is as large as the breadth: and he measured the city with the reed, twelve thousand furlongs. The length and the breadth and the height of it are equal. And he measured the wall thereof, an hundred and forty and four cubits, according to the measure of a man, that is, of the angel. (Revelation 21:15-17) There is no city on earth that we can compare to the New Jerusalem—it is beyond comparison. The New Jerusalem **lieth foursquare.** The length and the width are the same—twelve thousand furlongs. One furlong is 1/8th of a mile. Therefore, 12,000 furlongs is 1,500 miles. This Heavenly city is 1500 miles square. It would cover a space from Massachusetts to Florida to Texas to Colorado and back to Massachusetts—about ⅔'s the size of the United States. In addition, it is also 1,500 miles high. This amounts to a total of 2,250,000 square miles.

What a city! The walls were measured and found to be 144 cubits. A cubit is approximately eighteen inches making the walls 260 feet thick. In his book on *"Heaven: My Father's Country,"* Ivor Powell quotes an unknown author who had fed the dimensions of Heaven into a computer and came up with the following ...

"The city itself is said to be 12,000 furlongs. (1,500 miles) square. If it descended upon the earth, it would cover two thirds of the United States of America. Its walls would be 260 feet across, which is the length of a city block. They would contain 401,850 cubic feet of pure jasper. If the city were laid out into blocks 500 feet square, and if the streets were 100 feet wide, there would be 15,840 blocks to each side of the city. If each residence were 100 by 200 feet wide, or 20,000 square feet, there would be 12 residences in each block. This would total 3 billion, 10 million, 867,200 residences on the ground floor alone.

Allowing 20 feet for each floor, the city would be 396,000 floors high. The Empire State Building is only 103 floors high. The top floor would, according to the Bible, reach to a height of 1,500 miles. If we multiply the number on the ground floor by the total floors in height, we have the fantastic total of 1 quadrillion, 192 trillion, 303 billion, 411 million, 2 hundred thousand residences. Assuming there were 10 inhabitants occupying each residence, we would have as neighbors 11 quadrillion, 923 trillion, 34 billion, 112 million inhabitants."

Such a place cannot be fully comprehended. However, we do see that this is going be a massive city prepared by God. It is also the place where the Lord Jesus Christ will dwell with His bride.

The Splendor of the City

And the building of the wall of it was of jasper: and the city was pure gold, like unto clear glass. And the foundations of the wall of the city were garnished with all manner of precious stones. The first foundation was jasper; the second, sapphire; the third, a chalcedony; the fourth, an emerald; The fifth, sardonyx; the sixth, sardius; the seventh, chrysolyte; the eighth, beryl; the ninth, a topaz; the tenth, a chrysoprasus; the eleventh,

a jacinth; the twelfth, an amethyst. (Revelation 21:18-20) Human words cannot fully describe the splendor of this city. The city is made of **pure gold.** Gold so pure that it is transparent, as clear glass. The purest form of gold known to man is twenty-four-carat gold. However, the New Jerusalem is built of gold so pure that it is transparent **like unto clear glass.** The city is built on foundation stones inlaid with twelve gems. There is **jasper,** a crystal-like rock that is green in color. A **sapphire** stone which is blue. The **chalcedony** is green. The **emerald** is green. The **sardonyx** is brown and white, **sardius** is blood red, **chrysolyte** is yellow. The **beryl** is green. Topaz is yellow. The **chrysoprasus** is green. The **jacinth** is a combination of red, violet, and yellow. The **amethyst** is purple. These stones reflect the magnificent and brilliant glory of God and speak of the New Jerusalem's perfect beauty.

And the twelve gates were twelve pearls; every several gate was of one pearl: (Revelation 21:21a) Also mentioned are the **pearls.** The gates of the New Jerusalem are constructed of pearl, a single pearl for each gate. The gates of pearl remind us of the Lord's parable of the pearl of great price.

> **Again, the kingdom of heaven is like unto a merchant man, seeking goodly pearls: Who, when he had found one pearl of great price, went and sold all that he had, and bought it. (Matthew 13:45-46)**

The gates of pearl will be a reminder that Christ loved the church and gave Himself for it (Ephesians 5:25). John Phillips makes the following comments concerning these pearls:

> *How appropriate! All other precious gems are metals or stones, but a pearl is a gem formed within the oyster-the only one formed by living flesh. The humble oyster receives an irritation or a wound, and around the offending article that has penetrated and hurt it, the oyster builds a pearl. The pearl, we might say, is the answer of the oyster to that which injured it. The glory land is God's answer, in Christ, to wicked men who crucified heaven's beloved and put Him to*

open shame. How like God it is to make the gates of the new Jerusalem of pearl. The saints as they come and go will be forever reminded, as they pass the gates of glory, that access to God's home is only because of Calvary. Think of the size of those gates! Think of the supernatural pearls from which they are made! What gigantic suffering is symbolized by those gates of pearl! Throughout the endless ages we shall be reminded by those pearly gates of the immensity of the sufferings of Christ. Those pearls, hung eternally at the access routes to glory, will remind us forever of One who hung upon a tree and whose answer to those who injured Him was to invite them to share His home."

... and the street of the city was pure gold, as it were transparent glass. (Revelation 21:21b) We are further told that the city and even the streets are **pure gold, like unto clear glass.** I have no problem taking this literally. To create such a city would be no problem at all for the Omnipotent God. The gold is described as **like unto clear glass.** Imagine gold so pure that it is transparent, and the streets are paved with it. The emphasis of the passage is on the priceless value and infinite beauty of the Holy City—our eternal home.

THE DISTINCTION

The New Jerusalem is a unique and distinct city. It is the place that Jesus Christ is preparing for His people. As we have already seen there is no other place like it.

Concerning The Sanctuary

And I saw no temple therein: for the Lord God Almighty and the Lamb are the temple of it. (Revelation 21:22) There will be **no temple** in the New Jerusalem. This is an interesting declaration that John makes here. I have been to hundreds of cities here in the United States and many cities in other countries and I have never been to a city without there being some sort of a place to worship. Everywhere you go there is a place of worship— a church, a mosque, a basilica, etc. But in the New Jerusalem there will be no need for a temple **the Lord God**

Almighty and the Lamb are the temple of it. In the Temple of the Old Testament God dwelt in the Holy of holies. Because of His holiness and man's sinfulness, God limited His presence among men. Only the priest could enter the presence of God and then only with great preparation and caution. It is a serious and sobering thing to enter God's presence. However, with man in his glorified state there will be nothing to hinder his access to or his fellowship with God. He will openly occupy the whole city and we will have direct access to Him.

Concerning The Sun

And the city had no need of the sun, neither of the moon, to shine in it: for the glory of God did lighten it, and the Lamb is the light thereof. (Revelation 21:23) The New Jerusalem does not have any source of light other than **the glory of God ... and the Lamb** who is the light thereof. There will be no electricity in the New Jerusalem. The New Jerusalem will glow with the Shekinah glory of God. Jesus is the light (John 1:7-9; 3:19; 8:12; 12:35). Heaven is Christ centered.

And the nations of them which are saved shall walk in the light of it: and the kings of the earth do bring their glory and honour into it. ... And they shall bring the glory and honour of the nations into it. (Revelation 21:24, 26) Who are these kings and nations? These are probably the peoples who will not follow Gog and Magog when Satan is loosed for a little season. Remember when Satan is loosed, he will reach out to the four corners of the earth to get people to follow him. Multitudes will fall for his temptation and follow him. However, there will be multitudes who will not follow him. These are the kings and great men who will refuse to align with him, and they will make up the saved nations. The saved of all generations will have continual access to the Lamb of God and His city—they will come to praise and glorify God.

Concerning The Security

And the gates of it shall not be shut at all by day: for there shall be no night there. And there shall in no wise enter into it any thing that defileth, neither whatsoever worketh

abomination, or maketh a lie: but they which are written in the Lamb's book of life. (Revelation 21:25, 27)** There is no reason to lock the city down. In eternity there will be no dangers! There will no thieves, murderers, or tempters to disturb the eternal happiness of God's people. Satan will be confined to the lake of fire where he can never again disturb God's people. The gates of New Jerusalem will never close, nor will there ever be night there—this will be the eternal day.

THE DELIGHTS

In this section we get a glimpse inside the New Jerusalem. It is interesting that what we see here are the same objects that are referred to in the first chapter of the Bible. The Bible begins with a Paradise, and it ends with a Paradise. Genesis is a book of beginnings, and Revelation is a book of endings. That which was lost in Genesis is restored in the book of Revelation.

The Supply

And he shewed me a pure river of water of life, clear as crystal, proceeding out of the throne of God and of the Lamb. (Revelation 22:1) There is a delightful river that flows through the New Jerusalem. One day God's people will drink the water that flows from the throne of God. The Psalmist said:

> **There is a river, the streams whereof shall make glad the city of God, the holy place of the tabernacles of the most High. (Psalm 46:4)**

The **water of life** spoken of here has as its source **the throne of God and of the Lamb.** The water is described as being **clear as crystal.** This isn't stagnant water, rather it is described as a **pure river.** This water speaks of pureness, pleasure, and prosperity (Psalm 1:3; 36:8; Zechariah 14:8 and Joel 3:18). Throughout the New Testament salvation is oftentimes spoken of as water. Jesus said ...

> **But whosoever drinketh of the water that I shall give him shall never thirst; but the water that I shall give him shall be in him a well of water springing up into everlasting life. (John 4:14)**

This is not a muddy or contaminated stream. It is not a stagnant pool. It is not polluted, rather it is **a pure river of water of life**. This is satisfying water flowing fresh from the throne of God. This river is symbolic of the fullness and blessings of everlasting life.

The Sustenance

In the midst of the street of it, and on either side of the river, was there the tree of life, which bare twelve manner of fruits, and yielded her fruit every month: (Revelation 22:2a) The **tree of life** will be located in the **midst** of the street. Its branches will be large enough to spread on **either side of the river.** Because of Adam's fall, man was cut off from the tree of life back in the garden of Eden. Our God had a gracious reason for blocking man's access to the tree of life.

> **And the LORD God said, Behold, the man is become as one of us, to know good and evil: and now, lest he put forth his hand, and take also of the tree of life, and eat, and live for ever: Therefore the LORD God sent him forth from the garden of Eden, to till the ground from whence he was taken. So he drove out the man; and he placed at the east of the garden of Eden Cherubims, and a flaming sword which turned every way, to keep the way of the tree of life. (Genesis 3:22-24)**

God did not want fallen man to eat of the tree of life and live eternally in a state of sin. One can imagine what a miserable existence that would be. However, in the New Jerusalem man will again have access to the tree of life. There will be no more curse—eternity will be a state of perfect holiness. Thus, in eternity mans will have access to **the tree of life.** This tree will be different from anything man has ever seen. It will bear twelve different kinds of fruit, yield a harvest every thirty days, and the leaves will be for the healing of the nations.

... and the leaves of the tree were for the healing of the nations. (Revelation 22:2b) Why would there be a need for healing in Heaven? The obvious answer is that there would be. God has made it clear that there is no disease or death in Heaven.

The New Jerusalem

God's curse has been removed and the New Jerusalem will be a perfect place. Thus no one will enter the city of God with disease. It is interesting to note that the word **healing** comes from a Greek *"therapeia"* and is the word from which we get *"therapeutic or health giving."* These leaves will, in some mysterious way, add to the joyous existence of the redeemed.

The Satisfaction

And there shall be no more curse: (Revelation 22:3a) The sin that has cursed our world will have no effect in this wonderful paradise of God. That man once again has access to the Tree of Life is proof that the curse has been lifted. This tree will serve as a continual reminder of God's gracious provision of eternal life.

The Servants

... but the throne of God and of the Lamb shall be in it; and his servants shall serve him: And they shall see his face; and his name shall be in their foreheads. (Revelation 22:3b-4) The **throne of God and of the Lamb** speaks of the absolute sovereignty and power of God and the Son. We also see here that it is the source of grace and blessing. Every believer **shall see his face.** Imagine being able to look into the face of God. Jesus said ...

> **Blessed are the pure in heart: for they shall see God. (Matthew 5:8)**

The Psalmist said:

> **... I will behold thy face in righteousness: I shall be satisfied, when I awake, with thy likeness. (Psalm 17:15)**

Mortal man cannot see the face of God and live, but in Heaven when in our glorified state we will be able to look upon Him.

The Shinning

And there shall be no night there; and they need no candle, neither light of the sun; for the Lord God giveth them light: and they shall reign for ever and ever. (Revelation 22:5) Again, we are reminded that the Shekinah glory of God will illuminate the New Jerusalem. His glory will be the eternal light of eternity—no darkness can exist in His presence. What a day that will be when we are with our Saviour. Wilbur M. Smith describes the New Jerusalem this way:

> "All the glorious purposes of God, ordained from the foundation of the world, have now been attained. The rebellion of angels and mankind is all and finally subdued, as the King of kings assumes his rightful sovereignty. Absolute and unchangeable holiness characterizes all within the universal Kingdom of God. The redeemed, made so by the blood of the Lamb, are in resurrection and eternal glory. Life is everywhere and death will never intrude again. The earth and the heavens both are renewed. Light, beauty, holiness, joy, the presence of God, the worship of God, service to Christ, likeness to Christ-all are now abiding realities. The vocabulary of man, made for life here, is incapable of truly and adequately depicting what God has prepared for those that love him."

What a wonderful place! We are not to spiritualize these things away as many have. All of these things mentioned here are real. The river, the tree, the throne, the Lamb's face, and the Shekinah glory of God are real and will be in Heaven. In all of these things there is the perpetual reminder of the grace and glory of God.

THE PROTECTED BOOK
Revelation 22:6-10, 18-19

As John's vision comes to an end he is brought back to the present and given a final warning and one final invitation. The angel bears witness to John of the authenticity of the things which he was allowed to see.

THE ACCURACY OF GOD'S WORD

And he said unto me, These sayings are faithful and true: and the Lord God of the holy prophets sent his angel to show unto his servants the things which must shortly be done (Revelation 22:6) Well there you have it! Heaven's testimony concerning the Word of God! **These sayings are faithful and true.** In the context He is speaking specifically of the book of Revelation. However, it includes the whole Bible. God Himself guarantees that we can trust His Word. Understand that God's Word is dependent upon God's character and God never goes back on His Word. While many today have little or no respect for the Bible, God still hold His Word in high regard. His Word is _Pure_, _Perfect_, _Preserved_ and _Permanent_.

> **The words of the LORD are pure words: as silver tried in a furnace of earth, purified seven times. Thou shalt keep them, O LORD, thou shalt preserve them from this generation for ever. (Psalm 12:6-7)**

God dogmatically states that He gave us His Word, that it is pure, and He assures us that He is going to preserve it forever. The Bible is so important to God that His name rests upon it.

> **I will worship toward thy holy temple, and praise thy name for thy loving kindness and for thy truth: for thou hast magnified thy word above all thy name. (Psalm 138:2)**

God has magnified His word above His name. Surely God will keep His Word! Also notice the duration of preservation, God said that He would preserve them. (His Words) **from this**

generation for ever. God's Word is guaranteed to be eternal. Time and time again God assures us that His Word is preserved.

> **For ever, O LORD, thy word is settled in heaven. (Psalm 119:89)**
>
> **Thy word is true from the beginning: and every one of thy righteous judgments endureth for ever. (Psalm 119:160)**
>
> **The grass withereth, the flower fadeth: but the word of our God shall stand for ever. (Isaiah 40:8)**
>
> **Being born again, not of corruptible seed, but of incorruptible, by the word of God, which liveth and abideth for ever. (1 Peter 1:23)**

The Bible contains the mind of God, the condition of man, and the clear, simple plan of salvation. Christ is the wonderful and glorious theme of the Bible. His salvation shines forth from its pages as a guiding light to all who desire to be saved. All who reject its message will be judged by its Words. Imagine that all those who hate and ridicule the Word of God will someday stand under its authority and be judged by the Righteous God of the Bible they reject.! The Word of God will be at the Judgment. The Bible is the inspired, infallible, inerrant, preserved Word of the living God—**These sayings are faithful and true.**

THE AUTHORITY OF GOD'S WORD

The angel speaks to John concerning the power and authenticity of God's Word.

The Promised Return

Behold, I come quickly: (Revelation 22:7a) The word **quickly** does not mean that He will come in a short amount of time. Back in chapter 3, we learned that the word quickly comes from *"tachu"* and carries the idea of *"prompt and swift."* Jesus is saying that when He comes the events spoken of in this book will unfold rapidly.

The Persistent Responsibility

... blessed is he that keepeth the sayings of the prophecy of this book. (Revelation 22:7b) God's Word is authoritative—

we are to obey it. John said, **blessed is he that keepeth the sayings of the prophecy of this book.** We are to keep these words—that is, we are to obey the commands of the Bible. It is an authoritative book. So many are not blessed today because they do not follow the Bible. There is no other book to follow if we are to experience God's blessing. The Word of God is the final authority in all matters of faith and practice.

> **The grass withereth, the flower fadeth: but the word of our God shall stand for ever. (Isaiah 40:8)**

So many lives are messed up today because folks do not know the Word of God. David said:

> **Through thy precepts I get understanding: therefore I hate every false way. (Psalm 119:104)**

David knew and despised the false ways because he was familiar with the precepts of God. Jesus said:

> **Ye do err, not knowing the scriptures.... (Matthew 22:29)**

Too many today have learned their doctrine from a college professor, a textbook, a radio preacher, or some way other than a consistent diet of God's Word. Granted there are good textbooks and there are solid preachers and trustworthy teachers that we can learn from. However, it is upon the solid rock of Scripture that we must establish our doctrine. The Word of God is food for our spiritual lives. It is the final authority in all matters. Christ declared that ...

> **Man shall not live by bread alone, but by every word that proceedeth out of the mouth of God. (Matthew 4:4)**

The physical man lives by bread, but the spiritual man lives by every word that proceeds from our heavenly Father. No wonder Job said:

> **I have esteemed the words of his mouth more than my necessary food. (Job 23:12)**

Think about the trials that Job was going through! What a lesson! God's Word was more precious to him during his trials than anything else he could imagine. David said:

> **Unless thy law had been my delights, I should then have perished in mine affliction. (Psalm 119:92)**

The spiritual man lives according to the Word. Its nourishment strengthens and sustains him.

The Perplexing Reaction

And I John saw these things, and heard them. And when I had heard and seen, I fell down to worship before the feet of the angel which shewed me these things. (Revelation 22:8) John was so overwhelmed with what he saw that he fell down to worship the angelic messenger. There is a lot of angel worship going on today. Even people who claim to know Christ as Saviour have just about abandoned the Lord in pursuit of angels. Popular and blasphemous programming like *"Touched By An Angel"* has led hordes of undiscerning people astray.

The Powerful Rebuke

Then saith he unto me, See thou do it not: for I am thy fellowservant, and of thy brethren the prophets, and of them which keep the sayings of this book: worship God. (Revelation 22:9) Those who pray to angels should seriously consider these words. The Angel strongly rebuked John and said **See thou do it not: for I am thy fellowservant.** The angel took his place of submission and led John to **worship God.** God's angels do not seek the worship which only belongs to God.

THE ACCESSIBILITY OF GOD'S WORD

And he saith unto me, Seal not the sayings of the prophecy of this book: for the time is at hand. (Revelation 22:10) John was commanded not to seal up words of the prophecy. Daniel, however, was to seal up his visions.

> **But thou, O Daniel, shut up the words, and seal the book. (Daniel 12:4)**

There was yet another dispensation to come before the vision would be fulfilled. However, John was not to seal the prophecy he received—he was to publish it. The reason given is **for the time is at hand.** The book of Revelation was the completion of

God's revelation to man. God's word for man is now complete and available. There is no excuse for folks being ignorant of God's Word. We have easy access to the Word of God. Throughout the Bible it is clear that as Christians we have a duty to study and acquaint ourselves with God's Word.

> **Study to show thyself approved unto God, a workman that needeth not to be ashamed, rightly dividing the word of truth. (2 Timothy 2:15)**

The Bible is the greatest book in the world; it is the book above all other books. The Bible is a library of sixty-six books on the grandest theme possible, Christ and His redemptive work.

No Christian will ever be spiritually mature and equipped for God's service without a working knowledge of the Scriptures.

> **Study to shew thyself approved unto God, a workman that needeth not to be ashamed, rightly dividing the word of truth. (2 Timothy 2:15)**

> **All scripture is given by inspiration of God, and is profitable for doctrine, for reproof, for correction, for instruction in righteousness; that the man of God may be perfect, thoroughly furnished unto all good works. (2 Timothy 3:16-17)**

Those who study and **rightly divide** the word of truth will be **thoroughly furnished unto all good works.**

THE AVENGER OF GOD'S WORD

For I testify unto every man that heareth the words of the prophecy of this book, If any man shall add unto these things, God shall add unto him the plagues that are written in this book: And if any man shall take away from the words of the book of this prophecy, God shall take away his part out of the book of life, and out of the holy city, and from the things which are written in this book. (Revelation 22:18-19) God will protect His book and He will deal severely with those who mess with it! There are several of these warnings in the Word of God.

> **Ye shall not add unto the word which I command you. (Deuteronomy 4:2)**

And again:

> **... thou shalt not add thereto. (Deuteronomy 12:32)**

Solomon wrote:

> **... add thou not unto his words, lest he reprove thee, and thou be found a liar. (Proverbs 30:6)**

These verses are a Divine warning to anyone who would tamper with God's Word. This ought to serve as a warning to the Bible of The Month Club. The market has been flooded with so-called up-to-date and better translations. There are well over one hundred modern English versions of the Bible today. These modern translations water down and attack many fundamental doctrines of the Christian faith. In the name of scholarship, they delete the Deity of Christ, the Virgin birth, the Infallibility and Inerrancy of the Bible, Salvation by faith alone, the Trinity and more. Depending on which one you are using there are between 5,000 and 50,000 changes in them.

Satan and his ungodly crowd hate the Word of God and make every attempt to destroy it. Infidels attack it; scoffers sneer at it, and heretics deny it, the scholars mutilate it, but God preserves it. Continually men have tried to destroy the Bible, but praise to God, His Word lives on.

> **The words of the LORD are pure words: as silver tried in a furnace of earth, purified seven times. Thou shalt keep them, O LORD, thou shalt preserve them from this generation for ever. (Psalm 12:6-7)**

We have preserved for us a perfect copy of God's Word in the wonderful old King James Bible. We Baptists believe in Biblical Authority. We insist that the Bible is the Word of God and the final authority in all matters of faith and practice. We do not rely upon hand me down tradition and manmade teachings. We simply take God at His Word—we believe and obey the Bible.

THE OLD ACCOUNT IS SETTLED
Revelation 22:11-15

God assures us of our final and fixed state after death. Regardless of what religion teaches or what men think, God has the final say. Whether men are wicked or whether they are righteous—in whatever state God finds men in the end, that will be their eternal condition. Those who are saved can rejoice that the old account was settled at Calvary, and those who are lost must come to Christ, or die eternally lost.

THE FINAL STATE

He that is unjust, let him be unjust still: and he which is filthy, let him be filthy still: and he that is righteous, let him be righteous still: and he that is holy, let him be holy still. (Revelation 22:11) This solemn verse speaks of the final state—a time when there will be no more opportunity for change. The tragedy of this is that the man who dies in his sin will be forever lost and doomed eternally to the lake of fire. That is why the Bible places such importance on salvation.

> **... behold, now is the accepted time; behold, now is the day of salvation. (2 Corinthians 6:2)**

At the moment of death, everyone's spiritual condition is forever fixed. Many false teachers promote the idea of a second chance for salvation after death. Nothing could be further from the truth. The eternal state of the lost is forever settled the moment they die. Whether **unjust** and **filthy,** or **righteous** and **holy,** when one dies, that is the way he will be for eternity. Luke chapter 16 illustrates this truth.

> **And it came to pass, that the beggar died, and was carried by the angels into Abraham's bosom: the rich man also died, and was buried. (Luke 16:22)**

The beggar died saved and went to Paradise, the rich man died lost and went to Hell. Liberals and modernists can try all they want to air condition Hell, but it still burns hot. The lost man then asked for Lazarus to come to him with a few drops of water to cool his tongue—notice how this unfolds.

> **And he cried and said, Father Abraham, have mercy on me, and send Lazarus, that he may dip the tip of his finger in water, and cool my tongue; for I am tormented in this flame. But Abraham said, Son, remember that thou in thy lifetime receivedst thy good things, and likewise Lazarus evil things: but now he is comforted, and thou art tormented. And beside all this, between us and you there is a great gulf fixed: so that they which would pass from hence to you cannot; neither can they pass to us, that would come from thence. (Luke 16:24-26)**

Both the beggar and the rich man had entered their final state. This would be their condition for eternity. The beggar would be **righteous** and **holy** for eternity and the rich man would be **unjust** and **filthy** for eternity.

> **And as it is appointed unto men once to die, but after this the judgment. (Hebrews 9:27)**

Death is coming to all. One man draws his last breath his destiny is sealed. Where will you be? After death there is not a second chance—only judgment.

THE FAMILIAR SAYING

Often times in Scripture God repeats a statement or saying. Here He reiterates the fact of Christ's rewarding of His saints.

The Return Of The Saviour

And, behold, I come quickly; and my reward is with me, (Revelation 22:12a) Once again have the comforting promise of Christ's swift return for His people. God reiterates this promise to emphasize the significance of it. Dr. W. A. Criswell wrote:

> "First, the Saviour is to come that He might be crushed, bruised, crucified and made an offering for sin. He is to come to die as the Redeemer for the souls of men. After God made that promise in Eden,

hundreds of years passed, millenniums passed, and the Lord did not come. When finally He did arrive, He came unto His own and His own received Him not. He was in the world and the world was made by Him and the world knew Him not. The thousands of humanity had forgotten the promise or else they scoffed at its fulfillment. When finally, the announcement came that he had arrived, the learned scribes pointed out the place where He was to be born, but never took the time to journey the five miles from Jerusalem to Bethlehem to welcome this promised Saviour of the world. But, however long he delayed and however men forgot and scoffed and however few of a faithful band waited for the consolation of Israel, as old Simeon, yet He came. In keeping with the holy, faithful promise of God, the Lord Jesus came. It is thus in the text that God speaks in closing His Bible, Surely, I come quickly. Here a second time, however infidels may scoff and however others may reject and however the centuries may grow into the millenniums, this is the immutable Word and promise of the Lord God, Surely, I come."

This imminent return was the hope of the early Church. The Scriptures continually admonish believers to **watch** and **be ready.** Sadly, many professing Christians have lost sight of the blessed hope. The popular greeting of the early was **Maranatha. (1 Corinthians 16:22)** It expressed their hope and belief in the imminent return of Christ for His Church. Paul wrote:

> **For our conversation is in heaven; from whence also we look for the Saviour, the Lord Jesus Christ. (Philippians 3:20)**

Notice that Paul was looking for Christ's return and that his looking was present tense. He expected Christ to appear at any moment. As God's people, we are to be ...

Looking for that blessed hope, and the glorious appearing of the great God and our Saviour Jesus Christ. (Titus 2:13)

Yes, Jesus is coming again. In fact, God's people could be caught out immediately, or at any moment. The heart of every believer ought to be occupied with his or her Saviour's return.

The Rewarding Of The Saint

... to give every man according as his work shall be. (Revelation 22:12b) There are five rewards mentioned in Scripture that a believer can earn for faithful service. These rewards will be determined by Christ at the Judgment Seat.

- The Incorruptible Crown (1 Corinthians 9:25).
- The Crown of Rejoicing (1 Thessalonians 2:19).
- The Crown of Righteousness (2 Timothy 4:8).
- The Crown of Glory (1 Peter 5:2-3).
- The Crown of Life (Revelation 2:10).

All that a Christian has done, even to the giving of the cup of cool water in the name of the Lord Jesus, will be rewarded. Everything that a believer has done for God's glory will be rewarded.

THE FAITHFUL SAVIOUR

I am Alpha and Omega, the beginning and the end, the first and the last. (Revelation 22:13) After proclaiming His imminent return and promising a reward for faithfulness, He reminds us that He is the Eternal God. Jesus is the Self-existent, Eternal, Sovereign, Omniscient, Omnipresent and Omnipotent God of the universe. He is the Alpha and Omega, the beginning and the ending. Alpha is the first letter of the Greek alphabet and Omega is the last. He is the:

Author and finisher. (Hebrews 1:2)

Lehman Strauss said, *He is the one who created, controls, and will consummate all things (Ephesians 1:10; Colossians 1:16-17).* Jesus is the first and the last. In other words, He is everything! Here is another declaration of the Divinity of Christ. The Lord

Jesus is the all-sufficient, eternal God. Jesus was here before this world was created and He will be here when it is gone. He is the eternal Son of God.

THE FORGIVEN SAINTS

Blessed are they that do his commandments, that they may have right to the tree of life, and may enter in through the gates into the city. (Revelation 22:14) Redeemed by the precious blood of the Lamb, God's people will enter into the new Jerusalem with its tree of life. (Revelation 2:7) Many have stumbled here and confused grace and works because of the phrase **they that do his commandments.** However, the Bible clearly teaches that salvation is in Jesus Christ and Him alone without any mixture of works on our part.

> **For by grace are ye saved through faith; and that not of yourselves: it is the gift of God: Not of works, lest any man should boast. (Ephesians 2:8-9)**

> **Not by works of righteousness which we have done, but according to his mercy he saved us, by the washing of regeneration, and renewing of the Holy Ghost. (Titus 3:5)**

The Bible is clear on the matter of salvation and God does command that we believe in Christ to be saved.

> **And this is his commandment, That we should believe on the name of his Son Jesus Christ... (1 John 3:23a)**

Believing in the Lord Jesus Christ is the primary command of God. When we come to Him, our sin is forgiven, we are declared righteous, and Heaven becomes our home. Our own filthy rags of self-righteousness will not do, but it is the righteousness of Jesus Christ by which we gain Heaven.

> **And be found in him, not having mine own righteousness, which is of the law, but that which is through the faith of Christ, the righteousness which is of God by faith. (Philippians 3:9)**

This is imputed righteousness. Imputation means to put something against. All of Christ's righteousness is put to the sinner's account when he is saved. When a sinner comes to Christ for forgiveness all his sins are put to Christ's account. His blood made the payment in full for the sins of the world.

> **For he hath made him to be sin for us, who knew no sin; that we might be made the righteousness of God in him. (2 Corinthians 5:21)**

Believers are made the righteousness of God because all of Christ's righteousness is put to the believer's account. The child of God stands clothed in Christ's righteousness. Those who enter Heaven do not do so with a holier than thou attitude, but by merit of Christ's righteousness alone.

THE FORBIDDEN SINNERS

For without are dogs, and sorcerers, and whoremongers, and murderers, and idolaters, and whosoever loveth and maketh a lie. (Revelation 22:15) Entrance to the holy city will be denied to all who are unrighteous. As we read earlier:

> **... there shall in no wise enter into it any thing that defileth, neither whatsoever worketh abomination, or maketh a lie: but they which are written in the Lamb's book of life. (Revelation 21:27)**

Heaven is a restricted place. The lost man forever bars himself from Heaven because it is a perfect and pure place of righteousness. Hell is a place for those who will not be saved. There are many who will not gain access to Heaven. They will not come to Christ and have their sins forgiven and washed away. Jesus said:

> **And ye will not come to me, that ye might have life. (John 5:40)**

What sad words! With salvation purchased and paid for, many will still refuse His offer and remain lost for all eternity.

GOD'S FINAL INVITATION
Revelation 22:16-17

Having warned the lost that when the end comes there will be no more opportunities for salvation, God brings this book to a close with another wonderful invitation to be saved. God wants no one to go to Hell. God had given His Son as a sacrifice for the lost. God's desire for the lost is clear throughout the Bible.

> **As I live, saith the Lord GOD, I have no pleasure in the death of the wicked; but that the wicked turn from his way and live ... (Ezekiel 33:11)**

We are told God is:

> **... not willing that any should perish, but that all should come to repentance. (2 Peter 3:9)**

God's great desire is that the lost be saved. He takes no pleasure in the eternal death of the damned. So, it is here after warning man of the coming judgment, God closes this book with another invitation. Let's notice ...

THE PERSON OF THE INVITATION

I Jesus ... It is Christ who is speaking here. Jesus authenticates the message of this book by putting His name to it.

The Testimony Declared

I Jesus have sent mine angel to testify unto you these things in the churches. (Revelation 22:16a) Notice that this message is to be testified to **in the churches.** The Book of Revelation is to be proclaimed. Many are ignoring it but thank God for the faithful preachers who stand up and teach the message of Revelation.

... in the churches. (Revelation 22:16b) This is the first time the Church appears since the third chapter in the Book of Revelation. All during the Tribulation Period, there is no mention of the Church, since it is in Heaven with the Lord. The Lord tells John that the book of Revelation was given to testify to the Churches so that we would know God's plan for the end times.

The Titles Designated

I am the root and the offspring of David, (Revelation 22:16c) The Davidic Covenant promised that One from the lineage of David would inherit His throne: (2 Samuel 7; Matthew 1:1). As the **root** Jesus is David's preexistent Lord. Scripture clearly teaches us that Jesus existed long before King David. As his **offspring**, He is David's son, the incarnate Christ.

... the root and the offspring of David, (Revelation 22:16d) By announcing Himself with this title, Jesus is laying claim to David's throne and proclaiming He is King of kings. This was prophesied by Isaiah and is a fulfilled prophecy.

> **And there shall come forth a rod out of the stem of Jesse, and a Branch shall grow out of his roots. (Isaiah 11:1)**

Concerning these titles, Dr. H. A. Ironside comments:

> *It is noteworthy that when the blessed Lord introduced Himself by His personal name and declared His official title in connection with Israel and His special title in connection with the church, the Spirit and the bride alike are aroused to send up the invitation shout, Come. We read, I Jesus have sent mine angel to testify unto you these things in the churches. I am the root and the offspring of David. (16) He is the root of David because David sprang from Him—David's Creator and Lord, who called him to guide His people Israel. And He is the offspring of David, for as man He was born from a daughter of David. And He is the bright and morning star.*

With these titles the Lord Jesus Christ associates Himself with the nation Israel. He is the Saviour of all—He died for every man. Time and time again the Bible emphatically declares Jesus to be the only way to Heaven.

> For there is one God, and one mediator between God and men, the man Christ Jesus. **(1 Timothy 2:5)**

Speaking of Jesus Peter declared:

> **Neither is there salvation in any other: for there is none other name under heaven given among men, whereby we must be saved. (Acts 4:12)**

Jesus is the one Who paid man's sin debt and He is the one who saves. Without Christ and His atoning work there would be no invitation to be saved. He is the Person of the invitation.

> **... and the bright and morning star. (Revelation 22:16e)**

The morning star is the star that rises at dawn when it is darkest. This title of Christ is referenced in other places in Scripture. It is a title of glory and power.

> **... there shall come a Star out of Jacob, and a Sceptre shall rise out of Israel, and shall smite the corners of Moab, and destroy all the children of Sheth. (Numbers 24:17b)**

> **We have also a more sure word of prophecy; whereunto ye do well that ye take heed, as unto a light that shineth in a dark place, until the day dawn, and the day star arise in your hearts: (2 Peter 1:19)**

> **And I will give him the morning star. (Revelation 2:28)**

In the natural realm the morning star signals the sunrise of a new day. The return of Christ in His glory at the end of the Tribulation Period will be like the dawning of a new day, with the establishing of the Millennial Kingdom. When Jesus returns the light of His glory will flood the earth.

THE POWER OF THE INVITATION

The power of the invitation is **the Spirit. (Revelation 22:17)** No one gets saved without the Holy Spirit's involvement. Just before completing His earthly ministry Jesus said:

> **Nevertheless I tell you the truth; It is expedient for you that I go away: for if I go not away, the Comforter will not come unto you; but if I depart, I**

> **will send him unto you. And when he is come, he will reprove the world of sin, and of righteousness, and of judgment: Of sin, because they believe not on me; Of righteousness, because I go to my Father, and ye see me no more; Of judgment, because the prince of this world is judged. (John 16:7-11)**

The Holy Spirit will **reprove the world of sin.** The word **reprove** means to charge with a fault to the face; to chide; to reprehend. One of the main ministries of the Holy Spirit is to convict mankind of sin—mainly the sin of unbelief. Herein lies one of the missing elements in today's soul winning methods. Too many are going forth with a program, but they have no power. Where the Holy Spirit is not at work to convict of sin there will be no souls saved. When the Holy Spirit is present and working there will be conviction of sin. When a sinner repents it is the result of the Holy Spirit's work—not some slick plan of evangelism. The Bible declares that:

> **.. no man can say that Jesus is the Lord, but by the Holy Ghost. (1 Corinthians 12:3)**

The Holy Spirit calls the sinner, condemns his sin, and converts his soul. The whole process of conversion begins with and is carried out by the Holy Spirit of God.

THE PEOPLE OF THE INVITATION

The people involved in winning others to Christ are identified as the **bride. (Revelation 22:17)** While no one will be saved without the Holy Spirit, the Word of God is equally as clear on the fact that God uses His people to witness to the lost. Every Christian is commanded to be a soul-winner. I often hear people talk about the so-called gift of evangelism. My friend, evangelism is not a gift—it is a command. One of the most important things that any Christian can do is to win souls to Jesus Christ. Contrary to popular opinion, soul winning is not just the preacher's business. It is the duty of every Christian to be occupied with the heavenly business of bringing souls to Jesus Christ. The command of Christ to His Church is:

> **Go ye therefore, and teach all nations, baptizing them in the name of the Father, and of the Son, and of the Holy Ghost. (Matthew 28:19)**

The **go ye** applies to every child of God. It is the command of God that we go with the Gospel! Dear Christian, if you are not consistently involved in getting the gospel out, you are a disobedient Christian. When our Lord said go ye, He was not simply making a suggestion. He was issuing marching orders for His people. Solomon said:

> **... he that winneth souls is wise. (Proverbs 11:30)**

A wise man understands the importance of getting the gospel to a lost and dying world. If the man who wins souls is wise, what would a man who does not win souls be called?

THE PREREQUISITE OF THE INVITATION

And let him that is athirst come. And whosoever will, let him take the water of life .... (Revelation 22:17) The invitation is given. This is the last invitation of the Word of God. This has been the call of God to sinful man throughout the ages.

> **Ho, every one that thirsteth, come ye to the waters, and he that hath no money; come ye, buy, and eat; yea, come, buy wine and milk without money and without price. (Isaiah 55:1)**

In the Bible, thirst is sometimes used symbolically depicting spiritual poverty. As a man who is physically thirsty looks for something to drink, so the man who is spiritually thirsty seeks God.

> **Blessed are they which do hunger and thirst after righteousness: for they shall be filled. (Matthew 5:6)**

Jesus is the answer to man's spiritual thirst.

> **Jesus stood and cried, saying, If any man thirst, let him come unto me, and drink. He that believeth on me, as the scripture hath said, out of his belly shall flow rivers of living water. (But this spake he of the Spirit, which they that believe on him should**

> receive: for the Holy Ghost was not yet given; because that Jesus was not yet glorified) (John 7:37-39)

Jesus said to the Samaritan woman:

> But whosoever drinketh of the water that I shall give him shall never thirst; but the water that I shall give him shall be in him a well of water springing up into everlasting life. (John 4:14)

Eternal life, like an eternal spring of water, never runs dry and ever satisfies the thirsty soul of the redeemed. As God's children we may have a lot of needs, but once saved we will never need to be thirsty again—it is eternal.

THE PROMISE OF THE INVITATION

What a precious promise! He that has a thirst may **take of the water of life freely.** The promise is precious—the water of life is **freely** given. If God were to charge for salvation, no one could afford it. Let us not forget that it was with the shed blood of His only begotten Son that God Almighty purchased our salvation. The Bible says:

> ... ye are bought with a price. (1 Corinthians 6:20)

Salvation is free to us, but to the father it was the most expensive thing He ever bought.

> **Forasmuch as ye know that ye were not redeemed with corruptible things, as silver and gold, from your vain conversation received by tradition from your fathers; But with the precious blood of Christ, as of a lamb without blemish and without spot. (1 Peter 1:18-19)**

What kind of a dollar amount could be put on the Blood of Jesus? The human mind couldn't even comprehend such an astronomical amount. Almighty God, Who created and owns all things never had to make a purchase of any kind until it came to lost man. It was then that God paid the ultimate price for our salvation.

EVEN SO COME, LORD JESUS
Revelation 22:20-21

Revelation closes with yet another promise of our Lord's return. This important theme is sounded in one out of every twenty-five or so verses of the New Testament. We are not to lose sight of the fact that the return of Christ is coming. There are four main thoughts in these closing verses.

THE PROMISE

Surely I come quickly. (Revelation 22:20a) This is the last thing that Jesus ever said in the Word of God. It is a warning that the events of this book will come to and that His return is swift and certain. We are assured of our Lord's imminent return. Rapture is a precious and powerful doctrine for the believer.

> **Beloved, now are we the sons of God, and it doth not yet appear what we shall be: but we know that, when he shall appear, we shall be like him; for we shall see him as he is. (1 John 3:2)**

Think about those words, **we shall be like Him.** God the Father's desire for every believer will be realized at last. This verse speaks of the glorification of the Christian.

> **For whom he did foreknow, he also did predestinate to be conformed to the image of his Son, that he might be the firstborn among many brethren. (Romans 8:29)**

When God looked down through time and saw those who would be saved, He predestined them to be like His Son. We have a hope—the glorious return of Christ. Jesus said:

> **Let not your heart be troubled: ye believe in God, believe also in me. In my Father's house are many mansions: if it were not so, I would have told you. I go to prepare a place for you. And if I go and prepare a place for you, I will come again, and**

receive you unto myself; that where I am, there ye may be also. (John 14:1-3)

Even now, as we walk and labor for Him, He is preparing a place for us and has plans to return for us. When that day comes, we will be like Him. Our glorified bodies will be like Christ's resurrected body.

For our conversation is in heaven; from whence also we look for the Saviour, the Lord Jesus Christ: Who shall change our vile body, that it may be fashioned like unto his glorious body, according to the working whereby he is able even to subdue all things unto himself. (Philippians 3:20-21)

This is the grand promise of the Saviour to His people. The believer will be like Christ and forever be with Christ.

THE PRAYER

Amen. Even so, come, Lord Jesus. (Revelation 22:20a) As the Revelation winds down John overwhelmingly responds, **Amen. Even so, come, Lord Jesus.** The word **amen** means so be it. John was ready for Christ's return. To the Christian who is living for God, nothing is more precious than the hope of Christ's return.

THE PROVISION

The grace of our Lord Jesus Christ be with you all. Amen. (Revelation 22:21) Isn't it wonderful that the Bible closes with grace. Oh! How we need grace! And God's grace is sufficient. Things are tough in these last days. Paul said:

For the mystery of iniquity doth already work. (2 Thessalonians 2:7)

The mystery of iniquity has been at work since the days of the Apostles. The word **iniquity** means *"violation of the law, wickedness, injustice and unrighteousness."* It is a word that carries the general idea of lawlessness. God's people have always had to deal with lawlessness. It was a lawless mob that yelled, "Crucify Him" just before Jesus was nailed to the cross. A lawless mob stoned Stephen for preaching the gospel. Paul was beheaded for the gospel's sake. Peter was crucified upside-down because of his stand for the Lord. John was exiled to the Isle of Patmos for his testimony. Lawlessness will continue until the antichrist is revealed and dealt with by Christ Himself. The Bible plainly teaches that the last days will be marked by lawlessness. Certainly, we live in the last days.

> **This know also, that in the last days perilous times shall come. (2 Timothy 3:1)**

The word **perilous** comes from *"chalepos"* and means *"dangerous; difficult, fierce, hazardous, full of risk."* Yes, the last day will be dangerous and difficult days. However, God has given us His **grace** so that we can:

> **... endure hardness as a good soldier of Jesus Christ. (2 Timothy 2:3)**

God said to Paul:

> **My grace is sufficient for thee ... (2 Corinthians 12:9)**

God said, "My grace." This is God's grace, Divine grace. Grace is the wonderful provision of God to all who will come to Him. We are Sought by grace, _Saved_ by grace, _Sanctified_ by grace, _Secured_ by grace, and _Sustained_ by grace. The Christian life from Salvation to Heaven is a portrait of God's grace. Praise God, we are not left to ourselves to make out the best we can. We are assured of His grace and mercy, and He will see us through.

THE PRIORITY

Jesus said, **Surely I come quickly. (Revelation 22:20)** Regardless of what the scoffers and unbelievers say, Jesus is coming back. What if He were to come right now? Would you be ready to meet Him? Salvation isn't based on anything that you have done or can do; it is based entirely on what Jesus Christ has done for you. Only by receiving Him as your Saviour can you become a Christian and have eternal life. Christ promises that:

> **Whosoever shall call upon the name of the Lord shall be saved. (Romans 10:13)**

No one need be excluded from God's wonderful salvation.

For God so loved the world, that he gave his only begotten Son, that whosoever believeth in him should not perish, but have everlasting life. (John 3:16)

It is as simple as turning to Christ and trusting in Him for your salvation.

But as many as received him, to them gave he power to become the sons of God, even to them that believe on his name. (John 1:12)

If Jesus is speaking to you, won't you receive Him now? This may be the last time the Holy Spirit will trouble your heart concerning salvation.

If you are saved, you have been bought by the precious blood of Christ. You belong to the Lord because you have, by faith, accepted the provision He made on Calvary's altar. Bow your head and thank God for the forgiveness of sin and the life you possess in Christ Jesus and tell others about the free gift of salvation that saves sinners from eternity in Hell.

www.ingramcontent.com/pod-product-compliance
Lightning Source LLC
Chambersburg PA
CBHW071233160426
43196CB00009B/1036